M000087850

Competitive Agents in Certain and Uncertain Markets

Competitive Agents in Certain and Uncertain Markets

Robert G. Chambers

OXFORD
UNIVERSITY PRESS

OXFORD
UNIVERSITY PRESS

Oxford University Press is a department of the University of Oxford.
It furthers the University's objective of excellence in research, scholarship,
and education by publishing worldwide. Oxford is a registered trade mark of
Oxford University Press in the UK and certain other countries.

Published in the United States of America by Oxford University Press
198 Madison Avenue, New York, NY 10016, United States of America.

Library of Congress Control Number: 2020946802
ISBN 978-0-19-006301-6

1 3 5 7 9 8 6 4 2
Printed by
Integrated Books International, United States of America

For Michelle and Evan

Contents

Preface

The material in this book forms the backbone of a course on topics in applied microeconomics offered at the University of Maryland for a little over two decades. The topics covered in that course were and are somewhat idiosyncratic. That idiosyncrasy was a natural outgrowth of the course's intended purpose of augmenting the treatment of microeconomic topics that are of special interest to students of agricultural, environmental, and resource economics, but for which first-year theory courses only offer exposure at an introductory level.

For many years, despite their obvious similarities, I treated the core topics in that course as relatively distinct. And while I tried to emphasize the inherently identical mathematical structure of many of them, each was still posed and examined separately. Eventually, it seemed that a more efficient approach would be first to teach the basic mathematics behind the pervasive "tangency conditions" and then to drop out consumer theory, producer theory, equilibrium theory, and decision making under uncertainty as important special cases. As with all intellectual experiments, the results were mixed. Some find this integrative approach appealing, others are repelled. The most frequent objection of the latter group is that this different perspective confused them about material that they already understood. For better or worse, I took that perspective as encouraging, and this book is the result.

This material hinges on the idea that economics always reduces to comparing alternatives. Thus, the focus here is on what can be learned from *pairwise* comparisons. Should we build A rather than B? Will I be better off if I eat D rather than C? How much will it cost me to produce F instead of E? Can I use G to produce H? Many, if not most, times analyzing the differences is easier than analyzing, say, A and B separately and then comparing results. These differences are portrayed mathematically as *variations* from a particular point. And the basic economic idea is: *If a variation is bad, don't do it.* Moreover, to characterize the best possible outcome, an obvious strategy is to find a point from which one cannot find an improving variation.

The material is intentionally written in general terms. Some readers may be required to learn some new math. This is especially true in the first few chapters. While these ideas may be unfamiliar, they are simple conceptually. Still, experience has taught me that many will struggle. Because the concepts are simple, I believe this happens because they are also abstract. So, for example, where you are often coached to characterize constrained optima in mechanical terms involving Lagrangians and partial derivatives, here you will be asked to characterize optima abstractly and in a manner that does not always lend itself to brute-force computation. That requires asking oneself the seemingly obvious question of what it really means to be at an optimum. Answering that question requires some ability to think in terms of the abstract essence of the problem. But again, one should not confuse *abstract* with complicated or unfamiliar. I try to illustrate this in the initial chapter by providing six simple and hopefully familiar figures that I believe encapsulate all the basic ideas in these notes.

The presentation also presumes that you "know" a lot of basic microeconomics. The course that these lectures supported was part of a first-year graduate microeconomics curriculum. Therefore, they presume a familiarity with basic producer and consumer theory, decision making under uncertainty, and simple general-equilibrium theory at the advanced undergraduate level. I should also add that the voice that I chose to adopt throughout is that of a professor talking to first-year graduate students. To any of you who do not fit into this category, my apologies if the result strikes you as overly pedantic.

The book is not intended to introduce you to those theories. Instead, the intent is to convey an integrated perspective that emphasizes similarities rather than dissimilarities. At times the discussion is terse. That's not because the material is not important. Rather, it's because the basic argument was made in an earlier part of the book, and I want to encourage you to extend the argument to the case at hand. If you can't, then I at least want you to try. So, in what follows, you will see, for example, that many more words are devoted to the "expenditure-minimization" problem than to the "revenue-maximization" problem. The challenge for you is to recycle arguments made in one context into its mirror image. The ultimate goal is to help you develop the ability to take a basic theoretical model and then to extend it to suit the needs of a particular applied problem.

The organizing principle of the book is that most of the analyses of consumer theory, producer theory, equilibrium theory, and decision making under uncertainty are "alike, 'tho infinitely various" (William Blake). They can be formulated using a common structure amenable to analysis using fundamental principles of conjugacy theory and convex analysis. Consequently, there is no shortage of mathematical manipulation in what follows. Still, these *are not* lectures on mathematical economics. Some readers might be surprised to learn that a course organized along these lines is taught (indeed required) in an *applied economics* department. Much, of course, depends on what one means by *applied.* My definition of an *applied economist* (and I consider myself one) is someone whose primary interest lies in solving practical problems that have clear origins in the real world, the kind of problems readers of good-quality newspapers routinely encounter on a daily basis. In my experience, that translates into economic analysis that maintains roughly an even split between applied theorizing and data analysis.

I would never argue, however, that a mathematical approach is the only way to do economic analysis. But it does carry important and well-known advantages that include precision of thought and communication as well as the ability to extend from the special case to the more general. Even more importantly, however, by providing a clear foundation for analyzing problems, it also provides a mechanism for recognizing the same economic phenomenon when dressed in different guises. All too often, we applied economists waste too much time solving "new problems" that are really "old problems" in other areas of economics but that appear to us in disguised form. Mathematical analysis, of course, also has many shortcomings when it comes to doing economics. For completeness sake, I should really list a few. But I won't because you can always ask a sociologist, an historian, or a psychologist to explain how economists get it all wrong with their models and the attendant mathematics.

Hopefully, this book provides a guide to a simple, but surprisingly powerful, way of looking at things. And that entails some mathematics. If you can truly take a limit, all should be well. Moreover, all too often what follows is only quasi-rigorous. There are many undotted "*i's*" and uncrossed "*t's*". That does not mean that I believe such details to be unimportant. Indeed, just the opposite is true, experience has often taught me that getting a "detail" right has taught me something fundamental about economics. When more detail is needed, I try to mention where to go to get the "real stuff." Precious few (and certainly not me) can keep all of the math essential to different areas of economics in our heads at any one time. But knowing where to look is more often than not half the battle. Here are some books that I have found particularly valuable: R. T. Rockafellar, *Convex Analysis*; G. Pólya, *How to Solve It;* D. G. Luenberger, *Optimization by Vector Space Methods;* D. G. Luenberger, *Microeconomic Theory;* C. Berge, *Topological Spaces*; J-B Hiriart-Urruty and C. LeMaréchal, *Fundamentals of Convex Analysis;* J. Aczél, *Lectures on Functional Equations and Their Applictions;* C. Aliprantis and K. Border, *Infinite Dimensional Analysis: A Hitchhiker's Guide*;[1] P. C. Fishburn,

[1] Aliprantis and Border is particularly complete. If you need a basic mathematical result for economics, a good place to start is with them.

Mathematics of Decision Theory; F. H. Clarke, *Optimization and Nonsmooth Analysis;* D. M. Kreps, *A Course in Microeconomic Theory;* C. Chambers and F. Echenique, *Revealed Preference Theory;* J.-P. Aubin, *Mathematical Methods of Game and Economic Theory;* E. A. Ok, *Real Analysis with Economic Applications;* and H. Nikaido, *Convex Structures and Economic Theory.*

To close this preface, I present quotes from Savage (1954, p. viii) and Gale (1960, p. 28). They were intended for the audiences of *The Foundations of Statistics* and *The Theory of Linear Economic Models,* respectively, but they apply equally well for anyone reading this book.

> In the first place, it cannot be too strongly emphasized that a long mathematical argument can be fully understood on first reading only when it is very elementary indeed, relative to the reader's mathematical knowledge. If one wants only the gist of it, he may read such material *once* only; but otherwise he must expect to read it at least once again. Serious reading of mathematics is best done sitting bolt upright on a hard chair at a desk. Pencil and paper are nearly indispensable; for there are always figures to be sketched and steps in the argument to be verified by calculation. In this book, as in many mathematical books, when exercises are indicated, it is absolutely essential that they be read and nearly essential that they be worked, because they constitute part of the exposition, the exercise form being adopted where it seems to the author best for conveying the particular information at hand. (Savage 1954)

> It need hardly be mentioned here that one exercise worked by the reader is worth three paragraphs of explanation from us. (Gale 1960)

Acknowledgments

The original set of notes from which this book evolved were intended to give my graduate students at Maryland a relatively complete mathematical treatment of the lecture material. My reasoning was that providing detailed notes would obviate the need for the more frantic notetaking in which graduate students engage. That, I hoped, would let them focus on the intuitive content of the lectures. It didn't work out that way. And so, my first acknowledgment goes to those unintended victims whose struggles with the resulting material taught me more about it than I probably taught them. Much of what is said in this book traces back to a long-ago conversation that I had over cappuccino with Rolf Färe. It convinced me that the perspective on microeconomics taken in this book had much more to offer than I then understood. Rolf also read and commented on early versions of those lecture notes. *Tack så mycket*, Rolf. David Pervin, then with Oxford University Press, convinced me "to let the reviewers decide" and to include an early version of Chapter 1 in the manuscript. The form that chapter ultimately took has its roots in a lunchtime conversation with Steve Salant. I benefited greatly from the comments of anonymous reviewers for Oxford University Press. They encouraged me, among other things, to include a discussion of Revealed Preference in the final product. That effort taught me a lot. And Chris Chambers was kind enough to comment on the outcome. Readers will encounter many ideas that were developed jointly with Tigran Melkonyan and John Quiggin. My thanks to them both for sharing so generously and for long and fruitful (on my part) collaborations. Even though I never talk economics with them, I want to thank Paul and Frank for many decades of enduring friendship. Good friends are truly the scarcest and thus the most valuable good. As a boy, I was an avid fan of the Washington Senators who eventually became the Minnesota Twins. While in Washington, they were chronically in last place in the American League. "Washington, first in war, first in peace, and last in the American League" is perhaps the first quote that I memorized. They were so bad that there was even a play (and later a movie) about it, *Damn Yankees!*. My dad, a Red Sox fan, once consoled me by saying that it "took a strong team to hold up all of the others in the standings." As with many of the lessons he taught me, the idea that last doesn't mean worst is something that I've never forgotten.

So with that in mind, I want to end my acknowledgments by thanking those most important to me: my boys, Chris, Geoff, and Tim (in alphabetic order), Chris's family (Vanja and Evan), and my long-suffering, ever-supportive, and deeply loved wife, Michelle. I hope that I have brought to your lives a fraction of the happiness and fulfillment that you've brought to mine.

1
What's Covered

The easiest way to illustrate our subject matter is with some pictures. If you have a reasonable background in intermediate microeconomics, all should be familiar. You have likely seen several of these graphics multiple times in perhaps different contexts. These are Figures 1 to 6, which follow.[1] Before reading any further, I would ask that you attempt the following.

> **Pop Quiz (Basic Micro)** For Figures 1 through 6, do several things. First, for each one, choose a context in which you feel the figure illustrates a fundamental economic concept. Once that is done, label the figure, especially its axes, appropriately. Then tell an intuitive economic story that explains that concept.[2]

If you were not able to do this quiz without consulting a textbook (be honest with yourself), you need to supplement this material with remedial reading on intermediate microeconomics. The goal is for you to be readily conversant with each of these figures in a variety of different economic contexts. In doing that reading, it's probably best to concentrate on developing your intuition while not worrying too much about the mathematics.

Regardless of what text you choose, what follows presumes that you are thoroughly conversant, at the intermediate micro level, with the following concepts (plus others): indifference curves, isoquants, budget lines, cost lines, expansion paths, isocost curves, transformation curves (production possibilities frontiers), supply curves, compensated demand curves, uncompensated demand (Marshallian, Walrasian) curves, Pareto optimality, Pareto inferior, Pareto superior, market equilibrium, general equilibrium, utility maximization, cost minimization, expenditure minimization, profit maximization, marginal cost, marginal revenue, marginal utility, returns to scale, diminish-

[1] In referencing figures, the convention is as follows. For figures that are presented within this chapter, I will refer to figures as Figure 1, 2, 3,... If I should happen to reference any of these figures in another chapter, they will be referred to as Figure #.x where # corresponds to the chapter number and x to the number within the chapter.

[2] The idea for this Pop Quiz originated from a conversation with Steve Salant to whom I am indebted.

Competitive Agents in Certain and Uncertain Markets. Robert G. Chambers, Oxford University Press (2021).

DOI: 10.1093/oso/9780190063016.001.0001

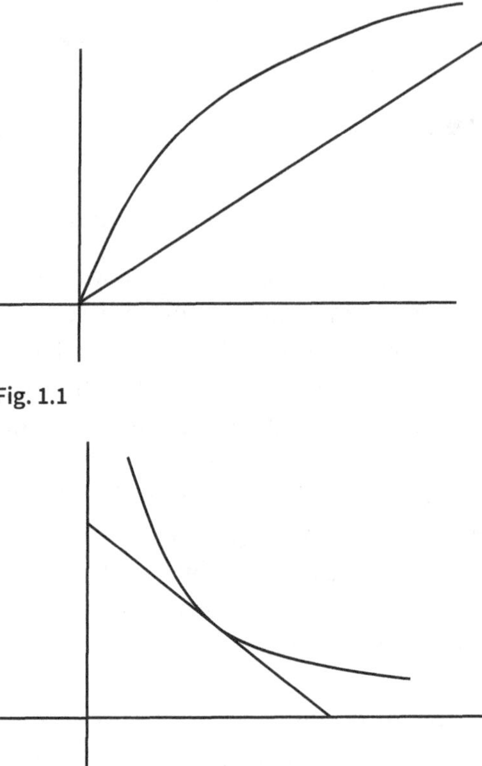

Fig. 1.1

Fig. 1.2

ing marginal returns, increasing marginal returns, constant returns to scale, decreasing returns to scale, increasing returns to scale, inferior goods, normal goods, Giffen goods, expected-utility maximization, and so on and so on.

Now that you've taken the Pop Quiz, let's take another look at Figures 1 to 6. Figures 1 to 4 are nicely symmetric. Figure 1 is a mirror image of Figure 3, and Figure 2 is a mirror image of Figure 4. My guess is that you have probably encountered both in studying firm behavior. In that context, the vertical axes in Figures 1 and 3 would represent dollars (euros, yen, etc.), and the horizontal axes input use and output produced, respectively. The (concave) curve in Figure 1 might then represent revenue earned by applying the input, while the straight line from the origin would represent input expenditure. Similarly, in Figure 3, the (convex) curve might depict cost of producing the output, and the straight line, revenue from sale of the output. In both Figure 1 and Figure 3, the vertical distance between the illustrated line and curve would represent profit. And the economic problem is to pick input and output, respectively, to maximize that profit.

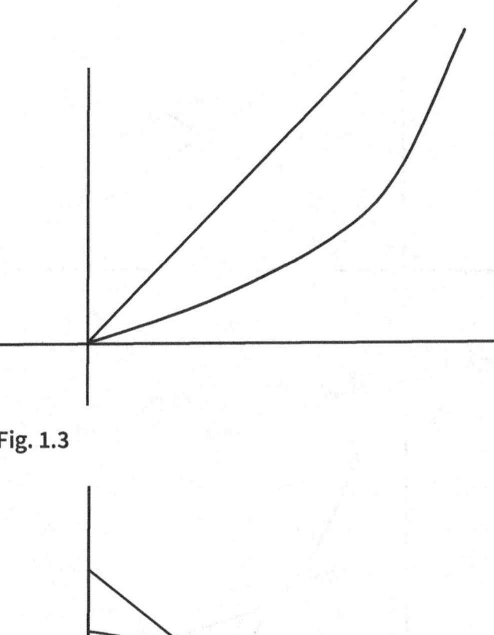

Fig. 1.3

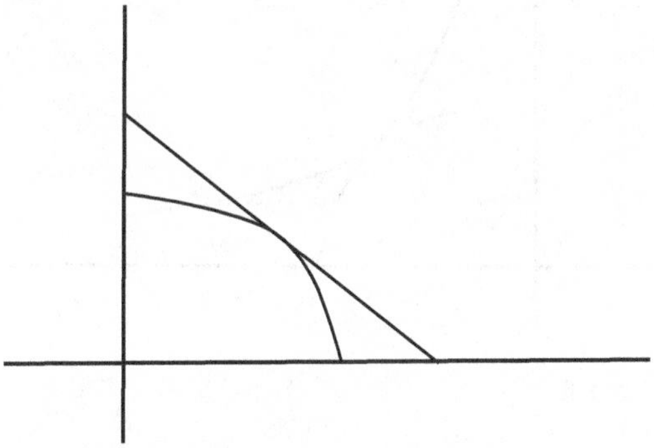

Fig. 1.4

Following this metaphor, Figures 2 and 4 illustrate optimality conditions for (slightly) generalized versions of the choice problems in Figures 1 and 3. Figure 2 would be drawn in input space, the convex to the origin curve would represent an isoquant, and the straight line would be an isocost line for fixed-input prices. Similarly, the concave to the origin curve in Figure 4 would represent a (multiple-output) isocost curve, and the straight line an isorevenue line for fixed-output prices. The "kissing" tangencies are familiarly interpreted as equating marginal rates of substitution to relative input prices and equating marginal rates of tranformation to relative output prices.

If these aren't the interpretations you offered, no worries. They are only some of the possible examples you will encounter in what follows. Myriad economic decision problems, when stripped to their essential kernel, have remarkably similar representations. For example, I will try to convince you that Figure 1, in addition to representing profit maximization, also represents

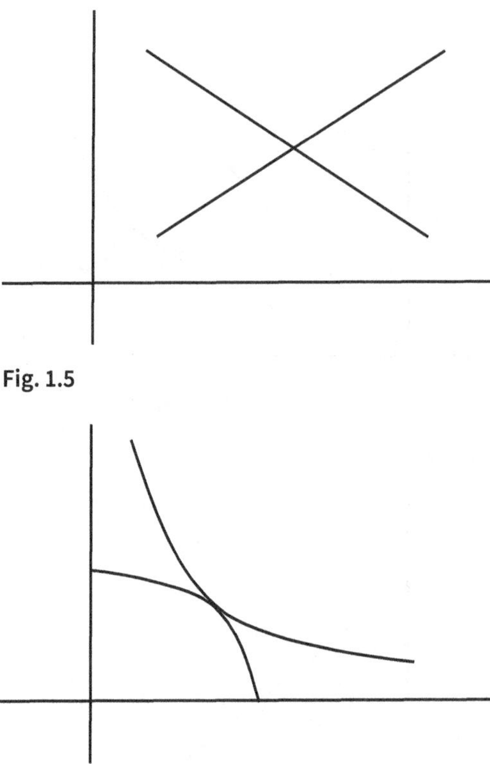

Fig. 1.5

Fig. 1.6

both expenditure minimization and utility maximization. Figure 2 is also interpretable as a way to determine relative probabilities. I chose the firm metaphor at this point to illustrate that, in that context, the two pairs illustrate different perspectives on the same problem (profit maximization). One concentrates on inputs, and the other on outputs. Heuristically, the two solutions should be connected, and they are. Moreover, they are nicely symmetric.

Figures 5 and 6 were chosen to illustrate this symmetry in a different fashion. The odds are strong that you labeled the vertical axis in Figure 5 in dollar terms and the horizontal axis in quantity terms. The downward-sloping curve would then represent demand and the upward-sloping curve supply. Their intersection represents a market equilibrium. Maintaining that metaphor, in a multiple-output setting, Figure 6 could depict two different offer curves for two different individuals oriented toward different origins. The depicted tangency would then illustrate a trading equilibrium between the two.

Again, do not worry if these are not the interpretations you chose. Many different economic problems can be illustrated in this same setting. For example, another interpretation of both involves the decision process of a multiplant firm allocating input across different plants. Yet another involves representing general equilibria and Pareto-optimal allocations.

These six figures form our core material. My first goal is to convince you that each illustrates an essentially identical concept; all reflect a common mathematical structure; each depicts a special case of a generic optimization program; and optimization problems can be easily solved even when the calculus is not applicable (but we should never forget the lessons the calculus has taught us). Then I try to demonstrate exactly why consumer theory, producer theory, decision theory, general-equilibrium theory, decision making under uncertainty, and equilibrium under uncertainty are all special cases of that problem. Many years ago, Paul Samuelson (1947) remarked that in studying economics he often found himself "simply proving the same theorems a wasteful number of times." My hope is to convince you that many of us do the same thing when we study those six topics as if they were independent. If I am successful in those goals, hopefully you will be able to extend and refine these same arguments in your applied research.

Most microeconomics books relegate the discussion of fundamentally mathematical concepts to appendices. These lectures pursue a different tack. Here that material is front and center as the next chapter. That's done to emphasize the common mathematical structure lying behind Figures 1 to 6. These structures can be analyzed using tools borrowed from convex analysis and optimization. In many instances, important concepts in modern microeconomics reflect special cases of mathematical objects that are immediately familiar to students of these areas. And while the mathematical material is "up front," so to speak, I have attempted to temper the discussion using verbiage and pictorial representations familiar to students with a sound grasp of intermediate micro.

2
Differentials and Convex Analysis

Almost a century ago, Frank Knight (1921) wrote that "mathematical economics in particular seems likely to remain little more than a cult, a closed book to all except a few of the 'initiated' " (Knight 1921). Times have changed! You cannot function as an applied microeconomist unless you understand the standard mathematical representations of consumer and producer behavior. At one time, that meant being able to set up simple constrained maximization problems, take a derivative to represent their first-order conditions, interpret those first-order conditions in a rote, but hopefully intuitive, fashion, differentiate those first-order conditions, formulate a bordered Hessian, solve the resulting differential equation system to obtain comparative-static results, and then interpret those results in a rote, but hopefully intuitive, fashion. While one is still expected to be able to do those things, it's no longer enough. Standard microeconomics moved past that framework roughly four decades ago in general economics and roughly three decades ago in more applied areas such as agricultural, environmental, and resource economics. The basic difference between the "old" way of looking at things and the "newer" way was the realization that most of what is truly predictable about economic behavior results **not** from structure placed on preferences, the technology, and their functional representations. Instead, they are immediate consequences of the problems we pose (for example, consumer preference maximization or producer profit maximization), the setting in which we pose those problems (for example, competitive markets), and our presumption of a precise form of rationality.

Perhaps the most basic assumption of neoclassical economics is that rational individuals optimize. That can be interpreted in different ways, but few would dispute that a sound understanding of the principles of mathematical optimization is essential for any professional economist. Considered as a distinct field of mathematics,

> [o]ptimization has an unusual status.... It really has to stand on three legs. One is a basic theory like convex analysis. Another is the understanding of the various ways of formulating problems, what are important things, not important things—

Competitive Agents in Certain and Uncertain Markets. Robert G. Chambers, Oxford University Press (2021).

DOI: 10.1093/oso/9780190063016.001.0001

> in other words artful mathematical modelling. What are the tools for that? In a new subject, you are obliged to develop new tools. The third leg on which optimization stands is computation . . . the models you set should be ones for solving problems effectively. The challenges of modeling and computation inspire advances in theory. (Rockafellar 2011)

Similar points pertain to microeconomic analysis. It, too, rests on three legs. The basic theory is that of rational behavior. For better or worse, rational behavior is closely identified with optimization. The second, and perhaps most crucial, leg is artful problem formulation. One typically relies on the principle of abstraction to focus attention on the kernel of the problem. Abstraction, however, is a two-edged sword. It can be used to pare a problem to its essentials to permit an informative resolution. Or it can be used to neuter the problem. If the paring is done properly, solving it frequently involves learning or developing new tools (often mathematical). And that is the third leg, which is using the tools appropriate to solve the true problem. Often, however, this is where things go awry. All too frequently, those averse to learning or developing new tools use abstraction as license to neuter the problem while ensuring that it fits tools in which they have become highly specialized. Forcing an applied problem to fit a preordained set of tools is not unlike forcing one's foot into nicely designed but ill-fitting shoes. Both appear attractive initially, but . . .

This chapter develops some basic tools that will be used repeatedly in what follows. As such, it is the longest and, perhaps, the most intensive chapter in the book. More often than not, it will prove wise to take Savage's admonition quoted in the Preface to heart. Slogging is definitely required at times. When that happens, and it will, my experience has always been that the best way to absorb detailed mathematical arguments is to skim them first to get the basic gist. And only then, go back and do the pencilling and figure sketching that understanding requires.

Nevertheless, the ideas are simple and common to a surprisingly broad array of problems. And these problems can be illustrated with pictures familiar to anyone having a smattering of undergraduate micro theory. That's the point of the earlier Pop Quiz. Moreover, the striking similarity between those pictures and the mathematical ideas that follow is not a coincidence. Many of the ideas developed in optimization theory were often motivated by unresolved problems in economics and its closely related cousin, operations research.[1]

[1] Today, the disciplines are often viewed as distinct. But not so long ago, graduate texts covered both topics. Baumol's (1961) text *Economic Theory and Operations Analysis* is a well-known example that

Although the ideas are simple, they are abstract and perhaps unfamiliar to some. So some may struggle even though they are well prepared mathematically. Much rests on whether you are well prepared mathematically in *computational* or *heuristic* terms. I've found that some students who excel at taking derivatives, setting up Lagrangians, integrating by parts, etc., struggle with what follows, when others who have little or no preparation absorb the ideas quite easily. The reverse of course is also true.

As you study these tools, it's well to remember that the mathematics developed stand alone on the stated axioms and assumptions. In and of themselves, they have no innate economic content. Instead, they are tools (albeit abstract) for consistent reasoning. How we interpret them economically involves what Fishburn (1972) has memorably coined *extramathematical reasoning*. But, for us, the mathematics are not a final goal; that's left to mathematicians and not economists. Rather, the goal is logical reasoning from precisely specified economic problems to understandable economic results. That requires the ability to distinguish the difference between analysis supported by the mathematics and intuitive analyses outside of the mathematical framework.

1 Correspondences

Many, if not most, times visualizing economic concepts enhances understanding. Thus, graphical depictions abound in economic discussions. Sometimes functions are graphed. But almost as frequently, upper or lower contour sets of a given function are depicted graphically. Here you can think of an indifference curve and a preference set. An indifference curve gives the set of points one finds indifferent to a particular point, and a preference set (or at-least-as-good set) everything at least as good as a point. Both sets are examples of *correspondences*.

Correspondences are *point-to-set mappings*. So, like a function, they take a point, say $y \in \mathbb{R}^M$, and map it into another (or possibly the same) real space, call it $\mathbb{R}^N$. But instead of mapping it into a single point as functions do, they map it into a collection of points. As noted, a prominent example of a

still proves rewarding reading for economists. More importantly, some very famous economic principles (the *revelation principle* being an especially prominent example) were originally articulated in operation research journals.

correspondence is the mapping defining the *at-least-as-good set* for $y \in \mathbb{R}^M$ defined by

$$V(y) \equiv \{x \in \mathbb{R}^M : x \text{ is at least as good as } y\}.$$

Most of you will visualize this as an upturned bowl tilted toward the northeast. Its lower boundary, the image of another correspondence, is the indifference curve.

It's convenient to differentiate correspondences from functions notationally. In what follows, a correspondence V that maps $\mathbb{R}^M$ into subsets of, say, $\mathbb{R}^N$ is denoted by $V : \mathbb{R}^M \rightrightarrows \mathbb{R}^N$. But be aware: Others often write the same concept as $V : \mathbb{R}^M \to 2^{\mathbb{R}^N}$, where the notation $2^{\mathbb{R}^N}$ denotes the set of all subsets of $\mathbb{R}^N$.

We have (or rather you should be familiar with) a notion of continuity for functions (defined formally as single-valued mappings); a corresponding property proves convenient for correspondences. A function $f : \mathbb{R}^N \to \mathbb{R}$ is *continuous* if and only if for every open subset Y of $\mathbb{R}$ the set

$$\begin{aligned} f^{-1}(Y) &\equiv \{x \in \mathbb{R}^N : f(x) = y, y \in Y\} \\ &\equiv \{x \in \mathbb{R}^N : f(x) \in Y\}, \end{aligned}$$

the inverse image of Y under f in $\mathbb{R}^N$, is an open subset of $\mathbb{R}^N$.

When speaking of a correspondence, $\Gamma : \mathbb{R}^l \rightrightarrows \mathbb{R}^m$, (at least) two natural ways exist to generalize the concept of an inverse image. This happens because where $f(x)$ denotes a singleton set, $\Gamma(x)$ does not. Thus, one can legitimately replace $f(x) \in Y$ with $\Gamma(x) \subset Y$ or with $\Gamma(x) \cap Y \neq \varnothing$.

Each alternative leads to a different notion of an inverse. Using the first gives the so-called *upper inverse of* $Y \subset \mathbb{R}^m$ *under* Γ (more simply the upper inverse of Γ):[2]

$$\Gamma^+(Y) = \{x \in \mathbb{R}^l : \Gamma(x) \subset Y\}.$$

Using the second gives the so-called *lower inverse of Y under* Γ :

$$\Gamma^-(Y) = \{x \in \mathbb{R}^l : \Gamma(x) \cap Y \neq \varnothing\}.$$

[2] A word on notation. I find the subset operators $\subseteq$ and $\supseteq$ visually displeasing. Therefore, notationally I always use either $\subset$ or $\supset$ to denote set inclusion. I do not notationally distinguish between strict and weak inclusion except where it is absolutely necessary. Then you can expect to see a footnote.

Exercise 1. *Prove that if $f : \mathbb{R}^N \to \mathbb{R}$, the correspondence $\Gamma : \mathbb{R}^N \rightrightarrows \mathbb{R}$ induced by*

$$\Gamma(x) = \{f(x)\},$$

where f is single-valued satisfies $\Gamma^+ = \Gamma^-$.

Exercise 2. *Consider the correspondence $\Gamma : \mathbb{R} \rightrightarrows \mathbb{R}$*

$$\Gamma(x) = \begin{cases} \bar{y} & x \leq x_1 \\ [y_1, y_2] & x_1 < x < x_2 \\ \bar{y} & x \geq x_2 \end{cases}$$

with $\bar{y} \in (y_1, y_2)$. Graph it. Derive its upper and lower inverses for $Y = (y_1, y_2)$. Graph both of them.

A correspondence, $\Gamma : \mathbb{R}^l \rightrightarrows \mathbb{R}^m$, Γ is *upper hemicontinuous* if $\Gamma^+(Y)$ is open for every Y open. A correspondence, $\Gamma : \mathbb{R}^l \rightrightarrows \mathbb{R}^m$, is *lower hemicontinuous* if $\Gamma^-(Y)$ is open for every Y open.[3] A correspondence that is both lower and upper hemicontinuous is *continuous*. The set

$$Gr(\Gamma) = \{(x, y) \in \mathbb{R}^l \times \mathbb{R}^m : y \in \Gamma(x)\}$$

is called the *graph of the correspondence.*

Exercise 3. *Consider the correspondence $\Gamma : \mathbb{R} \rightrightarrows \mathbb{R}$*

$$\Gamma(x) = \begin{cases} \bar{y} & x \leq x_1 \\ [y_1, y_2] & x_1 < x < x_2 \\ \bar{y} & x \geq x_2 \end{cases}$$

with $\bar{y} \in (y_1, y_2)$. Is it upper hemicontinuous? Is it lower hemicontinuous?

We're primarily interested in upper and lower hemicontinuity because of Berge's Maximum Theorem, which is fundamental to modern economics and to which you should have been introduced in Math Camp. I repeat a version of it here.

Theorem 1 (Berge's Maximum Theorem). *Suppose that $f : \mathbb{R}^k \times \mathbb{R}^l \to \mathbb{R}$ is continuous, and let $\Gamma : \mathbb{R}^k \rightrightarrows \mathbb{R}^l$ be a nonempty valued, compact valued, continuous correspondence.*[4] *Then the following two statements hold:*

[3] Another semantic alert. Some authors call hemicontinous *semicontinuous*, although this is becoming increasingly rare. I reserve the latter terminology for functions.

[4] A correspondence is *nonempty valued* if for all x, $\Gamma(x) \neq \varnothing$. It is *compact valued* if for all x, $\Gamma(x)$ is a compact set.

- *The function $g : \mathbb{R}^k \to \mathbb{R}$ defined by*

$$g(x) = \max\{f(x, y) : y \in \Gamma(x)\}$$

  is continuous.
- *The correspondence $G : \mathbb{R}^k \rightrightarrows \mathbb{R}^l$ defined by*

$$G(x) = \arg\max\{f(x, y) : y \in \Gamma(x)\}$$

  is upper hemicontinuous.

Proof. Go to Berge (1963). □

Remark 1. *While both upper and lower hemicontinuity are important, in most applied settings they're typically regularity conditions. As such, you can feel free in reading what follows to simply assume these are satisfied. In fact, it's hard to find real-world data sets that can't be made consistent with some version of hemicontinuity. So feel free to rely on Berge's Maximum Theorem whenever you need it. That said, you should read Berge (1963) carefully at some point in your graduate career. Aliprantis and Border (2006, Chapter 17) provides a detailed treatment of correspondences, various continuity notions, the Maximum Theorem, and related results.*

2 Differentiability?

If mathematics is the language of economics, the calculus is truly one of its chief dialects. And for a very long time, the calculus was the main dialect. When I first studied economics, the main difference between an undergraduate micro class and a graduate one was that the latter used the calculus. And students had finely honed, but largely mechanical, skill at forming Lagrangians, first-order conditions, and bordered Hessians.

Unfortunately, calculus-honed intuition often struggles when the world is not nicely smooth. In many instances, such departures may not be economically important because they often occur on "sets of measure zero." Put perhaps more visually, "kinks" typically occur at single points, and the latter correspond to sets of measure zero. The intuitive argument is that because we are talking "tiny sets" over which problems can exist, we can safely ignore them and proceed with our convenient calculations. This is sound enough advice, *provided nothing economically important happens on those tiny sets.*

It's harder for a mapping to be differentiable than it is for it to be continuous. Mathematically, that implies that differentiability requires more complicated rather than less complicated structures. If you only know the calculus, you may think of continuous but nondifferentiable structures as the more complicated, but that really means that you are confounding the definitions of complicated and familiar. It's also clear that when imposed on economic functions, *differentiability carries extra behavioral assumptions* about how real people respond. It makes for less rather than more realistic modeling.

Unfortunately, we've discovered that in many instances, those sets of measure zero can be important both theoretically and empirically.[5] And ignoring them, while insisting that observed phenemona fit our easily manipulable smooth models, can impede our understanding of the real world. As Samuelson (1947, p. 6) once wrote, such mental gymnastics are "unrewarding from the standpoint of advancing the science."

A familiar, but simple, example of when such a "set of measure zero" is important helps illustrate.

Exercise 4. *Take $x \in \mathbb{R}^N$. Define*

$$s(x) \equiv \left(\frac{1}{N} \sum_n |x_n - \mu|^2 \right)^{\frac{1}{2}}$$

Does $s(x)$ look familiar? Your answer should be yes. Mathematically, it's a member of the family of norms, which are fundamental to measuring distances in both economics and statistics. Can you give it a meaningful statistical interpretation? Again, the answer should be yes. Now attempt the following: Apply the Fermat–Leibniz Theorem[6] to solve the following problem $\min_x \{s(x)\}$.

[5] Witness, for example, the extended debate in environmental and experimental economics on whether perceived (better to say, empirically measured) gaps between willingness-to-pay and willingness-to-accept are "consistent with theory." (See Chapter 10 for a more detailed discussion of "Willingness-to-Pay and Willingness-to-Accept Discrepancies.") If you live in a smoothly differentiable world such things can be puzzling. In fact, they were very puzzling for approximately a decade to experimentalists and environmental economists. In a world that admits kinks, they aren't.

[6] Fancy language, designed to show you just how old this rule really is, for taking a derivative and setting it to zero. This is likely not the Fermat Theorem you are familiar with. That one is his "Last Theorem," which was only successfully proved in the last few decades. This one dates to 1636 and was converted into a calculus algorithm by Leibniz about fifty years later. Recall that Newton and Leibniz independently laid the foundations for modern calculus at about this time.

Remark 2. *Although Fermat's Theorem is very old, our current notions (there are many) of a derivative in the multidimensional case are, in fact, surprisingly recent. Fréchet's definition dates to around the 1920s, while Weierstrass's definition, which was introduced even earlier, only appeared in published form around 1930.*

The solution to Exercise 4 is obvious. Intuitively, you're looking for the point $x \in \mathbb{R}^N$ that is "closest" to $(\mu, \mu, \ldots, \mu) \in \mathbb{R}^N$. Naturally, the closest point to any point is the point itself. Even Homer Simpson would get this. The solution is to set all x_n equal to μ. But taking derivatives won't get you there. If you don't know why, sketch on a piece of paper the graph of the relationship:

$$f(x) = |x| .$$

Where is its global min? Is $f(x)$ differentiable at that point?

So there can be problems with a purely derivative-based approach to optimization. And that also means that there will be a problem with a derivative-based approach to economics. That doesn't mean, however, that we should throw out the baby with the bath water. The essential idea behind taking derivatives is nice, fundamental to optimization, and thus important in virtually every area of economics. Moreover, it's very intuitive. In fact, as I shall try to emphasize, *there is an innate link between economic functionals being differentiable (in a generalized sense), maximization, minimization, and rational behavior.*

So that leaves us in the following position: The essential idea behind derivatives in economics is nice, but the world, unfortunately, often isn't smooth. So a concept is needed that captures the essence of a derivative (more properly a *gradient*) but that can accommodate kinks if need be.

Let's first recall what a derivative is. For $f : \mathbb{R} \to \mathbb{R}$, its derivative is defined (if it exists) as something like

$$f'(x) = \lim_{\lambda \to 0} \left\{ \frac{f(x+\lambda) - f(x)}{\lambda} \right\}. \tag{2.1}$$

So (by the concept of a limit), it's the *unique* quantity, $f'(x) \in \mathbb{R}$, such that for λ sufficiently small

$$f(x+\lambda) - f(x) \approx f'(x)\,\lambda.$$

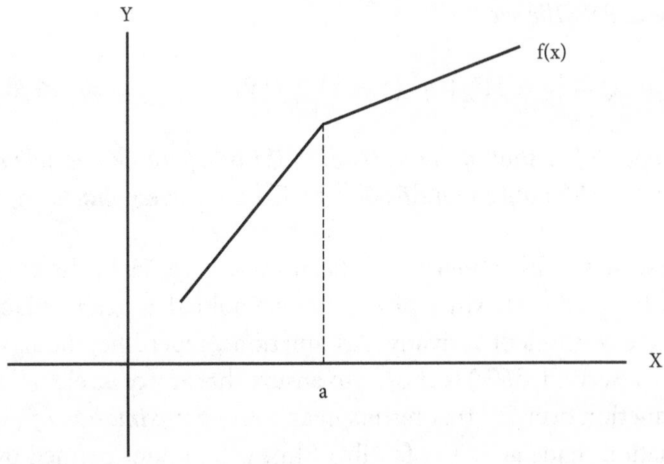

Fig. 2.1 Nondifferentiable Function

Or, in words, it defines a linear approximation to the difference $f(x+\lambda) - f(x)$ at x. Visually, you would interpret $f'(x^o)$ as the slope of the line (hyperplane) tangent to *the graph of* $f(x)$,

$$Gr(f) \equiv \{(x,y) : y = f(x)\},$$

at $(x^o, f(x^o))$.

The trouble occurs when $f(x)$ can be visualized as in Figure 2.1, and the graph of the function has a kink in it. At that point, there are literally an infinity (a continuum) of linear approximations (supporting lines) to the function. Hence, the limit does not exist. So, we're definitely talking a tiny set, but we're aso talking about one where "tiny" differences in one direction or another matter a lot.

To handle such cases, something more general is needed. Here's something that works for the figure. (*Notation:* For arbitrary x and y belonging to $\mathbb{R}^N$, the notation $x^\top$ is the transpose of x, and $x^\top y$ denotes the (standard) inner product. My convention is that all vectors are written in column form and transposes in row form. The same convention is applied for matrices and matrix products.)

Definition 1. $f : \mathbb{R}^N \to \mathbb{R}$ *is superdifferentiable at* x *if there exists* $q \in \mathbb{R}^N$ *such that*

$$q^\top (y - x) \geq f(y) - f(x),$$

for all $y \in \mathbb{R}^N$. The set

$$\partial f(x) = \{q \in \mathbb{R}^N : q^{\top}(y - x) \geq f(y) - f(x) \text{ for all } y \in \mathbb{R}^N\}$$

is the superdifferential of f at x. (Notice, if f is superdifferentiable at x, then $\partial f(x) \neq \emptyset$. Also notice that $\partial f : \mathbb{R}^N \rightrightarrows \mathbb{R}^N$ is a correspondence.)

Let's first be specific about what's been done here. First, the concept of a derivative (or gradient), which gives a unique point, has been replaced with a set. So where we think of derivatives as functions, superdifferentials are correspondences. Second, $\partial f(x)$ is chosen to ensure that any of its elements defines a linear function over $\mathbb{R}^N$ that results in an *over approximation of* $f(y)$ for an approximation made at x. The family of linear functions defined over $\mathbb{R}^N$ is given by the set $\mathbb{R}^N$.[7] Thus, each $q \in \partial f(x)$ defines a linear function that over-approximates the change in the function value from x to any other $y \in \mathbb{R}^N$—hence, the terminology *super*differential. The set $\partial f(x)$ consists of linear functions, each of which might be thought of in calculus terms as a *supergradient.*

There are *caveats.* First, some authors call what I am calling a superdifferential a *subdifferential* and superdifferentiability subdifferentiability. Second, there is a separate notion of subdifferentiability that is defined by reversing the inequality in this definition (please see below). Some also use the term "supergradients" for superdifferentials; there's considerable variability in terminology. Hence, it's easy to get confused if you don't get a good intuitive grasp of this notion.

Second, $\partial f(x)$, as we have defined it, requires that $q \in \partial f(x)$ satisfy a *global* property. Thus, unlike a derivative or a partial derivative, it is not based on the notion of a local linear approximation. This has pluses and minuses. One minus is that many mappings that are differentiably smooth in a local sense will not be superdifferentiable. A plus is that you can understand a superdifferential even if you are on shaky ground when it comes to taking limits. Another plus, as we shall see below, is that all concave functions are typically superdifferentiable. For this reason, many authors (including Rockafellar 1970) restrict the notion of a superdifferential to apply only to concave (convex) functions. Others (for example, Aubin 2007, Ok 2007, or Hiriart-Urruty and LeMaréchal 2001) do not.

Problem 1. *For Figure 1, determine graphically what is the superdifferential of $f(x)$. Write it mathematically?*

[7] Be careful here not to confuse a linear function with an affine function.

A geometric interpretation of $\partial f(x)$ slightly recycles the intuitive idea that the derivative of a function, $f'(x)$, defines an affine approximation to $f : \mathbb{R} \to \mathbb{R}$. Geometrically, that interpretation of the derivative means the graph of the affine function $a : \mathbb{R} \to \mathbb{R}$,

$$a(x) \equiv f'(x^o)x - (f'(x^o)x^o - f(x^o)),$$

with slope $f'(x^0)$, is tangent to $Gr(f)$ at $(x^o, f(x^o))$. (*N.B You are strongly encouraged to draw a picture.*)

The superdifferential generalizes this geometric idea by replacing $Gr(f)$ with its *hypograph* that consists of all points falling on or below $Gr(f)$, and by replacing *tangency* with the closely related notion of *support*. Formally, the *hypograph* of $f : \mathbb{R}^N \to \bar{\mathbb{R}}$,[8] denoted as $hyp(f)$, is defined as:

$$hyp(f) \equiv \{(x, y) \in \mathbb{R}^{N+1} : f(x) \geq y\}.$$

An affine function $A : \mathbb{R}^N \to \bar{\mathbb{R}}$

$$A(x) \equiv q^\top x - (q^\top x^o - f(x^o))$$

supports $hyp(f) \in \mathbb{R}^{N+1}$ *from above* at $(x^o, f(x^o))$ if

$$hyp(f) \subset hyp(A).$$

Visually, that means $Gr(A)$ is tangent to $Gr(f)$ at $(x^o, f(x^o))$ and lies above (no lower than) $hyp(f)$ everywhere.[9] Figure 2.2 illustrates.

Rewriting the definition of ∂f slightly yields closely related interpretations that prove essential in studying optimization. For example,

$$\partial f(x) = \{q \in \mathbb{R}^N : q^\top (y - x) \geq f(y) - f(x) \text{ for all } y \in \mathbb{R}^N\}$$

easily converts to

$$\partial f(x) = \{q \in \mathbb{R}^N : f(x) - q^\top x \geq f(y) - q^\top y \text{ for all } y \in \mathbb{R}^N\},$$

[8] $\overline{\mathbb{R}}$ denotes the set consisting of $\mathbb{R}$ and its limits $-\infty$ and ∞. Some write this as $[-\infty, \infty]$, which is meant to denote the closure of the set of reals with $-\infty$ and ∞ appended. Care should be taken in conducting basic algebraic operations involving $\pm\infty$. Where such things are paid attention to in the following, the conventions established in Rockafellar (1970) are followed.

[9] By construction, $(x^o, f(x^o))$ belongs to both $Gr(f)$ and $Gr(A)$.

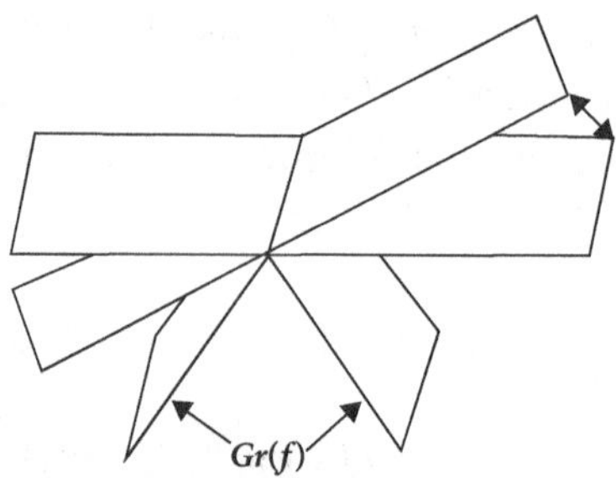

Fig. 2.2 Elements of the Superdifferential

or equivalently

$$\partial f(x) = \{q \in \mathbb{R}^N : q^\top y - f(y) \geq q^\top x - f(x) \text{ for all } y \in \mathbb{R}^N\}.$$

Thus, $q \in \partial f(x)$ requires $f(x) - q^\top x$ to provide an upper bound for $f(y) - q^\top y$ over $\mathbb{R}^N$ and (equivalently) requires that $q^\top x - f(x)$ provide a lower bound for $q^\top y - f(y)$ over $\mathbb{R}^N$. We state this fact as a theorem to emphasize its importance and for easy reference.

Theorem 2. *$q \in \partial f(x) \Longleftrightarrow q^\top y - f(y) \geq q^\top x - f(x)$ for all $y \in \mathbb{R}^N$ and $q \in \partial f(x) \Leftrightarrow f(x) - q^\top x \geq f(y) - q^\top y$ for all $y \in \mathbb{R}^N$.*

Theorem 2 simply reveals that we have engineered the definition of $\partial f(x)$ so that the informal idea of "taking a derivative and setting it to zero" can be formalized globally to identify optima for a broad class of problems of peculiar interest to economists.

Taking the special case $0_N \in \partial f(x)$ gives:

Corollary 1. *(Fermat–Leibniz) $0_N \in \partial f(x) \Leftrightarrow f(x) \geq f(y)$ for all $y \in \mathbb{R}^N$.*

A parallel notion of *subdifferentiability* is obtained by reversing the inequality in the definition of superdifferentiability.

Problem 2. *Define*

$$\partial^- f(x) = \{q \in \mathbb{R}^N : q^\top (y - x) \leq f(y) - f(x) \text{ for all } y \in \mathbb{R}^N\},$$

and say that f is subdifferentiable at x if $\partial^- f(x) \neq \emptyset$. Repeat the preceding discussions replacing superdifferentiable with subdifferentiable. True, false, explain why: $\partial^- f(x)$ is closed and convex. Interpret the result intuitively.

Example 1. *Consider minimizing*

$$\left(\frac{1}{N}\sum_n |x_n|^2\right)^{\frac{1}{2}}.$$

This function is kinked at $x = 0_N$ *which is clearly the minimizer. The minimal version of Corollary 1 is*

$$0 \in \partial^- f(x) \iff f(x) \leq f(y) \text{ for all } y \in \mathbb{R}^N.$$

The definition of $\partial^- f(x)$ *requires that*

$$q \in \partial^- f(0_N) \iff q^\top y \leq \left(\frac{1}{N}\sum_n |y_n|^2\right)^{\frac{1}{2}} \text{ for all } y \in \mathbb{R}^N.$$

It's obviously true that

$$0 = 0_N^\top y \leq \left(\frac{1}{N}\sum_n |y_n|^2\right)^{\frac{1}{2}} \text{ for all } y \in \mathbb{R}^N$$

so that $0_N \in \partial^- f(0_N)$ *as required.*

The next property of superdifferentials proves of special importance for *comparative-static* analysis. A correspondence $m : \mathbb{R}^N \rightrightarrows \mathbb{R}^N$ is *cyclically monotone*[10] if for all $q^k \in m\left(x^k\right)$, $k = 1, 2, \ldots, K$ with K arbitrary

$$\left(x^2 - x^1\right)^\top q^1 + \left(x^3 - x^2\right)^\top q^2 + \ldots + \left(x^1 - x^K\right)^\top q^K \geq 0. \tag{2.2}$$

Taking $K = 2$ gives

$$\left(x^2 - x^1\right)^\top q^1 + \left(x^1 - x^2\right)^\top q^2 \geq 0,$$

[10] This terminology merits an explicit comment. There exists an alternative definition of *cyclical monotonicity* that reverses the sign of the inequality. Following a similar argument to the one I make, it's easy to show that the *subdifferential* if it exists, is cyclically monotone in that sense. To distinguish between the two, one might wish to think of the version in (2.2) as *cyclically monotone decreasing* and the alternative as *cyclically monotone increasing*.

which can be rewritten as

$$(q^2 - q^1)^{\top} (x^2 - x^1) \leq 0. \tag{2.3}$$

The following argument shows that ∂f *is cyclically monotone over the set*

$$eff(\partial f) \equiv \{x \in \mathbb{R}^N : \partial f(x) \neq \emptyset\},$$

which corresponds to the points where f is superdifferentiable. For $q^k \in \partial f(x^k)$ and $x^k \in eff(\partial f), k = 1, 2, \ldots, K$

$$\begin{aligned}
(x^2 - x^1)^{\top} q^1 &\geq f(x^2) - f(x^1), \\
(x^3 - x^2)^{\top} q^2 &\geq f(x^3) - f(x^2), \\
&\vdots \\
(x^1 - x^K)^{\top} q^K &\geq f(x^1) - f(x^K).
\end{aligned}$$

Adding these K expressions gives (2.2).

In the one-dimensional case, cyclical monotonicity reduces to the correspondence $m(x)$ monotonically decreasing in x. Thus, cyclical monotonicity can be viewed as a natural extension of this concept for correspondences to higher dimensions. When applied to superdifferentials, cyclical monotonicity generalizes the notion of differentiable functions $f : \mathbb{R} \to \mathbb{R}$ possessing derivatives that are monotonically decreasing over $\mathbb{R}$. Although we have yet to define them, this same property characterizes the behavior of concave differentiable functions $f : \mathbb{R} \to \mathbb{R}$.

Superdifferentials and subdifferentials relate naturally to frequently encountered visual images associated with a "primal" view of economics where quantities are picked in response to fixed prices. As you have undoubtedly noticed, tangency conditions are the guts of most economic explanations of optima. (Recall the figures in the first chapter.) For example, cost minimization is explained by equating the slope of an isoquant, usually referred to as *the marginal rate of technical substitution*, to the slope of an isocost line. This visual intuition is so firmly grounded in most economists' psyches that it can be easily extended visually to cases where the marginal rate of technical substitution is not well defined because the isoquant has a kink. (Think Leontief.) Look for where the indifference curve just sits on the isocost line without going below it. When the functions of interest lack smoothness, that intuition proves correct, but the "function-based" notions of derivatives typically used to define marginal rates of technical substitution are replaced by "correspondence-based" notions. Superdifferentials and subdifferentials are those notions.

Superdifferentials and subdifferentials thus let one deal with optimization in a basic, but abstract, manner that emphasizes understanding the essential structure of the problem at hand. But it does not provide a cookbook approach that is applicable even if one doesn't fully grasp the basic ideas.

As such, there are definite drawbacks associated with the use of superdifferentials. The most obvious is that often they are difficult to compute. So, in many practical settings, it may be easier for you to just ignore them. This is the approach that many of us applied economists take, and it often serves us well. However, it also places firm limits on what one can do in the absence of a "cookbook." What happens then is the true test of what it means to be a "good applied economist."

As it turns out, many important economic concepts such as demand and supply functions can be identified with the superdifferentials of what economists think of as expenditure, cost, or profit functions. These superdifferentials naturally have an optimization interpretation in that setting as well, and this lies at the heart of duality theory. However, from an applied perspective the cyclical monotonicity of those superdifferentials may be even more important because they imply, among other results, an inverse relationship between derived-demand correspondences and prices and a positive relationship between supply correspondence and prices. *These are precisely the topics at the center of usual comparative-static analysis of derived demand and supply.* Cyclical monotonicity of superdifferentials in that setting encapsulates the fundamental results that one can obtain from those types of comparative-static exercises. When appropriately recycled, cyclical monotonicity thus translates into derived-demand curves being downward sloping in their own prices and supply functions being upward sloping in their own prices. Thus, the nexus between superdifferentiability and cyclical monotonicity is more than just a mathematical curiosity. It lies at the very heart of the type of behavior that we expect competitive economic agents to undertake. Ultimately, it reflects just how powerful the assumption of price-taking behavior in the pursuit of maximizing economic gain actually is.

3 Do You Prefer to Be Constrained or Penalized?

The optimization problem posed in Exercise 4, even though kinked, is easily managed because the kink occurs at a convenient place. More generally, kinks may not be so cooperative. An easy method to solve nonsmooth optimization problems would then prove convenient. Theorem 2 provides the core of such an approach for unconstrained problems. But most, if not all, economic problems involve constraints. Therefore, if Theorem 2 is to be truly useful, it must accommodate the presence of constraints. We now consider a general, but abstract, method for incorporating constraints into the analysis. Lagrangian, Kuhn–Tucker, and Hamiltonian methods are all special cases of this general approach.

Put intuitively, the basic idea, taken from *variational analysis,* is simple.[11] Convert constrained problems into unconstrained problems by introducing a *penalty function.* Suppose one wishes to solve

$$\max\{f(x) : x \in C\}$$

where $f : \mathbb{R}^N \to \mathbb{R}$ is continuous and $C \subset \mathbb{R}^N$ is a closed and bounded set. The Weierstrass Theorem ensures a solution exists. The practical problem is to find it.

Enter the variational approach.[12] For the set C, define its *indicator function,*[13] $\delta : \mathbb{R}^N \to \bar{\mathbb{R}}$, by

$$\delta(x \mid C) \equiv \begin{cases} 0 & x \in C \\ -\infty & x \notin C \end{cases}.$$

The following equivalence is immediate:

$$\max\{f(x) : x \in C\} = \max_{x \in \mathbb{R}^N}\{f(x) + \delta(x \mid C)\}.$$

Adding the indicator function to the objective function converts the constrained maximization problem into an unconstrained one using the

[11] *Variational analysis* is the field of mathematics that generalizes the theories of convex optimization and the calculus of variations, among other fields. It provides the essential mathematical tools required to solve a broad range of very practical, important, but uncooperative optimization problems in a broad range of fields. The *locus classicus* is R. T. Rockafellar and R. J-B. Wets (1998), *Variational Analysis*, from which the name is derived.

Its math requirements go well beyond this class, but the historical notes that it provides with each chapter provide a particularly informative view on how the struggle with very practical problems led to important, new theoretical developments.

[12] The key ideas here are traceable to Fenchel through Moreau (1962) and Rockafellar (1963).

[13] Indicator functions are usually written in the form

$$\tau(y \mid C) = \begin{cases} 0 & y \in C \\ \infty & y \notin C \end{cases},$$

which is more convenient when dealing with minimization and convex functions rather than concave functions. The definition used here is motivated by our primary focus on optimization as maximization and concave structures.

abstract device of imposing an arbitrarily large penalty for diverging from C. Given appropriate regularity conditions, the unconstrained problem's solution occurs where

$$0 \in \partial \left(f(x) + \delta \left(x \mid C \right) \right).$$

Minimization is handled similarly. To minimize $g : \mathbb{R}^N \to \mathbb{R}$ subject to a constraint recognize that

$$\min \left\{ g(x) : x \in C \right\} = \min_{x \in \mathbb{R}^N} \left\{ g(x) - \delta \left(x \mid C \right) \right\},$$

with solution characterized by

$$0 \in \partial^- \left(g(x) - \delta \left(x \mid C \right) \right).$$

This is so simple and elegant that you might ask why one bothers with Lagrangians or Hamiltonians at all. There are both historical and practical reasons. One is that indicator functions can be difficult to operationalize. Thus, while we have an abstract approach to solving problems that always works, we don't yet have a set of tools that can be routinely applied to give us readily interpretable solutions. The notions of convexity and concavity, to which we now turn, play an important role in developing those tools.

4 Convex Structures

One of the most common mathematical properties encountered in economics is *convexity*. It comes in at least two forms: *set convexity* and *functional convexity*. The two are integrally linked.

A set $C \subset \mathbb{R}^N$ is *convex* if for any $c^o \in C$ and $c' \in C$

$$c^o + \lambda \left(c' - c^o \right) \in C, \quad \lambda \in (0, 1),$$

which can be rewritten, perhaps more familiarly, as

$$\lambda c' + (1 - \lambda) c^o \in C, \quad \lambda \in (0, 1).$$

The first version proves particularly convenient for considering variations. Visually, it's depicted by locating any two ordered pairs, c^o and c', that fall in C and then connecting them with a straight line. The points on that straight line (known more formally as the *line segment connecting* c^o and c'),

$c^o + \lambda(c' - c^o)$, are the *convex combinations* of c^o and c'.[14] These points are obtained by starting at c^o and then moving toward c' in small increments by varying λ. When C is convex, all the points on that line also belong to C. For an arbitrary set $D \subset \mathbb{R}^N$, its *convex hull*, denoted $Co\{D\}$, is the intersection of all convex sets in $\mathbb{R}^N$ containing D. $Co\{D\}$ is the smallest convex set containing D.

Some familiar convex sets repeatedly prove important. An *affine hyperplane*, $\bar{H}(\alpha, p) \subset \mathbb{R}^N$, is a set of the form

$$\bar{H}(\alpha, p) = \{z \in \mathbb{R}^N : p^\top z = \alpha, \alpha \in \mathbb{R}\}.$$

We'll often refer to such sets more casually as *hyperplanes*. They're clearly convex (prove this to yourself). They also correspond to the parallel translations of the *linear hyperplane*

$$\bar{H}(0, p) = \{z \in \mathbb{R}^N : p^\top z = 0\},$$

which is the vector in $\mathbb{R}^N$ that is *orthogonal (perpendicular) to* $p \in \mathbb{R}^N$.[15] p is the *normal* of $\bar{H}(\alpha, p)$ and $\bar{H}(0, p)$. Economic examples of hyperplanes include *budget (isoexpenditure)* and *isocost* lines.

Another way to conceptualize $\bar{H}(\alpha, p)$ is as a *level set* of linear functions, $l_p : \mathbb{R}^N \to \mathbb{R}$, of the form

$$l_p(z) = p^\top z = p_1 z_1 + p_2 z_2 + \ldots + p_N z_n.$$

The linear hyperplane, $\bar{H}(0, p)$, is the level set of $l_p(z)$ that passes through the origin.

Exercise 5. *Prove that if $z \in \bar{H}(\alpha, p)$ then $z \in \bar{H}(\mu\alpha, \mu p)$ for $\mu > 0$.*

Exercise 6. *Prove that if $z \in \bar{H}(\alpha, p)$ and $z' \in \bar{H}(\alpha, p)$, then $z - z' \in \bar{H}(0, p)$. Illustrate visually.*

Exercise 7. *Prove that if $z \in \bar{H}(\alpha, p)$, then $p \in \bar{H}(\alpha, z)$. Illustrate visually and explain intuitively.*

[14] With the endpoints c^o, c' included, that line segment also represents the *convex hull* of the set $\{c^o, c'\}$.

[15] You may sometimes see this expressed as

$$\bar{H}(0, p) = \{p\}^\perp,$$

where the right-hand side denotes the *orthogonal complement* of the singleton set p.

Hyperplanes generate another important class of convex sets. A *half-space* (technically, a *closed* half-space) is a set of the form[16]

$$H(\alpha, p) = \{z \in \mathbb{R}^N : p^\top z \geq \alpha, \alpha \in \mathbb{R}\},$$

which consists of the *upper contour set* of the linear function l_p at $l_p(z) = \alpha$. Visually, half-spaces are the points lying on or above hyperplanes. Prove to yourself that they are convex.

The most important mathematical results on convex sets for economists are the *Separating Hyperplane Theorem* and its corollary *Minkowski's Theorem.*

Theorem 3 (Separating Hyperplane Theorem). *Suppose K is compact, convex, and nonempty, C is closed, convex, and nonempty, and $K \cap C = \emptyset$, Then there exists $p \in \mathbb{R}^n \backslash \{0\}$ and $\epsilon > 0$ such that for all $x \in K$ and $y \in C$, $p^\top x + \epsilon \leq p^\top y$.*

Corollary 2 (Minkowski's Theorem). *A closed, convex set is the intersection of the closed half-spaces containing it.*

As Figures 1.1 to 1.6 illustrate, geometric representations of equilibria across different areas of microeconomic theory are extremely similar. Consumer theory, producer theory, international trade theory, general-equilibrium analysis, and welfare analysis are all replete with "price lines" nicely tangent to "boundary curves." That common visual representation suggests that all rest on a single unifying mathematical result. The Separating Hyperplane Theorem is that result.

Both theorems are visually obvious. Proving them, however, can be more difficult. (Luenberger 1969, Rockafellar 1970, Hiriart-Urruty and LeMaréchal 2001, and Ok 2007 are good sources to consult.) Theorem 3 shows that if two "nice" nonintersecting convex sets are isolated, a hyperplane can be drawn between them. One set lies in the half-space falling "above" the hyperplane and the other in the half-space below. Minkowski's Theorem isolates an algorithm for constructing a convex set by successively separating it with hyperplanes from its complement. For illustration, see Figure 2.3.

Direct consequences of the Separating Hyperplane Theorem are a series of essentially equivalent results on the existence of solutions to sets of linear equalities or inequalities that have come to be known generically as *Farkas's Lemma* or *Theorems of the Alternative.* (Gale 1960 provides an accessible treatment.)

[16] Some reverse the inequality in defining a half-space. In that case, a half-space would consist of all the points majorized by the hyperplane. Because $\alpha \in \mathbb{R}$, either definition can be made equivalent to the other, so which one you choose is a matter of personal preference.

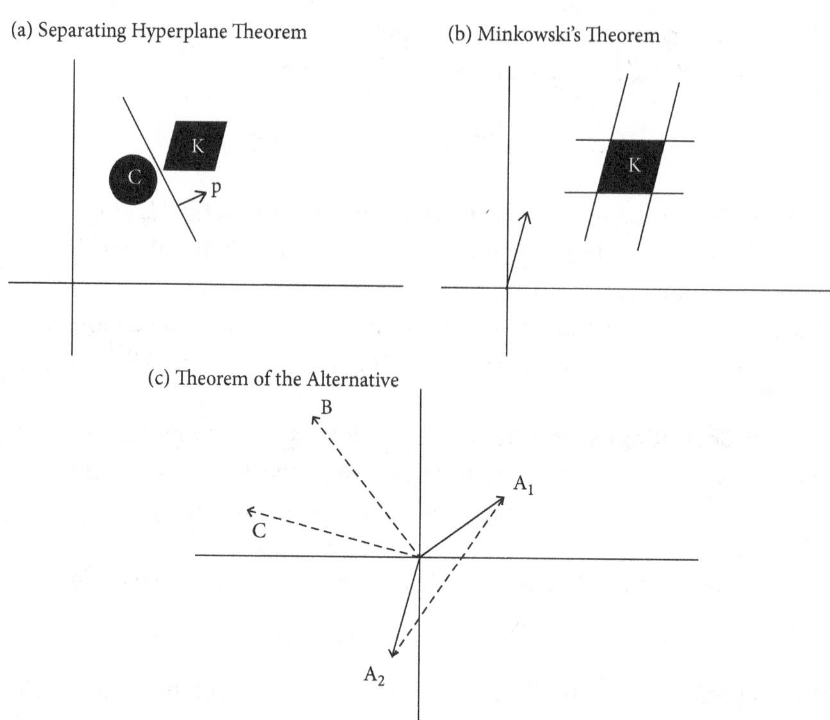

Fig. 2.3

Theorem 4. *Let A represent a* $K \times J$ *matrix. Then the following are true:*

(a) *Either* $z^{\top}A \leq 0$ *has a solution* $z \in \mathbb{R}^K_+ \backslash \{0\}$ *or* $Ay > 0$ *has a solution* $y \in \mathbb{R}^J_+$, *but not both.*
(b) *Either* $Ay > 0$ *has a solution, or* $z^{\top}A = 0$ *has a solution* $z \in \mathbb{R}^K_{++}$ *with* $\sum_k z_k = 1$, *but not both.*

4.1 Concave (Convex) Functions.

Our focus is on concave functions.[17] There are several equivalent definitions. One that illustrates its connection with set convexity is: $f : \mathbb{R}^N \to \bar{\mathbb{R}}$ is *concave*

[17] A common definition of concavity (in addition to what follows below) is: A function f is concave if $-f$ is convex. Thus, to study one is to study the other. Many mathematical discussions of concave and convex functions focus exclusively on convex functions, which mathematicians take to be of natural interest. Similarly, in studying optimization problems, mathematicians routinely focus on minimization rather than maximization. There are historic and analytic reasons for this focus. Economists, on the other hand, routinely find concave functions, and *pari passu* maximization, to be of inherent interest. To that end, our primary focus is on concavity, and we often leave the direct extension to convexity to the interested reader.

if and only if its hypograph, $hyp\left(f\right)$, forms a convex set. Figure 1.1 illustrates for $f:\mathbb{R}\to\bar{\mathbb{R}}$. The concave function is the nonlinear function that emanates from the origin and increases at a decreasing rate. Its $hyp\left(f\right)\subset\mathbb{R}^2$ consists visually of all points falling on or below the graph of that function.

An equivalent definition[18] is that $f:\mathbb{R}^N\to\bar{\mathbb{R}}$ is concave if for all $\lambda\in(0,1)$ and $x,y\in\mathbb{R}^N$

$$f(x+\lambda\left(y-x\right))\geq f(x)+\lambda\left(f(y)-f(x)\right). \tag{2.4}$$

A function f is *convex* if $-f$ is concave or, equivalently, if its *epigraph* forms a convex set, where

$$epi\left(f\right)\equiv\left\{(x,y)\in\mathbb{R}^{N+1}:f(x)\leq y\right\}$$

denotes the epigraph of f. (See the nonlinear function in Figure 1.3 for an example.)

Problem 3. *Show that* $\left\{(x,y)\in\mathbb{R}^{N+1}:f(x)\geq y\right\}$ *is convex if and only if* $f(x+\lambda\left(y-x\right))\geq f(x)+\lambda\left(f(y)-f(x)\right)$ *for all* $\lambda\in(0,1)$ *and* $x,y\in\mathbb{R}^N$.

Our attention is almost exclusively focused on well-behaved concave (convex) functions, where well-behaved means *proper* and *closed.* In the main, we'll just assume that the concave functions we consider satisfy these criteria. Still, you should have an intuitive grasp of what that means. The *effective domain of a concave function*, f, is defined:[19]

$$dom\left(f\right)\equiv\left\{x\in\mathbb{R}^N:f(x)>-\infty\right\}.$$

In words, $dom\left(f\right)$ consists of the elements of $\mathbb{R}^N$ for which f doesn't plunge to $-\infty$. *A concave function is proper if* $dom\left(f\right)\neq\emptyset$, *and if* $f(x)<\infty$ *for all* $x\in\mathbb{R}$. A proper concave function, f, is *closed* if it is *upper semicontinuous*, that is, if its upper contour set

$$\left\{x\in\mathbb{R}^N:f(x)\geq y\right\}$$

is closed for all $y\in\mathbb{R}$.

[18] If this isn't the one you were expecting, play with it a bit. Writing it this way makes the differential properties of concave and convex functions that we are going to develop more tractable.

[19] Thus, the effective domain of a convex function is defined as

$$dom\left(f\right)=\left\{x:f(x)<\infty\right\}.$$

Example 2. *Consider*

$$f(x) = \begin{cases} -\infty & x < 0 \\ 0 & x \geq 0 \end{cases}.$$

f is proper concave because dom $(f) = \mathbb{R}_+$ and $f(x) < \infty$ for all $x \in \mathbb{R}$. Sketch it out.

Example 3. *Consider*

$$f(x) = \begin{cases} 0 & x < 0 \\ \infty & x \geq 0 \end{cases}.$$

Here f is concave but not proper. dom $(f) = \mathbb{R}_-$. Sketch it out.

Example 4. *Consider $f(x) = \ln x$. f is proper concave because dom $(f) = \mathbb{R}_{++}$ and $f(x) < \infty$ for all $x \in \mathbb{R}$.*

Remark 3. *To avoid further cluttering an already technical discussion, we often forego properly qualifying where particular properties apply. When this happens, you should assume that attention is being restricted to either dom (f) or its relative interior (see Remark 4 below). Properly speaking, many of the following arguments only apply there and should be properly qualified. So, for example, if you see*

$$f(x) = \alpha + \beta \ln x,$$

you should understand that we're restricting attention to $x > 0$ because that corresponds to dom (f).

Minkowski's Theorem (Corollary 2) offers a natural way to characterize concave functions using half-spaces. For f closed concave, *hyp* (f) is always a closed convex set belonging to $\mathbb{R}^{N+1}$, so that Minkowski's Theorem requires that

$$hyp\,(f) = \cap_{\alpha,q} \{H\,(\alpha, q, -1) \subset \mathbb{R}^{N+1} : hyp\,(f) \subset H\,(\alpha, q, -1)\},$$

with $q \in \mathbb{R}^N$. Notice, however, that as a subset $\mathbb{R}^{N+1}$

$$\begin{aligned} H\,(\alpha, q, -1) &= \{(x, y) : q^\top x - y \geq \alpha\} \\ &= \{(x, y) : q^\top x - \alpha \geq y\} \\ &= hyp\,(q^\top x - \alpha) \end{aligned}$$

The search for the half-spaces containing $hyp\,(f)$ thus reduces to searching for the hypographs of the affine functions

$$h_{q,\alpha}(x) = q^{\top}x - \alpha$$

majorizing f in the sense that $h_{q,\alpha}(x) \geq f(x)$ for all x. Thus, by Minkowski's Theorem:

$$hyp\,(f) = \cap_{\alpha,q}\left\{hyp\left(h_{q,\alpha}\right) : hyp\,(f) \subset hyp\left(h_{q,\alpha}\right)\right\} \tag{2.5}$$

Expression (2.5) is called the *envelope characterization of concave functions*.

To visualize, sketch a concave f on a sheet of paper. Pick any point on $Gr\,(f)$ and draw the line segment tangent to this point. This line segment, when extended throughout $\mathbb{R}^2$, is the graph of an affine function, whose slope is given by the slope of the tangent. Its graph never passes below the graph of f, and it intersects the vertical axis at $-\alpha$, so that $hyp\,(f)$ is entirely contained in its hypograph. Hence, that affine function and the associated half-space support $hyp\,(f)$. For f concave, every point in $Gr\,(f)$ has an affine function tangent to it that majorizes f in this fashion. Thus, every point on the graph is majorized by at least one affine function. If f is kinked at x, it has multiple such majorizing functions tangent at that point.

Exercise 8. *Develop the graphical representation of the intuitive discussion provided in the immediately preceding paragraph.*

Now, visualize the problem of using these majorizing affine functions, $h_{q,\alpha}(x)$, to find a particular point on the graph of the concave function, $(x, f(x))$. This is equivalent to finding the majorizing affine function with the smallest value for that x. The function isolated is, of course, the one supporting $Gr\,(f)$ at $(x, f(x))$ with slope q, so that

$$h_{q,\alpha}(x) = q^{\top}x - \alpha = f(x),$$

and thus

$$\alpha = q^{\top}x - f(x) \text{ and } q \in \partial f(x).$$

$Hyp\,(f)$ lies in $hyp\left(h_{q,\alpha}\right)$ for this (q, α) Repeating this process for all $(x, f(x)) \in Gr\,(f)$ and then taking the intersection of the hypographs for the approximating affine functions yields $hyp\,(f)$. More formally,

Lemma 1. *A closed concave function, f, is the pointwise infimum of the collection of all affine functions, $h_{q,\alpha}$, such that $h_{q,\alpha} \geq f$.*

4.2 Differential Properties of Concave Functions and Directional Derivatives.

Recall the definition of a superdifferential

$$\partial f(x) = \{q \in \mathbb{R}^N : f(x) + q^\top (y - x) \geq f(y) \text{ for all } y \in \mathbb{R}^N\}.$$

Geometrically, $\partial f(x)$ describes the hyperplanes supporting $hyp(f)$ at $(x, f(x))$. When $x \in \mathbb{R}$, each $q \in \partial f(x)$ is the slope of a line tangent to the graph of $f(x)$ at $(x, f(x))$ *that never passes below the graph of* $f(x)$. When $f : \mathbb{R} \to \mathbb{R}$ is concave, all points on the graph of $f(x)$ corresponding to finite values clearly have at least one such tangent hyperplane, its tangent hyperplanes majorize $hyp(f)$, and $hyp(f)$ is a convex set. Minkowski's Theorem ensures that visual intuition extends to concave $f : \mathbb{R}^N \to \mathbb{R}$ and the relative interior (ri) of $dom(f)$.

Remark 4. *It's probably not essential that you understand the difference between relative interior and interior, but it would be helpful if you did. Check Hiriart-Urruty and LeMaréchal (2001, pp. 33–34) for a particularly intuitive discussion of the notion of a relative interior.*

One way to think of it is to consider two points in $\mathbb{R}^2$, calling them x and y. Sketch them on a piece of paper, and draw a line segment that connects them. That line segment and x and y form a convex set; call it A. If you think of A's interior as a subset of $\mathbb{R}^2$, you will see that it is empty because any ε−ball drawn around any element of A contains points not belonging to A. The expression relative interior of A means relative to the affine subspace (more jargon) containing A. That affine subspace in the two-dimensional case consists of all points lying on the line segment defining A and its extension beyond points x and y. That line is a one-dimensional set and A has a well defined interior relative to it, the open set consisting of all points in A except its endpoints.

Define $y \in \mathbb{R}^N$ as a *variation around $x \in \mathbb{R}^N$ in the direction of $v \in \mathbb{R}^N$* if

$$y \equiv x + \lambda v$$

with $\lambda > 0$. By the definition of $\partial f(x)$:

$$q \in \partial f(x) \Rightarrow q^{\top} v \geq \frac{f(x+\lambda v) - f(x)}{\lambda}, \tag{2.6}$$

for all $\lambda > 0$ and v so that the inner products of the elements of $\partial f(x)$ and the direction of the variation v dominate the associated variation in f as normalized by $\lambda > 0$. In (2.4), set

$$y = x + v$$

to obtain for $\lambda \in (0, 1)$

$$\frac{f(x+\lambda v) - f(x)}{\lambda} \geq f(x+v) - f(x). \tag{2.7}$$

For f superdifferentiable and concave, expressions (2.6) and (2.7) taken together require that

$$q \in \partial f(x) \Rightarrow q^{\top} v \geq \frac{f(x+\lambda v) - f(x)}{\lambda} \geq f(x+v) - f(x), \quad \lambda \in (0, 1).$$

In words, the linear functions of the variation v defined by the elements of $\partial f(x)$ provide upper bounds for $\frac{f(x+\lambda v)-f(x)}{\lambda}$ and for $f(x+v) - f(x)$. Taking the limit as λ approaches zero from above in the former gives

$$q \in \partial f(x) \Rightarrow q^{\top} v \geq \lim_{\lambda \downarrow 0} \frac{f(x+\lambda v) - f(x)}{\lambda} \geq f(x+v) - f(x) \tag{2.8}$$

If the limit, which we represent notationally as

$$f'(x; v) \equiv \lim_{\lambda \downarrow 0} \frac{f(x+\lambda v) - f(x)}{\lambda},$$

exists, it is called the *(one-sided) directional derivative of f in the direction v.* Note the similarities and differences between (2.1) and $f'(x; v)$. Both involve taking limits, and so both involve tiny perturbations from x. But where (2.1) takes the limit as $\lambda \in \mathbb{R}$ approaches zero from both below (the "left") and above (the "right"), $f'(x; v)$ only takes the limit as $\lambda \in \mathbb{R}_{+}$ approaches zero from above (the "right"). In words, derivatives involve examining tiny perturbations to both the right and the left, while (one-sided) directional derivatives only examine tiny perturbations to one side. Second, the domain of f in (2.1) is $\mathbb{R}$, while that in $f'(x;v)$ is $\mathbb{R}^N$.

When $N = 1$, setting $v = 1$ yields what is almost universally known as the "right-hand" derivative of f, while setting $v = -1$ yields its "left-hand" derivative. The right-hand derivative, if it exists, details how f changes as x increases by an imperceptibly small, but positive, amount. The left-hand details how f changes as x is decreased by that same small amount. If the right-hand derivative equals minus the left-hand derivative, they both equal (2.1), and f is said to be *differentiable.* If both exist, but they are not equal, f is not differentiable, and that lack of differentiability is perceived visually as a "kink" in $Gr(f)$.

Figure 2.1 illustrates the "kinky" case. One visualizes $f'(a;1)$ as how f changes as point a is approached from the right, and $f'(a;-1)$ as it is approached from the left. Because $f(x)'s$ slope is smaller when approached from the right than from the left, the result is a kink in the graph of f at a.

The notation, $f'(x;v)$, emphasizes that the directional derivative depends on the point at which the limit is taken, x, and the direction of the variation, v. For arbitrary $f: \mathbb{R}^N \to \mathbb{R}$, there is no reason to believe that $f'(x;v)$ exists. But in a smooth world, there are no worries. The limit exists, and the directional derivative takes the form:

$$f'(x;v) = \nabla f(x)^{\top} v, \tag{2.9}$$

where $\nabla f(x) \in \mathbb{R}^N$ denotes the gradient of f at x.

Our current interest, however, is in a potentially "kinky" world. For univariate functions, directions, $v \in \mathbb{R}$, are clear-cut notions as Figure 2.1 illustrates. For example, in the figure points on the real line can either be "to the right of a," "to the left of a," or coincide with a.

Things are more complicated in higher dimensions, and hence the required departure from the univariate notions of right-hand and left-hand derivatives. Consider $\mathbb{R}^2$. When drawing it on a piece of paper, one would likely fix two axes and orient $\mathbb{R}^2$ relative to those axes. Pick any single point in $\mathbb{R}^2$, and call it x. What does it mean to approach x from the right? To visualize, draw a circle with unit radius around x. Each azimuth on the implied compass now becomes a natural direction v from which to approach x, or a natural direction in which to move away from x. You might say the "right" consists of those between 0° and 180°, but there are literally an infinity of such azimuths. In even higher dimensions, one visualizes this same phenomenon in terms of unit balls or spheres.

The directional derivative, $f'(x; v)$, thus measures how $f(x)$ changes in the limit as we move away from x *in the direction of* v, that is, as we move away from x along one of those azimuths in $\mathbb{R}^2$. But if one can move in the direction of v, one can also move in the direction of $-v$. There are two equivalent ways to capture such movements, one of which is to evaluate $f'(x; -v)$. Another is to replace the middle term in (2.8) by a limit taken as $\lambda < 0$ approaches 0 from below:

$$\lim_{\lambda \uparrow 0} \frac{f(x+\lambda v) - f(x)}{\lambda}.$$

The result, of course, is a slightly different notion of a (one-sided) directional derivative resulting from the change in signs of λ. A slight change of variables, however, reveals

$$\begin{aligned} \lim_{\lambda \uparrow 0} \frac{f(x+\lambda v) - f(x)}{\lambda} &= -\lim_{\gamma \downarrow 0} \frac{f(x-\gamma v) - f(x)}{\gamma} \\ &= -f'(x; -v), \end{aligned}$$

so that such movements can be analyzed by taking the negative of $f'(x; -v)$.

Directional derivatives have interesting and important properties. For $t > 0$,

$$\begin{aligned} f'(x; tv) &= \lim_{\lambda \downarrow 0} \frac{f(x+\lambda tv) - f(x)}{\lambda} \\ &= \lim_{\lambda t \downarrow 0} t \frac{f(x+\lambda tv) - f(x)}{\lambda t} \\ &= t \lim_{\lambda t \downarrow 0} \frac{f(x+\lambda tv) - f(x)}{\lambda t} \\ &= tf'(x; v), \end{aligned}$$

so that $f'(x; v)$ is *positively homogeneous in* v. Compare this to the smooth case where f is differentiable. Then, not only is $f'(x; v)$ positively homogeneous in v, but (2.9) reveals that

$$\begin{aligned} f'(x; v+v') &= \nabla f(x)^{\top} (v+v') \\ &= \nabla f(x)^{\top} v + \nabla f(x)^{\top} v' \\ &= f'(x; v) + f'(x; v') \end{aligned}$$

so that $f'(x; v)$ *is linear in the direction of the variation.*

Positive homogeneity of $f'(x;v)$ is a general property of directional derivatives. It is an important generalization of linearity, but it is not equivalent to the linearity that emerges for differentiable functions.[20] Why linearity of $f'(x;v)$ fails to emerge for nondifferentiable structures is again easily visualized using Figure 2.1.

In the figure, consider a small movement to the right of a by $v > 0$. The function responds by increasing by a small positive amount that corresponds to the slope of the function times v. Conversely, a slight movement to the left of a by the same amount has the function fall by an even larger amount because the slope of $f(x)$ to the left of a is greater than its slope to the right of a. Hence,

$$-f'(x;-v) > f'(x;v)$$

so that

$$f'(x;-v) + f'(x;v) \neq f'(x;v-v) = f'(x;0) = 0.$$

Thus, the kinkiness of the function, which signals a discontinuous change in the slope of the function, automatically robs the directional derivative of its linearity.

For f concave, positive homogeneity of $f'(x;v)$ in v can be strengthened to positive homogeneity and concavity in v. To demonstrate, consider

$$f'(x;v+\mu(v^o-v)) \equiv \lim_{\lambda\downarrow 0}\frac{f(x+\lambda(v+\mu(v^o-v)))-f(x)}{\lambda},$$

for $\mu \in (0,1)$. Concavity of f ensures successively that

$$\begin{aligned}\lim_{\lambda\downarrow 0}\frac{f(x+\lambda(v+\mu(v^o-v)))-f(x)}{\lambda} &\geq \lim_{\lambda\downarrow 0}\frac{(1-\mu)f(x+\lambda v)+\mu f(x+\lambda v^o)-f(x)}{\lambda}\\ &= \lim_{\lambda\downarrow 0}\begin{pmatrix}(1-\mu)\frac{f(x+\lambda v)-f(x)}{\lambda}\\ +\mu\frac{f(x+\lambda v^o)-f(x)}{\lambda}\end{pmatrix}\\ &= (1-\mu)\lim_{\lambda\downarrow 0}\frac{f(x+\lambda v)-f(x)}{\lambda}\\ &\quad +\mu\lim_{\lambda\downarrow 0}\frac{f(x+\lambda v^o)-f(x)}{\lambda},\end{aligned}$$

[20] All linear functions are positively homogeneous. The converse, however, is not true.

so that

$$f'(x; v + \mu(v^o - v)) \geq f'(x; v) + \mu\left(f'(x; v^o) - f'(x; v)\right) \text{ for } \mu \in (0, 1)$$

which establishes that f' is concave in v.

More can be said. For f is concave, Lemma 1 ensures that finite $f(x)$ is the pointwise infimum of the affine functions $h_{q,\alpha}$ that majorize f. Hence, a (q, a) exists such that

$$q^\top x - f(x) = \alpha,$$

and

$$q^\top z - q^\top x + f(x) \geq f(z) \text{ for all } z \in \mathbb{R}^N,$$

so that $q \in \partial f(x)$ and f is superdifferentiable everywhere on *ri dom* (f). Moreover, it is also true that everywhere on *ri dom* (f), $f'(x; v)$ exists (allowing the special cases of $-\infty$ and ∞),

$$f'(x; v) = \inf\{q^\top v : q \in \partial f(x)\}, \tag{2.10}$$

and

$$\partial f(x) = \{q \in \mathbb{R}^N : q^\top v \geq f'(x; v) \text{ for all } v \in \mathbb{R}^N\}. \tag{2.11}$$

(See Rockafellar 1970 and Hiriart-Urruty and LeMaréchal 2001 for the details.)[21] Thus, for f concave, a simple algorithm exists for calculating $f'(x; v)$: Find $\partial f(x)$, and then find the supergradient giving the minimal linear function of the variation, v.

Using (2.10) gives

$$\begin{aligned} f'(x; -v) &= \inf\{-q^\top v : q \in \partial f(x)\} \\ &= -\sup\{q^\top v : q \in \partial f(x)\}, \end{aligned}$$

from which we conclude that $-f'(x; -v) \geq f'(x; v)$. Hence, movements to the "left" of x in the direction of v evince larger changes in the value

[21] As subsequent developments will reveal, (2.11) implies that f' is the *support function* for the superdifferential when f is concave. Some treatments, for example, Hiriart-Urruty and LeMaréchal (2001), use this fact as an alternative definition of the superdifferential for concave functions. Our definition of the superdifferential in terms of supporting hyperplanes to *hyp* (f) is more general and applies regardless of the concavity of f.

of f than movements to the "right" in the direction of v. From your basic calculus, you should remember that the basic property of a differentiable concave function of a single variable is that its derivatives are nonincreasing functions of the argument. The requirement for f concave that $-f'(x;-v) \geq f'(x;v)$ along with the cyclical monotonicity of $\partial f(x)$ generalize that basic property to the nonsmooth case. For smoothly differentiable structures, the parallel requirement is that $\nabla_{xx'}f(x)$, *the Hessian matrix for f*, is negative semidefinite, which implies among other things that its diagonal elements are nonpositive.

To visualize, refer again to Figure 2.1. There it's visually apparent that $\partial f(a) = [b,c]$, with both b and c strictly positive and b corresponding to the slope of the function for points greater than a and c corresponding to the slope of the function for points below a. It's also clear that as we move to the right v units from a, the function changes by

$$\begin{aligned} bv &= \min\{qv : q \in [b,c]\} \\ &< cv. \end{aligned}$$

Conversely, as we move to the left v units, the function decreases by $-bv < -cv$.

Summarizing:

Lemma 2. *If f concave, it is superdifferentiable everywhere in ri dom* (f),

$$q \in \partial f(x) \Rightarrow q^\top v \geq \inf\{q^\top v : q \in \partial f(x)\} = f'(x;v) \geq f(x+v) - f(x), \tag{2.12}$$

$$\partial f(x) = \{q \in \mathbb{R}^N : q^\top v \geq f'(x;v) \ \ \textit{for all} \ \ v \in \mathbb{R}^N\},$$

and for $q^k \in \partial f(x^k)$

$$(x^2 - x^1)^\top q^1 + (x^3 - x^2)^\top q^2 + \ldots + (x^1 - x^K)^\top q^K \geq 0.$$

Problem 4. *Using (2.10), prove:* $f'(x;v)$ *is positively homogeneous and concave in v, and*

$$\begin{aligned} \lim_{\lambda \uparrow 0} \frac{f(x+\lambda v) - f(x)}{\lambda} &= -f'(x;-v) \\ &\geq f'(x;v) \\ &= \lim_{\lambda \downarrow 0} \frac{f(x+\lambda v) - f(x)}{\lambda}. \end{aligned}$$

Problem 5. *Suppose $f(x)$ is convex. Delineate the differential properties that correspond to Lemma 2.*

Because economic analysis depends crucially on the principle of optimization, the characterization of maxima or minima over different choice sets is of primary importance. As Theorem 2 demonstrates, isolating maxima or minima eventually boils down to identifying points of, respectively, superdifferentiability or subdifferentiability. It turns out that functional concavity implies very nice superdifferentiability properties, while functional convexity implies very nice subdifferentiability properties. Thus, when either property is applicable, optimization is greatly simplified because properties required for the existence of global solutions are imbedded directly in the underlying structure.

The close connection between concavity and superdifferentiability is not accidental. Superdifferentiability provides necessary and sufficient conditions for a maximum, while concavity ensures that nicely deterministic global maxima exist. In fact, one can show that the existence of ∂f over closed convex sets guarantees that f is concave over those same sets (Rockafellar 1970, Theorems 24.8 and 24.9). More generally, isolating a cyclically monotone $\rho : \mathbb{R}^N \rightrightarrows \mathbb{R}^N$ ensures that one can identify a concave function that accompanies it.

Theorem 5. *(Rockafellar) For $\rho : \mathbb{R}^N \rightrightarrows \mathbb{R}^N$, there exists a concave function, $f : \mathbb{R}^N \to \mathbb{R}$, for which $\rho(x) \subset \partial f(x)$ for all x if and only if ρ is cyclically monotone.*

That cyclical monotonicity of ρ is needed to ensure the existence of a concave f essentially follows from Lemma 2. Sufficiency is demonstrated by constructing a concave function for which $\rho(x) \subset \partial f(x)$. The algorithm, due to Rockafellar (1970, see especially pp. 238–40), works as follows. Pick any $(x_o, q_o) \in Gr(\rho)$ and consider creating affine functions $a(x)$ by proceeding from x_o to x via series of links along $Gr(\rho)$, $(x_1, q_2), (x_2, q_2), \cdots, (x_m, q_m)$ with successive steps determining the values of $a(x_n)$ by

$$\begin{aligned} 0 &= a(x_o) \\ (x_1 - x_o)^{\top} q_o &= a(x_1), \\ (x_2 - x_1) + (x_1 - x_o)^{\top} q_o &= a(x_2), \end{aligned}$$

until one reaches x. Then define $f(x)$ as the infimum over $Gr(\rho)$ of all such affine functions

$$f(x) \equiv \inf\left\{(x - x_m)^{\mathsf{T}} q_m + \cdots + (x_1 - x_o)^{\mathsf{T}} q_o\right\} \tag{2.13}$$

Because f is the infimum of a set of affine functions, Lemma 1 implies it's closed, concave, and it is proper because $f(x_o) = 0$ by construction. Now choose $q \in \rho(x)$ and define

$$(y - x)^{\mathsf{T}} q + (x - x_m)^{\mathsf{T}} q_m + \cdots + (x_1 - x_o)^{\mathsf{T}} q_o$$

where (x_n, q_n), $n = 1, \ldots, m$ are the optimizers for (2.13). By definition

$$(y - x)^{\mathsf{T}} q + (x - x_m)^{\mathsf{T}} q_m + \cdots + (x_1 - x_o)^{\mathsf{T}} q_o \geq f(y)$$
$$\Downarrow$$
$$(y - x)^{\mathsf{T}} q \geq f(y) - f(y),$$

so that $q \in f(x)$ and $\rho(x)$ as required. Because this same proof works for arbitrary $(x_n, q_n) \in Gr(\rho)$ in place of $(x_o, q_o) \in Gr(\rho)$ and then requires that $f(x_n) = 0$, it follows that the resulting $f(x)$ determined is only unique up to an additive constant.

5 Conjugate Duality

5.1 A Brief Word about Dual Spaces[22]

This section's title includes the word "duality." Duality has different meanings. In economics, it typically means analyzing economic behavior in terms of *prices* instead of *quantities.* Both prices and quantities are measured using real numbers, $\mathbb{R}$. Thus, a bundle of N commodities are conceptualized as a vector in $\mathbb{R}^N$. So too is the matching price vector. As mathematical objects, they're very similar.

Nevertheless, the duality terminology is neither vacuous nor nondescriptive. $\mathbb{R}^N$ is a special case of a more general mathematical object known as a *vector space.*[23] For a vector space X, its *dual space*, denoted X^*, is t*he space of*

[22] This section is dedicated to my good friend Rolf Färe who has persistently, but patiently, pestered me to say something in this section about where the duality terminology used in economics originated.

[23] Luenberger (1969) provides an excellent and accessible treatment of vector spaces and their properties.

the linear functionals on X. A function f defined on X is *linear* if for any two scalars α and β,

$$f(\alpha x + \beta y) = \alpha f(x) + \beta f(y)$$

for all $x, y \in X$. From your basic (vector) algebra, you know that linear functionals on $\mathbb{R}^N$ are always expressible in inner product form as

$$f(x) = a^\top x = \sum_{n=1} a_n x_n$$

where $a \in \mathbb{R}^N$. Thus, $\mathbb{R}^N$ forms the space of linear functions on $\mathbb{R}^N$, so that $\mathbb{R}^{N*} = \mathbb{R}^N$, which is often expressed as $\mathbb{R}^N$ being *self dual.*

If $x \in \mathbb{R}^N$ measures *quanitities*, the linear functions of x that are of the most natural interest to economists are those formed using *prices*, $q \in \mathbb{R}^{N*}$, that determine their value, $q^\top x$. As a result, economists call representations of economic phenomena in terms of prices *duals* and representations in terms of quantities *primal.*[24] This viewpoint highlights the intuitive manner in which economists might interpet our differential concepts. For example, a superdifferential can be equivalently stated as

$$\partial f(x) = \{q \in \mathbb{R}^{N*} : q^\top y - f(y) \geq q^\top x - f(x) \text{ for all } y \in \mathbb{R}^N\},$$

or, in words, as a subset of the dual space. So, if $f(x)$ denotes some *evaluative function*, ∂f is the correspondence that identifies the *price vectors* $q \in \mathbb{R}^{N*}$, for which the difference between price-based valuation of x and $f(x)$ is the least. It is, of course, well known that derivatives and partial derivatives play a similar role. Why might one prefer superdifferential concepts? One obvious answer is that interesting economic functions may not be differentiable. But even if we rule that out, superdifferentials are preferred because their global nature ensures that *they identify the potential prices that cannot be ignored in economic analysis.* Standard derivatives, being local in nature, only *identify prices that* ***may*** *be of interest.* To see a case where they are not, just envision what happens when first-order conditions are met, but second-order conditions aren't.

[24] Another way to look at this, which of course is closely related but also very important historically, emerges from activity analysis which casts linear programming problems in terms of equivalent *primal* and *dual* programs and speaks in terms of quantities and shadow prices. As we shall eventually show, this particular version of duality is a particular manifestation of Fenchel's Duality Theorem developed below.

5.2 Concave Conjugates[25]

Our next goal is to establish that if $f : \mathbb{R}^N \to \bar{\mathbb{R}}$ is concave,

$$f(x) = \inf_{q \in \mathbb{R}^N} \{q^\top x - f^*(q)\}, \tag{2.14}$$

where

$$f^*(q) \equiv \inf_{x \in \mathbb{R}^N} \{q^\top x - f(x)\}. \tag{2.15}$$

Both f and f^* map $\mathbb{R}^N$ to the reals. (The $*$ notation reminds us that $f^{*\prime}s$ domain is the dual space for $f's$ domain.) Both (2.15) and (2.14) involve choosing an element from the other's dual space. Thus, in deriving (2.15), the search is over the linear operators for $q \in \mathbb{R}^N$. And in (2.14), the search is over the linear operators for $x \in \mathbb{R}^N$.

When $x \in \mathbb{R}^N$ is interpreted as a vector of quantities and $q \in \mathbb{R}^{N*} = \mathbb{R}^N$ as a vector of prices, the problem posed in (2.15) is to minimize the difference between x*'s market value*, $q^\top x$, and its valuation via f. (Equivalently, maximize the difference $f(x) - q^\top x$.) If minimizing that difference governs economic behavior, solving (2.15) gives both the optimal benefit, $f^*(q)$, and a description of how x is optimally chosen. Important economic versions of f^* with which you are likely familiar include expenditure, cost, profit, and indirect utility functions.

It's not particularly surprising that information embedded in f^* can be used to infer *something* about f. For example, it doesn't require rocket science to infer that limited expenditures on consumption signal the likely existence of a constraint on expenditure. What was surprising to discover is that f^* provides an exact and exhaustive description of f under appropriate circumstances. In those instances, the two approaches to examining optimizing behavior are equivalent. This equivalency then demonstrates that neither provides a *more fundamental* or *more basic* method to examine optimizing behavior, and both are equally basic.

Expressions (2.14) and (2.15) constitute *dual conjugate* mappings. The function $f^*(q)$ has different aliases. We'll call it the *(concave) conjugate*

[25] Different perspectives on viewing dual relationships exist. I focus almost exclusively on conjugacy theory because it provides a particularly convenient match for functional tools developed later in the book to represent preference structures, constraint sets, and production technologies. Moreover, it facilitates an approach that relies almost exclusively on superdifferential and subdifferential concepts to identify optimizing behavior.

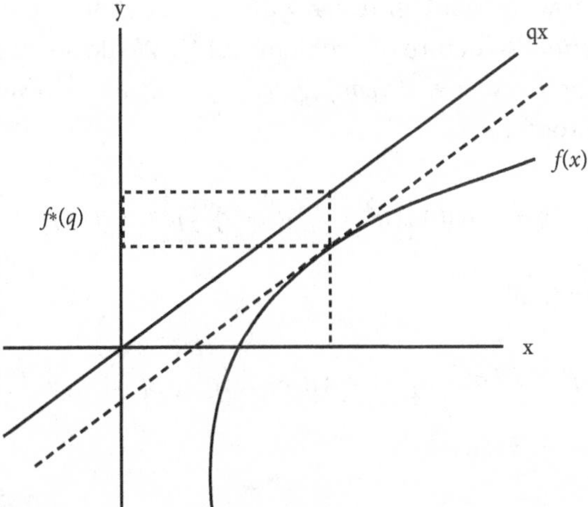

Fig. 2.4 The Concave Conjugate

of f.[26] Thus, the goal is to show that for f concave, f is the concave conjugate of its concave conjugate f^*. (The concave conjugate of the concave conjugate, f^*, denoted as $\left(f^*\right)^* = f^{**}$, is often referred to as $f's$ *biconjugate.* In these terms, the goal is to show that $f's$ biconjugate is f.)

5.2.1 Intuition and Sketch of a Demonstration

Figure 2.4, a slightly recycled and redrawn version of Figure 1.1, illustrates problem (2.15) as minimizing the vertical distance between the line passing through the origin with slope q and $Gr\left(f\right)$. To illustrate the dual problem (2.14), however, all one need do is relabel the vertical axis in Figure 2.4 in units of f^* and the horizontal axis in units of q. And (2.14) reduces to minimizing the vertical difference between the line passing through the origin with slope x and $Gr\left(f^*\right)$.

The solution techniques and illustrations for (2.15) and (2.14) are structurally identical. The only difference is that one, (2.15), treats q as given and chooses x. The other, (2.14), treats x as given and chooses q. In considering these two problems, it's important to remember that by the self-dual structure of $\mathbb{R}^N$, the inner product, $q^\top x$ for $q, x \in \mathbb{R}^N$, is interpretable both as a linear function of x (where q defines the linear function) and as a linear function of q (where x defines the linear function).

[26] Often, $f^*\left(q\right)$ is referred to simply as the *conjugate* of f. We use the terminology concave conjugate to distinguish it from the convex conjugate defined below. $f^*\left(q\right)$ is also often referred to as the *Fenchel transform* of $f(x)$.

We start by showing that Figure 2.4, with axes redefined in units of f^* and q, reflects the essential structure of problem (2.14). We do so by demonstrating that *regardless of f's shape, its conjugate, f^*, is always concave in $q \in \mathbb{R}^N$.* Here's a quick proof. Let

$$\hat{x} \in \arg\inf\left\{\left(q^0 + \lambda\left(q^1 - q^0\right)\right)^\top x - f(x)\right\}$$

for $\lambda \in (0, 1)$, so that

$$f^*\left(q^0 + \lambda\left(q^1 - q^0\right)\right) = \left(q^0 + \lambda\left(q^1 - q^0\right)\right)^\top \hat{x} - f(\hat{x}).$$

By definition

$$\begin{aligned} q^{0\top}\hat{x} - f(\hat{x}) &\geq f^*\left(q^0\right) \\ q^{1\top}\hat{x} - f(\hat{x}) &\geq f^*\left(q^1\right). \end{aligned}$$

Multiplying the first by $(1 - \lambda)$, the second by λ with $\lambda \in (0, 1)$, adding, and rearranging gives

$$f^*\left(q^0 + \lambda\left(q^1 - q^0\right)\right) \geq f^*\left(q^0\right) + \lambda\left(f^*\left(q^1\right) - f^*\left(q^0\right)\right),$$

which produces the desired result.

Lemma 3. *The concave conjugate of $g : \mathbb{R}^N \to \bar{\mathbb{R}}$,*

$$g^*(q) \equiv \inf_x\left\{q^\top x - g(x)\right\},$$

is concave in q.

We next develop a fundamental result. Known as Fenchel's Inequality, its logical basis is simple but it has profound implications. From the definition of f^*,

$$f^*(q) \leq q^\top x - f(x),$$

for all $x \in \mathbb{R}^N$, $q \in \mathbb{R}^N$, so that

$$f^*(q) + f(x) \leq q^\top x, \qquad \text{(Fenchel's Inequality)} \tag{2.16}$$

for all $x \in \mathbb{R}^N$ and $q \in \mathbb{R}^N$. Fenchel's Inequality says two distinct things. First,

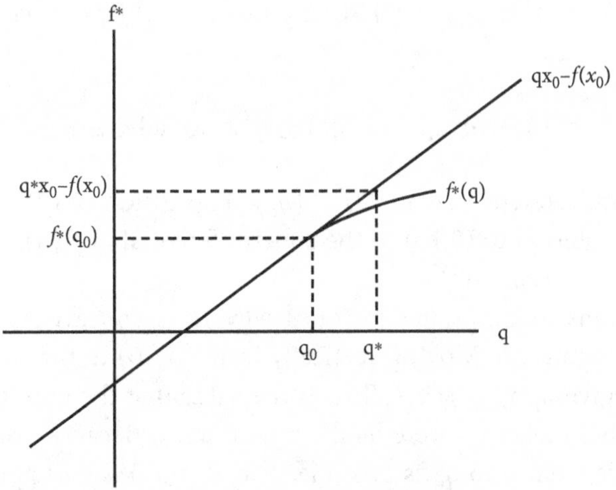

Fig. 2.5 Concave Conjugates are Concave

$$f^*(q) \le q^\top x - f(x), \text{ for all } q \in \mathbb{R}^N$$

so that *the affine function of* q, $q^\top x - f(x)$, always dominates (*majorizes*) $f^*(q)$. Second,

$$f(x) \le q^\top x - f^*(q), \text{ for all } x \in \mathbb{R}^N$$

so that *the affine function of* x, $q^\top x - f^*(q)$, always majorizes $f(x)$.

Figure 2.5 illustrates (2.16). For q_o in the figure, let x_o solve (2.15), so that

$$q_o \in \partial f(x_o).$$

That $x_o \in \mathbb{R}$ defines an affine function of q, depicted pictorially as $qx_o - f(x_o)$. By construction, $f^*(q_o) = q_o x_o - f(x_o)$, so that $Gr(qx_o - f(x_o))$ and $Gr(f^*)$ coincide at $(q_o, f^*(q_o))$. Moreover, because $qx_o - f(x_o) \ge f^*(q)$ for all q, $hyp(f^*) \subset hyp(qx_o - f(x_o))$. Thus, $qx_o - f(x_o)$ *supports* $hyp(f^*)$ at $(q_o, f^*(q_o))$, so that its normal, x_o, belongs to $\partial f^*(q)$, whence

$$q_o \in \partial f(x_o) \Rightarrow x_o \in \partial f^*(q_o). \tag{2.17}$$

Any solution to (2.15) must fall in the superdifferential of f^*. Thus, if a solution to (2.15) exists for q, $f^*$is superdifferentiable at q. This visual intuition is confirmed a bit more formally by recognizing that $q_o \in \partial f(x_o)$

implies $f(x_o) = q_o^{\top} x_o - f^*(q_o)$. Using this fact while evaluating (2.16) at x_o gives

$$f^*(q) + q_o^{\top} x_o - f^*(q_o) \leq q^{\top} x_o \text{ for all } q \in \mathbb{R}^N,$$

so that it is indeed true that $x_o \in \partial f^*(q_o)$. Expression (2.17), which relates the optimal solution to (2.15) to the superdifferential of $f^*(q)$, is commonly called *Shephard's Lemma.*[27]

The same visual intuition illustrates why f^* is concave. Consider a q_* above q_o in Figure 2.5. Moving vertically from $(q_*, 0)$ to the affine function $qx_o - f(x_o)$ gives $q_* x_o - f(x_o)$. This is the value that the objective function for (2.15) would take if x were held constant at x_o. Because not responding to the change from q to q_* is possible, $q_* x_o - f(x_o)$ is an upper bound on the best response for the change in q. Thus, because we are minimizing, the best response value, $(q_*, f^*(q_*))$, should fall below $Gr(qx_o - f(x_o))$ and certainly never above it. This suggests, as illustrated, a concave response surface. Extending the same argument to all possible q further indicates that $hyp(f^*)$ should always be supported from above by affine functions constructed using solutions to (2.15) for the varying q. As is visually apparent, that can only happen if f^* is concave in q.

From the second version of Fenchel's Inequality, one also obtains

$$f(x) \leq q^{\top} x - f^*(q)$$

for all x and q. Thus, it must be true that

$$f(x) \leq \inf_q \{q^{\top} x - f^*(q)\},$$

and moreover, whenever $f^*(q)$ is finite, we must have $f(x) = q^{\top} x - f^*(q)$, so that

$$f(x) = \inf_q \{q^{\top} x - f^*(q)\}.$$

But if f is concave, Lemma 2 ensures that it is superdifferentiable everywhere on $ri(dom(f))$. There must exist (q, x) such that $q \in \partial f(x)$, $x \in \partial f^*(q)$, and $f(x) = q^{\top} x - f^*(q)$. This is what we wanted to show.

[27] After Ronald Shephard (1953, 1970). The nomenclature is a bit imprecise because Shephard actually proved the analogue of what is referred to as the generalized envelope condition below.

5.3 A More Formal Argument

Lemma 1 lets us tighten these intuitive arguments. For f concave, let the set of affine functions majorizing f be denoted:

$$F \equiv \{(q,\alpha) \in \mathbb{R}^{N+1} : f(x) \leq q^{\top}x - \alpha, \forall x\}.$$

Thus, $(q,\alpha) \in F$ if and only if

$$\alpha \leq q^{\top}x - f(x), \quad \forall x,$$

and, in particular,

$$\begin{aligned} \alpha &\leq \inf_{x}\{q^{\top}x - f(x)\} \\ &= f^{*}(q), \end{aligned} \tag{2.18}$$

so that we can rewrite the definition of F as

$$\begin{aligned} F &= \{(q,\alpha) \in \mathbb{R}^{N+1} : \alpha \leq f^{*}(q)\} \\ &= hyp\left(f^{*}\right). \end{aligned}$$

Using Lemma 1 now gives

$$\begin{aligned} f(x) &= \inf_{\alpha,q}\{q^{\top}x - \alpha : (q,\alpha) \in F\} \\ &= \inf_{\alpha,q}\{q^{\top}x - \alpha : (q,\alpha) \in hyp\left(f^{*}\right)\} \\ &= \inf_{\alpha,q}\{q^{\top}x - \alpha : \alpha \leq f^{*}(q)\} \\ &= \inf_{q}\{q^{\top}x - f^{*}(q)\} \\ &\equiv f^{**}(x) \end{aligned} \tag{2.19}$$

which establishes, as desired, that *concave f is its biconjugate, f^{**}*.

Example 5. *Let $f(x) = \ln x$. Recall $dom\left(f\right) = \mathbb{R}_{++}$. Its concave conjugate is*

$$f^{*}(q) = \inf_{x \in \mathbb{R}_{++}} \{qx - \ln x\},$$

Solving establishes that:

$$f^{*}(q) = 1 + \ln q.$$

for which dom $(f^*) = \mathbb{R}_{++}$*. Taking the concave conjugate of* $f^*(q)$ *gives, symmetrically,*

$$\begin{aligned} f^{**}(x) &= \inf_{q\in\mathbb{R}_{++}} \{qx - 1 - \ln q\} \\ &= \inf_{q\in\mathbb{R}_{++}} \{qx - \ln q\} - 1 \\ &= 1 + \ln x - 1 \\ &= \ln x. \end{aligned}$$

Example 6. *Let* $f(x) = -\frac{x^2}{2}$ *with dom* $(f) = \mathbb{R}$*. Its concave conjugate is*

$$f^*(q) = \inf_x \left\{qx + \frac{x^2}{2}\right\}.$$

Solving gives

$$f^*(q) = -\frac{q^2}{2},$$

and symmetrically

$$f^{**}(x) = -\frac{x^2}{2}.$$

Remark 5. *One point related to Lemma 3 deserves special emphasis. Take* $\hat{f}: \mathbb{R}^N \to \mathbb{R}$ *that is closed* ***but not concave****. Its concave conjugate,*

$$\hat{f}^*(q) = \inf_x \left\{q^\top x - \hat{f}(x)\right\},$$

is concave by Lemma 3. But that same lemma also establishes that $\hat{f}^{*\prime}s$ *conjugate (the biconjugate)*

$$\hat{f}^{**}(x) \equiv \inf_q \left\{q^\top x - \hat{f}^*(q)\right\}$$

is concave in x*. Because* $\hat{f}$ *was chosen as nonconcave, we must, therefore, conclude that*

$$\hat{f}^{**}(x) \neq \hat{f}(x),$$

or in other words that $\hat{f}'s$ *biconjugate does not equal* $\hat{f}$*.*

The conjugacy mapping, expression (2.19), when applied to $\hat{f}^*$ for $\hat{f}$ nonconcave does not yield $\hat{f}$. *Instead from Fenchel's Inequality, we have that for all x and q*

$$\hat{f}(x) \leq q^\top x - \hat{f}^*(q),$$

whence

$$\hat{f}(x) \leq \inf_q \left\{q^\top x - \hat{f}^*(q)\right\} = \hat{f}^{**}(x) \text{ for all } x$$

so that the biconjugate always majorizes $\hat{f}(x)$.

What $\hat{f}^{**}$ does generate is best understood using $hyp\left(\hat{f}\right)$. Because $\hat{f}$ is not concave, $hyp\left(\hat{f}\right)$ is not convex. But taking its convex hull, $Co\left\{hyp\left(\hat{f}\right)\right\}$, yields a convex set. The dashed line segment in Figure 2.6 illustrates the hulling operation for a nonconcave f. Define the ***upper-bound function,*** *$u_C : \mathbb{R}^N \to \mathbb{R}$, for an arbitrary $C \subset \mathbb{R}^{N+1}$ by*

$$u_C(x) \equiv \sup\left\{r \in \mathbb{R} : (x, r) \in C, x \in \mathbb{R}^N\right\}.$$

If C is convex, u_C is concave because $(x^o, u_C(x^o)) + \lambda[(x^*, u_C(x^*)) - (x^o, u_C(x^o))] \in C$ for $\lambda \in (0, 1)$, whence

$$u_C(x^o + \lambda(x^* - x^o)) \geq u_C(x^o) + \lambda\left[u_C(x^*) - u_C(x^o)\right]$$

which establishes the desired concavity. Using the upper-bound function, we can show that

$$\hat{f}^{**}(x) = u_{Co\{hyp(\hat{f})\}}(x),$$

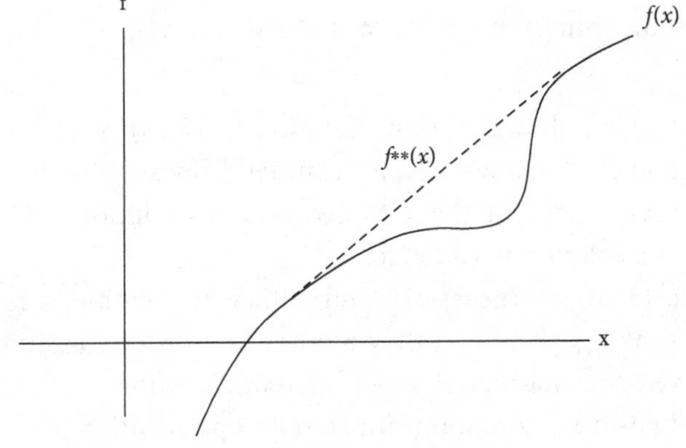

Fig. 2.6 Nonconcave $f(x)$ and $f^{**}(x)$

so that $\hat{f}^{**}(x)$ *corresponds to the upper-bound function for the convex hull of hyp* $(\hat{f})$. *In this sense,* $f^{**}(x)$ *can be thought of as the "concavification" of* $\hat{f}(x)$. $u_{Co\{hyp(\hat{f})\}}$ *is often referred to as the closed, convex hull of* $\hat{f}$. *For more details on this argument, see Proposition B.2.5.2 and Theorem E.1.3.5 in Hirriart-Urruty and LeMaréchal (2001) and the surrounding discussions.*

Example 7. *Take* $f(x) = \frac{x^2}{2}$, *which is convex. Its concave conjugate is the improper concave function*

$$f^*(q) = \inf_{x \in \mathbb{R}} \left\{ qx - \frac{x^2}{2} \right\} = -\infty.$$

We have already seen that Fenchel's Inequality generates a generalized version of Shephard's Lemma. To complete the story, let's suppose that for x_o, $(q_o, f^*(q_o))$ solves (2.19) so that

$$x_o \in \partial f^*(q_o).$$

It follows immediately that the affine function (now of x) $q_o^\top x - f^*(q_o)$ majorizes $f(x)$ and that their graphs coincide at $(x_o, f(x_0))$. Hence, q_o must belong to the superdifferential of f at x establishing that

$$x_o \in \partial f^*(q_o) \Rightarrow q_o \in \partial f(x_o),$$

which when combined with (2.17) gives for concave f that

$$q \in \partial f(x) \Leftrightarrow x \in \partial f^*(q), \quad \text{(Generalized Envelope Theorem)} \tag{2.20}$$

or equivalently

$$x \in \arg\min_{\hat{x}} \{q^\top \hat{x} - f(\hat{x})\} \Leftrightarrow q \in \arg\min_{\hat{q}} \{x^\top \hat{q} - f^*(\hat{q})\}.$$

Expression (2.20) shows that any solution to (2.15) must belong to the superdifferential of f^*. Conversely, for concave f any solution to (2.19) must belong to the superdifferential of f. Moreover, x is a solution to (2.15) for q if and only if q is a solution to (2.19) for x.

Conditions (2.20) are necessary and sufficient conditions for optimality. Strictly speaking, therefore, they are not first-order conditions. But we expressly developed notions of superdifferentials whose optimality conditions mimic first-order conditions for smooth optimization problems. Thus, in a nicely smooth world, expression (2.20) shows that the first-order conditions for the *primal* problem (2.15) are the envelope conditions for the *dual* problem (2.19). Conversely, the first-order conditions for the dual problem (2.19) are the envelope conditions for the *primal* problem (2.15).

As already noted, which problem is *primal* and which is *dual* mathematically is a matter of perspective. Both cases treat choices over $\mathbb{R}^N$. In economics, it's standard to identify the primal problem as choosing $x \in \mathbb{R}^N$, standing for economic quantities, for given $q \in \mathbb{R}^N$, prices. The dual problem turns this on its head and chooses prices for given quantities.

The ultimate reason that these dual relationships are important is embedded in Rockafellar's earlier quote for this chapter: "the models you set should be ones for solving problems effectively." Very frequently, it turns out that problems cast in what economists view as their traditional primal form are more effectively and informatively solved when set in their dual form. That means understanding the dual relationships conveys a significant advantage to the informed over the uninformed in solving practical problems. And when it comes to econometric modeling of those practical problems, the dual form has made problems once viewed as empirically intractable empirically tractable using straightforward and basic econometric techniques.

Summarizing:

Theorem 6. *(Fenchel, Rockafellar): If f is proper concave and closed,*

$$f^*(q) = \inf_x \{q^\top x - f(x)\},$$

$$f(x) = \inf_q \{q^\top x - f^*(q)\},$$

$$f(x) + f^*(q) \le q^\top x \quad \forall x, q,$$

and $x \in \partial f^*(q) \Longleftrightarrow q \in \partial f(x)$.

5.4 And for Nonconcave Structures?

Everyday experience teaches us that many interesting phenomena, including production relationships, are neither concave nor convex. Indeed, intermediate microeconomic theory routinely introduces students to a single-output production function whose characteristic lazy *S*-shape exhibits progressively increasing marginal returns, decreasing marginal returns, and finally negative marginal returns. Taking that starting point, it's natural to approach models based on concave (convex) structures skeptically.

In economic analysis, skepticism is always merited and usually well rewarded. And so, if one's perspective on modeling is that economic models should be firmly grounded, for example, in realistic representations of actual technologies, truly serious study of potential nonconvexities is definitely merited.

If, however, your perspective on economic modeling is that economic models should be formulated in terms of *reasonable economic behavior*, the reliance on concavity or convexity to structure our models may be less problematic. The reason, which seems ultimately traceable to innovations in statistical mechanics and thermodynamics J. Willard Gibbs made in the late nineteenth century, is that reasonable equilibrium behavior can be modeled, without true loss of generality, AS IF the underlying structures were suitably concave or convex. Put another way, replacing f with its concavification $u_{Co\{hyp(f)\}}$ may not inhibit our ability to accurately describe economic behavior.

The reasoning is a bit abstract but fundamentally simple. By and large, economists borrow their notion of a *stable equilibrium* as coinciding with the solution of an appropriate extremum or optimization problem from thermodynamics. The existential nexus between superdifferentiability (subdifferentiability) and extrema, therefore, identifies properties that need to be satisfied for these equilibria to arise. Cast mathematically, that means economic behavior is typically analyzed AS IF individuals solve either a maximization or a minimization problem.

For example, let's suppose that one wants to maximize the nonconcave function f illustrated in Figure 2.7. As you prefer, you can think of this as an unrestricted maximization problem or a restricted one that has been converted to an unrestricted one using a suitable mathematical trick. As drawn, the function in Figure 2.7 is not globally convex, not globally concave, not everywhere smooth, not everywhere continuous, and its effective domain, $dom(f)$, is given by (a, b). Nevertheless, it's visually apparent that the maximum is at point A, where it is superdifferentiable, and that f is also superdifferentiable at B, C, and D.

Because f is not everywhere smooth, the basic calculus cannot be used to either isolate or characterize the optimum. But because superdifferentials do exist, they can be used. For example, at both B and C, the respective superdifferentials signal that rightward movement is merited, while at D the signal is to move to the left. Moreover, each of the elements of the respective superdifferentials (all are not illustrated) describes a half-space that majorizes $hyp(f)$. And if one isolated all the points of superdifferentiability and the associated half-spaces, they can be used to construct $Co\{hyp(f)\}$ and

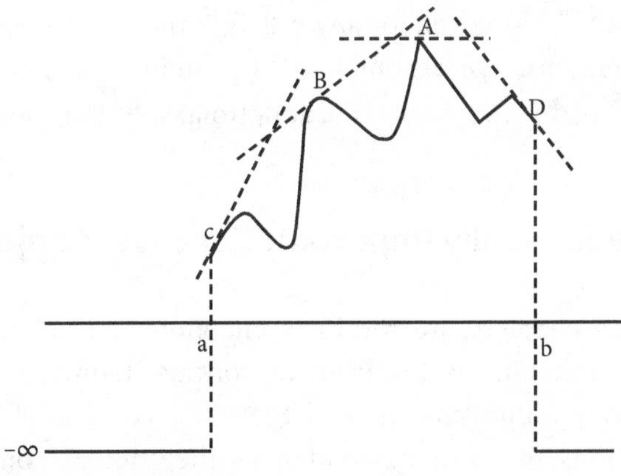

Fig. 2.7 Nonconcave $f(x)$

$u_{Co\{hyp(f)\}}$. So imagine replacing $Gr\left(f\right)$ in Figure 2.7 with $Gr\left(u_{Co\{hyp(f)\}}\right)$ and using the latter as the basis for analysis.

Several points are important. First, and most importantly, the max still occurs at A, so that the qualitative behavior for the true f and its concavification is the same. Second, while not everywhere smooth, $u_{Co\{hyp(f)\}}$ is both concave and continuous. Therefore, it is almost everywhere differentiable on (a, b), everywhere superdifferentiable, and because it is concave both gradients (when they exist) and elements of its superdifferentials always signal the correct *global* direction in which to move. Thus, considerable computational tractability has been purchased at the loss of no true generality in identifying the optimal behavior. The reason this occurs is the same as Gibbs identified in the nineteenth century. The conditions required for global optimality ensure some degree of (in this case) concavity. Thus, replacing the original objective function with its *most conservative concave approximation* ensures that the optimal choice for the original problem remains optimal for the concavified version.[28]

This intuitive argument is phrased a bit more directly by noting that Theorem 2 demonstrates that isolating points of superdifferentiability is equivalent to identifying the points where x can fall into the solution set for

$$\inf_{x}\{q^{\top}x - f(x)\}$$

[28] It's not true, however, that the solution sets for both problems are identical. However, they must overlap, and the solution set for the concavified problem must contain the solution set for the original problem.

for some $q \in \mathbb{R}^N$.[29] Moreover, for any $q \in \mathbb{R}^N$, the solution set to this minimization problem must correspond to $\partial f^*(q)$ and $u_{Co\{f\}}(x) = f^{**}(x) = f(x)$. Hence, $u_{Co\{f\}}(x)$ and f always coincide at optimal solutions $\inf_x \{q^\top x - f(x)\}$.

5.5 Two Economically Important Concave–Conjugate Pairs

In the following chapters, we routinely encounter two classes of concave (convex) functions. One is the class of concave (convex) functions that are also positively homogeneous, and the other consists of those concave (convex) functions that can be written as the sum of concave (convex) functions. We now develop each in turn, paying particular attention to their conjugates.

Support Functions

For the set $C \subset \mathbb{R}^N$, recall that its indicator function, $\delta : \mathbb{R}^N \to \bar{\mathbb{R}}$, is defined by

$$\delta(x \mid C) \equiv \begin{cases} 0 & x \in C \\ -\infty & x \notin C \end{cases}.$$

If C is closed convex, $\delta(x \mid C)$ is closed and proper concave. This is easily established by noting that

$$\begin{aligned} hyp(\delta) &\equiv \{(x, y) \in \mathbb{R}^{N+1} : \delta(x \mid C) \geq y\} \\ &= (C, \mathbb{R}_-) \end{aligned}$$

is convex, while $dom(\delta) = C$. Its concave conjugate, the (lower) *support function for C*,

$$\begin{aligned} \delta^*(q \mid C) &= \inf_{x \in \mathbb{R}^N} \{q^\top x - \delta(x \mid C)\} \\ &= \inf\{q^\top x : x \in C\}, \end{aligned}$$

[29] For subdifferentiability, the equivalent statement is that the points identified can fall in the potential solution sets for

$$\sup_x \{f(x) - q^\top x\}.$$

is also proper concave and closed. If C is closed convex,

$$\begin{aligned}\delta^{**}(x \mid C) &= \inf\{q^{\top}x - \delta^{*}(q \mid C)\}\\ &= \delta(x \mid C).\end{aligned}$$

If C is not convex $\delta^{**}(x \mid C)$ is the indicator function for $Co\{C\}$.

Recalling the definition of $H(\alpha, q)$ as

$$H(\alpha, q) = \{x : q^{\top}x \geq \alpha\},$$

reveals that

$$\begin{aligned}\delta^{*}(q \mid C) &= \inf\{q^{\top}x : x \in C\}\\ &= \inf\{\alpha : C \subset H(\alpha, q)\}.\end{aligned}$$

Thus, solving for the support function can be recast as finding the $H(\alpha, q)$ that *supports* C, as illustrated in Figure 2.8. (Note the similarity to Figure 1.2.) Because half-spaces are homogeneous of degree zero in (α, q), it follows that for $\mu > 0$

$$\begin{aligned}\delta^{*}(\mu q \mid C) &= \inf\{\alpha : C \subset H(\alpha, \mu q)\}\\ &= \mu \inf\left\{\frac{\alpha}{\mu} : C \subset H\left(\frac{\alpha}{\mu}, q\right)\right\}\\ &= \mu\delta^{*}(q \mid C),\end{aligned}$$

so that $\delta^{*}(q \mid C)$ is positively homogeneous. Because it is also a concave conjugate, $\delta^{*}(q \mid C)$ is, therefore, simultaneously concave and positively homogeneous in q. Functions that are positively homogeneous and concave are *superlinear.*

Superlinear functions are the simplest concave generalizations of linear functions. A function $l : \mathbb{R}^N \to \mathbb{R}$ is *linear* if for all $(x^0, x^1) \in \mathbb{R}^N \times \mathbb{R}^N$ and $(\mu^0, \mu^1) \in \mathbb{R} \times \mathbb{R}$

$$l(\mu^0 x^0 + \mu^1 x^1) = \mu^0 l(x^0) + \mu^1 l(x^1).$$

Linear functions are thus simultaneously (weakly) concave and convex. Geometrically, their hypographs and epigraphs are convex cones[30] because, for example,

[30] A set $K \subset \mathbb{R}^N$ is a *cone* if $x \in K \Rightarrow \lambda x \in K$ for $\lambda > 0$.

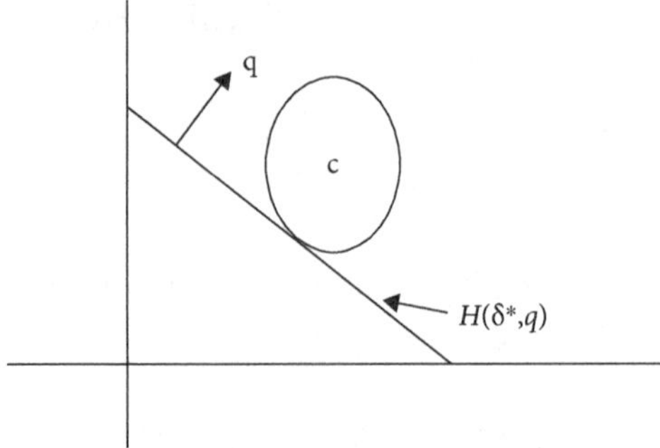

Fig. 2.8 Solving for C's Support Function

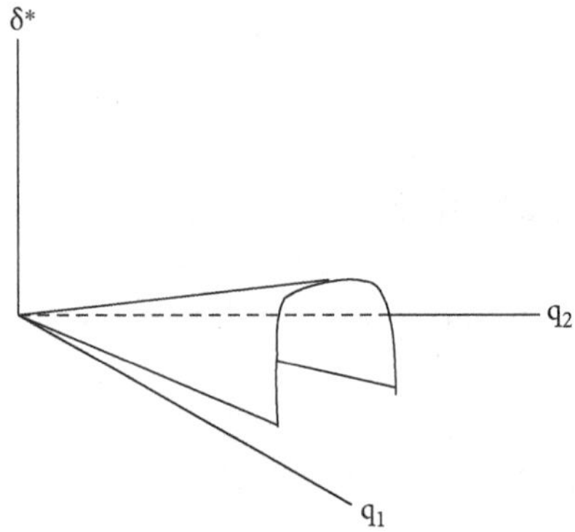

Fig. 2.9 Superlinear Function

$$(x, y) \in hyp\,(l) \Longleftrightarrow (\mu x, \mu y) \in hyp\,(l) \quad \mu > 0.$$

Superlinearity (and its natural complement sublinearity) generalizes linearity by requiring the hypograph (epigraph) but not the epigraph (hypograph) of the function to be a convex cone. Figure 2.9 illustrates the superlinear case. Equivalently, $s : \mathbb{R}^N \to \bar{\mathbb{R}}$ is *superlinear* if and only if for all $(x^0, x^1) \in \mathbb{R}^N \times \mathbb{R}^N$ and $(\mu^0, \mu^1) \in \mathbb{R}_{++} \times \mathbb{R}_{++}$

$$s\left(\mu^0 x^0 + \mu^1 x^1\right) \geq \mu^0 s\left(x^0\right) + \mu^1 s\left(x^1\right),$$

and *sublinear* if and only if

$$s\left(\mu^0 x^0 + \mu^1 x^1\right) \leq \mu^0 s\left(x^0\right) + \mu^1 s\left(x^1\right).$$

Functions that are both superlinear and sublinear are linear.

Problem 6. *Show that*

$$s\left(\mu^0 x^0 + \mu^1 x^1\right) \geq \mu^0 s\left(x^0\right) + \mu^1 s\left(x^1\right),$$

for all $\left(x^0, x^1\right) \in \mathbb{R}^N \times \mathbb{R}^N$ *and* $\left(\mu^0, \mu^1\right) \in \mathbb{R}_{++} \times \mathbb{R}_{++}$ *if and only if (a) s is concave and positively homogeneous, (b) s is superadditive, that is,*

$$s\left(x^0 + x^1\right) \geq s\left(x^0\right) + s\left(x^1\right)$$

and positively homogeneous, and (c) hyp (s) is a closed, convex cone.

Example 8. *Consider the closed convex set* $C = \{(x_1, x_2) : |x_1| \leq 1, |x_2| \leq 1\}$ *that can be visualized in two dimensions as a square box containing the origin with its respective vertices at* $(1,1), (1,-1), (-1,-1)$, *and* $(-1,1)$. *Its support function is*

$$\begin{aligned}\delta^*(q \mid C) &= \inf_q \{q_1 x_1 + q_2 x_2 : |x_1| \leq 1, |x_2| \leq 1\} \\ &= \inf_{q_1} \{q_1 x_1 : |x_1| \leq 1\} + \inf_{q_2} \{q_2 x_2 : |x_2| \leq 1\} \\ &= -|q_1| - |q_2|\end{aligned}$$

$\delta^*(q \mid C)$ is not the first superlinear function we've encountered. Eventually, we will encounter many more. But for the moment, it's enough to recall that the one-sided directional derivative for concave $f : \mathbb{R}^N \to \bar{\mathbb{R}}, f'(x; v)$ is positively homogeneous and concave v. Moreover, by Lemma 2 for f concave

$$f'(x; v) = \inf\{q^\top v : q \in \partial f(x)\}.$$

The structural similarity of $f'(x; v)$ to

$$\delta^*(q \mid C) = \inf\{q^\top x : x \in C\},$$

is not accidental. $f'(x; v)$ *is the support function for* $\partial f(x)$, or in that notation

$$f'(x; v) = \delta^*(v \mid \partial f(x)).$$

More generally, an innate connection exists between superlinearity and support functions (Rockafellar 1970; Hiriart-Urruty and Le Maréchal 2001). All support functions are superlinear, and all superlinear functions are support functions for some closed convex set.

Lemma 4. *A function $f : \mathbb{R}^N \to \bar{\mathbb{R}}$ is superlinear if and only if there exists a closed, convex $C \subset \mathbb{R}^N$ such that*

$$\begin{aligned} f(x) &= \inf\{x^\top v : v \in C\} \\ &= \inf_{v \in \mathbb{R}^N} \{x^\top v - \delta(v \mid C)\} \\ &= \delta^*(x \mid C) \end{aligned}$$

and

$$C = \{v : x^\top v \geq f(x) \text{ for all } x \in \mathbb{R}^N\}.$$

The convex analogue of superlinearity is sublinearity. More formally, $f : \mathbb{R}^N \to \bar{\mathbb{R}}$ is *sublinear* if $-f$ is superlinear, so that sublinearity corresponds either to convexity and positive homogeneity or subadditivity and positive homogeneity.[31] Exactly parallel to Lemma 4, we have:

Lemma 5. *A function $f : \mathbb{R}^N \to \bar{\mathbb{R}}$ is sublinear if and only if there exists a closed, convex $D \subset \mathbb{R}^N$ such that*

$$f(x) = \sup\{x^\top v : v \in D\}$$

and

$$D = \{v : f(x) \geq x^\top v \text{ for all } x \in \mathbb{R}^N\}.$$

Besides directional derivatives, economic manifestations of support functions include cost functions, expenditure functions, revenue functions and profit functions. Each is either superlinear or sublinear, and each can be recognized as the support function for a set derived from preferences or technologies.

More generally, virtually any optimization program framed in $\mathbb{R}^N$can be recognized as a special case of support function, now defined over $\mathbb{R}^{N+1}$. Consider

$$\delta^*(q, p \mid C) \equiv \inf_{x \in \mathbb{R}^N, y \in \mathbb{R}} \{q^\top x + py : (x, y) \in C \subset \mathbb{R}^{N+1}\}.$$

[31] As with superlinearity, either one implies the other. Alternatively, f is sublinear if $epi(f)$ is a cone.

Taking $C = epi\,(f)$ then reveals, for example, that

$$\delta^*\left(0,1 \mid epi\,(f)\right) = \inf_{x,y}\{y : y \geq f(x)\}$$
$$= \inf\{f(x)\},$$

and the requirement for the optimum is that

$$0 \in \partial^- f(x).$$

Supremal Convolutions

Another class of concave functions that we'll frequently encounter are the concave functions obtained by allocating a fixed quantity, $x \in \mathbb{R}^N$, across different concave functions to maximize their sum. Microeconomic examples of this problem abound. One classic example is that of the multiplant firm allocating its purchased input bundle across plants to maximize its profits. Another, less obvious, but important, example is that of calculating Paretian equilibria.

For $f_1, \ldots, f_N$ with each $f_n : \mathbb{R}^N \to \mathbb{R}$ closed and proper concave for all n define their *supremal convolution* by

$$\Diamond f(x) \equiv \sup\left\{\sum_{n=1}^{N} f_n\left(x_n\right) : x_n \in \mathbb{R}^N, \sum_{n=1}^{N} x_n = x\right\}$$
$$= \sup\left\{f_1\left(x - \sum_{n=2}^{N} x_n\right) + \sum_{n=2}^{N} f_n\left(x_n\right)\right\}.$$

That $\Diamond f : \mathbb{R}^N \to \mathbb{R}$ is concave is easily established. Let x_n^o for $n = 1, \ldots, N$ denote an optimal allocation for x^o and x_n^* an optimal allocation for x^*. Clearly, $x_n^o + \mu\left(x_n^* - x_n^o\right)$ for $\mu \in (0,1)$ represents a feasible allocation for $x^o + \mu\left(x^* - x^o\right)$. Thus,

$$\Diamond f(x^o + \mu\left(x^* - x^o\right)) \geq \sum_{n=1}^{N} f_n\left(x_n^o + \mu\left(x_n^* - x_n^o\right)\right)$$
$$\geq \sum_{n=1}^{N} f_n\left(x_n^o\right) + \mu\left[f_n\left(x_n^*\right) - f_n\left(x_n^o\right)\right]$$
$$= \Diamond f(x^o) + \mu\left[\Diamond f(x^*) - \Diamond f(x^o)\right]$$

where the first inequality follows by the definition of $\diamond f$ and the second by the concavity of $f_1, \ldots, f_N$. Thus, the supremal convolution of concave functions is, indeed, concave.

Any optimal allocation, $(\hat{x}_1, \ldots, \hat{x}_N)$, solving the supremal convolution problem must satisfy:

$$\cap_{n=1}^{N} \partial f_n(\hat{x}_n) \neq \varnothing \text{ and } \sum_{n=1}^{N} \hat{x}_n = x.$$

This condition that requires the superdifferentials of all f_n to overlap is easily established using Theorem 2 and the second version of the supremal convolution definition to obtain for all x_n,

$$\begin{aligned} 0 &\in \partial\left(f_n(\hat{x}_n) + f_1\left(x - \sum_{n=2}^{N} x_n\right)\right) \\ &= \partial f_n(\hat{x}_n) - \partial f_1(\hat{x}_1), \end{aligned}$$

which establishes that $\partial f_n(\hat{x}_n)$ and $\partial f_1(\hat{x}_1)$ must overlap (that is, have a nonempty intersection).[32] Because this has to be true for all $n = 2, \ldots, N$, optimality requires

$$\cap_{n=1}^{N} \partial f_n(\hat{x}_n) \neq \varnothing.$$

When each of the f_n is smooth, this overlapping condition (often referred to as the *Dubovitsky–Milyutin* condition) reduces to equalizing partial derivatives (or gradients) across all $n = 1, 2, \ldots, N$.

Write any solution, $(\hat{x}_1, \ldots, \hat{x}_N)$, to the supremal convolution problem as

$$\diamond f(x) = f_1\left(x - \sum_{n=2}^{N} \hat{x}_n\right) + \sum_{n=2}^{N} f_n(\hat{x}_n).$$

Because $\diamond f(x)$ is concave, it is superdifferentiable. A straightforward extension of the envelope theorem then implies that

[32] As a general rule, superdifferentials and subdifferentials need not obey the rules of addition in the same manner that derivatives do. However, they do for proper concave and convex functions (see, for example, Hiriart-Urruty and LeMaréchal (2001, Theorem D.4.1.1).

$$\begin{aligned}\partial\Diamond f(x) &= \partial f_1\left(x - \sum_{n=2}^{N}\hat{x}_n\right)\\ &\subset \cap_{n=1}^{N}\partial f_n\left(\hat{x}_n\right).\end{aligned} \tag{2.21}$$

The concave conjugate of $\Diamond f$ proves of particular interest in the following chapters:

$$\begin{aligned}(\Diamond f)^*(q) &= \inf\left\{q^\top x - \sup\left\{\sum_{n=1}^{N} f_n(x_n) : \sum_{n=1}^{N} x_n = x\right\}\right\}\\ &= \inf\left\{q^\top \sum_{n=1}^{N} x_n - \sum_{n=1}^{N} f_n(x_n)\right\}\\ &= \sum_{n=1}^{N}\inf\{q^\top x_n - f_n(x_n)\}\\ &= \sum_{n=1}^{N} f_n^*(q).\end{aligned} \tag{2.22}$$

Thus, $(\Diamond f)^*$ equals the sum of concave conjugates of the individual $f_n's$, $n = 1, 2, \ldots, N$. The concavity of the individual $f_n's$ ensures that:

$$\left(\sum_{n=1}^{N} f_n^*(q)\right)^* = (\Diamond f)^{**} = \Diamond f(x),$$

from which we obtain the following superdifferential relationship:

$$q \in \partial\Diamond f(x) = \cap_{n=1}^{N}\partial f_n(\hat{x}_n) \Leftrightarrow x \in \partial\left(\sum_{n=1}^{N} f_n^*(q)\right) = \sum_{n=1}^{N}\partial f_n^*(q), \tag{2.23}$$

by Theorem 6.

5.6 Convex Conjugates

Parallel conjugacy relationships apply for convex functions. Because, a function f is convex if $-f$ is concave, the essentials are captured by making four changes: replacing the infimum used in defining concave conjugates with supremum, replacing superdifferentials with subdifferentials, reversing inequalities, and looking at Figures 1.3 and 1.4. Thus,

Theorem 7. *(Fenchel, Rockafellar): If f is proper*[33] *convex and closed,*

$$f^*(q) = \sup_x \{q^\top x - f(x)\},$$
$$f(x) = \sup_q \{q^\top x - f^*(q)\},$$
$$f(x) + f^*(q) \geq q^\top x \quad \forall x, q,$$

and

$$x \in \partial^- f^*(q) \Longleftrightarrow q \in \partial^- f(x).$$

Establishing Theorem 7 is mainly a matter of recycling the concave–conjugate discussion. The essential observation is that convexity of f implies that $epi(f)$ forms a convex set. Minkowski's Theorem implies that convex f is fully characterized by the closed half-spaces containing $epi(f)$. Each of those half-spaces consists of those elements of $\mathbb{R}^{N+1}$ lying to one side of a hyperplane described, as before, by

$$\{z : p^\top z = \alpha\}.$$

But instead of looking below the hyperplane, we look above it at sets of the form (after renormalization),

$$H^+(\alpha, p) = \{(x, y) : q^\top x - \alpha \leq y\},$$

that correspond to the epigraphs of affine function. From this observation, the crucial result is:

Lemma 6. *A closed convex function is the pointwise supremum of the collection of all affine functions, h, such that $h \leq f$.*

Problem 7. *Using Lemma 6, develop an argument supporting the statement of Theorem 7.*

[33] A convex function is proper if $dom(f) \neq \emptyset$, and if $f(x) > -\infty$ for all x.

Problem 8. *For C closed and convex, $\delta(x \mid C)$ is proper concave and closed. Therefore, $-\delta(x \mid C)$ is proper convex and closed. The (upper) support function for C is defined by*

$$\begin{aligned}(-\delta)^*(q \mid C) &= \sup\{q^\top x + \delta(x \mid C)\}\\ &= \sup\{q^\top x : x \in C\},\end{aligned}$$

where $(-\delta)^*(q \mid C)$ denotes the convex conjugate of $-\delta(x \mid C)$. Prove that $(-\delta)^*(q \mid C)$ is sublinear and that

$$-\delta^*(-q \mid C) = (-\delta)^*(q \mid C).$$

Problem 9. *For $f_1, \ldots, f_M$ closed and proper convex, with $f_n : \mathbb{R}^N \to \mathbb{R}$ their infimal convolution is defined as*

$$\bigvee f[x] = \inf\left\{\sum_{m=1}^{M} f_m(x_m) : \sum_{m=1}^{M} x_m = x\right\}.$$

Prove that it is convex and develop its convex conjugate.

Remark 6. *At this juncture, it is perhaps helpful to recall some problems that you have encountered in intermediate microeconomics. For example, one invariably encounters two versions of the profit-maximization problem in undergraduate classes. One is posed as picking quantities, interpreted as outputs, to maximize the difference between the revenue received from selling those quantities and their cost of production.*

If we let $y \in \mathbb{R}^M$ denote output quantities, p their prices, and $C(y)$ the associated cost, the resulting profit maximization problem is

$$C^*(p) = \max_y \{p^\top y - C(y)\}.$$

One usually thinks in terms of outputs having marginal costs that are positive and increasing in y. Mathematically, this is typically expressed by assuming that C is convex in y. Thus, the profit maximization problem reduces simply to one of finding the convex conjugate of $C(y)$, and the solution occurs where

$$p \in \partial^- C(y),$$

which is an elegant way of saying price is equated to marginal cost. But it also follows that the solution satisfies

$$y \in \partial^{-} C^{*}(p),$$

which is often referred to as Hotelling's Lemma.

Another way to view profit maximization is as picking quantities, interpreted as inputs and denoted x, to maximize the difference between the value of the output produced and the cost of acquiring the inputs. Let the prices of inputs expressed in units of the output (in economic jargon take the output as the numeraire good) be q and the "production function" be $f(x)$. Then this version of the profit-maximization problem is written

$$\begin{aligned}\max_x \{f(x) - q^{\top}x\} &= -\min_x \{q^{\top}x - f(x)\} \\ &= -f^{*}(q)\end{aligned}$$

so that it reduces to finding the concave conjugate of $f(x)$. The solution occurs where

$$q \in \partial f(x),$$

which is an elegant way of saying "equate marginal products to input prices normalized by the price of output," and it satisfies

$$x \in \partial f^{*}(q).$$

5.7 Fenchel's Duality Theorem

Consider two functions, $f : \mathbb{R}^N \to \bar{\mathbb{R}}$ proper concave and closed and $g : \mathbb{R}^N \to \bar{\mathbb{R}}$ proper convex and closed. From preceding developments, it seems clear that either

$$\sup_{x\in\mathbb{R}^N} \{f(x) - g(x)\},$$

or

$$\inf_{x\in\mathbb{R}^N} \{g(x) - f(x)\},$$

should be relatively easy to solve using the methods that we have already developed. The former objective function is concave, and the latter is convex. Therefore, if maxima or minima exist, they should be relatively well behaved. However, the duality theory that we have already developed offers yet another way to pose and solve either problem. We show the result for the supremum version and leave the development of the infimum version to you.

By Fenchel's Inequality

$$q^\top x \geq f(x) + f^*(q), \text{ and}$$
$$g(x) + g^*(q) \geq q^\top x,$$

for all x and q. Moreover, whenever x is optimal, each inequality becomes an equality. Adding the inequalities together gives

$$g(x) + g^*(q) \geq f(x) + f^*(q),$$

whence

$$g^*(q) - f^*(q) \geq f(x) - g(x),$$

for all x and q. The left-hand side is independent of x and the right-hand side is independent of q, from which it follows immediately that

$$\inf_{q \in \mathbb{R}^N} \{g^*(q) - f^*(q)\} \geq \sup_{x \in \mathbb{R}^N} \{f(x) - g(x)\}.$$

This inequality reduces to an equality under weak regularity conditions,[34]

$$\inf_{q \in \mathbb{R}^N} \{g^*(q) - f^*(q)\} = \sup_{x \in \mathbb{R}^N} \{f(x) - g(x)\}, \qquad \textit{(Fenchel's Duality Theorem)} \tag{2.24}$$

Remark 7. *Notice that*

$$\sup_{x \in \mathbb{R}^N} \{f(x) - g(x)\},$$

can be rewritten as

$$\sup_{x \in \mathbb{R}^N} \{f(x) - g(y) \; : \; x - y = 0\},$$

[34] Either the relative interiors of *dom* (f) and *dom* (g) intersect or the relative interiors of their conjugate duals intersect.

so that Fenchel's Duality Theorem can be treated as a special case of a supremal convolution. Develop its properties from this perspective.

Fenchel's Duality Theorem has particularly important implications for the representations of economic equilibria. As a simple example, one might consider the generic problem of choosing an economic quantity, x, to maximize the difference between a concave economic benefit function given by $f(x)$ and a convex economic cost function given by $g(x)$. The well-known solution is to equate *marginal benefit* to *marginal cost,* which is expressed mathematically as

$$\partial f(x) \cap \partial^{-} g(x) \neq \varnothing,$$

so that the appropriate superdifferential (measuring marginal benefit) and subdifferential (measuring marginal cost) overlap. Fenchel's Duality Theorem reveals that same problem can be equivalently posed as one of choosing a dual variable $q \in \mathbb{R}$, which we will think of as either a price or a shadow price to minimize the difference between the two conjugates so that

$$\partial^{-} g^{*}(q) \cap \partial f^{*}(q) \neq \varnothing,$$

which requires the optimal solutions to the primal problems to overlap. There are many such manifestations of this latter result, but the most common one is simply that demand for an economic quantity equals its supply. Notice that for concave f and convex g, the equilibrium condition of equating marginal benefit to marginal cost is reflected in the tangency condition represented by Figure 1.6, while the intersecting demand and supply are represented in Figure 1.5.

6 Chapter Commentary

The material on correpondences and the Maximum Theorem derives from Berge (1963). The discussion of generalized notions of differentiability draws from several sources. In rough rank of order of importance, they are Rockafellar (1970), Luenberger (1969), Hiriart-Urruty and Le Maréchal (2001), Aliprantis and Border (2007), Clarke (1983), Rockafellar and Wets (1998), and Ok (2007). The material on convex analysis and conjugate duality mainly derives from Rockafellar (1970). However, more than a few of the ideas in that discussion were drawn from other sources, including Hiriart-Urruty and Le Maréchal (2001), Gale (1960), and Aliprantis and Border (2007).

3
Orders and Their Representations

1 What Is an Order?

Much of modern economic analysis is based on the concept of a binary relation or an order (partial) of some real dimensional space. I will almost exclusively use the order terminology. Although this approach may strike some as mathematically imprecise, it's less clumsy than repeatedly writing or saying "binary relation."[1] Regardless, the examples are many. They encompass most of the basic concepts in consumer theory, producer theory, decision theory, and decision making under uncertainty.

An order does exactly what it says: It orders something. We consider orders that order sets, the most typical of which is $\mathbb{R}^N \times \mathbb{R}^M$, where N may or may not be equal to M.

One order that you may be familiar with is the greater than or equal to order, denoted by $\geq$. How does $\geq$ order $\mathbb{R}^N \times \mathbb{R}^N$? Well, $x \geq y$ means that every element of the vector $x \in \mathbb{R}^N$ is at least as large its corresponding element in $y \in \mathbb{R}^N$. Thus, it lets you compare, or in the sense used here, order elements of $\mathbb{R}^N$. It's *transitive* because if $x \geq y$ and $y \geq z$, then $x \geq z$. It's also *reflexive* because $x \geq x$ for all $x \in \mathbb{R}^N$. Finally, it's an *incomplete order* because there exist x and y for which neither of the following two statements is true $x \geq y$ or $y \geq x$. Take $x = (2, 1)^\top$ and $y = (1, 2)^\top$ for an example.

The $\geq$ order is both familiar and interesting. Unfortunately, unless your approach to economics is totally Leontief, $\geq$ may not carry you very far. More is needed. But we try to add parsimoniously. In particular, we try to avoid adding more than necessary. Still, in many instances, $\geq$ defines an interesting (and economically meaningful) polar case of the general orders that we do study.

[1] In the following, the terms "order" and "ordering", when used as nouns, are interchangeable. It is common to reserve the term "order" for binary relations that satisfy specified properties, for example, reflexivity and transitivity. That convention is not followed here.

Competitive Agents in Certain and Uncertain Markets. Robert G. Chambers, Oxford University Press (2021).

DOI: 10.1093/oso/9780190063016.001.0001

I consider orderings of $\mathbb{R}^N \times \mathbb{R}^M$ that I will denote by $\succeq(y)$ for $y \in \mathbb{R}^M$. This is not standard notation.[2] What does $x \succeq (y)$ mean? That depends on the problem that we're interested in.

For example, suppose that $M = N$, so that both x and y belong to $\mathbb{R}^N$. One familiar interpretation of $x \succeq (y)$ is that the consumption bundle x is *at least as good as* the consumption bundle y. I'll leave it to you as an exercise to decide what "at least as good as" means.

Exercise 9. *Imagine a bowl that contains three pieces of fruit (an apple, an orange, and a pear). Write down formally what would constitute an at-least-as-good set for that bowl of fruit for you.*

In general, there is no reason to believe that $\succeq(y)$ preserves the $\geq$ order. By that I mean that $x \geq y$ does not necessarily imply $x \succeq (y)$. Why? Those of you who are aspiring environmental economists should knock this softball out of the park. Those of you who aren't: How many Big Macs can you eat? In fact, *a priori*, there's not much reason to suppose that $\succeq(y)$ satisfies any specific properties. That doesn't mean we won't impose such properties later on. We will. But they should be recognized as assumptions and, thus, restrictive.

Is there another way to interpret $\succeq(y)$? Again that's easy and illustrates the need for my nonstandard notation. Let's take $y \in \mathbb{R}^M$, where M is not the same as N, and read the order as $x \in \mathbb{R}^N$ *can produce* y. Then, $\succeq(y)$ orders $\mathbb{R}^N \times \mathbb{R}^M$ by isolating those bundles of inputs that can produce the output bundle y. Notice that we are specifically thinking of a multi-output technology as the general case.

By now, hopefully, you are forming visual images of these examples of orderings. Specifically, consumer and/or producer theory would suggest something similar to Figures 1.2 and 1.4. Try instead to visualize the case where $M = N$ and both x and y are *random variables*. Random variables can always be thought of as vectors. Many times they're infinite-dimensional vectors, but they're still vectors. If you don't understand or believe this, I'm not surprised, but it is true and later chapters explain why. So if both x and y are random variables, then yet another interpretation of $x \succeq (y)$ is that *x is at least as risky as y*. One of the take-away messages I want to leave you with is that the visual interpretation of x is at least as risky as y is intimately related to the visual representation of y is at least as good as x.

[2] Note, however, that Jehle and Reny (2011), which is an excellent resource, uses a similar notation for a related, but distinct, concept.

Do you believe that the idea that x is at least as risky as y is a reasonable notion for economists to study? Do you know what this means? Suppose a noneconomist challenged you to explain it, could you? Let's see.

Exercise 10. *Suppose we have two random variables, x and y. Define what it means for x to be more risky than y.*

Exercise 11. *Assume that $x \succeq (y)$ means that x is at least as good as y. Draw a visual representation of what this means to you.*

Exercise 12. *Assume that $x \succeq (y)$ means that x can produce y. Draw a visual representation of what this means to you.*

Exercise 13. *If there are any similarities between the figures you have drawn, explain why you drew them that way.*

Exercise 14. *Detail the mathematical assumptions that you have imposed in drawing these figures.*

2 Some Structure (Assumptions)

Now that you've drawn some pictures and thought about orders visually, it's time to impose some assumptions. Depending on the application, the assumptions will differ. Moreover, regardless of the application, it's usually true that exceptions exist.

The first assumption, however, is relatively harmless. It's a technical assumption, and virtually any observed body of economic data can be made consistent with a version of it. At a philosophical level, there are many reasons that still might cause one to hesitate to make such an assumption, but this is applied economics and not philosophy.

I call this assumption *continuity*, and in the following it will typically come in three versions, each of which is distinguished by the (visual) perspective one takes on correspondences that are generated by $\succeq (y)$

Assumption: $(CA) \succeq (y)$ is *continuous from above*. That is,

$$V(y) \equiv \{x \in \mathbb{R}^N : x \succeq (y)\},$$

is closed.

Assumption: $(CB) \succeq (y)$ is *continuous from below.* That is,

$$Y(x) \equiv \{y \in \mathbb{R}^M : x \succeq (y)\}$$

is closed.

Assumption: (C) $\succeq (y)$ *is continuous.* That is,

$$Gr(\succeq (y)) \equiv \{(x, y) \in \mathbb{R}^{N+M} : x \succeq (y)\}$$

is closed.

The second assumption is not relatively harmless. In fact, as my earlier Big Macs query suggests, it's easy to find counterexamples. Therefore, it is very definitely an assumption. For now, we will call it *monotonicity*, although we will later encounter it under the moniker of *disposability* that reflects the current jargon of production economists. Monotonicity also comes in three versions, all reflecting a similar logic—namely, that specific inferences can be made by observing that $x' \geq x$ and $x \succeq (y)$ or that $y' \leq y$ and $x \succeq (y)$.

Assumption: $(MA) \succeq (y)$ is *monotonic from above* if

$$x' \geq x \succeq (y) \Rightarrow x' \succeq (y),$$

or equivalently

$$x' \geq x \in V(y) \Rightarrow x' \in V(y).$$

Assumption: $(MB) \succeq (y)$ is *monotonic from below if*

$$x \succeq (y) \Rightarrow x \succeq (y') \text{ for } y' \leq y,$$

or equivalently

$$y' \leq y \in Y(x) \Rightarrow y' \in Y(x).$$

Assumption: (M) $\succeq (y)$ is *monotonic if it is monotonic from above and from below.*

Exercise 15. *"Jack Spratt could eat no fat, His wife could eat no lean, But between them both, They licked the platter clean" is a familiar nursery rhyme. But in* *a two-good world of* $\left(x_{fat}, x_{lean}\right) \in \mathbb{R}^2$, *it also represents a statement about the preferences of Mr. and Ms. Spratt.*[3] *Derive an explicit representation of* $\succeq (y)$ *defined on* $\mathbb{R}^2$, *interpreted as an at-least-as-good order, for Mr. and Ms. Spratt. Does the order satisfy MA, MB, or M?*

3 Cardinal Representations of Orders

Often people argue that cardinality is overly restrictive, which in economics typically means bad. It depends. For example, people often insist that preference orderings should be ordinal. Taken precisely, that's perfectly sensible. But any ordinal, monotonic, upper semicontinuous utility function has a cardinal representation. In fact, we shall show that cardinal representations of orders, preference or otherwise, can be developed under even weaker conditions.

To demonstrate, assume that $\succeq (y)$ is continuous from above (CA) and monotonic from above (MA). For $g \in \mathbb{R}_+^N \backslash \{0\}$ define

$$\begin{aligned} d(x, y; g) &\equiv \max\{\beta \in \mathbb{R} : x - \beta g \succeq (y)\} \\ &\equiv \max\{\beta \in \mathbb{R} : x - \beta g \in V(y)\} \end{aligned}$$

if there exists β such that $x - \beta g \succeq (y)$ and $-\infty$ otherwise.[4] I claim that $d(x, y; g)$ represents $\succeq (y)$ in the sense that

$$d(x, y; g) \geq 0 \Leftrightarrow x \succeq (y) \qquad (Indication) \qquad (3.1)$$

Expression (3.1) is referred to as the *Indication Property* because it *indicates* whether or not $x \succeq (y)$. It implies that $d(x, y; g)$ is a *function representation* of $\succeq (y)$ so that $d(x, y; g) \geq 0$ and $x \succeq (y)$ are informationally equivalent. We'll refer to $d(x, y; g)$ as either a *directional distance function* or a *distance function*. Its mathematical roots trace at least to Blackorby and Donaldson (1980) and Luenberger (1992a). The "directional" terminology is due to Chambers, Chung, and Färe (1996).[5]

[3] Here, an informational constraint forces me to presume that Jack Spratt's wife chooses not to go by her maiden name.

[4] The notation $\mathbb{R}_+^N \backslash \{0\}$ refers to the nonnegative N orthant with the origin excluded. Another way to write the same notion is to require $x \geq 0$ and $x \neq 0$ for $x \in \mathbb{R}^N$.

[5] Personally, I have often regretted being party to introducing what is clearly clumsy terminology. But, as is so often the case with bad ideas, it seemed like a good idea at the time. Unfortunately, many papers, as of this writing, have taken up the terminology, and so it's impossible to go back now.

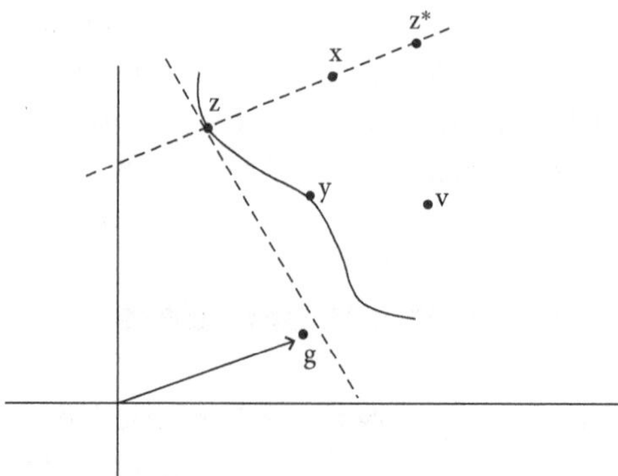

Fig. 3.1 Distance Function

Before proving (3.1), let's look at what $g \in \mathbb{R}^N_+ \setminus \{0\}$ is, what $d(x, y; g)$ is, and what is being assumed. There are different ways to interpret g. Mathematically speaking, it is a point in the nonnegative orthant. That is, each coordinate of g, denoted g_n, is no smaller than zero, and g has at least one coordinate that is strictly positive. We've been talking about $x \succeq (y)$ in an at-least-as-good sense. One obvious way to interpret g is as a bundle of goods and services, or in perhaps more familiar jargon, a market basket of goods and services. Given that interpretation, $d(x, y; g)$ is the maximal (real) number of units of this market basket that can be subtracted from bundle x (or added to it) while leaving the resulting bundle of goods and services, $x - \beta g$, at least as good as y. Hence, g can be viewed as a yardstick, denominated in real commodity units, of whether x is at least as good as y. That yardstick can also be thought of as a *numeraire*. This may strike some as strange because economic numeraires are typically single commodities, but that interpretation can be placed in perspective by reminding yourself, for example, that the consumer price index is a price index for a representative bundle of consumption commodities.

Figure 3.1 illustrates $d(x, y; g)$. The frontier passing through point y should be interpreted as the "boundary" of $V(y)$ generated by $\succeq (y)$. By *CA* it is included in $V(y)$. *MA* ensures that points lying to its northeast satisfy $x \succeq (y)$. The vector labeled g is the numeraire bundle of the two commodities or goods. The movement $x - \beta g$ is visualized as translating point x in the direction of the numeraire (if $\beta > 0$, one envisions this as sliding x along the dotted line segment parallel to g to the southwest, and $\beta < 0$ to the northeast). As drawn, β needs to be positive, and x needs to be translated to point z on the curve so that $d(x, y; g) = \frac{\|xz\|}{\|g\|}$.

Let's now show why $d(x,y;g)$ is a function representation of $\succeq(y)$. To go one way (the easiest way), I need to show that

$$d(x,y;g) \geq 0 \Leftarrow x \succeq (y).$$

This follows almost by definition because $x \succeq (y)$ obviously implies $x - 0g \succeq (y)$, so that the max in the definition can be no smaller than 0. Now to go the other way (a bit harder but still easy), I need to show that

$$d(x,y;g) \geq 0 \Rightarrow x \succeq (y).$$

Because $g \in \mathbb{R}^N_+ \backslash \{0\}$, $d(x,y;g) \geq 0$ requires that $x \geq x - d(x,y;g)\,g$. By definition, $x - d(x,y;g)\,g \succeq (y)$, and *MA* now yields the result.

It's worth emphasizing how the sufficiency part ($d(x,y;g) \geq 0 \Rightarrow x \succeq (y)$) of the proof works. It argues that $x - d(x,y;g)\,g \succeq (y)$ for $d(x,y;g) \geq 0$ implies that $x \succeq (y)$. And that follows by *MA*, which requires that $x \succeq (y)$ preserves $x \geq y$'s monotonicity property. Notice, however, that any alternative assumption ensuring that

$$x - \lambda g \succeq (y) \text{ for } \lambda \geq 0 \Rightarrow x \succeq (y),$$

would also suffice to complete the sufficiency part of the proof.

So, for example, suppose we instead impose *$\hat{g}$–monotonicity*, which requires that

$$x \succeq (y) \Rightarrow x + \lambda \hat{g} \succeq (y), \qquad \lambda \geq 0 \tag{3.2}$$

where $\hat{g}$ is a *fixed* direction (numeraire) in $\mathbb{R}^N_+ \backslash \{0\}$. Under $\hat{g}$-monotonicity, it follows that

$$d(x,y;\hat{g}) \geq 0 \Longleftrightarrow x \succeq (y).$$

Thus, the ability to represent $\succeq(y)$ cardinally is preserved under weaker versions of monotonicity than *MA*. As $\hat{g}$–monotonicity illustrates, what's crucial is that the chosen numeraire, $g \in \mathbb{R}^N$, represents a direction in which movements always preserve the binary relation as in (3.2).

Problem 10. *Let's reconsider Mr. and Ms. Spratt's preferences as discussed in Exercise 15. Derive, if you can, cardinal representations of his and her preferences that satisfy the Indication Property.*

Why is it important to have a function representation of $\succeq (y)$? Some introspection might help. You've undoubtedly encountered an *ordinal* utility function, $u : \mathbb{R}^N \to \mathbb{R}$. That function assigns a real number to any element of $\mathbb{R}^N$ such that all $x, y \in \mathbb{R}^N$ can be ranked according to $u(x)$ and $u(y)$. Why do economists need such a concept? Why did you need it? What did you learn from it? Most importantly, how did you use it? (*Not rhetorical questions; give them some thought.*)

Using the at-least-as-good interpretation of $\succeq (y)$, $u(x)$ necessarily has an order embedded in it because $u(x) \geq u(y)$ can be taken to imply that $x \succeq (y)$. Therefore, if a utility function exists, an associated order $\succeq (y)$ must also exist. Think, for example, of u inducing an at-least-as-good order, $\succeq (y)$ via:

$$u(x) \geq u(y) \Rightarrow x \succeq (y)$$

Problem 11. *Prove (disprove) that if $u(x)$ is upper semicontinuous[6] and nondecreasing that the order defined by*

$$u(x) \geq u(y) \Leftrightarrow x \succeq (y)$$

satisfies continuity from above, monotonicity from above, and monotonicity from below.

Problem 12. *For the order induced by u, define $d(x, y; g)$ and state and prove its properties.*

These problems were designed to convince you that having a utility function necessarily implies the existence of a $\succeq (y)$ satisfying certain regularity properties. The next is designed to determine if you can go the other way.

Problem 13. *True, false, explain why. If there exists an ordering of $\mathbb{R}^N \times \mathbb{R}^N$ denoted $\succeq (y)$ that satisfies continuity from above and monotonicity from above, there exists an ordinal utility function, $u : \mathbb{R}^N \to \mathbb{R}$ such that all $x, y \in \mathbb{R}^N$ can be ranked according to the (ordinal) value of the utility function and all such rankings are consistent with $\succeq (y)$.*

[6] $u : \mathbb{R}^N \to \mathbb{R}$ is upper semicontinuous if

$$\{x \in \mathbb{R}^N : u(x) \geq y\}$$

is closed for all $y \in \mathbb{R}$.

4 Properties of *d (x, y; g)*

Naturally, $d(x, y; g)$ has some properties. Perhaps the most important is its Indication Property. Another is the *Translation Property.* It says:

$$d(x + \lambda g, y; g) = d(x, y; g) + \lambda,$$

for $\lambda \in \mathbb{R}$. Showing Translation is mainly a matter of manipulating the definition:

$$\begin{aligned} d(x + \lambda g, y; g) &= \max\{\beta : x + \lambda g - \beta g \succeq (y)\} \\ &= \max\{\beta : x - (\beta - \lambda) g \succeq (y)\} \\ &= \max\{\lambda + \beta - \lambda : x - (\beta - \lambda) g \succeq (y)\} \\ &= \lambda + \max\{\beta - \lambda : x - (\beta - \lambda) g \succeq (y)\} \\ &= d(x, y; g) + \lambda. \end{aligned}$$

You can visualize this proof as follows. Adding λg to x is equivalent, for example, to sliding x in Figure 3.1 $\frac{\|xz^*\|}{\|g\|} = \lambda$ units along the dotted line segment passing through x to point z^*. The distance function for z^* projects it onto the frontier at z, which is exactly where it also projects x, with $d(z^*, y; g) = \frac{\|zz*\|}{\|g\|} = \frac{\|zx\|}{\|g\|} + \frac{\|xz^*\|}{\|g\|}$.

Why is this called the Translation Property? Try thinking of it this way. Suppose one visualizes $\mathbb{R}^N$. If you were asked to represent it pictorially, I imagine most would draw a picture of $\mathbb{R}^2$ similar to Figure 3.1, with the usual orthonormal vectors defining the origin and the axes. Go ahead and do this. Now suppose that to each point in that picture you added, say, the vector $(2, 1)$ and represented the result on a new pair of axes. The old origin $(0, 0)$ would now correspond to $(2, 1)$, and the "new" origin would correspond to the old $(-2, -1)$. Visually, the new axes would have every point from the old axes (x_1, x_2) slid (*translated*) over to $(x_1 + 2, x_2 + 1)$.

The Translation Property says that if one "translates" $x \in \mathbb{R}^N$ λ units in the direction of the numeraire $g \in \mathbb{R}^N$ *(a variation in the direction of g)*, $d(x, y; g)$ changes by precisely the same amount. Hence, any redefinition of the origin in the direction of g changes d by precisely the same amount. Put another way, a variation in the direction of g "renormalizes" $d(x, y; g)$.

Exercise 16. *Suppose that $\succeq (y)$ represents an at-least-as-good order. Provide a convincing economic interpretation of the Translation Property. Does the Translation Property fail if $\succeq (y)$ is not monotonic?*

The Translation Property has many implications. In more applied readings, you will encounter some of these. But right now, it's time to see if $d(x, y; g)$ satisfies any other properties. Here's a conjecture worth considering:

Conjecture 1. *If* $\succeq (y)$ *is monotonic from above, then*

$$x' \geq x \Rightarrow d(x', y; g) \geq d(x, y; g).$$

If $\succeq (y)$ *is monotonic from below,* $y' \leq y \Rightarrow d(x, y'; g) \geq d(x, y; g)$.

Problem 14. *Prove: If* $\succeq (y)$ *is monotonic from above, then*

$$x' \geq x \Rightarrow d(x', y; g) \geq d(x, y; g).$$

If $\succeq (y)$ *is monotonic from below,* $y' \leq y \Rightarrow d(x, y'; g) \geq d(x, y; g)$.

Translatability and monotonicity of $d(x, y; g)$ repeatedly prove very convenient in what follows. Another that you might have seen elsewhere, but in a somewhat different form, is *homogeneity,* namely,

$$d(x, y; tg) = t^{-1} d(x, y; g) \qquad t > 0.$$

Here's the proof

$$\begin{aligned} d(x, y; tg) &= \max\{\beta : x - \beta tg \succeq (y)\} \\ &= \max\left\{\frac{t}{t}\beta : x - \beta tg \succeq (y)\right\} \\ &= t^{-1} \max\{t\beta : x - \beta tg \succeq (y)\} \\ &= t^{-1} d(x, y; g). \end{aligned}$$

In words, renormalizing g's units by multiplying each of its components by the positive scalar t, renormalizes the resulting d measure by the same t.

It's time to collect results.

Lemma 7. *If* $\succeq (y)$ *is continuous from above:*

a) $d(x + \lambda g, y; g) = d(x, y; g) + \lambda$, $\lambda \in \mathbb{R}$ *(Translation);*

b) $d(x, y; tg) = t^{-1} d(x, y; g)$, $t > 0$.

If $\succeq (y)$ *is continuous from above and monotonic from above:*

a) $d(x + \lambda g, y; g) = d(x, y; g) + \lambda$, $\lambda \in \mathbb{R}$ *(Translation);*

b) $d(x,y;tg) = t^{-1}d(x,y;g)$, $t > 0$;
c) $d(x,y;g) \geq 0 \Leftrightarrow x \succeq (y)$ *(Indication); and*
d) $x' \geq x \Rightarrow d(x',y;g) \geq d(x,y;g)$.

Problem 15. *Show that if* $\succeq (y)$ *satisfies C,* $d(x,y;g)$ *is continuous in* x.

5 Superdifferentiability and *d(x, y; g)*

Denote the superdifferential of d in x by $\partial d(x,y;g)$ so that

$$q \in \partial d(x,y;g) \Rightarrow q^{\top}(z-x) \geq d(z,y;g) - d(x,y;g) \text{ for all } z \in \mathbb{R}^N.$$

We have:

Proposition 1. *(a)* $q \in \partial d(x,y;g) \Leftrightarrow q \in \partial d(x+\lambda g,y;g)$ *for all* $\lambda \in \mathbb{R}$ *(Translation Invariance); (b)* $q \in \partial d(x,y;g) \neq \varnothing \Rightarrow q^{\top}g = 1$ *(Normalization); and (c) if* $\succeq (y)$ *satisfies MA,* $q \in \partial d(x,y;g) \neq \varnothing \Rightarrow q \in \mathbb{R}^N_+$.

Both Translation Invariance and Normalization are consequences of the Translation Property of $d(x,y;g)$ (Lemma 7.a). To establish (a), note that Lemma 7.a ensures that

$$q^{\top}(z-x) \geq d(z,y;g) - d(x,y;g), \text{ for all } z$$
$$\Updownarrow$$
$$q^{\top}(z+\lambda g - x - \lambda g) \geq d(z+\lambda g,y;g) - d(x+\lambda g,y;g), \text{ for all } z+\lambda g,$$

whence $q \in \partial d(x,y;g) \Leftrightarrow q \in \partial d(x+\lambda g,y;g)$. To establish (b), take $z = x+g$ in the definition of $\partial d(x,y;g)$. Then if $q \in \partial d(x,y;g)$, it must be true that

$$\begin{aligned} q^{\top}g &\geq d(x+g,y;g) - d(x,y;g) \\ &= 1, \end{aligned}$$

where the equality follows by Lemma 7.a (the Translation Property). Now take $z = x - g$, and a symmetric argument shows that $q \in \partial d(x,y;g) \Rightarrow -q^{\top}g \geq -1$, whence $q^{\top}g \leq 1$. Together, they require $1 \leq q^{\top}g \leq 1$, so that $q^{\top}g = 1$.

Using Figure 3.1 helps visualize Translation Invariance. Imagine, first, the level set (not drawn) for $d(x, y; g)$ passing through point x in the figure. If a hyperlane supports it at x, $d(x, y; g)$ is superdifferentiable there and $\partial d(x, y; g) \neq \emptyset$. The invariance property then requires that the same hyperplane support the level set (again not drawn) passing through z^* and that $\partial d(z^*, y; g) \neq \emptyset$. Now take the smooth curve passing through z and y as the level set

$$\{\hat{x} \in \mathbb{R}^N : d(\hat{x}, y; g) = d(z, y; g) = 0\},$$

that defines the boundary of $V(y)$. That set is supported at z by the hyperplane defined by the dotted line segment tangent. Hence, $\partial d(z, y; g) \neq \emptyset$, and $d(z, y; g)$ is superdifferentiable. But z equals $x - d(x, y; g)\,g$. Applying the invariance property of the superdifferential gives that $\partial d(z, y; g) = \partial d(x, y; g)$ and thus $\partial d(z, y; g) = \partial d(z^*, y; g)$. *The distance function, $d(x, y; g)$, inherits the superdifferential properties of the distance function evaluated at the point on the frontier of $V(y)$ to which $d(x, y; g)$ translates x.* So, as illustrated in this case, both $\partial d(x, y; g)$ and $\partial d(z^*, y; g)$ are nonempty. On the other hand, points such as v and y *whose distance functions map them onto points on the frontier not supported by hyperplanes have* $\partial d(v, y; g) = \emptyset = \partial d(y, y; g)$, as will all translations of them in the direction of the numeraire g.

Problem 16. *Let $d(x, y; g)$ be everywhere differentiable in x. Prove that $\nabla_x d(x, y; g) = \nabla_x d(x + \lambda g, y; g)$ for all $\lambda \in \mathbb{R}$ and that $\nabla_x d(x, y; g)^\top g = 1$.*

Before discussing Normalization, let's show part (c). Consider x and its variation $x + \delta^n$ where $\delta^n \in \mathbb{R}^N$ is a vector of zeroes except in the *nth* coordinate and there equals one. That variation keeps all but the *nth* coordinate constant while increasing the *nth* by one. For any $q \in \partial d(x, y; g)$, it must be true

$$q^\top \delta^n \geq d(x + \delta^n, y; g) - d(x, y; g),$$

while Lemma 7.d (*MA*) requires that $d(x + \delta^n, y; g) - d(x, y; g) \geq 0$. Hence, under *MA*

$$q_n \geq 0.$$

Because n was chosen arbitrarily, it follows that $\partial d(x, y; g) \subset \mathbb{R}^N_+$.

Given MA, superdifferentiability of $d(x,y;g)$ requires that *at least one nonnegative vector* $q \in \mathbb{R}^N_+$ exists whose inner product with the numeraire, $q^\top g$, equals one. Moreover, that q must be the normal to a hyperplane that supports $V(y)$ at x. If $\succeq(y)$ were taken to be a preference order, most economists would interpret such nonnegative vectors as containing *marginal utilities* whose ratios determine marginal rates of substitution giving the rate at which the individual trades off one commodity against another so as to keep her level of well-being constant. And, in a market setting, first principles tell us that equilibrium requires equating those marginal rates of substitution to market-price ratios. That realization has led economists to refer to such q's as defining the individual's *internal (shadow) prices* for x.

Interpreted in this light, Normalization means that the individual's internal valuation of the numeraire bundle always equals one. You will recall, however, that the role of the numeraire is to transform our order $\succeq(y)$ into cardinal terms so that it can be measured accurately by a real valued function, $d(x,y;g)$. Normalization then implies that the individual's internal valuation of the numeraire bundle should always equal one, which is precisely the value to which we always set numeraire values. That's because the role of the numeraire is to provide a real basis on which to measure nominal values. Hence, Normalization just ensures that internal or shadow values associated with $\succeq(y)$ are well behaved.

5.1 A Basic Result on Internal (Shadow) Prices

Now that we know internal prices exist, let's see what we can learn about them. Suppose that $d(y,y;g) = 0$ for all y (a strong version of MA ensures that this is true). Then because $x \succeq (y)$ implies $d(x,y;g) \geq 0$, it follows that $d(x,y;g) - d(y,y;g) \geq 0$ for all $x \succeq (y)$. Thus, if $d(x,y;g)$ is superdifferentiable (as a function of x) at $y \in \mathbb{R}^N$,

$$q \in \partial d(y,y;g) \Rightarrow q^\top(x-y) \geq d(x,y;g) \text{ for all } x \in \mathbb{R}^N$$

with $\partial d(y,y;g) \subset \mathbb{R}^N_+$. Indication, however, ensures that

$$x \succeq (y) \Leftrightarrow d(x,y;g) \geq 0.$$

Putting the two together gives

$$x \succeq (y) \Rightarrow q^{\top}(x-y) \geq 0,$$

for $q \in \partial d(y, y; g)$.

To make things more concrete, assume for the rest of this section that $x \succeq (y)$ means that x is at least as good as y. If $d(y, y; g)$ is superdifferentiable, then for any (and thus every) x that is at least as good as y, at least one nonnegative vector of internal prices exists for which x is at least as costly as y. These vectors of internal prices are determined by the hyperplanes supporting $hyp(d)$ at $(y, d(y, y; g) = 0)$.[7]

Economically speaking, for the internal prices $q \in \partial d(y, y; g)$, y is the cheapest way to get something at least as good as y. This is one interpretation of Figure 1.2, and this observation is the foundation for many basic results in both producer and consumer theory.

Still more can be said. Suppose a $q \in \mathbb{R}_{+}^{N}$ exists such that $x \succeq (y) \Rightarrow q^{\top}(x-y) \geq 0$ and $q^{\top}g = 1$. Because q is nonnegative, it can be thought of as a price vector. Does finding such a price vector tell us anything about $d(y, y; g)$? If you guessed that it implies that $d(y, y; g)$ is superdifferentiable, you're right.

To show this, we proceed by contradiction. That is, suppose that such a $q \in \mathbb{R}_{+}^{N}$ exists, but that $d(y, y; g)$ is not superdifferentiable. If $d(y, y; g)$ is not superdifferentiable, at least one $x \in \mathbb{R}^{N}$ must exist such that

$$\begin{aligned} q^{\top}(x-y) &< d(x, y; g) - d(y, y; g) \\ &= d(x, y; g). \end{aligned}$$

Because $q^{\top}g = 1$, this inequality implies

$$q^{\top}(x - d(x, y; g)g - y) < 0. \tag{3.3}$$

By definition, however,

$$x - d(x, y; g)g \succeq (y),$$

and thus expression (3.3) contradicts the assumption that for q, $x \succeq (y) \Rightarrow q^{\top}(x-y) \geq 0$ and $q^{\top}g = 1$. Hence, if a nonnegative vector of prices exists such that $x \succeq (y) \Rightarrow q^{\top}(x-y) \geq 0$, $q^{\top}g = 1$, then $q \in \partial d(y, y; g)$.

[7] We say vectors here because if $\partial d(y, y; g)$ is not a singleton set, the boundary of $hyp(d)$ has a kink in it, which is inherited by $\bar{V}(y)$. You can think of this intuitively as there being multiple marginal rates of substitution at y.

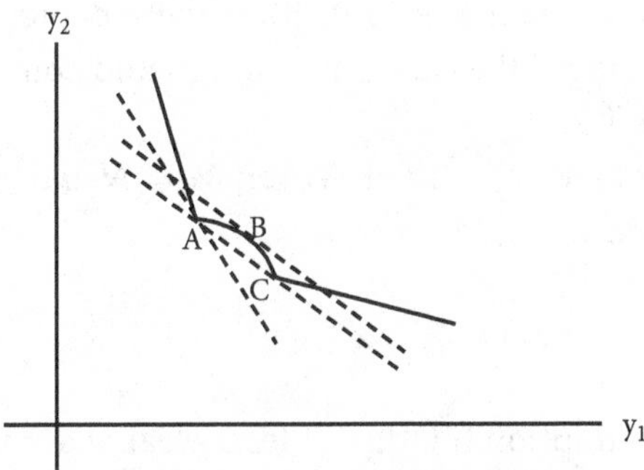

Fig. 3.2 Superdifferentials and $V(y)$

Taken together:

Lemma 8. *Suppose* $g \in \mathbb{R}^N_{++}$ *and that* $\succeq (y)$ *for* $y \in \mathbb{R}^N$ *satisfies continuity from above, strict monotonicity from above, transitivity, and reflexivity, then*

$$q \in \partial d(y, y; g) \Leftrightarrow q^{\top}(x - y) \geq 0 \text{ for all } x \succeq (y),$$

with $q \in \mathbb{R}^N_+$ *and* $q^{\top}g = 1$.

An innate connection exists between superdifferentiability and rational choice. Lemma 8 is illustrated visually in Figure 3.2. There, three points, A, B, and C, fall on the boundary of $V(y)$. Superdifferentials exist at A and C, but not at B because points falling on the hyperplane defined by the tangent at B pass through $V(y)$. The following problem asks you to consider this basic result in the producer context.

Problem 17. *Suppose that* $x \succeq (y)$ *is read as* x *can produce* y*. Does it make sense to assume reflexivity? If not, restructure the proof of Lemma 8 to arrive at a parallel result. Hint: If reflexivity does not make sense, how would you restructure the argument and the derivation?*

6 Turning the Bowl Over

This section is brief, but its brevity does not imply lack of importance. Rather, it recognizes that arguments made for $V(y)$ are easily recyclable in terms of $Y(x)$. The "bowl" is the imaginary bowl that we often ask undergraduate students to visualize in discussions of $V(y)$. Whether $V(y)'s$ boundary is an indifference curve or an isoquant, it's usually depicted as an upturned bowl tilted toward the northeast, nicely smooth and convex to the origin, as illustrated in Figure 1.2.

Just as important as $V(y)$ is $Y(x)$. When $M = N$ and $\succeq (y)$ represents an at-least-as-good ordering,

$$Y(x) = \{y : x \succeq (y)\} = V^{-}(x)$$

gives all of the consumption bundles at least weakly dominated by x. Alternatively, one can think of $Y(x)$ as the *not-better-than set for* x. It's particularly important in the study of various types of opportunity costs. $Y(x)$ is also essential in isolating conditions on observable behavior that are consistent with complete ordering of preferences (see Chapter 5).

On the other hand, if $M \neq N$, $Y(x)$ might naturally be conceptualized in a production context as an *output correspondence*, that is, as the collection of outputs that can feasibly be produced by x. (Other, perhaps more familiar but equivalent, terminology might include *production possibilities set* or *producible output set.*) If asked to visualize $Y(x)$, most would likely flip that upturned bowl over. So now instead of thinking in terms of Figure 1.2, you should be thinking in terms of Figure 1.4.

What's been established applies equally to $Y(x)$ as to $V(y)$. Anything that can be derived for $Y(x)$ can obviously be developed from $V(y)$ because

$$y \in Y(x) \Leftrightarrow x \in V(y).$$

But there are advantages to looking at $Y(x)$, without first going through $V(y)$.[8]

This section provides a cardinal tool. It, too, is a directional distance function or distance function and defined, with an abuse of notation,[9] for $g \in \mathbb{R}_{+}^{M} \backslash \{0\}$ as

[8] In considering why different ways of looking at the same phenomena may be important, one might well recall the parable of the blind men and the elephant. When three blind men were confronted with what to them was an unknown beast called an *elephant,* they decided to identify its nature by examining it by touch. The first man, who touched its side, declared it to be a wall. The second, who touched its ear, declared it to be a type of fan. And the third, who felt its tail, opined that it was a snake. The moral of the parable isn't that economists operate as though they are blind, but that looking at things from different perspectives conveys different bits of information.

[9] My apologies for using g to denote both an N dimensional numeraire and an M dimensional numeraire, but introducing new notation or subscripts to distinguish the two numeraires strikes me as visually untidy.

$$t(y,x;g) \equiv \min\{\beta \in \mathbb{R} : y - \beta g \in Y(x)\}$$
$$= \min\{\beta \in \mathbb{R} : x \geq (y - \beta g)\},$$

if there exists $\beta \in \mathbb{R}$ such that $y - \beta g \in Y(x)$ and $-\infty$ otherwise. How t is interpreted depends on the context. For example, if Y is thought of as an output correspondence, $t(y,x;g)$ measures how much y needs to be shrunk if it is to be producible using x.

With little true loss of generality, we impose continuity from below in what follows. We have:

Lemma 9. *If* $\geq (y)$ *is continuous from below:*
a) $t(y + \lambda g, y; g) = t(y,x;g) + \lambda, \lambda \in \mathbb{R}$;
b) $t(y,x;\mu g) = \mu^{-1} t(y,x;g), \mu > 0.$
If $\geq (y)$ *is continuous from below and monotonic from below:*
a) $t(y + \lambda g, x; g) = t(y,x;g) + \lambda, \lambda \in \mathbb{R}$ *(Translation);*
b) $t(y,x;\mu g) = \mu^{-1} t(y,x;g), \mu > 0.$
c) $t(y,x;g) \leq 0 \Leftrightarrow x \geq (y)$ *(Indication); and*
d) $y \geq y' \Rightarrow t(y,x;g) \geq t(y',x;g)$.

Problem 18. *Prove Lemma 9.*

Lemma 9 reveals that $t(y,x;g)$ satisfies properties very similar to $d(x,y;g)$. Under appropriate monotonicity conditions, t provides a function representation of $\geq (y)$ and is monotonic in y. It automatically satisfies versions of the Translation Property and homogeneity properties associated with d. Because t essentially provides a representation of the lower contour set associated with $\geq (y)$, intuition should suggest that its subdifferentials satisfy an appropriately modified version of Lemma 8. We have:

Lemma 10. *Suppose* $g \in \mathbb{R}^N_{++}$ *and that* $\geq (y)$ *for* $y \in \mathbb{R}^N$ *satisfies continuity from below, monotonicity from below, transitivity, reflexivity, then*

$$p \in \partial^{-} t(x,x;g) \Leftrightarrow p^{\top}(x - y) \geq 0 \text{ for all } y \in Y(x),$$

with $p \in \mathbb{R}^N_{+}$ *and* $p^{\top} g = 1$.

Problem 19. *Provide a detailed demonstration of Lemma 10. Discuss the underlying economic intuition.*

7 Three Types of Convexity Restrictions

Three different notions of convexity for $\succeq (y)$ prove of particular interest. Each represents a subtly different curvature and smoothness criterion imposed upon $\succeq (y)$. And, as with the notions of continuity and monotonicity, each is designed with a different perspective of $\succeq (y)$ in mind.

Assumption: *(CON)* $\succeq (y)$ *is convex if*

$$x \succeq (y) \text{ and } x' \succeq (y') \Rightarrow x' + \lambda (x - x') \succeq (y' + \lambda (y - y')) \qquad \lambda \in (0, 1).$$

Assumption: *(CONA)* $\succeq (y)$ *is convex from above if V(y) is a convex set.*

Assumption: *(CONB)* $\succeq (y)$ *is convex from below if Y(x) is a convex set.*

Problem 20. *Convexity of* $\succeq$ *implies convexity from above and convexity from below. True, false, explain why: convexity from above does not imply convexity from below.*

Problem 21. *Illustrate visually each of the three different types of convexity. In your illustration, you may assume that* $\succeq (y)$ *satisfies: continuity (C), monotonicity (M), reflexivity, and transitivity. Your illustration should also illustrate your answer to the previous problem.*

Problem 22. *True, false, explain why:* $x \succeq (y)$ *and* $x' \succeq (y') \Rightarrow x' + \lambda (x - x') \succeq (y' + \lambda (y - y'))$, $\lambda \in (0, 1)$ *implies that the correspondence* $Y : \mathbb{R}^N_+ \rightrightarrows \mathbb{R}^M_+$ *defined by*

$$Y(x) \equiv \{y : x \succeq (y)\}$$

satisfies $Y(x)$ *is a convex set for all* $x \in \mathbb{R}^N_+$.

Problem 23. *True, false, explain why:* $x \succeq (y)$ *and* $x' \succeq (y') \Rightarrow x' + \lambda (x - x') \succeq (y' + \lambda (y - y'))$, $\lambda \in (0, 1)$ *implies that the correspondence* $V : \mathbb{R}^M_+ \rightrightarrows \mathbb{R}^N_+$ *satisfies* $V(y)$ *is a convex set for all* $y \in \mathbb{R}^M_+$.

Problem 24. *True, false, explain why:* $x \succeq (y)$ *and* $x' \succeq (y') \Rightarrow x' + \lambda (x - x') \succeq (y' + \lambda (y - y'))$, $\lambda \in (0, 1)$ *implies that*

$$Gr(V) = Gr(Y) = \{(x, y) : x \succeq (y)\},$$

is a convex set.

Problem 25. *What does* $x \succeq (y)$ *and* $x \succeq (y') \Rightarrow x \succeq (y' + \lambda(y - y'))$, $\lambda \in (0,1)$ *imply for* $V : \mathbb{R}_+^M \rightrightarrows \mathbb{R}_+^N$? *Illustrate your answer visually.*

Problem 26. *What does* $x \succeq (y)$ *and* $x' \succeq (y) \Rightarrow x' + \lambda(x - x') \succeq (y)$, $\lambda \in (0,1)$ *imply for* $Y : \mathbb{R}_+^N \rightrightarrows \mathbb{R}_+^M$? *Illustrate your answer visually.*

8 Why Three Types of Convexity?

The different types of convexity have different implications for $d(x, y; g)$. I will show you two. The remaining one is left to you as an exercise. Start with convexity from above *CONA*. If $\succeq (y)$ satisfies *CONA*, $d(x, y; g)$ is concave in x. That implies that $d(x, y; g)$ satisfies both Lemma 8 and Lemma 2. Here's the proof. Consider

$$d(x, y; g) = \max\{\beta : x - \beta g \succeq (y)\},$$

and

$$d(x', y; g) = \max\{\beta : x' - \beta g \succeq (y)\}.$$

Because $x' - d(x', y; g) g \succeq y$ and $x - d(x, y; g) g \succeq y$, *CONA* implies

$$x' - d(x', y; g) g + \lambda(x - d(x, y; g) g - x' + d(x', y; g) g) \succeq (y), \quad \text{for } \lambda \in (0,1).$$

And thus

$$x' + \lambda(x - x') - [d(x', y; g) + \lambda(d(x, y; g) - d(x', y; g))] g \succeq (y).$$

Therefore, it must be true that

$$\begin{aligned} d(x' + \lambda(x - x'), y; g) &= \max\{\beta : x' + \lambda(x - x') - \beta g \succeq (y)\} \\ &\geq d(x', y; g) + \lambda(d(x, y; g) - d(x', y; g)), \end{aligned}$$

which shows the desired concavity.

Lemma 11. *If* $x \succeq (y)$ *satisfies CONA,* $d(x, y; g)$ *is concave in* x.

Problem 27. *Suppose that* $\succeq (y)$ *is continuous from above, monotonic from above, reflexive, transitive, and convex from above for* $y \in \mathbb{R}^N$*. Also suppose that you have strengthened monotonicity from above to ensure that* $d(y, y; g) = 0$*. Provide an economic interpretation of*

$$V(y) = \{x \in \mathbb{R}^N : d(x, y; g) \geq 0\},$$

in terms of an at-least-as-good preference order.

Now suppose that from y*, you were asked the following question: how much in real terms would you be willing to pay for an arbitrarily small increment in your commodity bundle from* y *to* $y + h$*, where* $h \in \mathbb{R}^N$*? How would you answer the parallel question: how much would you have to be paid to get you to sell an arbitrarily small amount of* h *out of your commodity bundle* y*? Are the answers always the same? If not, provide a simple economic intuition for why they are not.*

Problem 27 is one of our first forays into economics. It was chosen specifically for students interested in environmental economics and, in particular, for those students interested in the valuation of environmental amenities.

Next we consider a convex order (*CON*). Obviously, it implies that $d(x, y; g)$ is concave in x because it implies convexity from above. Does it imply anything more? Let's investigate. Because

$$x' - d(x', y'; g)\, g \succeq (y'), \text{ and}$$
$$x - d(x, y; g)\, g \succeq (y),$$

convexity of the order implies

$$x' + \lambda(x - x') - [d(x', y'; g) + \lambda(d(x, y; g) - d(x', y'; g))]\, g$$
$$\succeq (y' + \lambda(y - y'))\, \lambda \in (0, 1).$$

Thus, $d(x', y'; g) + \lambda(d(x, y; g) - d(x', y'; g))$ represents a feasible choice for

$$d(x' + \lambda(x - x'), y' + \lambda(y - y'); g)$$

leading us to conclude that

$$\begin{aligned} &d\left(x' + \lambda\left(x - x'\right), y' + \lambda\left(y - y'\right); g\right) \\ &\quad = \max\left\{\beta : x' + \lambda\left(x - x'\right) - \beta g \succeq \left(y' + \lambda\left(y - y'\right)\right)\right\} \\ &\quad \geq d\left(x', y'; g\right) + \lambda\left(d\left(x, y; g\right) - d\left(x', y'; g\right)\right), \quad \lambda \in (0, 1). \end{aligned}$$

Lemma 12. *If $x \succeq (y)$ satisfies CON, $d(x, y; g)$ is concave in (x, y).*

That leaves convexity from below. As I said, that's left to you. Here's a hint to help you on your way.

$$V^{-}(x) = \left\{y \in \mathbb{R}^{M} : x \succeq (y)\right\}.$$

Problem 28. *Prove that if $\succeq (y)$ satisfies CON, $t(y, x; g)$ is convex in (y, x).*

9 Chapter Commentary

This chapter is idiosyncratic. The order notion that I use, beyond saying it is a binary relation, is not standard. And so, if you consult, for example, Fishburn (1972) or Ok (2007), you will see things defined differently. There's a reason that I have chosen a nonstandard notation. The common mathematical structures supporting consumer theory, producer theory, equilibrium theory, and decision making under uncertainty are readily apparent. But, for example, where production economists frame their axioms in terms of production correspondences, decision theorists frame theirs in terms of order relations. One can induce a correspondence from a binary relation. And one can induce a binary relation from a correspondence. But the perspectives and jargon remain different. And such differences inhibit exploiting existing intellectual arbitrages. Concepts that are well understood in one context can appear unfamiliar or even exotic when encountered in another. An overarching goal of this book is to erase those apparent exoticisms by revealing the common structural core. The order notation used here is an attempt to present a general setup that has different problems of interest drop out as special cases. The framing of properties in "from above" and "from below" terms has firm geometric roots. "From below" properties are properties usually cast in terms of lower contour sets, and "from above" are those usually cast in terms upper contour sets.

Distance functions trace their roots to Minkowski functionals (gauge functions) as measures of distance in real space. Versions of what I call radial distance functions, to which you will be introduced in Chapter 6, appear in Konüs (1939),[10] Debreu (1951), Malmquist (1953), and Shephard (1953). Earlier versions of the directional version appear in Blackorby and Donaldson (1980) and Luenberger (1992). Chambers, Chung, and Färe (1996) showed how versions of the Blackorby–Donaldson–Luenberger (1992a) concepts could be used to obtain function representations of production technologies and efficiency measures. I believe Lemmata 8 and 10 to be original, but both have antecedents in basic conjugacy theory; see Chambers and Quiggin (2007) and Chambers (2014).

[10] A translation of an even earlier Russian article by the same author.

4
Squiggly Economics

We've spent a lot of time looking at optimization theory, basic results from convex analysis, $\succeq(y)$, and its function representation, $d(x, y; g)$. At times, I'm sure it's been difficult to decipher how all this relates to standard microeconomics. For example, you've been told that Lemma 8 and its counterpart, Lemma 10, contain the essence of producer and consumer theory, but I've not said why. This chapter investigates why by considering three standard problems in microeconomics: expenditure (cost) minimization, revenue maximization, and profit maximization. Each can be solved by applying Theorem 2. The relationship between $\succeq(y)$ and its economic manifestation is captured by either Theorem 6 or Theorem 7.

The discussion is intentionally generic. Rather than referring to consumption or production, I refer to "squiggle behavior."[1] That's done to identify the core principles that guide economic behavior for the varying interpretations attached to $\succeq(\cdot)$. This may strike some as overly abstract and unintuitive. Perhaps so. But this chapter represents a first, and not a final, step. It's meant to lay an analytic foundation for the economic behavior that characterizes price-taking agents. Once that's done, more textured analyses can be developed as needed. All the chapters that follow build upon this foundation. And so, Chapter 5 treats consumer behavior in a nonstochastic setting, Chapter 6 treats producer behavior in a nonstochastic setting, and Chapter 7 treats the equilibrium interaction between those consumers and producers. Chapters 8 and 9 then revisit these topics in a stochastic decision setting, while Chapter 10 closes the book by using that foundation to study several more specialized topics.

In reading this chapter, you may wish to interpret "squiggle" in the manner that you find the most intuitive. But once you've done that, it's worth recycling the discussion using something that was less intuitive to start. The more times you recycle the discussion using different notions of "squiggling," the better you will grasp the fundamental ideas. The presentation intentionally becomes more terse as the chapter develops. That's because the needed optimization

[1] Squiggle is the term I use to describe the $\succeq(\cdot)$ symbol in classroom discussion.

Competitive Agents in Certain and Uncertain Markets. Robert G. Chambers, Oxford University Press (2021).

DOI: 10.1093/oso/9780190063016.001.0001

tools, Theorems 6 and 7, were developed earlier. So once you're shown how to apply them for one problem, the next challenge is to apply them to others. I could do this for you, but long experience has taught me and many others that your analytic skills will be best honed by working through the details on your own.

1 A Standard Problem: Expenditure Minimization

For a given vector of prices, $q \in \mathbb{R}^N_{++}$, consider:

$$\begin{aligned} E(q;y) &\equiv \min\{q^\top x : x \succeq (y)\} \\ &= \min\{q^\top x : x \in V(y)\} \\ &= \min\{q^\top x : d(x,y;g) \geq 0\}, \end{aligned} \tag{4.1}$$

if $V(y)$ is nonempty and ∞ otherwise. Going from the definitional equality to the third assumes that $d(x,y;g)$ characterizes $\succeq (y)$. That condition is always satisfied if, for example, $\succeq (y)$ satisfies monotonicity from above (*MA*). I refer to $E(q;y)$ as a *McKenzie expenditure function.*[2]

You should recognize $E(q;y)$ as a natural generalization of the expenditure and cost functions that you encountered in intermediate microeconomics and elsewhere. Instead of giving you the cheapest way to attain a given level of utility, $E(q;y)$ gives the cheapest way to *squiggle* y. $E(q;y)$, therefore, is a *"money-metric" squiggle function* showing how much money one would spend to squiggle y. Put another way, it's the *willingness-to-pay*, at market prices q, to squiggle y.

Problem 29. *Write problem (4.1) as*

$$E(q;y) = \min\{q^\top x : x \in V(y)\}.$$

True or false, explain why: $E(q;y)$ is continuous in q and y.

It's just a hunch, but I'm willing to bet that if you were asked to solve (4.1), you would form the Lagrangian

$$L(x,q;y) = q^\top x - \lambda d(x,y;g),$$

[2] McKenzie (1957, p. 185) defines his version of the expenditure function as "the minimum income which allows the consumer to obtain a commodity vector at least as good as x when the commodity price vector is p."

with λ a nonnegative Lagrange multiplier. Then, you might proceed to rely on Kuhn–Tucker theory to solve the associated minimization problem using a saddlepoint argument.

Good! This is exactly what you've been trained to do. Moreover, it underlines the computational importance of having a function representation of $\succeq (y)$. Let's proceed in this fashion for a simple, but specific, $d(x, y; g)$:

Problem 30. *Suppose $y \in \mathbb{R}^N_+$ and that*

$$d(x, y; g) = \min\left\{\frac{x_1 - y_1}{g_1}, ..., \frac{x_N - y_N}{g_N}\right\},$$

where $g_n > 0$ for all n. Using the Lagrangian expression:

$$L(x, q; y) = q^\top x - \lambda \min\left\{\frac{x_1 - y_1}{g_1}, ..., \frac{x_N - y_N}{g_N}\right\},$$

where $\lambda \in \mathbb{R}_+$ is a Lagrangian multiplier, characterize rigorously the solution to (4.1). (That means necessary and sufficient conditions. No hand-waving allowed!) Illustrate visually the solution to your problem, and provide an intuitive interpretation of all of your arguments.

Problem 30's solution is straightforward, but you will not get there by taking partial derivatives. $V(y)$ has a Leontief structure with *L-shaped* boundaries. I conjecture that in Problem 30:

$$V(y) = y + \mathbb{R}^N_+.$$

Under this conjecture, the solution is immediate because the problem reduces to

$$\min_{z \in \mathbb{R}^N_+} \{q^\top (y + z)\}.$$

Naturally, the solution is set $z = 0$.

Exercise 17. *If $d(x, y; g) = \min\left\{\frac{x_1 - y_1}{g_1}, ..., \frac{x_N - y_N}{g_N}\right\}$, derive the associated $V(y)$.*

Under the conjecture, the solution to the problem is trivial. Would you have thought of the conjecture on your own? If your honest answer is no and/or your first impulse was to take partial derivatives of the Lagrangian, you'll need to develop a different approach for solving such problems. We now turn to developing those tools.

2 Expenditure Minimization without Lagrangians

2.1 McKenzie Expenditure from an Indicator Function

Using the indicator function for $V(y)$ gives:

$$\begin{aligned} E(q;y) &\equiv \min\{q^{\top}x : x \in V(y)\} \\ &= \min_{x\in\mathbb{R}^N}\{q^{\top}x - \delta(x \mid V(y))\} \\ &= \delta^{*}(q \mid V(y)). \end{aligned}$$

$E(q;y)$ is the support function for $V(y)$ and $\delta(x \mid V(y))'s$ concave conjugate. Lemma 3, therefore, implies that, regardless of the properties of $\succeq(y)$, $E(q;y)$ is concave in q, and $E(q;y)'s$ concave conjugate is

$$\begin{aligned} \delta^{**}(x \mid V(y)) &= \min_{q\in\mathbb{R}^N_+}\{q^{\top}x - \delta^{*}(q \mid V(y))\} \\ &= \min_{q\in\mathbb{R}^N_+}\{q^{\top}x - E(q;y)\}. \end{aligned}$$

Thus, if $\delta(x \mid V(y))$ is closed and proper concave, Theorem 6 implies $\delta^{**}(x \mid V(y)) = \delta(x \mid V(y))$. One also easily shows that, regardless of the properties of $\succeq(y)$, $E(q;y)$ is nondecreasing and positively homogeneous in q so that it is nondecreasing and superlinear in q.

Exercise 18. *Prove that $E(q;y)$ is nondecreasing and positively homogeneous in $q \in \mathbb{R}^N$.*

Problem 31. *Suppose $V(y)$ is monotonic from above, closed, and convex, and use the fact that $\delta(x \mid V(y)) = 0$ for $x \in V(y)$ and the conjugate dual relation to show that $x \in V(y)$ if and only if $q^{\top}x \geq E(q;y)$ for all $q \in \mathbb{R}^N_{++}$. That is,*

$$V(y) = \{x : q^{\top}x \geq E(q;y) \text{ for all } q \in \mathbb{R}^N_{++}\}.$$

Remark 8. *Note the slight difference between the domains used in the qualifiers for*

$$C = \{v : x^{\top} v \geq f(x) \text{ for all } x \in \mathbb{R}^N\}$$

in Lemma 4 and

$$V(y) = \{x \in \mathbb{R}^N : q^{\top} x \geq E(q; y) \text{ for all } q \in \mathbb{R}^N_{++}\}.$$

One uses $\mathbb{R}^N$ *and the other* $\mathbb{R}^N_{++}$. *The latter emerges because, properly speaking,* $E : \mathbb{R}^N_{++} \times \mathbb{R}^M \to \bar{\mathbb{R}}$. *Because one only searches over* $q \in \mathbb{R}^N_{++}$ *and not all* $\mathbb{R}^N$, *closedness and convexity of* $V(y)$ *no longer suffice for duality. Limiting the search to* $q \in \mathbb{R}^N_{++}$ *and* $x \in \mathbb{R}^N$ *requires the further regularity condition of monotonicity from above (MA) to ensure duality. This is a technical detail that you may soon forget, but at least make note of it.*

Putting facts together gives:

Theorem 8. *If* $\succeq (y)$ *satisfies monotonicity from above (MA), continuity from above (CA), and convexity from above (CONA)*

$$\begin{aligned} E(q; y) &= \min_{x \in \mathbb{R}^N} \{q^{\top} x - \delta(x \mid V(y))\} \\ &= \delta^*(q \mid V(y)) \\ \delta(x \mid V(y)) &= \min_{q \in \mathbb{R}^N_{++}} \{q^{\top} x - \delta^*(q \mid V(y))\}, \\ E(q; y) + \delta(x \mid V(y)) &\leq q^{\top} x, \text{ for all } x \in \mathbb{R}^N \text{ and } q \in \mathbb{R}^N_{++} \end{aligned}$$

and

$$x \in \partial E(q; y) \Leftrightarrow q \in \partial \delta(x \mid V(y)).$$

Theorem 8 demonstrates the duality that exists between $E(q; y)$ and $\succeq (y)$ as represented by the indicator function for $V(y)$. The last line in Theorem 8 contains a general version of *Shephard's Lemma*. That is, expenditure-minimizing demands (McKenzie demands) can be retrieved, in the smooth case, as partial derivatives of $E(q; y)$ and more generally as elements of its superdifferential.

It is this observation that reveals the fundamental economics behind the superlinearity of $E(q; y)$. If $V(y)$ did not permit substitution (as in

Problem 30), the solution to the McKenzie expenditure minimization problem would be invariant to changes in q and fixed at, say, $\hat{x}(y) \in \mathbb{R}_{+}^{N}$. Thus,

$$E(q;y) = q^{\top}\hat{x}(y),$$

which is linear in q and satisfies

$$\hat{x}(y) \in \partial E(q;y)$$

for all q. It's also trivially superlinear. If $V(y)$ permits substitution, changes in q can induce adjustments in x directed toward minimizing expenditures. Thus, $E(q;y)$ need not be linear. The superlinearity of $E(q;y)$ reflects that ability to improve upon "standing pat" by substituting in response to price changes.

Shephard's Lemma ensures that expenditure-minimizing demands to squiggle y can be derived from the superdifferential of $E(q;y)$. The concavity of $E(q;y)$ and the cyclical monotonicity of $\partial E(q;y)$ guarantee that if $x^k \in \partial E(q^k;y)$, $k = 1, 2, ..., K$, then

$$(q^2 - q^1)^{\top} x^1 + (q^3 - q^2)^{\top} x^2 + ... + (q^1 - q^K)^{\top} x^K \geq 0.$$

Taking $K = 2$ gives

$$(q^2 - q^1)^{\top} x^1 + (q^1 - q^2)^{\top} x^2 = (q^2 - q^1)^{\top} (x^2 - x^1) \leq 0. \qquad (4.2)$$

Expression (4.2) effectively solves the most basic comparative-static problem that can be posed for individuals who minimize the expenditure required to squiggle y: How do their expenditure-minimizing demands change as prices change? Taking q^2 and q^1 to be the same except for their *kth* elements reveals, for example, that

$$(q_k^2 - q_k^1)^{\top} (x_k^2 - x_k^1) \leq 0,$$

for all elements of the superdifferential. Expenditure-minimizing demand correspondences vary inversely with price adjustments. Hence, in the smooth case when ∂E consists of singleton sets, expenditure-minimizing demand functions vary inversely with their own-price adjustments, and derived demand curves will never increase in their own prices. As shall be shown later in this section, concavity E and the associated cyclical monotonicity of

∂E have even more comparative-static bite when we restrict attention to a smooth world.

Because these arguments do not rely on any specific restriction placed on $V(y)$, it cannot be emphasized strongly enough that *these properties of $E(q;y)$ are consequences of assuming that economic agents are rational and face fixed prices*, and not various regularity conditions imposed on $\succeq(y)$. Thus, whether these predictions are sustainable rests upon whether those assumptions, and not ones placed on $\succeq(y)$, reasonably approximate the decision scenario.

Reversing the process, using $E(q;y)$ to resurrect the original $V(y)$, however, does require some regularity conditions, as Theorem 8 demonstrates. But if those regularity conditions are not satisfied by $V(y)$, there will exist an input correspondence described by

$$\begin{aligned}\hat{V}(y) &\equiv \{x \in \mathbb{R}_+^N : \delta^{**}(x \mid V(y)) = 0\} \\ &= \{x \in \mathbb{R}_+^N : q^\top x \geq E(q;y) \text{ for all } q \in \mathbb{R}_+^N\},\end{aligned}$$

with $V(y) \subset \hat{V}(y)$ for which the regularity conditions are satisfied. $\hat{V}(y)$ is often referred to as the *free-disposal convex hull of* $V(y)$, the smallest convex set consistent with monotonicity from above (*MA*) that contains $V(y)$.[3] To visualize, draw $V(y)$ as closed and nonempty but not satisfying either monotonicity from above or convexity from above (*CONA*). Now construct the *smallest* set containing $V(y)$ that is also consistent with monotonicity and convexity from above. That's $\hat{V}(y)$.

To whom exactly does $\hat{V}(y)$ belong? And, more importantly, why do we get it and not $V(y)$? The first answer is that $\hat{V}(y)$ belongs to $V(y)$'s economically rational clone. That clone is identical to $\succeq(y)$ in all but two ways. Its $\succeq(y)$ is monotonic from above and convex from above. But in every other way it reflects the same squiggle behavior as $\succeq(y)$. (Also see Remark 5 and Section 2.5.3.)

It's been well known for a long time that rational individuals in this price-taking setting will not operate on portions of boundary curves for $V(y)$ that do not satisfy these properties. Perhaps the clearest early explanation is in Samuelson's (1947) *Foundations*. Solving the following problem may help you visualize what's happening.

[3] Mathematically, it corresponds to

$$\hat{V}(y) = \{x : x \geq \lambda x^0 + (1-\lambda)x^1 \text{ for all } x^0, x^1 \in V(y), \lambda \in [0,1]\}.$$

Problem 32. *In two-dimensional space, draw a picture of $V(y)$ that is nonempty and closed but that does not satisfy either MA or CONA. Using that $V(y)$, visually solve the McKenzie expenditure-minimization problem for $V(y)$ for strictly positive prices. Identify whether it is possible to obtain a solution where $V(y)$ is locally inconsistent with either MA or CONA.*

We now connect some mathematical objects, one-sided directional derivatives and concave conjugates, with an important economic object, the McKenzie expenditure function, $E(q;y)$. Positive homogeneity of $E(q;y)$ requires that

$$\begin{aligned} E'(q;y;q) &= \lim_{\lambda \downarrow 0} \frac{E(q+\lambda q;y) - E(q;y)}{\lambda} \\ &= \lim_{\lambda \downarrow 0} \frac{(1+\lambda)E(q;y) - E(q;y)}{\lambda} \\ &= \lim_{\lambda \downarrow 0} \frac{\lambda E(q;y)}{\lambda} \\ &= E(q;y), \end{aligned}$$

so that the $E(q;y)$ is interpretable as its own one-sided directional derivative in the direction of q. The fact that

$$E(q;y) = E'(q;y;q)$$

generalizes *Euler's Theorem for Homogeneous Functions* to the superdifferentiable case and leads to yet another interpretation of $E(q;y)$ as the support function for its superdifferential, which we know from Shephard's Lemma, includes its McKenzie demands. That is,

$$E(q;y) = E'(q;y;q) = \min\{q^{\top}x : x \in \partial E(q;y)\}.$$

What this superdifferential property says economically is that a slight proportional increase in q increases expenditure by exactly $E(q;y)$ but does not affect the optimal solution set to the expenditure minimization problem. This is an economic manifestation of the fact that proportional (radial) changes in q do not alter the expenditure-minimizing solution, $\partial E(q;y)$. In words, *McKenzie demands are homogeneous of degree zero in q.* Here's how homogeneity of degree zero is shown using Shephard's Lemma and the superlinearity of $E(q;y)$:

$$
\begin{gathered}
x \in \partial E(q; y) \\
\Updownarrow \\
x^{\top}(\hat{q} - q) \geq E(\hat{q}; y) - E(q; y) \text{ for all } \hat{q} \\
\Updownarrow \\
x^{\top}(\mu\hat{q} - \mu q) \geq E(\mu\hat{q}; y) - E(\mu q; y) \text{ for all } \mu\hat{q} \\
\Updownarrow \\
x \in \partial E(\mu q; y) \quad \mu > 0,
\end{gathered}
$$

where the second $\Updownarrow$ (from the top or the bottom) follows by the superlinearity of $E(q; y)$. In economic jargon, *only real (relative) prices matter* to the expenditure-minimizing solution.

In a nicely smooth setting, homogeneity of degree zero has structural implications for cross-price effects associated with McKenzie derived demands. Writing the McKenzie demand for x_k as $x_k(q; y)$, we have

$$
x_k(\mu q; y) = x_k(q; y).
$$

Differentiating this expression with respect to μ and evaluating the result at $\mu = 1$ gives

$$
\sum_n \frac{\partial x_k(q; y)}{\partial q_n} q_n = 0. \tag{4.3}
$$

Recognizing that

$$
\frac{\partial x_k(q; y)}{\partial q_n} = \frac{\partial^2 E(q; y)}{\partial q_k \partial q_n}
$$

applying Young's Theorem on the symmetry of cross-partial derivatives and using the consequence of zero homogeneity gives, respectively,

$$
\frac{\partial x_k(q; y)}{\partial q_n} = \frac{\partial^2 E(q; y)}{\partial q_k \partial q_n} = \frac{\partial^2 E(q; y)}{\partial q_n \partial q_k} = \frac{\partial x_n(q; y)}{\partial q_k} \text{ for all } k, n, \text{ and}
$$

$$
\sum_n \frac{\partial x_n(q; y)}{\partial q_k} q_n = 0. \tag{4.4}
$$

Expressions (4.3) and (4.4) both imply that the Jacobian matrix of $(x_1(q; y), \ldots, x_N(q; y))^{\top}$ in q, which equals the Hessian of $E(q; y)$ in q, is singular. Expression (4.3) demonstrates this by showing that when elements of the Jacobian are multiplied by an appropriate price and summed across columns (along a row), the resulting sum is zero. Hence, the columns must be linearly dependent, and the resulting matrix is singular. Expression (4.4) demonstrates a parallel result for rows. Coupling this result with the well-known fact that the Hessian of a concave function is negative semidefinite, we conclude that the Hesssian of $E(q;y)$ in q is singular and negative semidefinite.

Remark 9. *This section recycles, with a bit more economic explanation, the discussion surrounding Lemma 4 characterizing superlinear functions as the concave conjugates of indicator functions for convex sets.*

2.2 McKenzie Expenditure Function from a Distance Function

Indicator functions provide one approach to generating $E(q;y)$. But they can be difficult to deploy. Another approach is to maintain monotonicity from above (MA) and use $d(x,y;g)$. The basic idea behind using $\delta(x \mid C)$ and $d(x,y;g)$ is the same. Each takes x and "corrects it" according to whether or not it falls in $V(y)$. The indicator function attaches an arbitrarily large penalty to x not lying in $V(y)$. The distance function corrects x to ensure that

$$x - d(x,y;g)\,g \succeq (y).$$

The "corrected" x squiggles y. For prices q, that corrected point cannot be cheaper than the cheapest way to squiggle y. Thus,

$$q^{\top}(x - d(x,y;g)\,g) \geq E(q;y).$$

$E(q;y)$ is a lower bound for the value of the "corrected" x. If that lower bound is achieved, the result is a calculating formula for finding $E(q;y)$—namely, minimize the quantity on the left.

If a finite $E(q;y)$ exists, the lower bound is achievable. For then, an x^* exists such that

$$E(q;y) = q^{\top}x^*,$$

whence

$$\begin{aligned} q^{\top}x^* &= q^{\top}(x^* - 0g) \\ &= E(q;y) \\ &\leq q^{\top}(x - d(x,y;g)\,g) \end{aligned}$$

for all x. Summarizing:

Proposition 2. *If* $\succeq (y)$ *satisfies MA and a finite minimum exists for the McKenzie expenditure-minimization problem:*

$$\begin{aligned} E(q;y) &= \min_x \{q^{\top}x - d(x,y;g)\,q^{\top}g\} \\ &= q^{\top}g \min_x \left\{\frac{q^{\top}}{q^{\top}g}x - d(x,y;g)\right\} \\ &= q^{\top}g d^*\left(\frac{q^{\top}}{q^{\top}g}, y; g\right) \\ &\equiv \min_x M(x,q;y) \end{aligned} \tag{4.5}$$

$E(q;y)$ is a positive multiple of the concave conjugate of $d(x,y;g)$ expressed in prices normalized by the value of the numeraire. The intuitive connection with the indicator function approach is clear. Using the indicator function translates a constrained problem into an unconstrained one by the device of placing arbitrarily large penalties on $x's$ not falling $V(y)$. Hence, rational individuals always avoid such choices. The distance-function approach translates $x's$ to ensure that the translated value falls within $V(y)$.

Before solving it, we note an indeterminacy associated with (4.5). Denote an element of the solution set to (4.5) by

$$\tilde{x} \in \arg\min\{q^{\top}(x - d(x,y;g)\,g)\}.$$

For $\alpha \in \mathbb{R}$, the Translation Property requires $d(\tilde{x} + \alpha g, y; g) = d(\tilde{x}, y; g) + \alpha$ so that

$$\tilde{x} + \alpha g - d(\tilde{x} + \alpha g, y; g)\,g = \tilde{x} - d(\tilde{x}, y; g)\,g.$$

We conclude, therefore, that

$$\begin{aligned} E(q; y) &= q^\top (\tilde{x} - d(\tilde{x}, y; g) g) \\ &= q^\top (\tilde{x} + \alpha g - d(\tilde{x} + \alpha g, y; g) g), \end{aligned}$$

and

$$\tilde{x} + \alpha g \in \arg\min \{q^\top (x - d(x, y; g) g)\},$$

for $\alpha \in \mathbb{R}$. If a solution exists to (4.5), there are an infinity of such solutions that all cost the same amount.

This happens because an $\tilde{x}$ that solves (4.5) is not necessarily an "expenditure minimizing" x. Instead,

$$\tilde{x} - d(\tilde{x}, y; g) g$$

is the expenditure-minimizing x, and it is found by translating any solution, $\tilde{x}$, to (4.5) $d(\tilde{x}, y; g)$ units in the direction of g. That brings $\tilde{x}$ back to the expenditure-minimizing point on the boundary of $V(y)$.

You can visualize as follows. Find a solution to the expenditure-minimization problem. Now draw a ray parallel to g through that solution. Visually, $\tilde{x}$ can represent any point on that ray in the direction of the numeraire, g, that passes through the solution. There are an infinity of such points, but once translated in the direction of g by $d(\tilde{x}, y; g)$, all map into the same expenditure-minimizing point. One way to resolve the indeterminacy is to set d to zero to ensure that the point chosen lies in $V(y)$.[4]

Lemma 13. *If*

$$\tilde{x} \in \arg\min \{q^\top (x - d(x, y; g) g)\}$$

then,

$$\tilde{x} + \alpha g \in \arg\min \{q^\top (x - d(x, y; g) g)\} \text{ for } \alpha \in \mathbb{R}.$$

[4] In effect, when you write the expenditure-minimization problem as

$$\min_x \{q^\top x : d(x, y; g) \geq 0\},$$

this is exactly what you are doing. The price for getting rid of the Lagrangian multiplier in the optimization problem is the possibility of the infinity of solutions.

Applying Theorem 2 gives

Proposition 3. $\tilde{x} \in \arg\min \{q^\top (x - d(x, y; g) g)\}$ *if and only if:*

$$\frac{q}{q^\top g} \in \partial d(\tilde{x}, y; g). \tag{4.6}$$

Variants of (4.6) are so familiar as to be taken for granted. Mechanically, they seem to represent first-order conditions for the McKenzie cost-minimization problem. But they are not first-order conditions. Instead they are global conditions for a solution to (4.5). Recall our earlier *caveat.* The definition of superdifferentiability is global and not local. Thus, one might encounter a situation where, for example,

$$\frac{q}{q^\top g} = \nabla d(x, y; g),$$

but $\frac{q}{q^\top g} \notin \partial d(x, y; g)$. This is what happens in the smooth case when second-order conditions are not met. Of course, when $d(x, y; g)$ is concave in x, any minimum must be global.[5]

Reconsidering Problem 30 illustrates. Recall that the Lagrangian for that problem is written

$$\min_x \left\{ q^\top x - \lambda \min \left\{ \frac{x_1 - y_1}{g_1}, \ldots, \frac{x_N - y_N}{g_N} \right\} \right\}$$

with λ a nonnegative Lagrange multiplier and $\min\left\{\frac{x_1-y_1}{g_1}, \ldots, \frac{x_N-y_N}{g_N}\right\}$ as $d(x, y; g)$. Reformulate it using $d(x, y; g)$ as a "correction" to obtain:

[5] Just in case you suspect that I am solving a different problem, consider the Lagrangian formulation of this problem:

$$L(x, \lambda; y, g) = q^\top x - \lambda d(x, y; g),$$

where λ is the Lagrangian multiplier. By Theorem 2 the solution must satisfy

$$\frac{q}{\lambda} \in \partial d(x, y; g).$$

Proposition 1 implies

$$\left(\frac{q}{\lambda}\right)^\top g = 1,$$

whence our condition becomes

$$\frac{q}{q^\top g} \in \partial d(x, y; g),$$

which is identical to the condition derived in the text.

$$\min_x \left\{ q^\top x - \min\left\{ \frac{x_1 - y_1}{g_1}, \ldots, \frac{x_N - y_N}{g_N} \right\} q^\top g \right\}.$$

You can establish that $\min\left\{\frac{x_1-y_1}{g_1}, \ldots, \frac{x_N-y_N}{g_N}\right\}$ is concave in x. Therefore, it has a superdifferential, even though it is not smooth. The expression, $\min\left\{\frac{x_1-y_1}{g_1}, \ldots, \frac{x_N-y_N}{g_N}\right\}$, is the $d(x, y; g)$ induced by the $\geq$ ordering of $\mathbb{R}^N \times \mathbb{R}^N$.

Pictorially the solution seems obvious. Choose $x = y$ to ensure that $d(x, y; g) = 0$ and $M(y, q; y) = q^\top y$. We have a visually appealing and intuitively obvious solution to the problem. But a formal argument hasn't been given. There are at least two strategies to employ. One is to derive the answer by solving the superdifferential condition. This is clear cut and mechanical. But you need to be able to calculate ∂f. If $d(x, y; g)$ were smooth, it would be easy. You could simply apply the calculus. But this $d(x, y; g)$ is not everywhere smooth, so that approach won't work.

The second strategy is to start at the suspected solution and work backwards. In other words, make an intuitive guess, and then see if the conditions for a minimum are satisfied. So, let's do that. Our visualization suggests $x = y$ is the solution. Setting $x = y$ gives $d(x, y; g) = 0$ and $M(y, q; y) = q^\top y$. It's definitely a feasible choice for a solution. Now consider an arbitrary *variation*, $v \in \mathbb{R}^N$, around y, $y + \lambda v$ with $\lambda > 0$. Direct evaluation gives

$$\begin{aligned} M(y + \lambda v, q; y) &= \left[q^\top (y + \lambda v) - \min\left\{ \frac{y_1 + \lambda v_1 - y_1}{g_1}, \ldots, \frac{y_N + \lambda v_N - y_N}{g_N} \right\} q^\top g \right] \\ &= q^\top y + \lambda \left[q^\top v - \min\left\{ \frac{v_1}{g_1}, \ldots, \frac{v_N}{g_N} \right\} q^\top g \right] \\ &= q^\top y + \lambda \sum_n q_n \left(v_n - \min\left\{ \frac{v_1}{g_1}, \ldots, \frac{v_N}{g_N} \right\} g_n \right) \\ &= q^\top y + \lambda \sum_n q_n g_n \left(\frac{v_n}{g_n} - \min\left\{ \frac{v_1}{g_1}, \ldots, \frac{v_N}{g_N} \right\} \right). \end{aligned}$$

In words, we've perturbed our supposed solution in the direction of the arbitrary variation. Obviously,

$$\left(\frac{v_n}{g_n} - \min\left\{ \frac{v_1}{g_1}, \ldots, \frac{v_N}{g_N} \right\} \right) \geq 0,$$

for all n. And, therefore, because $q \in \mathbb{R}^N_{++}$,

$$\lambda \sum_n q_n g_n \left(\frac{v_n}{g_n} - \min\left\{ \frac{v_1}{g_1}, \ldots, \frac{v_N}{g_N} \right\} \right) \geq 0.$$

Hence, any such variation around y (note, there is no requirement that λ be small) must increase the value of M, and we conclude that y has to be the optimal solution.

Alternatively, we can check the superdifferential requirement for an optimum. Written out formally, it requires that

$$\frac{q}{q^{\top}g} \in \partial d\,(y,y;g) \Leftrightarrow \frac{q^{\top}}{q^{\top}g}\,(x-y) \geq \min\left\{\frac{x_1-y_1}{g_1},\ldots,\frac{x_N-y_N}{g_N}\right\} \text{ for all } x.$$

The last inequality can be rewritten (after multiplying each $\frac{q_n}{q^{\top}g}$ by one in the form $\frac{g_n}{g_n}$) as requiring

$$\sum_n \frac{q_n g_n}{q^{\top}g}\frac{(x_n-y_n)}{g_n} \geq \min\left\{\frac{x_1-y_1}{g_1},\ldots,\frac{x_N-y_N}{g_N}\right\} \text{ for all } x.$$

Because $\frac{q_n g_n}{q^{\top}g} \geq 0$ for all n and $\sum_n \frac{q_n g_n}{q^{\top}g} = 1$, the left-hand side is a weighted average of the elements of $\left(\frac{x_1-y_1}{g_1},\ldots,\frac{x_N-y_N}{g_N}\right)$. The inequality always holds. Hence,

$$\frac{q}{q^{\top}g} \in \partial d\,(y,y;g)$$

for this specific structure.[6] Either way, we've shown that our guess is correct.

At this juncture, it doesn't hurt to emphasize the obvious. When verifying a mathematical result, it *always pays to use the definitions.* This argument illustrates this point. Rather than attempting to mechanically "take" the

[6] For

$$d\,(x,y;g) = \min_n\left\{\frac{x_n-y_n}{g_n}\right\},$$

$$\begin{aligned}\partial d\,(y,y;g) &= \left\{q : q^{\top}(x-y) \geq \min_n\left\{\frac{x_n-y_n}{g_n}\right\} \text{ for all } x\right\} \\ &= \left\{q : q^{\top}v \geq \min_n\left\{\frac{v_n}{g_n}\right\} \text{ for all } v\right\} \\ &= Co\left\{\frac{e_1}{g_1},\ldots,\frac{e_N}{g_N}\right\}\end{aligned}$$

where $Co\{X\}$ denotes the convex hull of set X and $e_n \in \mathbb{R}^N$ corresponds to the *nth* element of the usual orthonormal basis from which it follows immediately that

$$\frac{q}{q'g} \in \partial d\,(y,y;g).$$

superdifferential, $\partial d(x, y; g)$, for arbitrary x and then evaluating the result at $x = y$, I wrote down what the definition of the superdifferential of $\partial d(y, y; g)$ required and then checked.

Remark 10. *Pólya (1945), which is highly recommended, refers to this second type of reasoning as the "heuristic approach to problem solving." Heuristic signals that the approach involves guessing. Roughly put, it prescribes the following: assemble all the relevant information; state what constitutes a solution; draw some pictures to help visualize the problem; and then make your informed guess. Once that is done, you check to see if your informed guess is correct. Simply put, it emphasizes inspiration over either perspiration and/or computation in problem solving. You will find surprisingly often that informed guessing and checking is a better approach than the more computationally oriented algorithm of setting up a Lagrangian, calculating the first-order conditions, and then solving them. That's especially true when (a) behavior cannot be accurately characterized by smooth functionals, or (b) when it can, but those smooth functionals do not have closed-form solutions. Cobb–Douglas functions do; that's one of the reasons they are so popular—but they are much more an exception than the rule.*

2.3 *d* and *E* as Concave Conjugates

Perhaps the most familiar notion of an *economic duality* is that between a technology and its economic counterpart, a cost (profit, restricted profit, revenue) function. If such a duality exists, knowledge of, say, the cost function is equivalent to knowing the technology. Because the cost function is traditionally deduced by combining producer rationality with the technology, it's not surprising that the cost function reflects characteristics of the technology. That the process is reversible, in hindsight, is also not surprising, especially if one understands Fenchel's Inequality. But at one time, it was a revelation to economists.

From the definition of $E(q; y)$,

$$
\begin{aligned}
E(q; y) &\leq q^{\top}(x - d(x, y; g)\, g) \\
&= q^{\top} g \left(\frac{q^{\top}}{q^{\top} g} x - d(x, y; g) \right), \quad \forall x \in \mathbb{R}_{+}^{N}, q \in \mathbb{R}_{+}^{N}.
\end{aligned}
$$

By the positive homogeneity of E,

$$E\left(\frac{q}{q^{\top}g};y\right) \leq \frac{q^{\top}}{q^{\top}g}x - d(x,y;g), \quad \forall x \in \mathbb{R}_{+}^{N}, q \in \mathbb{R}_{+}^{N}. \tag{4.7}$$

And trivially,

$$d(x,y;g) \leq \frac{q^{\top}}{q^{\top}g}x - E\left(\frac{q}{q^{\top}g};y\right), \quad \forall x \in \mathbb{R}_{+}^{N}, q \in \mathbb{R}_{+}^{N}. \tag{4.8}$$

$E\left(\frac{q}{q^{\top}g};y\right)$ and $d(x,y;g)$ are, respectively, lower bounds for affine functions of $\frac{q^{\top}}{q^{\top}g}$ and x.

Let

$$\tilde{x} \in \arg\min\left\{\frac{q^{\top}}{q^{\top}g}x - d(x,y;g)\right\},$$

so that

$$E\left(\frac{q}{q^{\top}g};y\right) = \frac{q^{\top}}{q^{\top}g}\tilde{x} - d(\tilde{x},y;g), \tag{4.9}$$

and

$$d(\tilde{x},y;g) = \frac{q^{\top}}{q^{\top}g}\tilde{x} - E\left(\frac{q}{q^{\top}g};y\right), \tag{4.10}$$

which demonstrates that these lower bounds are achievable by an appropriate choice of x and $\frac{q^{\top}}{q^{\top}g}$.

These observations, Lemma 1, and Theorem 6 probably incline you to conjecture that

$$\begin{aligned} E\left(\frac{q}{q^{\top}g};y\right) &= \min_{x\in\mathbb{R}_{+}^{N}}\left\{\frac{q^{\top}}{q^{\top}g}x - d(x,y;g)\right\} \\ &= d^{*}\left(\frac{q^{\top}}{q^{\top}g},y;g\right), \end{aligned} \tag{4.11}$$

$$d(x,y;g) = \min_{\frac{q}{q^{\top}g}\in\mathbb{R}_{+}^{N}}\left\{\frac{q^{\top}}{q^{\top}g}x - E\left(\frac{q}{q^{\top}g};y\right)\right\}.$$

That is, $E\left(\frac{q}{q^{\top}g};y\right)$ is the concave conjugate of $d\left(x,y;g\right)$, and $d\left(x,y;g\right)$ is the concave conjugate of $E\left(\frac{q}{q^{\top}g};y\right)$.

This is too tidy. In economics, there's usually a catch. Here, there are two. One is that for $E\left(\frac{q}{q^{\top}g};y\right)$ to be the concave conjugate of $d\left(x,y;g\right)$, the latter must satisfy the Indication Property. That requires monotonicity from above. When the axioms (assumptions) on $\succeq(y)$ were introduced, care was taken to emphasize that monotonicity from above (*MA*) is an assumption. If $\succeq(y)$ is not monotonic from above, the argument does not go through. d is not a true function representation of $\succeq(y)$, and in particular

$$E\left(\frac{q}{q^{\top}g};y\right) \neq \min_{x\in\mathbb{R}^N_+}\left\{\frac{q^{\top}}{q^{\top}g}x - d\left(x,y;g\right)\right\}.$$

The other catch is that if

$$\begin{aligned} d^{**}\left(x,y;g\right) &= \min_{\frac{q}{q^{\top}g}\in\mathbb{R}^N_+}\left\{\frac{q^{\top}}{q^{\top}g}x - E\left(\frac{q}{q^{\top}g};y\right)\right\} \\ &= \min_{\frac{q}{q^{\top}g}\in\mathbb{R}^N_+}\left\{\frac{q^{\top}}{q^{\top}g}x - d^{*}\left(\frac{q^{\top}}{q^{\top}g},y;g\right)\right\} \end{aligned}$$

is to equal $d\left(x,y;g\right)$, the latter needs to be concave in x because $d^{**}\left(x,y;g\right)$, as the concave conjugate of $E\left(\frac{q}{q^{\top}g},y\right)$, always is.

Neither monotonicity from above (*MA*) nor convexity from above (*CONA*) needs to be invoked to derive $E\left(q;y\right)$. But $d^{**}\left(x,y;g\right)$ is both concave and nondecreasing in x (you should be able to prove the latter yourself). To prove the Translation Property

$$d^{**}\left(x+\alpha g,y;g\right) = d^{**}\left(x,y;g\right) + \alpha,$$

all we need to do is to marshal its definition

$$\begin{aligned} d^{**}\left(x+\alpha g,y;g\right) &= \min_{\frac{q}{q^{\top}g}\in\mathbb{R}^N_+}\left\{\frac{q^{\top}}{q^{\top}g}\left(x+\alpha g\right) - E\left(\frac{q}{q^{\top}g};y\right)\right\} \\ &= \min_{\frac{q}{q^{\top}g}\in\mathbb{R}^N_{++}}\left\{\frac{q^{\top}}{q^{\top}g}x - E\left(\frac{q}{q^{\top}g};y\right)\right\} + \alpha. \end{aligned}$$

$d^{**}(x,y;\mu g) = \mu^{-1} d^{**}(x,y;g)$ for $\mu > 0$ is proved similarly (again you should be able to prove this yourself).

Hence, without requiring that $\succeq(y)$ be monotonic, we recapture something that is consistent with monotonicity from above and continuity from above, exhibits the Translation Property, and is homogeneous of degree minus one in g. That something can be construed as the directional distance function for some $\hat{\succeq}(y)$ that is continuous and monotonic from above. Applying Theorem 6 shows that if $\hat{\succeq}(y)$ were used to construct $E(q;y)$, the same $E(q;y)$ originally derived from $\succeq(y)$ would be obtained. Thus, even though $\hat{\succeq}(y)$ is not the original $\succeq(y)$, it predicts the same economic behavior (insofar as characterized by $E(q;y)$) as an individual possessing $\succeq(y)$.

Together, *MA* and *CONA* imply that $V(y)$ satisfies the principle of substitutability and exhibits a nonincreasing (diminishing) marginal rate of substitution. The bottom line is:

Claim 1. *$E(q;y)$ is superlinear and nondecreasing in $q \in \mathbb{R}^N_+$. If $\succeq(y)$ satisfies CA, MA, and CONA:*

$$E\left(\frac{q}{q^\top g}, y\right) = \min_{x \in \mathbb{R}^N_+} \left\{ \frac{q^\top}{q^\top g} x - d(x,y;g) \right\},$$

$$d(x,y;g) = \min_{\frac{q}{q^\top g} \in \mathbb{R}^N_+} \left\{ \frac{q^\top}{q^\top g} x - E\left(\frac{q}{q^\top g}; y\right) \right\},$$

$$\frac{q}{q^\top g} \in \partial d(x,y;g) \Leftrightarrow x \in \partial E\left(\frac{q}{q^\top g}; y\right).$$

I've called this a "claim" and not a theorem or a proposition. That's because while the sense of it is correct, I have not taken care of all the mathematical details required to make it exact. That requires some work, mostly technical detail, that's easily accessible elsewhere.

The third part of Claim 1 is Shephard's Lemma restated in terms of $d(x,y;g)$. In words, it goes something like this: any expenditure minimizing demand belongs to the superdifferential of the McKenzie expenditure function. Conversely, if x is expenditure-minimizing for $\frac{q}{q^\top g}$, $\frac{q}{q^\top g}$ belongs to the superdifferential of d at x.[7]

[7] Recall that the superdifferential of $d(x,y;g)$ is invariant to translations in the direction of g. Thus, the superdifferential remains invariant for all the potential solutions to the expenditure-minimization problem.

If one were to illustrate the equilibrium solutions to the dual conjugate problems in Claim 1 visually, one might draw a two-panel diagram. Both panels would likely contain figures quite similar to Figure 1.2. One panel (what economists typically refer to as the "primal") would have the axes labeled as x, and the curved portion would constitute the zero-level set for $d(x, y; g)$, $\bar{V}(y) \equiv \{x : d(x, y; g) = 0\}$, and the linear component would have slope $-\frac{q_1}{q_2}$. The other panel (illustrating the "dual") would have the axes labeled as $\frac{q}{q^{\top}g}$, the curved portion would represent a level set for $E\left(\frac{q}{q^{\top}g}; y\right)$, and the linear component would have slope $-\frac{x_1}{x_2}$.

In such a smooth case, relative price changes immediately elicit changes in optimal $\frac{x_1}{x_2}$ as the "price line" smoothly slides along the level set for $d(x, y; g)$. The dual reflection of this would be smooth changes in optimal $\frac{q_1}{q_2}$ as relative $\frac{x_1}{x_2}$ slides along the level set for $E\left(\frac{q}{q^{\top}g}; y\right)$ in the other panel. This, of course, is what happens in a smooth world. *Imposing smoothness has behavioral consequences because it suggests that tiny changes in* $\frac{q_1}{q_2}$ *will be matched by tiny changes in* $\frac{x_1}{x_2}$, and vice versa.

Figure 4.1 illustrates what happens in our more complicated, but still simple, "kinky" world. In the left panel, I have represented a portion of the level set for $d(x, y; g)$ with a kink at (x_1, x_2). (For visual clarity, I have drawn the part of the boundary illustrated as piecewise linear. More generally, kinks can emerge even in the absence of such structures.) As long as relative prices vary within the region depicted by the slopes of the two line segments defining the kink, the optimal solution remains at (x_1, x_2). Tiny, and even not so tiny, relative price changes do not elicit an economic response. Those price ratios that define the kink are depicted in the right panel by the vector (q_1, q_2) for the lower leg of the kink and (q_1^*, q_2^*) for the upper leg of the kink. When relative prices vary between those two rays, the isoexpenditure curve maintains a constant slope of $\left(-\frac{x_1}{x_2}\right)$ as illustrated in the figure. Thus, a kink in primal space corresponds to a flat in dual space. Following this method of argument, you can demonstrate that *kinks in dual space map into flats in primal space and vice versa.*

The general principle is simple. By Shephard's Lemma, if $\partial E\left(\frac{q}{q^{\top}g}; y\right)$ is a nonsingleton set, $E\left(\frac{q}{q^{\top}g}; y\right)$ has multiple supporting hyperplanes at $\frac{q}{q^{\top}g}$ and $E\left(\frac{q}{q^{\top}g}; y\right)$ is not differentiable. Visually, its isoexpenditure curve is kinked. Each of those elements of $\partial E\left(\frac{q}{q^{\top}g}; y\right)$ defining the kink corresponds to a

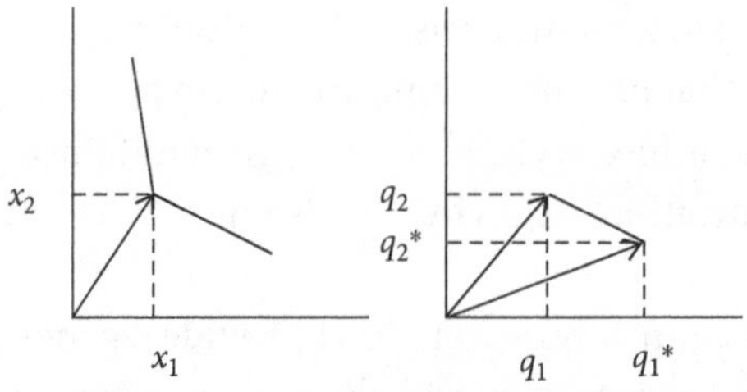

Fig. 4.1 Primal "Kinks" Imply Dual "Flats"

solution to the McKenzie expenditure-minimization problem, which then implies a linear portion for the level set of $d(x, y; g)$. Conversely, if $\partial d(x, y; g)$ is not a singleton set, $d(x, y; g)$ has multiple supporting hyperplanes at x, and it is not differentiable. The associated $\bar{V}(y)$ is kinked. That means x solves the McKenzie expenditure-minimization problem for a range of relative prices–hence the flat. Thus, Shephard's Lemma, besides defining optimality conditions, is also a statement about how the existence of and number of solutions relate to the smoothness or lack of smoothness of d and E.

2.4 Why Is Conjugacy (Duality) Important?

Why should we care about Theorem 8 and Claim 1? Part of the answer is historic. Generations of economists struggled to build a theory of economic behavior based on as few primitive assumptions as possible. The reason for the emphasis on minimizing the number of assumptions was to ensure the generality of the theory. One lesson from Theorem 8 and Claim 1 is that, starting with relatively few assumptions, we get individual behavior consistent with a somewhat longer list of assumptions. Why is that?

The answer lies in the behavioral assumptions that justify minimization. The idea that people always want to pay the smallest amount for anything is second nature to economists and many members of modern Western society. This is not a philosophy text, and so I will limit my comment to this: Being second nature doesn't make it either true or innocuous. Regardless of its plausibility, if you maintain minimization, you're describing behavior that is consistent with individuals who always want more in the sense of $\succeq(y)$ being monotonic from above.

The idea that individuals face linear prices for x isn't so much a behavioral assumption as it is a judgment about the decision environment. We're clearly thinking about individuals facing the type of market structures with which most of us are relatively familiar. If you go into Starbuck's, you don't negotiate the price of an espresso with the barista. If you don't pay the set price, you don't get it. To be useful, that pricing assumption doesn't have to be accurate. It just needs to be plausible in a stylized setting. If maintained and coupled with expenditure minimization, behavior consistent with convexity from above is obtained.

Theorem 8 and Claim 1, however, don't provide a general license to invoke those extra assumptions, or even to believe that they're plausible. Rather, it's an "AS IF" result. If we model the optimal behavior of individuals facing linear prices and trying to minimize expenditures, the behavior of individuals who act AS IF they have monotonic and convex from above $\succeq (y)$ will be recaptured. The mathematical reason is, at the same time, simple but beautifully obvious. Those twin assumptions allow us to segregate behavior according to closed and convex half spaces.

The ultimate usefulness of AS IF results lies in their ability to predict behavior in certain settings. Here's neither the time nor the place to judge how valuable economic theory has been or is in that regard. That's best left to other fora, and you as individuals will only be able to partake in the debate intelligently when you properly understand the fundamental issues and have learned a lot more than this book has to offer.

Another way to interpret Claim 1 is to start by making no assumptions on $\succeq (y)$. Instead, following Samuelson's (1938) revealed-preference suggestion, let's impose axioms on things we can directly observe such as individual demands and expenditures. So, for example, suppose we believe demands to be invariant to nominal price changes and, in some sense, downward sloping. We can formalize those beliefs by asserting that expenditures are characterized by $E\left(\frac{q}{q^{\top}g};y\right)$ with associated demands satisfying

$$x \in \partial E\left(\frac{q}{q^{\top}g};y\right),$$

and $E(q;y)$ nondecreasing and superlinear in q. Claim 1 shows that there exists an $\succeq (y)$ consistent with $d(x,y;g)$ nondecreasing and concave in x. How you interpret that $d(x,y;g)$ is up to you. Professional economists often choose to interpret it in at-least-as-good or production-feasibility terms.

Regardless of how you view things, the basic result is that you typically have (at least) two ways of looking at many economic phenomena. That provides considerable flexibility in attacking problems. That basic observation revolutionized empirical practice in a number of areas of applied economics. One reason that occurred was that strikingly few functional forms admit closed form solutions to problems formulated as solving Lagrangian problems posed in primal terms. The Cobb–Douglas does, as does the constant elasticity of substitution (CES) form—hence, their popularity. But both require homotheticity (more on this below), and both impose empirically problematic restrictions on the range and constancy of substitution relationships. The ability to formulate problems meaningfully in dual form rescued both empirical consumer and producer economics from that Cobb–Douglas–CES whirlpool and permitted a closer marriage between applied economics and its theoretical underpinnings.

2.5 $E(q;y)$'s Behavior in y

We've come a long way using very few assumptions. All that's been needed is continuity from above (*CA*), which is an extremely weak regularity condition. $E(q;y)$ has been found to be nondecreasing, superlinear, and superdifferentiable in q, to satisfy at least one part of Shephard's Lemma, and to possess cyclically monotone demand correspondences. That's a lot. It all emerges from rational[8] behavior. Moreover, as far as squiggly economics is concerned, monotonicity from above (*MA*) and convexity from above (*CONA*) are essentially superfluous. Even if not imposed, duality ensures that they come for free via $\hat{\succeq}(y)$ that can be constructed from $d^{**}(x,y;g)$

What we've not done is examine the behavior of $E(q;y)$ in y. The free lunch is over. Further assumptions are needed, and so we examine the consequences of monotonicity from below (*MB*) and convexity from below (*CONB*).

MB requires that if $x \succeq (y)$ then $x \succeq (y')$ for $y' \leq y$. So, if

$$x^* \in \arg\min\{q^\top x : x \succeq (y)\},$$

monotonicity from below ensures that $x^* \succeq (y')$ for $y' \leq y$. Thus, the minimal expenditure for squiggling y' can never exceed $q^\top x^*$. Hence,

$$E(q;y) \geq E(q;y') \qquad y \geq y'.$$

In economic jargon, the marginal cost or marginal expenditure of y is nonnegative if $\succeq (y)$ is monotonic from below.

[8] That is minimizing in this case.

Convexity from below (*CONB*) requires that

$$x \succeq (y^0) \text{ and } x \succeq (y^1) \Rightarrow x \succeq (y^0 + \lambda (y^1 - y^0)) \qquad \lambda \in (0,1).$$

Rewriting in terms of $V(y)$ gives

$$x \in V(y^0) \text{ and } x \in V(y^1) \Rightarrow x \in V(y^0 + \lambda (y^1 - y^0)) \qquad \lambda \in (0,1),$$

but because $x \in V(y^0)$ and $x \in V(y^1)$ is also expressible as $x \in V(y^0) \cap V(y^1)$ this becomes

$$V(y^0) \cap V(y^1) \subset V(y^0 + \lambda (y^1 - y^0)) \qquad \lambda \in (0,1).$$

Therefore, *CONB* requires that

$$q^\top x \geq E(q; y^0 + \lambda (y^1 - y^0)) \qquad \lambda \in (0,1),$$

for all $x \in V(y^0) \cap V(y^1)$. In words, anything that can squiggle both y^0 and y^1 can also squiggle their convex combination. Thus, anything in $V(y^0) \cap V(y^1)$ is at least as costly as the cheapest way to squiggle $y^0 + \lambda (y^1 - y^0)$. So, one way of thinking about this is that it's never cheaper to be prepared to squiggle two bundles than it is to squiggle any average of them. So, *CONB* gives some bite in explaining behavior, but it's an economic mouthful.[9] Abusing notation slightly,

$$E(q; V(y^0) \cap V(y^1)) \geq E(q; y^0 + \lambda (y^1 - y^0)) \qquad \lambda \in (0,1).$$

What gives more bite and is easier to digest intuitively is convexity of the order (*CON*). Let's revisit y^0 and y^1 and suppose that the solutions to least-cost squiggling them are, respectively, x^0 and x^1. By *CON*,

$$\lambda x^1 + (1 - \lambda) x^0 \succeq \lambda y^1 + (1 - \lambda) y^0 \qquad \lambda \in (0,1).$$

Thus, $x^0 + \lambda (x^1 - x^0)$ is a feasible choice for the cheapest way to squiggle $(y^0 + \lambda (y^1 - y^0))$. But that means

[9] On the other hand, as you will observe below, *CONB* has a very meaningful implication when it comes to explaining revenue-maximization behavior. In that case, CONA is considerably less intuitive than *CONB*.

$$E(q;\lambda y^1 + (1-\lambda) y^0) \leq q^\top (\lambda x^1 + (1-\lambda) x^0)$$
$$= \lambda E(q;y^1) + (1-\lambda) E(q;y^0)$$
$$= E(q;y^0) + \lambda (E(q;y^1) - E(q;y^0)) \qquad \lambda \in (0,1),$$

so that $E(q;y)$ is convex in y.

Together, monotonicity from below (*MB*) and convexity of the order (*CON*) ensure that the marginal cost of squiggling y is nonnegative and nondecreasing. Doubtless, you've seen numerous examples of marginal cost curves represented pictorially as upward-sloping curves in the northeast quadrant of $\mathbb{R}^2$. Herein lies the root cause of that behavior.

Proposition 4. *If* $\succeq$ *satisfies MB and CON,* $E(q;y)$ *is nondecreasing and convex in* y*. Moreover,* $m \in \partial_y^- E(q;y)$ *implies*

$$m^\top v \leq \sup\{m^\top v : m \in \partial_y^- E(q;y)\} = E^{y}(q;y;v) \leq E(q;y+v) - E(q;y),$$

and for $m^k \in \partial_y^- E(q;y)$

$$(y^2 - y^1)^\top m^1 + (y^3 - y^2)^\top m^2 + \ldots + (y^1 - y^K)^\top m^K \leq 0,$$

where

$$E^{y}(q;y;v) \equiv \lim_{\lambda \downarrow 0} \frac{E(q;y+\lambda v) - E(q;y)}{\lambda}.$$

Problem 33. *Suppose that* $E(q;y)$ *is superlinear and nondecreasing in* q *and convex and nondecreasing in* y*. Use the conjugacy relation to prove that there must exist a* $\hat{\succeq}(y)$ *that satisfies MA, MB, and CON.*

3 A Standard Problem: Revenue Maximization

It's time to exploit $t(y,x;g)$. Throughout this section, maintain continuity from below (*CB*) and monotonicity from below (*MB*). The economic essence of what follows has already been developed. Therefore, the discussion is brief to the point of terseness. Again this does not reflect its relative importance, but instead a desire not to recycle arguments already marshaled. By that I mean that we have already looked closely at the parallel problem of minimization under *CA* and *MA*. Now, I want you to use the intuition developed there, turn the bowl over so to speak, and apply it to the problem that follows. Undoubtedly, this will be more painful for you than if I had done the recycling for you, but this is truly an example of where the aphorism "the less pain, the less gain" applies.

The basic problem is

$$\begin{aligned} R(p;x) &\equiv \max_y \{p^\top y : x \succeq (y)\} \\ &= \max_y \{p^\top y : y \in Y(x)\} \\ &= \max_y \{p^\top (y - t(y,x;g)\,g)\}, \quad p \in \mathbb{R}^M_{++} \end{aligned}$$

if there exists y such that $x \succeq (y)$ and $-\infty$ otherwise. Our focus is on the third representation.[10]

Visually, the solution to the revenue-maximization problem is represented by Figure 1.4, where the straight line is interpreted as having slope given by relative prices, p, the axes are labeled as quantities of y, and the curved to the origin figure represents $Y(x)$. Perhaps the most familiar interpretation of $R(p;x)$ is that $\succeq (y)$ represents a technology, and Y an output correspondence depicting the outputs that can be produced using inputs $x \in \mathbb{R}^N_+$. $R(p;x)$ is then called a *revenue function* and represents the maximal revenue that a price-taking producer could generate from an input endowment of x for prices p. The applications of revenue functions are legion, and when recycled as GNP functions, they play an important role in both international trade and growth theory. All to the good, and it's a safe bet you can find textbook treatments of those topics. Moreover, Chapter 6 is devoted to a closer examination of technologies, and you will be asked to examine revenue functions much more closely there.

I suggest, however, that you also revisit Lemma 8 and Lemma 10 under the assumption that $x, y \in \mathbb{R}^N$. (Perhaps, it may be easiest then to think of $V(y)$ as an at-least-as-good set and $Y(x)$ as a not-better-than set.) Those lemmata give differential properties for alternative representations of $\succeq (y)$.

[10] Also note that if one defined the indicator function

$$\tau(y \mid C) = \begin{cases} 0 & y \in C \\ \infty & y \notin C \end{cases},$$

one can also write

$$\begin{aligned} R(p;x) &= \sup\{p^\top y - \tau(y \mid C)\} \\ &= \tau^*(y \mid C) \end{aligned}$$

as the convex conjugate of the indicator function. Complete dual relations can then be developed via this conjugacy relationship.

Lemma 8 shows that if $d(y, y; g)$ is superdifferentiable, all of the elements of its superdifferential, $\partial d(y, y; g)$, define internal prices for which y is the cheapest element of $V(y)$. Lemma 10, on the other hand, shows that if $t(x, x; g)$ is subdifferentiable, all of the elements of its subdifferential $\partial^{-} t(x, x; g)$, define internal prices for which x is the most expensive element of $Y(x)$.

Now let's set $x = y$ and consider $\partial d(y, y; g)$ and $\partial^{-} t(y, y; g)$. One is the superdifferential associated with $V(y)$, and the other is a subdifferential associated with $Y(y)$. (Drawing a picture here would help.) Is there a well-behaved order for which both $\partial d(y, y; g) \neq \emptyset$ and $\partial^{-} t(y, y; g) \neq \emptyset$? The answer is yes, as the $\geq$ order demonstrates. For that order

$$V(y) = \{x \in \mathbb{R}^N : x \geq y\},$$
$$Y(y) = \{x \in \mathbb{R}^N : y \geq x\},$$

and $V(y) \cap Y(y) = \{y\}$, so that the Separating Hyperplane Theorem now requires the existence of a $p \in \mathbb{R}^N_+$ such that $p^\top z \geq p^\top v$ for all $z \in V(y)$ and $v \in Y(y)$.[11] The economic message that can be drawn from Lemmata 8 and 10 is clear. *Superdifferentiability and subdifferentiability at a point y imply that y can be optimal in either of two ways.* It can be the most valuable element of a set of alternatives that are no better than it, or the cheapest element of a set of alternatives that are at least as good as it. $E(q; y)$ thus is interpretable as *willingness-to-pay for* y given prices q, and $R(p; y)$ as the *willingness-to-sell (accept) for* y given prices p.

We have:

Lemma 14. *If*

$$\hat{y} \in \arg\max \{p^\top (y - t(y, x; g) g)\},$$

then

$$\hat{y} + \alpha g \in \arg\max \{p^\top (y - t(y, x; g) g)\} \textit{ for } \alpha \in \mathbb{R}.$$

Problem 34. *Prove that if* $\succeq(y)$ *is continuous from below (CB) and convex from below (CONB):*

$$t(y + \lambda(y^o - y), x; g) \leq t(y, x; g) + \lambda(t(y^o, x; g) - t(y, x; g)), \quad \lambda \in (0, 1).$$

[11] Your picture should convince you that in fact an infinity of such hyperplanes exist.

Claim 2. *$R(p;x)$ is sublinear*[12] *and nondecreasing in $p \in \mathbb{R}^M_+$. If $\succeq(y)$ is continuous from below, monotonic from below, and convex from below:*

$$R\left(\frac{p}{p^\top g};x\right) = \max_y \left\{\frac{p^\top}{p^\top g}y - t(y,x;g)\right\},$$

$$t(y,x;g) = \max_{\frac{p^\top}{p^\top g}} \left\{\frac{p^\top}{p^\top g}y - R\left(\frac{p}{p^\top g},x\right)\right\},$$

$$\frac{p}{p^\top g} \in \partial^- t(y,x;g) \Leftrightarrow y \in \partial^- R\left(\frac{p}{p^\top g};x\right).$$

Problem 35. *Demonstrate Claim 2 and discuss its economic consequences. (Hint: Here you will want to think in terms of convex conjugates and not concave conjugates.)*

That leaves $R(p;x)'$ s behavior in x. What does your intuition suggest? In considering the behavior of $E(q;y)$ in y, which is the analogous property, we saw that monotonicity from below and convexity from below yielded results. So the natural suspects here would be monotonicity from above (*MA*), convexity from above (*CONA*), and convexity of the order (*CON*).

Problem 36. *Prove that if $\succeq(y)$ satisfies monotonicity from above and that convexity of the order $R(p;x)$ is nondecreasing and concave in x. Derive the implications of convexity from above for $R(p;x)$.*

4 A Standard Problem: Profit Maximization

For this final step in "squiggle economics," it seems most natural to think of $\succeq(y)$ in production-theoretic terms. The generic problem is

$$\pi(p,q) \equiv \max_{y,x}\{p^\top y - q^\top x : x \succeq (y)\}.$$

$\pi : \mathbb{R}^M_+ \times \mathbb{R}^N_+ \to \mathbb{R}$ is referred to as the *profit function*. It gives the maximum profit consistent with $\succeq(y)$ for prices (p,q). In a production context, it's natural to think of $p \in \mathbb{R}^M_+$ as output prices and $q \in \mathbb{R}^N_+$ as input prices.

[12] Recall that a function f is sublinear if $-f$ is superlinear. Therefore, f is sublinear if its epigraph is a convex cone.

Problem 37. *While the production-theoretic setting is perhaps the most natural, there are others. For example, consider the case of a "pure middle-man,"*[13] *operating in two distinct markets for the same commodities (so $M = N$), who is trying to take advantage of price differences between those markets. You might visualize this as two geographically distinct markets, location A and location B. Assuming that the middle-man's costs of transporting the commodities between the two are given by $c \in \mathbb{R}_+^N$, decide what is the appropriate $\succeq (y)$ ordering for the middle-man and develop a complete theory of his or her behavior.*

There are several distinct, but equivalent, ways to solve the profit-maximization problem. One is to proceed directly with developing properties of the solution after imposing suitable structure upon $\succeq (y)$. Another is to rely on the generalized *Bellman's Principle*[14] to decompose the problem as

$$\begin{aligned}
\pi(p,q) &= \max_{y,x}\{p^\top y - q^\top x : x \succeq (y)\} \\
&= \max_x\left\{\max_y\{p^\top y : x \succeq (y)\} - q^\top x\right\} \\
&= \max_x\{R(p,x) - q^\top x\} \\
&= -\min_x\{q^\top x - R(p,x)\} \\
&\equiv -R^*(p;q).
\end{aligned} \tag{4.12}$$

Yet another is to use Bellman's Principle to decompose it as

$$\begin{aligned}
\pi(p,q) &= \max_{y,x}\{p^\top y - q^\top x : x \succeq (y)\} \\
&= \max_y\left\{p^\top y - \min_x\{q^\top x : x \succeq (y)\}\right\} \\
&= \max_y\{p^\top y - E(q;y)\} \\
&= E^*(q;p).
\end{aligned} \tag{4.13}$$

Thus, $E(q;y)$, the McKenzie expenditure function, and $R(p;x)$ represent solutions to conditional or restricted profit-maximization problems. $E(q;y)$

[13] My apologies for departing from gender neutrality. I try not to do that, but sometimes the result is so disharmonious that it's merited. For me, this is one of those instances, while politically correct, "middle-person" strikes me as particularly dorky.

[14] Bellman (1957) refers to the decomposition approach illustrated by (4.12) as the *functional equation approach* to optimization.

involves choosing x to maximize the profit associated with a fixed y, and $R(p;x)$ chooses y to maximize profit associated with a fixed x. The second stages involve, respectively, choosing y and x optimally. The second-stage problem that invokes $R(p;x)$ is illustrated visually by Figure 1.1 and its solution principle is illustrated visually by Figure 1.2. The second-stage problem that invokes $E(q;y)$ is illustrated visually by Figure 1.3, and its solution principle is illustrated visually by Figure 1.4.

Remark 11. *Bellman's Principle (see, for example, Bellman 1957, pp. 7–10) is identified almost exclusively with dynamic programming problems. But the essential principle is applicable to any optimization problem involving multiple-choice variates. I'll illustrate the argument for (4.13) and leave it to you to extend it to other optimization problems. Let*

$$(x^*, y^*) \in \arg\max \{p^\top y - q^\top x : x \succeq (y)\}.$$

Now the question that we seek to answer is whether

$$x^* \in \arg\min \{q^\top x : x \succeq (y^*)\}$$

necessarily. To see that it must be, suppose the contrary. Then it must be true that there exists an $\hat{x} \succeq (y^*)$ for which $q^\top \hat{x} < q^\top x^*$. But that requires that $p^\top y^* - q^\top \hat{x} > p^\top y^* - q^\top x^*$, violating the assumed optimality of (x^*, y^*). That's a contradiction, and so we conclude that

$$x^* \in \arg\min \{q^\top x : x \succeq (y^*)\}$$

necessarily. But this means that at the optimum $\pi(p,q) = p^\top y^* - E(q;y^*)$. An exactly parallel argument then shows that necessarily

$$y^* \in \arg\max \{p^\top y - E(q;y)\}.$$

So, why do we want to proceed in this manner? The bottom line is that Bellman's Principle lets us decompose complicated multivariate optimization problems into simpler lower-dimensional problems. That has great analytic advantages, and as such, it is an AS IF argument that is repeatedly used in this book. Think of it this way. If you were asked to name the best strategy to consume an orange or any other sizable piece of fruit, few would answer: "stuff it whole into your mouth and chew."

The structure of (4.12) and (4.13) both lend themselves naturally to solution via superdifferential and subdifferential methods. By Theorem 2 and its subdifferential counterpart, the optimal solutions occur, respectively, where

$$q \in \partial_x R(p; x), \tag{4.14}$$

and

$$p \in \partial_y^- E(q; y). \tag{4.15}$$

Profit maximization requires equating the marginal revenue associated with an input to the input's price and equating marginal cost to the price of the output. Both should be familiar and intuitive.

Our focus here is on $\pi(p, q)$ as the *convex conjugate* of $E(q; y)$; denote it $E^*(q; p)$. Our previous discussion establishes that $E^*(q; p)$ is convex and nondecreasing in p. That it is also positively homogeneous in (p, q) follows by

$$\begin{aligned} E^*(\mu q; \mu p) &= \max_y \{\mu p^\top y - E(\mu q; y)\} \\ &= \max_y \{\mu p^\top y - \mu E(q; y)\} \\ &= \mu \max_y \{p^\top y - E(q; y)\}, \quad \mu > 0, \end{aligned}$$

where the second equality reflects the positive homogeneity of $E(q; y)$ in q. Positive homogeneity implies that nominal profits respond proportionally to equiproportional changes in prices. Real economic decisions, however, remain unaffected. The latter is demonstrated conveniently using either (4.14) or (4.15). Use the latter and recall that $E(q; y)$ is superlinear in q. By superlinearity, for $\mu > 0$

$$\begin{gathered} m \in \partial_y^- E(\mu q; y) \\ \Updownarrow \\ m^\top (v - y) \le E(\mu q; v) - E(\mu q; y) \text{ for all } v \\ \Updownarrow \\ \frac{m^\top}{\mu}(v - y) \le E(q; v) - E(q; y) \text{ for all } v \\ \Updownarrow \\ \frac{m}{\mu} \in \partial_y^- E(q; y). \end{gathered}$$

Therefore

$$\mu p \in \partial_y^- E(\mu q; y) \Leftrightarrow p \in \partial_y^- E(q; y),$$

so that nominal price changes do not change the optimal choice of y. A parallel argument using $\partial_x R(p, x)$ shows that nominal price changes do not change optimal x. Hence, the reaction to a nominal price change is to maintain the original economic choice, while nominal profit adjusts by the same proportion. As always, only real prices matter.

It is left to you to establish that $E^*(q; p)$ is nonincreasing in q. A simple argument establishes that $E^*(q; p)$ is subadditive in (p, q). Let

$$\tilde{y} \in \arg\max\left\{(p + p^o)^\top y - E(q + q^o; y)\right\}.$$

Obviously,

$$\begin{aligned} p^\top \tilde{y} - E(q; \tilde{y}) &\leq \pi(p, q), \text{ and} \\ p^{o\top} \tilde{y} - E(q^o; \tilde{y}) &\leq \pi(p^o, q^o), \end{aligned}$$

Adding these inequalities yields

$$p^\top \tilde{y} - E(q; \tilde{y}) + p^{o\top} \tilde{y} - E(q^o; \tilde{y}) \leq \pi(p, q) + \pi(p^o, q^o).$$

Recalling that $E(q; y)$ is superadditive in q, that is,

$$E(q + q^o; y) \geq E(q; y) + E(q^0; y),$$

establishes that

$$\begin{aligned} E^*(q + q^o; p + p^o) &= (p + p^o)^\top \tilde{y} - E(q + q^o; \tilde{y}) \\ &\leq p^\top \tilde{y} - E(q; \tilde{y}) + p^{o\top} \tilde{y} - E(q^o; \tilde{y}) \\ &\leq E^*(q; p) + E^*(q^o, p^o), \end{aligned}$$

which is the desired subadditivity. Combining subadditivity with positive homogeneity then establishes that $E^*(q; p)$ is sublinear (positively homogeneous and convex) in (p, q).[15]

[15] Alternatively, define $T \subset \mathbb{R}^N \times \mathbb{R}^M$ by

$$T = \{(x, y) : x \succeq (y)\}.$$

Then

$$\pi(q, p) = \sup\{p^\top y - q^\top x : (x, y) \in T\}$$

establishing that $\pi(q, p)$ is an upper support function for T and thus sublinear.

$E^*(q;p)$ and

$$E^{**}(q;y) = \max_p \{p^\top y - E^*(q;p)\},$$

are (convex) conjugate duals. $E^{**}(q;y)$ is necessarily nondecreasing and convex in y regardless of the properties that $E(q;y)$ possesses in y. The economic interpretation is straightforward. Just as $E(q;y)$ and $R(p;x)$ are dual to a $\hat{\succeq}(y)$ that exhibits monotonicity and convexity from above and monotonicity and convexity from below, respectively, the profit function is dual to a $\hat{\succeq}(y)$ that satisfies convexity of the order and monotonicity from above and below.[16] The intuition is the same as originally demonstrated by Samuelson (1947). If a rational individual faces a linear pricing structure (that is, he or she is a price taker), his or her rational choices will never occur on nonconvex or nonmonotonic segments of the graph of $\succeq$.

We have:

Claim 3. *$\pi(p,q) \equiv E^*(q;p)$ is sublinear and nondecreasing in $(-q,p)$. If $E(q;y)$ is nondecreasing and convex in y:*

$$E^*(q;p) = \max_y \{p^\top y - E(q;y)\},$$

$$E(q;y) = \max_p \{p^\top y - E^*(q;p)\}, \quad \text{and}$$

$$p \in \partial_y^- E(q;y) \Leftrightarrow y \in \partial_p^- E^*(q;p) = \partial_p^- \pi(p,q).$$

Problem 38. *Develop Claim 3 formally.*

Problem 39. *Prove: If $R(p;x)$ is nondecreasing and concave in x:*

$$\pi(p,q) = \max_x \{R(p;x) - q^\top x\}$$

$$R(p;x) = \min_q \{\pi(p,q) + q^\top x\}$$

$$q \in \partial_x R(p;x) \Leftrightarrow x \in -\partial_q^- \pi(p,q).$$

(Hint: Recall

$$\pi(p,q) = -R^*(p;q),$$

where $R^*(p;q)$ is the concave conjugate of $R(p;x)$. Proceed from here.)

[16] Recall that convexity of $\succeq$ and monotonicity from below are required to establish that marginal cost of y is nonnegative and nondecreasing. ($E(q;y)$ is nondecreasing and convex in y.)

Claim 3 and Problem 39 taken together establish what many recognize as *Hotelling's Lemma*. That is,

$$y \in \partial_p^- \pi(p, q) \text{ and } x \in -\partial_q^- \pi(p, q), \qquad \textit{(Hotelling's Lemma)}$$

profit-maximizing supplies of y and profit-maximizing derived demands for x are derivable as subdifferentials of the profit function in output and input prices, respectively. Because $\pi(p, q)$ is convex in (p, q), its subdifferentials are cyclically monotone. This ensures that $y^1 \in \partial_p^- \pi(p^1, q), y^2 \in \partial_p^- \pi(p^2, q)$ satisfy

$$(p^1 - p^2)(y^1 - y^2) \geq 0,$$

and $x^1 \in -\partial_q^- \pi(p, q^1), x^2 \in -\partial_q^- \pi(p, q^2)$ satisfy

$$(q^1 - q^2)(x^1 - x^2) \leq 0.$$

In words, supply correspondences vary positively with output price changes, and derived-demand correspondences vary inversely with input price changes. More familiarly, supply curves don't slope downward, and derived-demand curves don't slope upward.

Problem 40. *The sublinearity of $\pi(p, q)$ and Lemma 5 imply that $\pi(p, q)$ is the support function for the set*

$$T = \{(y, x) : p^\top y - q^\top x \leq \pi(p, q) \text{ for all } (p, q)\}.$$

Derive the properties of T and then discuss the economic intuition behind T.

Problem 41. *Suppose that $\pi(p, q)$ is twice continuously differentiable in all its arguments. Develop the consequences of the sublinearity of $\pi(p, q)$ for its Hessian matrix in (p, q). After this has been done, use Hotelling's Lemma and Shephard's Lemma to make inferences about the cross-price effects of the optimal solutions for the profit-maximizing problem. Provide a thorough economic explanation for each result.*

5 Superdifferentials, Subdifferentials, and Economic Behavior

If you systematically replaced the superdifferentials or subdifferentials in this chapter with gradients, relatively little would change. There would be simple cases (for example, affine or L-shaped level sets) that you couldn't handle properly. But in such instances the combination of a simple picture and a little handwaving should set you approximately straight. Even if you can't get the details straight, you get the gist of the argument.

So, if you can understand the basics only using the calculus, why bother with superdifferentials, subdifferentials, one-side directional derivatives and the like? If you have the mental discipline to avoid *the seductiveness of differentiability*, you might not need to bother. But if you don't, then you probably should.

What do I mean by the *seductiveness of differentiability*? Perhaps the best way to explain is to relate briefly a story that I once heard, although I can no longer remember from whom or the specific details. Anyway, the story runs like this: A very famous economist was challenged that his models did not fit the real-world facts. The purported response: "So much the worse for the real world." I have no way of verifying the veracity of this story, but it's surely indicative of a view many noneconomists (particularly sociologists and historians) seem to have of professional economists. And if you believe as I do that addressing real-world problems is what economics is really about, it's not very flattering.

I relate this story because experience has taught me that many of us applied economists frequently manifest a similar attitude. That's because very often our understanding of economics is so firmly grounded in calculus-based arguments that we often view nonsmooth behavior as contradictive of or a challenge to basic microeconomic theory. Few, if any, of us would be surprised to learn that in making a cake, it doesn't make sense to respond to a rise in the price of sugar by increasing the amount of flour. You can do that, but the result is a different-tasting product. On the other hand, if the literature on the divergence between willingness-to-accept and willingness-to-pay taught us anything, it's that many of us were genuinely surprised to learn that individuals frequently are willing to buy and sell at quite different prices because that seems to contradict what smooth theory predicts. The problem, of course, is that this is something we routinely observe in a variety of different settings. So, are we to conclude, as some have suggested, that these individuals are irrational?[17] If you've been seduced by the calculus to believe in immediate responsiveness, you might be so inclined, and many were. But if you view the world in the terms treated here, such behavior is not particularly surprising. It's exactly the type of behavior that superdifferentials or subdifferentials capture. Individuals can be operating at well-defined extrema, but those extrema may not be as locally sensitive as the calculus would suggest. Rationality and smoothness are not the same thing. It can be perfectly rational to hesitate or to refuse to trade even if smooth models suggest otherwise.

6 Chapter Commentary

The goal of this chapter is to translate the largely mathematical material in Chapters 2 and 3 into generic economic analyses familiar to microeconomists. Those analyses assume that agents optimize taking prices as given. Thus, the setting is that of a stylized competitive market. And the criterion-motivating individual behavior is rationality, which is interpreted mathematically as optimizing subject to various constraints. That's an unabashedly neoclassical perspective that relies on a legion of intellectual antecedents. Looking at matters in terms of conjugates is, perhaps, novel, but the ideas are well known and available in a variety of texts. The problems analyzed are the same as those in McFadden (1978). His summary of the argument bears repeating: "The definition of the cost function as the result of an optimization yields strong mathematical properties, and establishes the cost function as a 'sufficient statistic' for all the economically relevant characteristics of the underlying technology." Once you suitably substitute "cost function" and "underlying technology" for the relevant counterparts, the argument remains the same. Economic properties follow from the optimization hypothesis and the perceived market environment, and not from the structure imposed on technologies and/or preferences.

[17] For example, Coursey, Hovis, and Schulze (1987, p. 679) wrote: "Economic theory would suggest that individuals who exhibit a large disparity between WTP and WTA. . . . are behaving in an irrational manner." For more on this controversy, please see the related discussion in Chapter 10.

5
The Consumer Problem

The classic consumer problem is to allocate a fixed money income, $m \in \mathbb{R}_{+}$, among N commodities whose prices are given by $p^{*} \in \mathbb{R}_{++}^{N}$. In this chapter, we study that problem for an individual whose preference structure is given by $\succeq (y)$ where x and $y \in \mathbb{R}_{+}^{N}$. Throughout this chapter, assume that $\succeq (y)$ is continuous (C), transitive, and strictly monotonic in the sense that

$$y + \delta \succ (y), \qquad \delta \in \mathbb{R}_{+}^{N} \setminus \{0\},$$

where $\succ$ is to be read as *strictly better than*, which is taken to mean that

$$y + \delta \succeq (y) \text{ but } \neg y \succeq (y + \delta),$$

where $\neg$ denotes negation of the statement that follows, so that $\neg y \succeq (y + \delta)$ reads y is not at least as good as $y+\delta$. Strict monotonicity is invoked to simplify arguments. It can be relaxed, and essentially identical results are obtained. The generality gain, however, doesn't merit the bother. We write $x \sim (y)$, and say x and y are *indifferent*, if

$$x \succeq (y) \text{ and } y \succeq (x).$$

In one sense, I have just provided enough information to interpret precisely what the binary relation $\succeq (y)$ means in a consumer choice setting. Think again! Read carefully: All it really says is that comparisons of two N-dimensional vectors must obey certain rules. Nowhere have we detailed exactly what goes into each of those two vectors and what the decision framework really looks like. Let's take a simple example, comparing bundles of two goods, peanut-butter sandwiches and potato chips. That seems pretty clear, but really it's quite vague because we all know that both peanut butter and potato chips come in many different varieties. And speaking personally, I don't consider a peanut-butter sandwich made with *Skippy*© brand peanut butter to be the same thing as one made with *Jif*© even if both are made from identical bread. The same is true for potato chips, *Utz*© brand potato chips

Competitive Agents in Certain and Uncertain Markets. Robert G. Chambers, Oxford University Press (2021).

DOI: 10.1093/oso/9780190063016.001.0001

differ from *Lays*©. Thus, while the mathematical meaning of an element of $\mathbb{R}$ is precisely defined, its economic interpretation, especially in empirical settings, often is not. For the comparisons to be meaningful, the nth element of, say, y must contain *exactly* the same product as that in the *nth* element of x. The only way in which those components are allowed to differ is in quantity. In all other dimensions, they must be identical. Thus, our formal model is operating in very narrow and specific terms, where all potential sources of difference in products are recognized and properly taken into account.

In Einstein's model of the physical universe, in which I presume we operate, time is a dimension and thus a source of product variation. Thus, proper comparability only holds if time is held constant. After all, a candy bar now when you are hungry is not the same thing later when you're not. That doesn't mean intertemporal comparisons are necessarily ruled out, but if they are permitted, N must be chosen with care so that commodities can be properly indexed according to this dimension as well. This quickly leads us to infinite dimensional analysis, and so for the sake of brevity we assume here that all comparisons are for a given period in time. In other words, the theorizing we're doing is for a "timeless" economy. Unfortunately, when it comes to applying the theory, one rarely has the luxury of using data generated in a timeless setting.

It's also important in comparing, for example, x and y that the individual actually understands the true comparison. On paper, this is an easy assumption to make. But ensuring its relevance in a practical setting is something else. Psychologists have repeatedly shown economists that the context and the manner in which alternatives are framed play an important role in individual choice. No matter how precise one tries to be, actual experiences are always encountered in various shades of gray determined by their context and not in black and white as the mathematical manipulations require. One catchword for such effects is the "framing" of decisions. And because some quite famous economists have been caught out by framing effects, it's best neither to ignore nor to discount their practical importance. If the preference model, especially one that invokes transitivity, is to make any sense at all, the notation and the mathematical manipulations must be interpreted as only truly applying to a stylized setting where all such matters have been properly accounted for.

Right now, and probably for a long time to come, total control of an empirical setting that permits examining the theory in the formal terms in which it is cast seems out of reach. That's not a license to avoid either theorizing or empiricizing. Both are important, but imperfect, tools for the applied economist. Also, each has its own role to play in enhancing our understanding of the economic universe and for designing even better tools with which to examine it.

One way to think of the problem is that if the manipulations are done correctly, and there are no mathematical errors, the model must be correct. But being correct is not the same thing as being useful in a practical setting that departs from our idealized setting. For the model to be useful in that sense, its results should conform enough with realistic outcomes that we can reasonably order our thinking about economic phenomena AS IF the stylized world prevails.

1 The Budget Correspondence

Consumption possibilities for given p^* and m are given by the budget correspondence, $B^* : \mathbb{R}_+^{N+1} \rightrightarrows \mathbb{R}_+^N$:

$$B^*(p^*, m) = \{x \in \mathbb{R}_+^N : p^{*\top}x \leq m\}.$$

In words, $B^*(p^*, m)$ gives the consumption bundles that are affordable out of money income of when prices are p^*. For $m > 0$, $B^*(p^*, m)$ is nonempty, bounded, closed, and convex. Moreover,

$$\begin{aligned} B^*(p^*, m) &= \left\{x \in \mathbb{R}_+^N : \frac{p^*}{m}^{\top} x \leq 1\right\} \\ &= B^*\left(\frac{p^*}{m}, 1\right) \\ &\equiv B\left(\frac{p^*}{m}\right), \end{aligned}$$

where $B : \mathbb{R}_+^N \rightrightarrows \mathbb{R}_+^N$. Without true loss of generality, therefore, attention is restricted to normalized prices

$$p \equiv \frac{p^*}{m},$$

and $B(p)$.

Define the *budget-shortage function* as

$$\begin{aligned} b(x, p; g) &\equiv \min\{\beta \in \mathbb{R} : p^{\top}(x - \beta g) \leq 1\} \\ &= \min\left\{\beta \in \mathbb{R} : \frac{p^{\top}x - 1}{p^{\top}g} \leq \beta\right\} \\ &= \frac{p^{\top}x - 1}{p^{\top}g}. \end{aligned}$$

Its convex conjugate is

$$\begin{aligned} b^*(\hat{p},p;g) &= \sup_x \{\hat{p}^\top x - b(x,p;g)\} \\ &= \sup_x \left\{\hat{p}^\top x - \frac{p^\top x - 1}{p^\top g}\right\} \\ &= \begin{cases} \frac{1}{p^\top g} & \hat{p} = \frac{p}{p^\top g} \\ \infty & \text{otherwise} \end{cases}. \end{aligned}$$

Exercise 19. *Prove that* $x \in B(p) \Leftrightarrow b(x,p;g) \le 0$.

2 Rational Demand

The consumer decision problem is typically framed as maximizing utility subject to a budget constraint. But we have not introduced a utility function. Thus, we start our analysis by assuming that individual choice is guided by a more basic choice criterion. Namely, when faced with $B(p)$, a *rational individual* never chooses a consumption vector that is dominated by another feasible consumption vector. More formally:

Rationality Postulate: A feasible consumption vector $y \in B(p)$ is a *rational demand* only if there exists no $x \in B(p)$ such that

$$x \succ (y).$$

A definition facilitates characterizing rational-demand structures.

Definition 2. $y \in \mathbb{R}^N$ *is zero minimal for the problem*

$$\min_{x \in \mathbb{R}^N} \{f(x,y)\}$$

where $f: \mathbb{R}^N \times \mathbb{R}^N \to \mathbb{R}$ *if*

$$0 = f(y,y) \le f(x,y) \text{ for all } x \in \mathbb{R}^N.$$

$y \in \mathbb{R}^N$ *is zero maximal for the problem*

$$\max_{x \in \mathbb{R}^N} \{g(x,y)\}$$

if

$$0 = g(y, y) \geq g(x, y) \text{ for all } x \in \mathbb{R}^N.$$

We have:[1]

Theorem 9. *$y \in B(p)$ is a rational demand if and only if y is zero minimal for*

$$\begin{aligned}\min_{x \in \mathbb{R}_+^N} \{b(x, p; g) - d(x, y; g)\} &= \min_{x \in \mathbb{R}_+^N} \left\{ \frac{p^\top x - 1}{p^\top g} - d(x, y; g) \right\} \\ &= \min_{x \in \mathbb{R}_+^N} \left\{ \frac{p^\top x}{p^\top g} - d(x, y; g) \right\} - \frac{1}{p^\top g}.\end{aligned}$$

Proof. ⇒If we suppose that y is rational, it must be true that $b(y, p; g) = 0$. If $b(y, p; g) > 0$, it is not feasible. If $b(y, p; g) < 0$, $y - \frac{b(y,p;g)}{2} g$ is feasible and $d\left(y - \frac{b(y,p;g)}{2} g, y; g\right) > 0$, which represents an improvement. This contradicts the presumed rationality of y. Hence, if y is rational

$$b(y, p; g) - d(y, y; g) = 0.$$

Now suppose an x exists such that

$$b(x, p; g) - d(x, y; g) < 0,$$

which contradicts zero minimality of y. Then by the Translation Property applied to d

$$d(x - b(x, p; g) g, y; g) = d(x, y; g) - b(x, p; g) > 0,$$

with $x - b(x, g; g) g$ budget feasible. This contradicts the presumed rationality of y. Hence, if $y \in B(p)$ is rational,

$$b(x, p; g) - d(x, y; g) \geq 0$$

for all x. But, as shown, for y rational $b(y, p; g) - d(y, y; g) = 0$, proving zero minimality.

[1] The technique used here in establishing the equivalence of rational demand and zero minimality is borrowed from arguments made in a different context by Luenberger (1992b).

⇐To prove that zero minimality implies $y \in B(p)$ is rational, suppose zero minimality but that $y \in B(p)$ is not rational. There then exists an $x \in B(p)$ such that

$$\frac{p^{\top}x - 1}{p^{\top}g} \leq 0,$$

and

$$d(x, y; g) > 0,$$

which contradicts zero minimality. □

Remark 12. *Writing*

$$x_d - x_b = 0$$

gives

$$\min_{x_b, x_d \in \mathbb{R}^N_+} \{b(x_b, p; g) - d(x_d, y; g) : x_d - x_b = 0\} = \min_{x \in \mathbb{R}^N_+} \{b(x, p; g) - d(x, y; g)\}$$

so that Theorem 9 can be recast as: $y \in B(p)$ is a rational demand if and only if y solves an infimal convolution problem and the infimal convolution equals zero. The basic idea that equilibria can be identified by solving either an infimal convolution or a supremal convolution will be repeated multiple times in what follows.

Before discussing Theorem 9 intuitively, it's important to discriminate between what it does and what it doesn't accomplish. It provides necessary and sufficient conditions for rationality of y. Therefore, it identifies circumstances in which clearly enumerated criteria can be used to determine whether a particular y is rational. However, it does not provide a traditional calculating formula for determining a rational y because the indicated *optimization is always conditioned on y.* Hence, zero minimality here is better interpreted as providing a way, based on an optimization argument, to "check" whether a particular y is rational.

Intuitively, Theorem 9 is simple enough. For strictly monotonic preferences, rationality requires that a consumer simultaneously operates on the frontier of both the budget set and the at-least-as-good set. For a given x,

$b(x,p;g) - d(x,y;g)$ measures the difference between how far x is from the boundary of $B(p)$ and how far it is from the boundary of $V(y)$. Because rational y needs to lie on both frontiers, the distance to each should be zero, and thus the differences between the distances should also be zero.

Bundles that are inside both the budget set and above the least-as-good frontier satisfy

$$b(x,p;g) - d(x,y;g) \leq 0.$$

If the individual is strictly inside the budget set but on the frontier of the least-as-good set, leaving this inequality strictly negative, the consumer can afford to purchase a commodity bundle that strictly dominates y signaling that y is not rational. On the other hand, if the consumer is on the frontier of the budget set but strictly inside the least-as-good set for y, strict monotonicity ensures he or she can do better than y.

The second equality in Theorem 9 implies that rational-demand theory is treatable using the theory of concave conjugates and, thus, is a special case of the McKenzie expenditure-minimization problem. Therefore, everything that was said about McKenzie demand correspondences applies to rational-demand behavior. Visually, equilibrium rational-demand behavior is that illustrated by Figure 1.2, where a level curve representing $\bar{V}(y)$ just "kisses" the frontier of the budget set represented as the line segment. A bit more formally,

Corollary 3. *$y \in B(p)$ is an interior rational demand if and only if*

$$E(p;y) = 1,$$

$$\frac{p}{p^{\top}g} \in \partial d(y,y;g), \textit{ and}$$

$$y \in \partial E\left(\frac{p}{p^{\top}g};y\right).$$

Corollary 3 emphasizes an essential point. Analysis of the consumer's problem can be broken into two stages. First, one analyzes the McKenzie expenditure problem for an arbitrary $y \in \mathbb{R}^N_+$ to obtain demands that are conditional upon y (hence, *y-compensated demands*)-while being cyclically monotone in $\frac{p}{p^{\top}g}$. Once that's done, one checks y's consistency with the budget constraint. This is exactly analogous to the standard utility-function approach to demand theory. First, analyze Hicksian-compensated demand behavior via the utility-constant expenditure function and then ensure utility's consistency with the budget constraint. (See Section 6 below for more detail.) The difference is that rather than rely on the analytic, but imaginary, concept of "utility" that "aggregrates y," we rely on y itself.

This decomposition, as with many others in economics, is an AS IF analytic device. The argument is not that individuals act in this manner. Instead, the argument is that rational individual behavior is indistinguishable from that of one who does. And thus analyzing behavior as if individuals acted in this fashion involves no true loss of generaltiy. The usefulness of such AS IF devices lies not in exactly *describing* economic behavior but in promoting our ability to comprehend and ultimately *explain* economic behavior.

Decomposing demand decisions in this fashion seems attributable to Antonelli (1886), Slutsky (1915), and Hicks and Allen (1934).[2] The essential point is simple. y is rational only if it is the *cheapest* way, given prices p, to leave you at least as good as y. If there were a cheaper way, y could never be rational. This merits the focus on that particular y and implicitly on $\bar{V}(y)$. *Here it is essential that you not only recall but revisit Lemma 8 and the associated discussion.*

The demands captured by

$$y \in \partial E\left(\frac{p}{p^{\top} g}; y\right),$$

with $E(p; y) = 1$ are analogous to *Marshallian (Walrasian) demands* chosen to maximize utility subject to a budget constraint. If y is a McKenzie demand for itself and exhausts income, it is rational. This doesn't require y to be the only McKenzie demand for y at $\frac{p}{p^{\top} g}$. Depending on $\succeq(y)$, others might exist (see Example 9 below), but all must be McKenzie demands and together they must cost the same as y.

3 Price-Dependent Rational Demand

Provided $d(x, y; g)$ is concave in x, Fenchel's Duality Theorem (2.24) and Theorem 9 imply:

[2] Here, I presume you are already familiar with Hicksian-compensated demands and the Slutsky equation. If you're not, see Section 6 below.

Corollary 4. *$y \in B(p)$ is a rational demand if and only if $\frac{p}{p^{\top}g}$ is zero maximal for*

$$\max_{\hat{p}\in\mathbb{R}^N_+}\{d^*(\hat{p},y;g)-b^*(\hat{p},p;g)\}=\max_{\hat{p}\in\mathbb{R}^N_+}\{E(\hat{p},y)-b^*(\hat{p},p;g)\},$$

with $d^*(\hat{p},y;g)$ the concave conjugate of $d(x,y;g)$.

Corollary 4 presents a different perspective on the requirements for demand rationality. Demand y is rational only if the real prices that support it ensure that McKenzie expenditure exhaust real income, $E(\hat{p};y)=\frac{1}{p^{\top}g}$. This *price-dependent demand* perspective views quantities, y, as predetermined and elicits the consumer's *marginal willingnesses-to-pay* (read prices) for each commodity that ensure real income is exhausted.

The differential conditions for zero maximality require

$$\partial E\left(\frac{p}{p^{\top}g},y\right)\cap\partial b^*\left(\frac{p}{p^{\top}g},p;g\right)\neq\emptyset,$$

or equivalently

$$y\in\partial E\left(\frac{p}{p^{\top}g},y\right),$$

and

$$E\left(\frac{p}{p^{\top}g},y\right)=\frac{1}{p^{\top}g}\Leftrightarrow E(p,y)=1.$$

Naturally, this just repeats Corollary 3.

Solutions to this problem are referred to as *rational price-dependent demands.* As is usual with dual systems, these solutions are obtained via the general envelope relationship, Theorem 6, as

$$\frac{p}{p^{\top}g}\in\partial d^{**}(y,y;g).$$

When $d(x,y;g)$ is concave, $d=d^{**}$, so that $\partial d(y,y;g)$ is then the lower inverse of the McKenzie demand correspondence

$$\partial d(y,y;g)=\left\{\frac{p}{p^{\top}g}:y\in\partial E\left(\frac{p}{p^{\top}g};y\right)\right\}.$$

For this reason, price-dependent demands are often referred to as *inverse demands* or *indirect demands.*

When $d(x, y; g)$ is concave, our duality results ensure that the budget constraint and

$$\frac{p}{p^\top g} \in \partial d(y, y; g), \qquad \text{(Wold's Identity)} \qquad (5.1)$$

exhaustively characterize rational price-dependent demand behavior. This is the dual reflection of $\partial E\left(\frac{p}{p^\top g}; y\right)$ characterizing rational (quantity-dependent) demand behavior. *Wold's Identity,* therefore, rationalizes a system of price-dependent rational demands with predictable properties dual to those associated with the (quantity-dependent) rational demands. And just as $\partial E\left(\frac{p}{p^\top g}; y\right)$ represents a system of y-compensated demand curves, $\partial d(x, y; g)$ represents a system of *y-compensated price-dependent demands* (the *Antonelli demands*) that correspond to rational demands when $x = y$. Concavity of $d(x, y; g)$ ensures cyclical monotonicity of $\partial d(x, y; g)$. That is, for $q^k \in \partial d(x^k, y; g)$

$$(q^2 - q^1)^\top x^1 + (q^3 - q^2)^\top x^2 + \ldots + (q^1 - q^H)^\top x^H \geq 0,$$

and for $H = 2$

$$(q^2 - q^1)^\top (x^2 - x^1) \leq 0.$$

Antonelli demands are downward sloping in their own quantities. As you are asked to buy more and more of a commodity, your marginal willingness-to-pay decreases.

4 What's Rational?

If you know $\succeq(y)$ and $B(p)$, you can determine what is a rational-demand structure. But there's a catch. The knowledge may prove uninformative. An example illustrates.

Example 9. *Suppose* $d(x, y; g) = \min\left\{\frac{x_1-y_1}{g_1}, \ldots, \frac{x_N-y_N}{g_N}\right\}$. *This satisfies all maintained assumptions, except strict monotonicity. It's also concave. By Corollary 3, rational demands must satisfy Wold's Identity*

$$\frac{p}{p^{\top}g} \in \partial d(y, y; g).$$

For this preference structure, that requires

$$\frac{p}{p^{\top}g}^{\top}(x-y) \geq \min\left\{\frac{x_1-y_1}{g_1}, \ldots, \frac{x_N-y_N}{g_N}\right\},$$

for all x. However, for $g \in \mathbb{R}^N_{++}$, *this condition can always be rewritten as*

$$\sum_n \frac{p_n g_n}{p^{\top}g}\frac{(x_n-y_n)}{g_n} \geq \min\left\{\frac{x_1-y_1}{g_1}, \ldots, \frac{x_N-y_N}{g_N}\right\},$$

for all x. This is always true, so that

$$E(p, y) = p^{\top}y,$$

and the rational demands for $B(p)$ *are*

$$\bar{B}(p) = \{x : p^{\top}x = 1\}.$$

Thus, any $y \in \bar{B}(p)$ *is rational and exhibits no y-compensated price responsiveness.*

Everything that exhausts the budget constraint is rational for $\geq$. Thus, *a monotonic, convex from above, and reflexive order always exists that "rationalizes" any observed demand that exhausts the budget.* Because the associated order is $\geq$, that's not suprising. But it also means that the only criterion upon which to discriminate rational-demand behavior from *irrational*-demand behavior is whether an individual exhausts his or her budget. That leaves one dangerously close to having a theory that explains everything, which if we are to believe Popper means that it risks explaining nothing. And that leads us directly to utility functions.

5 A Utility Function?

Utility theory entered economics in the last part of the nineteenth century as an offshoot of the psychological doctrine of *hedonism (utilitarianism)*. The basic premise of hedonism is that individual behavior is driven by pleasure seeking and/or pain avoidance. The seemingly natural next steps were to identify pleasure with commodity consumption and to make utility a function of consumption. F. Y. Edgeworth (1881) then revolutionized formal economic analysis by using these utility functions to induce *indifference curves*.

Early writers took the existence of utility functions for granted. Moreover, utility was presumed to be measurable and, therefore, comparable across individuals. Gradually, both measurable and comparable utility fell into disrepute. Instead, attention was focused increasingly on Edgeworth's indifference curves expressed in terms of (unit-free) ratios of marginal utility and their comparison to market-based prices ratios. When Paul Samuelson (1938) unveiled what became known as the "revealed-preference approach," his stated goal was to remove "the last vestiges of utility analysis" from the pure theory of consumer behavior. Vestigial or not, eight decades on, utility functions still form the hard core of consumer theory.

We've not yet used utility functions. They've been referred to in passing, but only because they and their related concepts are so deeply entrenched in economic jargon that avoidance is impossible. One reason to resist the virtually irresistable impulse economists have to develop consumer theory in terms of utility is to reemphasize the essentially identical superstructure that supports seemingly disparate economic problems. Another is that rationalizing utility functions requires an assumption that many find problematic but that isn't associated with either measurability or comparability concerns. The issue is more basic and arises from the demands the assumption places on one's ability to compare different economic alternatives.

Many of us are unable to choose between two alternatives. If a utility function exists, such indecision reflects indifference. But speaking for myself, often I've been unable to choose simply because I couldn't properly compare the alternatives. That's especially true when the alternatives are unfamiliar. Imagine, for example, presenting a primitive man with a choice between an iPhone© or an Android© phone. Roughly translated, I would expect the answer to be "Huh?" Does that mean that the individual is irrational? I would argue not. Does it mean that the individual is truly indifferent? One could rationalize such behavior as indifference, but that threatens to erase the line between sophistry and science. Permitting the possibility that some things can't be compared, which we have so far done, seems both simpler and more realistic. Even Leonard Savage (1917–1971; the father of modern decision theory) opined that

> [t]here is some temptation to explore the possibilities of analyzing preference among acts as a *partial ordering*, ... admitting that some pairs of acts are incomparable. This would seem to give expression to introspective sensations of indecision or vacillation, which we may be reluctant to identify with indifference. (1954, p. 21, emphasis in original)

And so, our arguments have proceeded without using utility functions. But having done so, we've seen that the truly *predictable* components of rational-demand behavior, as encapsulated in $E(p,y)$ and its superdifferential $\partial E(p,y)$, are isomorphic to those obtained for Marshallian demand behavior. *All of the strong results available can be developed without a utility function.* Thus, specific results that are available using a utility function may prove robust to relaxing that assumption. Rather than weakening the case for using utility functions in demand analysis, this finding actually strengthens it because it suggests that regardless of whether individuals do possess and maximize a utility function, our analysis loses no true generality in assuming that individuals act AS IF this were true. And where rational-demand theory struggles to determine unique demand structures, a utility-based approach cuts that "Gordian Knot" by presuming all incomparability is removed.

The assumption that we have avoided is that $\succeq(y)$ is *complete.* That is, either

$$x \succeq (y),$$

or

$$y \succeq (x)$$

must be true for all $x, y \in \mathbb{R}_+^N$. All possible alternatives can be ranked, no matter how disparate or unfamiliar. One can easily visualize the difference between an incomplete $\succeq(y)$ and one that is complete with the aid of Figure 5.1. Figure 5.1 depicts $V(y)$ and $Y(y)$ for an incomplete preference ordering. As is apparent from the illustration, there are points $z \in \mathbb{R}_+^N$ (for example, those in the shaded areas) that do not fall in either the least-as-good or no-better-than sets for the chosen y. Because these points cannot be ranked relative to y, the underlying order does not completely order $\mathbb{R}_+^N \times \mathbb{R}_+^N$. The

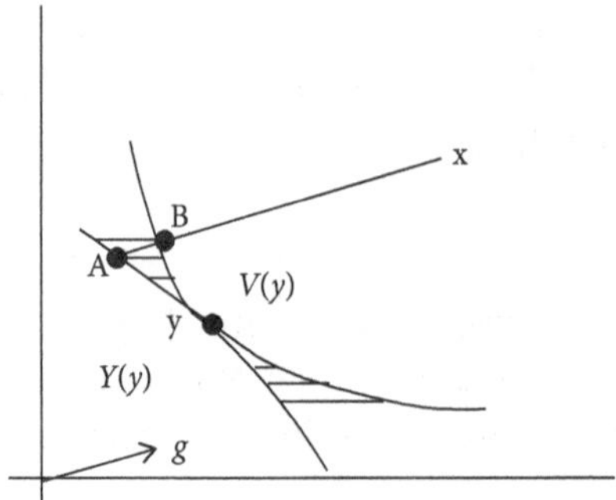

Fig. 5.1 An Incomplete Preference Order

preference order would be complete if all points, say, not falling in $Y(y)$ fell in $V(y)$ so that the two sets (assuming continuity) shared a common boundary.

Assumption: (CO) $\succeq(y)$ *satisfies complete ordering if* $\succeq(y)$ either

$$x \succeq (y),$$

or

$$y \succeq (x)$$

must be true for all $x, y \in \mathbb{R}_+^N$.

Now that we've agreed that we're going to construct a utility function, the next logical question is how to do it. I intend to use some old friends. The specific goal is to show that there exists a function $U : \mathbb{R}_+^N \to \mathbb{R}$ such that:

$$U(x) \geq U(y) \Leftrightarrow x \succeq (y).$$

The old friends are

$$d(x, y; g) = \max\{\beta \in \mathbb{R} : x - \beta g \in V(y)\}$$

and

$$t(y, x; g) = \min\{\beta \in \mathbb{R} : y - \beta g \in Y(x)\},$$

where g is the same in both cases and $g \in \mathbb{R}_{++}^N$.

Returning to Figure 5.1, one sees that for the illustrated x and g, $x - d(x,y;g)g$ brings us to point B while $x - t(x,y;g)g$ brings us to point A. Because preferences are incomplete, these points differ. However, if the shaded areas separating $Y(y)$ and $V(y)$ were eliminated, and a common boundary separated the two sets, A and B would be identical-requiring that $d(x,y;g) = t(x,y;g)$. In fact, requiring this equality to hold everywhere characterizes complete preference structures. We have:

Theorem 10. *A transitive, continuous and strictly monotonic* $\succeq(y)$ *satisfies CO on* $\mathbb{R}^N \times \mathbb{R}^N$ *if and only if* $d(x,y;g) = t(x,y;g)$ *for all* x *and* y.

Proof. Assume for arbitrary x that $d(x,y;g) = t(x,y;g)$. There are two possibilities, either both are nonnegative or both are negative. If both are nonnegative, then $d(x,y;g) \geq 0$ and Indication as in Lemma 7 implies that $x \succeq (y)$. If they are both negative, then $t(x,y;g) < 0$ and Indication as in Lemma 9 implies $y \succeq (x)$. Hence, $\succeq(y)$ must be complete. To go the other way, suppose that the structure is complete and suppose without loss of generality that $d(x,y;g) > t(x,y;g)$. Then it must be true by strict monotonicity that $d(x - t(x,y;g)g, y;g) > d(x - d(x,y;g)g, y;g) = 0$. Strict monotoncity and Indication in Lemmata 7 and 9 require simultaneously that $y \succeq (x - t(x,y;g)g) \succ (y)$, which establishes a contradiction. □

We can now use Theorem 10 to construct a utility function for $\succeq(y)$. As it turns out, the one constructed is *cardinal*—that despite the fact that we have not assumed that preferences are cardinal. This may seem paradoxical, but it's not. What economists really mean when they speak of assuming a *cardinal preference structure* is to assume that preferences are characterized completely by a *unique* cardinal (numeric) utility function that can be added and subtracted. We haven't done that. Instead, we've worked from the more primitive $\succeq(y)$ structure and shown that an appropriate version of monotonicity (actually an extremely weak version) suffices to guarantee the existence of a cardinal representation that completely characterizes $\succeq(y)$. But that cardinal representation is not a utility function, and indeed it need not be unique. In fact, if we employ the standard notion of monotonicity (M), it turns out that an infinity of such representations exist, each corresponding to a different choice of a numeraire. Instead of measuring utility, it measures the individual's willingness-to-pay to move from 0 to y in the units of the numeraire bundle. If we choose to call the result a utility function, doing so does not change its essential nature.

We choose to work with $d(0, y; g)$, which by Theorem 10 corresponds to $t(0, y; g)$. We have that

$$\begin{aligned} d(0, y; g) &= \max\{\beta \in \mathbb{R} : -\beta g \in V(y)\} \\ &= \max\{-\gamma \in \mathbb{R} : \gamma g \in V(y)\} \\ &= -\min\{\gamma \in \mathbb{R} : \gamma g \in V(y)\} \\ &\equiv -u(y; g), \end{aligned}$$

where $u(y; g)$ can be thought of as the *upper g-equivalent of y* and gives *the smallest number of units of the numeraire bundle that would leave the individual in the at-least-as-good set for y.*[3] All that remains now is to demonstrate that

$$\begin{gathered} -d(0, x; g) = u(x; g) \geq u(y; g) = -d(0, y; g) \\ \Updownarrow \\ x \succeq (y), \end{gathered}$$

so that $u(x; g)$ can be meaningfully interpreted as a utility function. To go one way, suppose $x \succeq (y)$. Strict monotoncity and transitivity require

$$-d(0, x; g)\, g \sim x \succeq (y) \sim -d(0, y; g)\, g$$

and $-d(0, x; g) \geq -d(0, y; g)$. Now suppose that $-d(0, x; g) \geq -d(0, y; g)$, uniqueness and strict monotonicity then ensure

$$x \sim -d(0, x; g)\, g \succeq -d(0, y; g)\, g \sim y,$$

and we are done.

Problem 42. *Use $t(0, y; g)$ to develop and characterize a cardinal utility function. Discuss the "intuitive" difference between it and $u(x; g)$.*

Distance functions generate utility functions under complete ordering (CO). In one sense, this isn't surprising. One can always think of a utility function as a willingness-to-pay (or accept) for y expressed in imaginary units that economists fondly refer to as *utils.* All we've done is to show that

[3] You may already be familiar with the notion of a *certainty equivalent* of a gamble. It is the special case of a g-equivalent that gives the smallest amount of the sure thing that is indifferent to the gamble. More on this connection later.

those *utils* can be translated into g-equivalent units. Our utility function is developed by using a tool for making *two-way comparisons* (x versus y) to make *a three-way comparison* (x versus 0, y versus 0, and then rank the results). This captures the essence of what complete ordering means. Written in terms of $d(x, y; g)$, complete ordering requires that for all $x, y \in \mathbb{R}_+^N$ either

$$d(x, y; g) \geq 0,$$

or

$$d(y, x; g) \geq 0,$$

must be true. Thus, if $d(x, y; g) < 0$, complete ordering (CO) ensures that $d(y, x; g) \geq 0$.

6 Marshallian Demand and the Slutsky–Hicks Equation

Let's agree that an ordinal "utility representation" exists that we shall denote by $U(y)$. As the previous section demonstrates, that structure could always be represented by $d(0, y; g)$ for an appropriate g, but consistency with established tradition elsewhere is better served by using U. This section studies the relationship between rational and McKenzie demand structures on the one hand and Marshallian and Hicksian-compensated demands on the other.

Marshallian demands are demands that have been chosen to maximize utility. That is, they are the solution to

$$\max_x \{U(x) : x \in B(p)\}.$$

Marshallian demands must be rational because they at least weakly dominate everything in $B(p)$. Because they're rational, they're also McKenzie demands by Corollary 3. Thus, Marshallian demand theory is rational demand theory for the special case of a utility function. The converse is not generally true. The existence of a McKenzie structure does not imply a Marshallian structure.

If a utility function exists,

$$\begin{aligned} E(p; y) &= \min_x \{p^\top x : x \succeq (y)\} \\ &= \min_x \{p^\top x : U(x) \geq U(y)\} \\ &= E^H(p; U(y)), \end{aligned} \tag{5.2}$$

where

$$E^H(p;u) \equiv \min_x \{p^\top x : U(x) \geq u\},$$

is the *Hicksian expenditure function*. Because it is a support function for, abusing notation,

$$V(u) = \{x : U(x) \geq u\},$$

E^H is superlinear in p and

$$E^H(p;u) = \delta^*(p \mid V^*(u)),$$

where

$$V^*(u) = \{x \in \mathbb{R}^N_+ : p^\top x \geq E^H(p;u) \text{ for all } p \in \mathbb{R}^N_+\},$$

and $V(u) \subset V^*(u)$. $E^H(p;u)$ is the consumer's *willingness-to-pay* (now measured in the same units in which p is denominated) for achieving utility level u. Thus, it is a cardinal measure of utility, and for that reason, it's often referred to as a *money-metric utility function.*

Brushing aside some mathematical detail, we'll assume that E^H is strictly increasing in u, which ensures: (a) that the marginal cost of an extra unit of u is strictly positive and (b) that the utility-maximization problem can be written

$$\max_u \{u : E^H(p;u) \leq 1\}.$$

The solution to this problem, called the *indirect utility function*, $I : \mathbb{R}^N_+ \to \mathbb{R}$, is the implicit solution to:

$$E^H(p; I(p)) = 1. \tag{5.3}$$

$I(p)$ represents the value of utility achieved from the optimal Marshallian demands. Letting

$$x^*(p) \in \arg\max \{U(x) : x \in B(p)\}$$

denote the Marshallian demands, that means $I(p) = U(x^*(p))$. Both $x^*(p)$ and $I(p)$ are obviously homogeneous of degree zero in p^* and m reflecting the property that nominal price and income changes do not affect the budget set. As a direct consequence of the fact that budget sets do not get larger as prices rise, $p' \geq p \Rightarrow I(p') \leq I(p)$.

Exercise 20. *Prove that* $B(p') \subset B(p)$ *for* $p' \geq p$.

That the indirect utility is nonincreasing in real prices is not surprising. If that weren't true, the underlying theory would necessarily be suspect because it would imply consumers like higher prices. A bit less obvious are the curvature properties of $I(p)$. We can't show that $I(p)$ is either convex or concave. But we can show that it is *quasi-convex* in p. That is,

$$I(p + \lambda(p' - p)) \leq \max\{I(p), I(p')\}, \quad \lambda \in (0, 1).$$

To derive this property, without loss of generality, take $I(p') \geq I(p)$. From our definitions, we know that

$$E^H(p; I(p)) = 1 = E^H(p'; I(p')), \tag{5.4}$$

and because E^H is strictly increasing in u, $I(p') \geq I(p)$ implies

$$E^H(p; I(p')) \geq 1. \tag{5.5}$$

Concavity of E^H in p, (5.4), and (5.5) together imply for $\lambda \in (0, 1)$ that

$$\begin{aligned} E^H(p + \lambda(p' - p), I(p')) &\geq E^H(p; I(p')) + \lambda(E^H(p'; I(p')) - E^H(p; I(p'))) \\ &\geq 1. \end{aligned}$$

Because $I(p + \lambda(p' - p))$ is determined by

$$E^H(p + \lambda(p' - p), I(p + \lambda(p' - p))) = 1,$$

strict monotonicity of E^H in u implies

$$I(p + \lambda(p' - p)) \leq I(p'),$$

as desired.

Intuitively, the two budget sets, $B(p)$ and $B(p')$, correspond to different sets of prices. Because $I(p') \geq I(p)$, $B(p')$ must be the *more favorable* in the eyes of the consumer. Quasi-convexity of $I(p)$ implies the consumer would rather stick with $B(p')$ than face any convex combination of $B(p)$ and $B(p')$.

So, quasi-convexity implies that *consumers lose from averaging more favorable budget sets with less favorable ones.* Waugh (1944), who discovered an early version of this result, suggested that it implied consumers were hurt by price-stabilization policies. Samuelson (1972) discredited this interpretation.

Exercise 21. *Visualizing the proof in the two-dimensional case should prove helpful. To that end, draw $B(p)$ and $B(p')$ so that they intersect, and then identify $I(p)$ and $I(p')$ via the usual tangency condition. Now draw $B(p+\lambda(p'-p))$ for $\lambda \in (0,1)$ and identify $I(p+\lambda(p'-p))$.*

We denote a *Hicksian-compensated demand* vector by $x^H(p;u)$ and note (from previous results) that

$$x^H(p;u) \in \arg\min_x \{p^\top x : U(x) \geq u\},$$

with $x^H(p;u) \in \partial E^H(p;u)$. Because $E^H(p;U(y)) = E(p;y)$, it follows immediately that Hicksian-compensated demands evaluated at $U(y)$ are simply McKenzie demands evaluated at y. Moreover, by the definition of $I(p)$, it's also true that Marshallian demands satisfy

$$x^*(p) = x^H(p; I(p)),$$

so that Marshallian demands can be interpreted as Hicksian-compensated demands evaluated at $I(p)$.

This manner of viewing Marshallian demands carries important analytic advantages. For example, for discrete price changes it implies that

$$\begin{aligned} x^*(p^o) - x^*(p) &= \overbrace{x^H(p^o; I(p^o)) - x^H(p^o; I(p))}^{\textit{income}} + \overbrace{x^H(p^o; I(p)) - x^H(p; I(p))}^{\textit{substitution}} \quad \text{Laspeyres} \\ &= \overbrace{x^H(p; I(p^o)) - x^H(p; I(p))}^{\textit{income}} + \overbrace{x^H(p^o; I(p^o)) - x^H(p; I(p^o))}^{\textit{substitution}} \quad \text{Paasche.} \end{aligned}$$

Marshallian demand adjustments to price changes can be decomposed into two components. There is a *u-compensated* component that describes adjustments to price change holding u constant. These involve what are referred to as *substitution effects* and involve movements along $\bar{V}(I(p))$ induced by the price change. In Figure 5.2, one would visualize the substitution process as the slope of the tangent line segment changing and leading to a new "kissing" tangency.

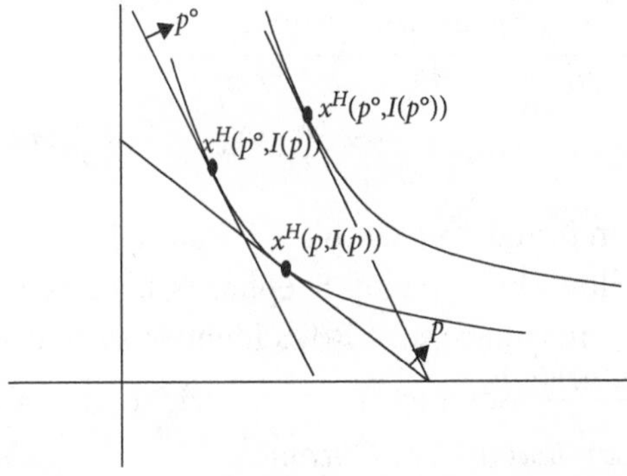

Fig. 5.2 u-compensated Demand Adjustment.

There is also the *real-income* effect, which is determined residually. It arises because price changes make an individual facing a fixed income (here held at one) either a bit richer or a bit poorer. One visualizes this in Figure 5.2 as the budget line pivoting outwards. That pivoting forces a rational individual off $\bar{V}(I(p))$ to a new one associated with $x(p^o)$. The real-income effect describes that movement, but now holding prices constant at p^o.

No doubt you will have noticed that the adjustment depicted in Figure 5.2 corresponds to what I have referred to as the Laspeyres version of the decomposition and not to the Paasche. The Laspeyres and Paasche jargon was chosen to remind the reader that, as with all such discrete decompositions, the labeling of effects is arbitrary and depends importantly on what one defines as the reference point. It only takes a second to verify, for example, that the Laspeyres substitution effect does not generally equal the Paasche substitution effect.

Problem 43. *Illustrate the Paasche version of the decomposition of $x^*(p) - x(p)$ and compare it to Figure 5.2. Derive necessary and sufficient conditions for*

$$x^H(p^o; I(p^o)) - x^H(p; I(p^o)) = x^H(p^o; I(p)) - x^H(p; I(p))$$

for all p, p^o.

Figure 5.2 treats discrete price changes. More normally, however, economists focus on differentially small changes when analyzing how consumers respond to price changes. So, for the remainder of this section, it's convenient to treat the arbitrarily smooth case. Differentiating (5.3) with respect to p_i and rearranging give:

$$-\frac{\partial E^H(p;I(p))}{\partial u}\frac{\partial I(p)}{\partial p_i} = \frac{\partial E^H(p;I(p))}{\partial p_i}$$
$$= x_i^*(p), \qquad \textit{(Roy's Identity)} \tag{5.6}$$

which is typically referred to (if a bit misleadingly) as *Roy's Identity.* The second equality follows by applying Shephard's Lemma in the smooth case to $E^H(p;I(p))$. You may have seen Roy's Identity written slightly differently. If so, recall that $\frac{\partial E^H(p;I(p))}{\partial u}$, which is the marginal cost of utility, is also the reciprocal of the *marginal utility of income.*

We're now ready to derive the *Slutsky–Hicks Equation*, which is the differential version of the decomposition of demand adjustments to price changes into two parts. Because,

$$x_i^*(p) = x_i^H(p, I(p)),$$

differentiation gives after substituting u for $I(p)$

$$\frac{\partial x_i^*(p)}{\partial p_j} = \frac{\partial x_i^H(p,u)}{\partial p_j} + \frac{\partial x_i^H(p,u)}{\partial u}\frac{\partial I(p)}{\partial p_j}$$
$$= \frac{\partial x_i^H(p,u)}{\partial p_j} - x_j^*(p)\frac{\partial x_i^H(p,u)/\partial u}{\partial E^H(p;u)/\partial u}, \tag{5.7}$$

where the second equality follows from Roy's Identity. This is the *Slutsky–Hicks Equation.*

The Slutsky–Hicks Equation reconfirms that demand adjustments can be broken into two parts. One, $\frac{\partial x_i^H(p,u)}{\partial p_j}$, is a *Hicksian-compensated* component that is usually identified as the *Hicksian substitution effect* (or more simply as the substitution effect). It corresponds to price-induced movements along an indifference curve, and it can be illustrated as in Figure 5.2. You will note that this part is extremely well behaved. Chapter 4 has shown us that these demands are homogeneous of degree zero and that demand curves are downward sloping. Cross-price effects are symmetric.

The second part, $-x_j^*(p)\frac{\partial x_i^H(p,u)/\partial u}{\partial E^H(p;u)/\partial u}$, is called the *income effect.* Intuitively, it too can be illustrated as in Figure 5.2. But there's a bit of a technical catch. Figure 5.2 depicts the income effect as $x^H(p^o;I(p^o)) - x^H(p^o;I(p))$, which is the difference in consumption at the new prices p^o attributable to the real-income change from $I(p)$ to $I(p^o)$. Expression (5.7) instead treats the income effect as $\frac{\partial x_i^H(p,u)}{\partial u}\frac{\partial I(p)}{\partial p_j}$, which is the difference in consumption evaluated at the original prices attributable to a real-income change. So, Figure 5.2 is perhaps better viewed as conveying the idea of what's involved in expression (5.7) rather than its actual content.

Income effects are typically messy and are the source of many "two-handed" answers. So, for example, if on the one hand a commodity is *normal*, raising real income (here we're talking u) raises its demand, so that $\partial x_i^H(p,u)/\partial u \geq 0$. Then, Marshallian demand curves are downward sloping in their own prices. But if on the other hand a commodity is inferior, things aren't so nice. In fact, one can even end up in "Giffen Land," where paradoxically

$$\frac{\partial x_i^*(p)}{\partial p_i} \geq 0.$$

The apocryphal example here involves Irish consumers and potatoes during the Great Potato Blight.

Exercise 22. *Here I have presumed that you know what is a normal commodity and what is an inferior commodity. Again, this should come from your background in basic intermediate micro. However, just to ensure that we continue to speak the same economic language, please discuss the concepts of of normal and inferior commodities and include an explanation of their underlying importance in the basic theory of consumer demand. As always, make the discussion both complete and completely intuitive.*

Remark 13. *A more standard presentation of the Slutsky–Hicks equation is in terms of demand functions expressed in terms of unnormalized prices, p^*, and nominal income, m. Slightly abusing notation, we have that indirect utility is now expressed as*

$$I(p^*,m) = \max\{u : E^H(p^*,u) = m\}.$$

This requires rewriting the Marshallian demand and Hicksian-compensated demands as requiring, again abusing notation,

$$x^*(p^*,m) = x^H(p^*; I(p^*,m)).$$

But it's also true that

$$x^H(p^*;u) = x^*(p^*, E^H(p^*,u)).$$

Both demand expressions contain the same information expressed in different form. Differentiation gives

$$\frac{\partial x_i^*(p^*,m)}{\partial p_j} = \frac{\partial x_i^H(p^*;I(p^*,m))}{\partial p_j} + \frac{\partial x_i^H(p^*;I(p^*,m))}{\partial u}\frac{\partial I(p^*,m)}{\partial p_j},$$

and

$$\frac{\partial x_i^H(p^*;u)}{\partial p_j} = \frac{\partial x_i^*(p^*,E^H(p^*,u))}{\partial p_j} + \frac{\partial x_i^*(p^*,E^H(p^*,u))}{\partial m}\frac{\partial E^H(p^*,u)}{\partial p_j}.$$

The first expression corresponds to (5.7). The second, which contains equivalent information, can be rewritten (after substituting m for $E^H(p^*,u)$ *and using Shephard's Lemma) as*

$$\begin{aligned}\frac{\partial x_i^*(p^*,m)}{\partial p_j} &= \frac{\partial x_i^H(p^*;u)}{\partial p_j} - \frac{\partial x_i^*(p^*,m)}{\partial m}\frac{\partial E^H(p^*,I(p))}{\partial p_j}\\ &= \frac{\partial x_i^H(p^*;u)}{\partial p_j} - x_j^*(p,m)\frac{\partial x_i^*(p^*,m)}{\partial m},\end{aligned}$$

so that the real-income effect here corresponds to the level of the Marshallian demand for good j times the income effect on good i.

Perhaps the most fundamental result of consumer theory is that optimal smooth demand behavior is exhaustively characterized by the negative semidefiniteness and singularity (the latter is implied by homogeneity of degree zero of Hicksian demands) of the Hicksian substitution matrix:

$$\begin{bmatrix} \frac{\partial x_1^H(p,I(p))}{\partial p_1} & \cdots & \frac{\partial x_1^H(p,I(p))}{\partial p_N} \\ \vdots & \ddots & \vdots \\ \frac{\partial x_N^H(p,I(p))}{\partial p_1} & \cdots & \frac{\partial x_N^H(p,I(p))}{\partial p_N} \end{bmatrix}.$$

These properties are the differentiable manifestations of the superlinearity of E^H in p.

7 Profit Maximization and Utility Maximization

The Slutsky–Hicks equation is an immediate consequence of decomposing the consumer utility maximization problem into two stages. In the first, the utility-constrained expenditure minimization problem is solved, and then utility is chosen to exhaust the budget constraint (yet another manifestation of Bellman's Principle). The analytic and historic importance of the Slutsky–Hicks equation is hard to overemphasize. It demonstrated conclusively that an economic theory based on rational behavior could explain a seemingly "perverse" empirical irregularity (upward-sloping demand curves) while simultaneously providing a core theoretical prediction for economically rational behavior (well-behaved substitution effects).[4]

The facts that indirect utility functions can be derived from expenditure functions, that expenditure functions and cost functions (please see Chapter 6) are equivalent mathematically, and that profit functions are derivable from cost functions suggest that other demand decompositions might be available. This is indeed true, and in fact a tight connection exists between profit-maximizing behavior and utility-maximizing behavior. Looking at matters from this perspective helps clarify the connection between rational demand behavior and developments in Revealed-Preference Theory. The connection is clearest when $U(y)$ is concave, and to keep matters simple we'll maintain that assumption for the remainder of this section. (We'll return to this briefly in a moment.)

The utility-maximization problem in its most usual form is

$$I(p) = \max_{y} \{U(y) : p^{\top} y \leq 1\}.$$

If a $\hat{y}$ exists such that $p^{\top}\hat{y} < 1$, the associated Lagrangian problem can be written as:[5]

$$I(p) = \min_{\lambda \geq 0} \max_{y \in \mathbb{R}_{+}^{N}} \{U(y) - \lambda p^{\top} y + \lambda\},$$

[4] Undoubtedly, this is "old hat" to most of you. That, however, signals its true importance and how pathbreaking it was when first discovered. It's one of those results that all individuals taking even basic microeconomics are taught.

[5] The primal Lagrangian for the utility-maximization problem is usually written as

$$\max_{x} \min_{\lambda \geq 0} \{U(y) - \lambda p^{\top} y + \lambda\}.$$

The expression in the text is its dual form. If U is concave, the two expressions coincide if Slater's constraint qualification condition holds. Nonemptiness of the interior of the budget set ensures the latter.

where λ is the Lagrange multiplier. By Bellman's Principle, this problem decomposes as

$$\begin{aligned} I(p) &= \min_{\lambda}\left\{\lambda + \max_{y}\{U(y) - \lambda p^{\top} y\}\right\} \\ &= \min_{\lambda}\left\{\lambda - \min_{y}\{\lambda p^{\top} y - U(y)\}\right\} \\ &= \min_{\lambda}\{\lambda - U^{*}(\lambda p)\} \end{aligned} \tag{5.8}$$

where $U^{*}(\lambda p)$, the concave conjugate of $U(y)$, is intuitively recognizable as minus a normalized "profit function" associated with "input prices," λp, that have been converted into utility units by λ (see, for example, Remark 6). Here "profit" represents the difference between utility derived from y (presumably expressed in "utils") and expenditure on the commodity bundle expressed in normalized prices λp. By Theorem 6, the optimal solution to the *utility-as-profit maximization* problem satisfies

$$\lambda p \in \partial U(y) \Rightarrow y \in \partial U^{*}(\lambda p) \Leftrightarrow \lambda p \in \partial U^{**}(y), \tag{5.9}$$

where as usual U^{**} denotes the concave biconjugate of U.

Problem 44. *A slightly different perspective on the utility-as-profit maximization problem is obtained from the formulation*

$$I(p) = \max_{u}\{u : E^{H}(p,u) \leq 1\}.$$

The associated Lagrangian problem (under appropriate regularity cond-tions) is

$$\begin{aligned} I(p) &= \min_{\gamma \geq 0}\max_{u}\{u - \gamma E^{H}(p,u) + \gamma\} \\ &= \min_{\gamma \geq 0}\{\gamma + E^{H^{*}}(\gamma p, 1)\}, \end{aligned}$$

where γ is a Lagrange multiplier and

$$E^{H^{*}}(\gamma p, 1) = \max_{u}\{u - E^{H}(\gamma p, u)\}$$

is the normalized profit function associated with E^{H} at prices γp expressed as the convex conjugate (in u) of E^{H}. You are asked to perform two tasks. Show the equivalence of the two approaches. Relate optimal γ here to optimal λ in (5.8).

Most standard treatments of consumer demand theory do not require U to be concave. Instead, U is usually taken to be *quasi-concave.*[6] There are a variety of reasons. One is that quasi-concavity of U is a minimal requirement for the existence of consumer demands consistent with the existence of a general equilibrium. It's also true that quasi-concavity of U suffices to allow the use of Kuhn–Tucker methods in analyzing consumer behavior. Another is that concavity is not preserved under the monotone transformations of utility required by ordinality, while quasi-concavity is. Nevertheless, relatively little true generality is lost by assuming U concave. The ultimate consequence of concavity is to ensure that the marginal utility of income is a decreasing function of income. Moreover, quasi-concavity of U requires $V(y)$ to be convex (*CONA*) so that $\succeq (y)$ is always completely characterizable by a concave distance function.

Thus, for U concave, the existence of an optimal consumer demand requires that there exist a concave function, U^{**}, such that optimal demands satisfy (5.9) for optimal λ. By the definition of a superdifferential, any optimal demand structure must satisfy

$$\lambda p^{\top}(z-y) \geq U^{**}(z) - U^{**}(x) \text{ for all } z \in \mathbb{R}^N \tag{5.10}$$

at optimal λ. Furthermore, the cyclical monotonicity of ∂U^{**} and ∂U^{*} ensures that demands y_m optimal for $\lambda_m p_m$ satisfy

$$(y_1 - y_0)^{\top} \lambda_0 p_0 + (y_2 - y_1)^{\top} \lambda_1 p_1 + \cdots + (y_0 - y_M)^{\top} \lambda_M p_M \geq 0 \tag{5.11}$$

for all possible pairs $(y_m, \lambda_m p_m)$ for arbitrary M. This, of course, translates into the requirement that $(y_m - y_n)^{\top}(\lambda_m p_m - \lambda_n p_n) \leq 0$ for all m and n. In words, that means that optimal demands must be downward sloping in their own "corrected prices," λp.

Using (5.8), optimal λ for the consumer program must satisfy (in addition to 5.9)

$$1 - U^{*\prime}(\lambda p; p) = 0 \tag{5.12}$$

for an interior solution where

$$\begin{aligned} U^{*\prime}(\lambda p; p) &= \lim_{\mu \downarrow 0} \frac{U^{*}((\lambda + \mu)p) - U^{*}(\lambda p)}{\mu} \\ &= \sup\{p^{\top} y : y \in \partial U^{*}(\lambda p)\}. \end{aligned}$$

[6] Recall that a function f is quasi-concave if $-f$ is quasi-convex. Thus, to obtain an exact mathematical expression for quasi-concavity, revisit our discussion of quasi-convex $I(p)$.

In short, λ is chosen to ensure that normalized optimal consumer expenditure equal one,[7] the budget constraint must respected at the optimum.

These arguments demonstrate that

$$x^{*}(p) \in \partial U^{*}(\lambda(p)p) \tag{5.13}$$

where $\lambda(p)$ represents the optimal value of the Lagrange multiplier and as before x^{*} is an optimal Marshallian demand vector. Thus, just as we earlier showed that Marshallian demands can be expressed as Hicksian-compensated demands evaluated at the optimal utility level, we now see that they can also be represented as "profit-maximizing input demands" evaluated at *normalized prices p converted into utility units by* $\lambda(p)$.

Demand adjustment to price changes, therefore, can be decomposed into two components. One is a direct relationship associated with the price change, referred to as the *substitution effect*. The other is an indirect adjustment associated with changes in $\lambda(p)$ induced by changes in p. Because this latter adjustment affects all prices p proportionately, it is isomorphic to rescaling money income, m. We refer to it as the *valuation effect* because it reflects adjustments in the rate at which nominal income, m, is converted into "real" income as expressed in units of U.

To keep the notation simple, assume that $\partial U^{*}(\lambda(p)p)$ is a singleton set whose only member is $x^{\pi}(\lambda p) \in \mathbb{R}^{N}$ where superscript π reminds us that it corresponds to the profit-maximizing demand associated with U^{**}. In discrete terms, we can decompose demand adjustments to price changes as follows:

$$\begin{aligned} x^{*}(p^{o}) - x(p) &= \overbrace{x^{\pi}(\lambda^{o}p^{o}) - x^{\pi}(\lambda^{o}p)}^{\textit{substitution}} + \overbrace{x^{\pi}(\lambda^{o}p) - x^{\pi}(\lambda p)}^{\textit{valuation}} \\ &= \overbrace{x^{\pi}(\lambda p^{o}) - x^{\pi}(\lambda p)}^{\textit{substitution}} + \overbrace{x^{\pi}(\lambda^{o}p^{o}) - x^{\pi}(\lambda p^{o})}^{\textit{valuation}}. \end{aligned}$$

Problem 45. *Identify necessary and sufficient conditions for*

$$x^{\pi}(\lambda p^{o}) - x^{\pi}(\lambda p) = x^{\pi}(\lambda^{o}p^{o}) - x^{\pi}(\lambda^{o}p)$$

for all (λ, p).

[7] This, of course, is equivalent to the standard first-order condition associated with λ from the Kuhn–Tucker Theorem.

For smooth structures, the associated demand decomposition is obtained by differentiating (5.13), for example, with respect to p_j:

$$\frac{\partial x_k^*(p)}{\partial p_j^*} = \lambda(p)\frac{\partial x_k^\pi(\lambda p)}{\partial(\lambda p_j)} + \sum_i \frac{\partial x_k^\pi(\lambda p)}{\partial(\lambda p_i)}\frac{\partial \lambda(p)}{\partial p_j}, \tag{5.14}$$

Marshallian demand adjustments to price changes consist of two components. The substitution effect is characterized in the smooth case by

$$\lambda(p)\begin{bmatrix} \frac{\partial x_1^\pi(\lambda p)}{\partial(\lambda p_1)} & \cdots & \frac{\partial x_1^\pi(\lambda p)}{\partial(\lambda p_N)} \\ \vdots & \ddots & \vdots \\ \frac{\partial x_N^\pi(\lambda p)}{\partial(\lambda p_1)} & \cdots & \frac{\partial x_N^\pi(\lambda p)}{\partial(\lambda p_N)} \end{bmatrix},$$

which is negative semidefinite. Its diagonal (own-price effects) elements are nonpositive, and its off-diagonal (cross-price effects) elements are symmetric. This substitution effect exhibits behavior similar to that of *Hicksian-compensated demands.* The valuation effect, $\sum_i \frac{\partial x_k^\pi(\lambda p)}{\partial(\lambda p_i)}\frac{\partial\lambda(p)}{\partial p_j}$, manifests "an income effect." Its proximate cause is the change in $\lambda(p)$ evinced by a normalized price change, $\partial\lambda(p)/\partial p_j$.

These substitution effects are not Slutsky–Hicks effects. The latter restrict attention to movements along an indifference curve. The substitution effects studied here permit individuals to adjust utility and thus move across indifference curves. Hence, they incorporate a real-income effect. The tricky part is that these real-income effects can never cause these compensated demands to be upward sloping in their own prices. The appropriate producer analogy for the Slutsky–Hicks effect are the adjustments made by a cost-minimizing producer responding to price changes. The appropriate analogy here is to the input adjustments made by a profit-maximizing producer to price changes. In production analysis, these real-income effects for derived demands are usually called "expansion effects" and are the source of the *LeChatelier relationship* between short- and long-run input demand adjustment (see, for example, Chambers 1988 and Chapter 6). Thus, the substitution relationships in this decomposition correspond to notions of *gross substitutability* in production analysis.

8 Revealed Preference

In developing consumer demands, we've worked in one direction, reasoning from a binary relation $\succeq(y)$ capturing an individual's attitudes toward consumption items through a budget constraint to potentially observable economic quantities that we've referred to as either rational or Marshallian (utility-maximizing) demands. These arguments have resulted in dual representations, $E(p,y)$ and $E^{H}(p,u)$, that are recognizable via Lemma 4 as support functions for closed, convex subsets of $\mathbb{R}^{N}$. Thus, given enough information on these dual representations, one could use our basic duality results to infer the existence of sets $V^{**}(y)$ and $V^{**}(u)$, slightly abusing notation, which can be interpreted as at-least-as-good sets derived, respectively, from a preference order and a utility function. A natural conjecture, therefore, is that an alternative approach to developing a systematic theory of consumer behavior is to obtain information on $E(p,y)$ and $E^{H}(p,u)$ and then to use that information to infer something about consumer preferences. Obvious building blocks of such an approach would be observed demands and prices, p.

So what obstructs such an approach? The answer lies in what is observable in a market setting and what is not. Typically, $x^{*}(p)$ is observed, but its compensated counterpart is not. And one can reason from $x^{*}(p)$ to $x^{H}(p,u)$ only through an intermittent step involving the circular relationship

$$x^{*}(p)=x^{H}(p,U(x^{*}(p))).$$

Thus, reasoning from observed demands using our constructs requires either knowledge of U or an assumption about how real-income effects impinge on $x^{*}(p)$.

Samuelson (1938) suggested as an alternative "a direct attack upon the problem." Instead of starting from a utility structure, he argued that consumer-demand theory be based on three postulates. The first two postulates are satisfied by assuming the existence of single-valued demand functions, $x_{n}(p)$, for the N commodities that are homogeneous of degree zero in p and that satisfy

$$p^{\top}x(p)=1.$$

So far, so good. Both our rational demands and their Marshallian counterparts meet these criteria.

His third postulate, however, nudges us away from our idealized world. It requires that we can *observe* these demands under *different market conditions* represented by *different market prices*. How this might be accomplished without the time frame or some other characteristic of the decision setting changing remains unclear. One way to accommodate this difficulty, which we adopt, is to assume that the demand functions for the commodities remain stable or stationary across the different price constellations. To that end, assume that we have K observations on the purchasing decisions of a single consumer, $x^k \in \mathbb{R}^N$ for price vectors $p^k \in \mathbb{R}^N_{++}$, $k = 1, ..., K$.

Consider the following binary relation on $\mathbb{R}^N$

$$p^{k\top} x^j \leq p^{k\top} x^k = 1 \Leftrightarrow x^j \preceq x^k$$

with strict counterpart

$$p^{k\top} x^j < p^{k\top} x^k = 1 \Leftrightarrow x^j \prec x^k.$$

Here are some things to note. First, $\preceq$ does not satisfy *CO*. But it is reflexive and monotonic in the sense that $x^m \preceq x^j$ and $x^j \preceq x^k$ implies $x^m \preceq x^k$. The information that $\preceq$ communicates is that the left-hand side was affordable at prices defined by the right-hand side but was not purchased. Here we need to remember that both x^k and x^j correspond to actual purchases. Thus, while $\preceq$ is only contingent on observed behavior, it does communicate information about the individual's choice behavior. Common jargon thus refers to $x^j \preceq x^k$ as implying that the latter is *revealed preferred* to the former. Samuelson's (1938) third postulate, which has come to be called the *weak axiom of revealed preference (WARP)*, requires that neither $x^j \preceq x^k \prec x^j$ nor $x^j \prec x^k \preceq x^j$ can hold. Rewriting $\preceq$ in terms of its definition, that requires that neither of the following can be true for any pair (p^j, x^j) and (p^k, x^k)

$$p^{k\top} x^j \leq p^{k\top} x^k \text{ and } p^{j\top} x^k < p^{j\top} x^j,$$

or

$$p^{k\top} x^j < p^{k\top} x^k \text{ and } p^{j\top} x^k \leq p^{j\top} x^j,$$

if WARP is to be satisfied. Notice that if either one of these conditions hold,

$$0 < \left(p^k - p^j\right)^\top \left(x^k - x^j\right),$$

and the observed demands cannot be cyclically monotone (decreasing) in p. Figure 5.3 illustrates a violation of WARP. For that case, x^2 is budget feasible

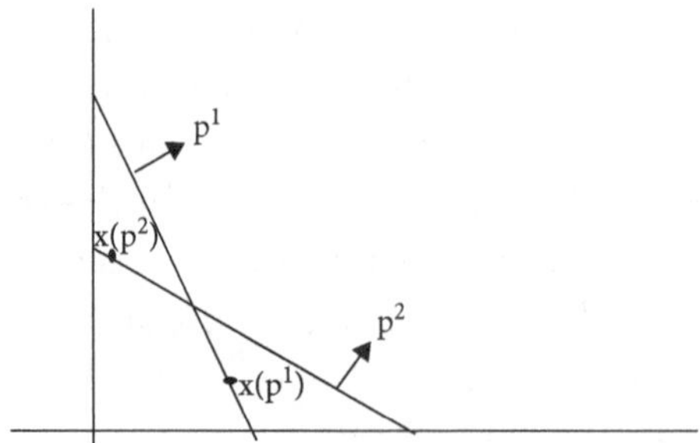

Fig. 5.3 Failure of Samuelson's Third Postulate

for p^1, and x^1 is budget feasible for p^2. Thus, if x^1 were chosen over x^2 when p^1 prevailed, and it was truly preferred to x^2, it should have been picked when p^2 prevailed because it remained budget feasible. Similarly, if x^2 was chosen over x^1 for prices p^2, it should also have been picked for prices p^1.

Whether WARP is a proper criterion upon which to base a theory of consumer demand is, ultimately, subjective. Much like any other criterion imposed by some individual, we as individuals are free to decide whether or not to accept it. But what is objectively true is that WARP, by itself, is not sufficient to generate consumer behavior that is consistent with the standard utility-maximization hypothesis. Something stronger is required. That property is known as the *Generalized Axiom of Revealed Preference* (GARP) and is due to Afriat (1967). It requires that any finite series of the observed demands and prices, $(x^{k_1}, p^{k_1}), (x^{k_2}, p^{k_2}), \ldots, (x^{k_m}, p^{k_m})$, can never satisfy

$$x^{k_1} \preceq x^{k_m} \preceq x^{k_{m-1}} \preceq \cdots \preceq x^{k_2} \preceq x^{k_1}$$

with at least one $\preceq$ replaced with an $\prec$. Suppose, for example, that for $(x^1, p^1), (x^2, p^2)$, and (x^3, p^3) that

$$x^1 \prec x^3 \preceq x^2 \preceq x^1,$$

violating GARP. Associating a meaningful utility function with these data and $\preceq$ would be impossible because it would require $U(x^1) \geq U(x^2) \geq U(x^3) > U(x^1)$, so that x^1 would have to be strictly preferred to itself. In words, GARP, therefore, requires that one can never build a chain of observations from the observed data set such that x^{k_1} is revealed strictly preferred to itself. Taking $m = 2$, it's easy to see that GARP implies WARP. The converse, however, is not generally true.

Afriat (1967) proved the following remarkable result:

Theorem 11. *(Afriat's Theorem) For a finite demand data set, the following are equivalent:*

(a) the demand data are consistent with utility-maximizing choice for a continuous, strictly monotonic, proper concave U^{**};
(b) the demand data satisfy GARP; and
(c) for each (x^k, p^k) there exist strictly positive real numbers (λ^k, U^{**k}) satisfying $\lambda^k p^{k\top}(x^j - x^k) \geq U^{**j} - U^{**k}$ for all $j \in \{1, 2, ..., K\}$.

We've already argued that the existence of a strictly monotonic utility function requires GARP. The discussion around expression (5.10) and the ordinal nature of utility functions shows why (a) requires something like (c). Reversing the argument to show that (c) requires (a) involves noting that (c) ensures that $(x^k, \lambda^k p^k)$, $k = 1, ..., K$ satisfy (5.11) with each $\lambda^k > 0$ interpreted as a strictly positive marginal utility of income. Hence, these $\lambda^k p^k$ are interpretable as images of a cyclically monotone correspondence. Theorem 5 is in force, and we can use a slightly transformed version of the algorithm detailed in (2.13) to construct a concave function that satisfies the requirements spelled out in (c).

To that end, define

$$U^{**}(x) \equiv \min\left\{(\hat{x}^2 - x^1)^\top \lambda^1 p^1 + (\hat{x}^3 - \hat{x}^2)^\top \hat{\lambda}^2 \hat{p}^2 + \cdots + (x - \hat{x}^m)^\top \hat{\lambda}^m \hat{p}^m\right\},$$

where the minimum is defined over $(\hat{x}^n, \hat{\lambda}^n \hat{p}^n) \in Gr\{(x^k, \lambda^k p^k), k = 1, ..., K\}$. Because U^{**} is defined as the minimum of a set of affine functions of x, it is closed concave by Lemma 1. Taking $x = x^1$ establishes that $U^{**}(x^1) = 0$, so it is also proper. That $\lambda^k p^{k\top}(x^j - x^k) \geq U^{**j} - U^{**k}$ for all $j \in \{1, 2, ..., K\}$ follows by choosing $(\hat{x}^n, \hat{\lambda}^n \hat{p}^n)$ such that

$$U^{**}(x^k) = (\hat{x}^2 - x^1)^\top \lambda^1 p^1 + (\hat{x}^3 - \hat{x}^2)^\top \hat{\lambda}^2 \hat{p}^2 + \cdots + (x^k - \hat{x}^m)^\top \hat{\lambda}^m \hat{p}^m.$$

Definitionally, however,

$$(\hat{x}^2 - x^1)^\top \lambda^1 p^1 + (\hat{x}^3 - \hat{x}^2)^\top \hat{\lambda}^2 \hat{p}^2 + \cdots + (x^k - \hat{x}^m)^\top \hat{\lambda}^m \hat{p}^m + (x^j - x^k)^\top \lambda^k p^k \geq U^{**}(x^j)$$

whence

$$(x^j - x^k)^\top \lambda^k p^k \geq U^{**}(x^j) - U^{**}(x^k).$$

To satisfy the criterion that all U^{**k} and U^{**j} be positive, note that for all k, the cyclical monotonicity of $\{(x^k, \lambda^k p^k), k = 1, ..., K\}$ requires that

$$(\hat{x}^2 - x^1)^\top \lambda^1 p^1 + (\hat{x}^3 - \hat{x}^2)^\top \hat{\lambda}^2 \hat{p}^2 + \cdots + (x^k - \hat{x}^m)^\top \hat{\lambda}^m \hat{p}^m \geq (x^k - x^1)^\top \lambda^k p^k,$$

so that taking the minimum of the left-hand side gives

$$U^{**}(x^k) \geq (x^k - x^1)^\top \lambda^k p^k,$$

which is always finite. Now find $min\{U^{**}(x^k)\}$. If it is negative, take β such that

$$min\{U^{**}(x^k)\} + \beta > 0,$$

to obtain a new utility function according to $U^{***}(x^j) = U^{**}(x^j) + \beta > 0$, which completes the demonstration.

That leaves demonstrating that (b) requires (c). Working through a detailed derivation is both lengthy and notationally burdensome. Therefore, in place of a formal argument, I offer a quick sketch that provides a flavor of the argument. The whole truth can be found in Chambers (not me) and Echenique (2016, pp. 38–46).[8]

Assume that GARP fails, and let indexes be chosen such that $x^1 \prec x^K \cdots \preceq x^2 \preceq x^1$. Converting into expenditure terms, this requires that

$$\begin{aligned} p^{1\top}x^2 &\leq p^{1\top}x^1, \\ p^{2\top}x^3 &\leq p^{2\top}x^2, \\ &\vdots \\ p^{K\top}x^1 &< p^{K\top}x^K. \end{aligned}$$

Multiplying each inequality by an arbitrary $\lambda^k > 0$ and then adding yield

$$\lambda^1 p^{1\top}(x^2 - x^1) + \lambda^2 p^{2\top}(x^3 - x^2) + \cdots + \lambda^K p^{K\top}(x^1 - x^K) < 0, \quad (5.15)$$

for all $(\lambda^1, \lambda^2, \cdots, \lambda^K) \in \mathbb{R}^K_{++}$. But that means it's impossible to find $(\lambda^1, \lambda^2, \cdots, \lambda^K) \in \mathbb{R}^K_{++}$ such that

$$\lambda^1 p^{1\top}(x^2 - x^1) + \lambda^2 p^{2\top}(x^3 - x^2) + \cdots + \lambda^K p^{K\top}(x^1 - x^K) \geq 0,$$

[8] Jehle and Reny (2011, Exercise 2.12, pp. 120–121) provide a detailed guide through a simplified version that can be easily worked by using methods developed in Chapter 2 of this book.

as required by the condition that $\lambda^k p^k (x^j - x^k) \geq U^{**j} - U^{**k}$ for k and j. Going the other way, suppose that (c) is satisfied, then a little manipulation reveals that $(\lambda^1, \lambda^2, \cdots, \lambda^K) \in \mathbb{R}^K_{++}$ and the data satisfy

$$\lambda^1 p^{1\top} (x^2 - x^1) + \lambda^2 p^{2\top} (x^3 - x^2) + \cdots + \lambda^K p^{K\top} (x^1 - x^K) \geq 0, \quad (5.16)$$

which is inconsistent with (5.15).

Finally, let's assume that GARP is satisfied. Therefore, for every sequence in the data, it has to be true

$$\begin{aligned} p^{1\top} x^2 &\leq p^{1\top} x^1, \\ p^{2\top} x^3 &\leq p^{2\top} x^2, \\ &\vdots \\ p^{k\top} x^1 &\geq p^{k\top} x^k. \end{aligned}$$

It follows immediately that there exists no $\mu > 0$ such that

$$\mu \begin{pmatrix} p^{1\top} (x^2 - x^1) \\ p^{2\top} (x^3 - x^2) \\ \vdots \\ p^{k\top} (x^1 - x^k) \end{pmatrix} < 0.$$

Thus, unless the k-dimensional vector in this expression is the zero vector, there must exist for each sequence a nonnegative $(\lambda^1, \lambda^2, ..., \lambda^k) \in \mathbb{R}^k_+ \backslash \{0\}$ such that

$$(\lambda^1, \lambda^2, ..., \lambda^k) \begin{pmatrix} p^{1\top} (x^2 - x^1) \\ p^{2\top} (x^3 - x^2) \\ \vdots \\ p^{k\top} (x^1 - x^k) \end{pmatrix} \geq 0,$$

which implies consistency with cyclical monotonicity of $(\lambda^k p^k, x^k)$, as desired. This gets us part of the way, but it still remains to be shown that $(\lambda^1, \lambda^2, ..., \lambda^K)$ is strictly positive and holds for all possible reorderings of the data. This can be accomplished by either enumeration or use of the Theorem of the Alternative.

Problem 46. *Building the argument up inductively should help you understand what's going on. This problem is intended to help you do that. You may want to consult Chambers and Echenique (2016) in attempting this problem.*

Let's first recall that optimality in the presence of a utility function requires

$$\lambda p \in \partial U^{**}(x),$$

with $\partial U^{**}(x)$ cyclically monotone. Thus, for any observed data set, we need to find $(U^{k**}, \lambda^k) \geq 0$ for all k such that

$$\lambda^k p^{k\top}(x^k - x^j) + U^{**j} - U^{**k} \leq 0,$$

for all k, j. Starting with the case $K = 2$, that requires there exist nonnegative λ^1 and λ^2 such that

$$(U^{**1}, U^{**2}, \lambda^1, \lambda^2)\begin{pmatrix} -1 & 1 \\ 1 & -1 \\ p^{1\top}(x^1 - x^2) & 0 \\ 0 & p^{2\top}(x^2 - x^1) \end{pmatrix} \leq 0.$$

If $p^{1\top}(x^1 - x^2)$ and $p^{2\top}(x^2 - x^1)$ are both nonpositive, I can easily do this using arbitrary $(\lambda^1, \lambda^2) > 0$ and U^{**k} (note that as in the discussion in the text, the U^{**k} can all be renormalized to be positive without any loss of generality), and it's easy to see that GARP is also satisfied. Now let $K = 3$. We now need to find $(\lambda^1, \lambda^2, \lambda^3)$ such that

$$\begin{pmatrix} U^{**1} \\ U^{**2} \\ U^{**3} \\ \lambda^1 \\ \lambda^2 \\ \lambda^3 \end{pmatrix}^{\top}\begin{pmatrix} -1 & -1 & 1 & 0 & 1 & 0 \\ 1 & 0 & -1 & -1 & 0 & 1 \\ 0 & 1 & 0 & 1 & -1 & -1 \\ p^{1\top}(x^1 - x^2) & p^{1\top}(x^1 - x^3) & 0 & 0 & 0 & 0 \\ 0 & 0 & \cdots & \cdots & 0 & 0 \\ 0 & 0 & 0 & 0 & p^{3\top}(x^3 - x^1) & p^{3\top}(x^3 - x^1) \end{pmatrix} \leq 0.$$

Recall that the Theorem of the Alternative requires that either $z^\top A \leq 0$ has a solution $z \in \mathbb{R}_+^K \backslash \{0\}$ or $Ay > 0$ has a solution $y \in \mathbb{R}_+^J$, ***but not both****, where K denotes the number of rows and J the number of columns. In this instance, failure of cyclical monotonicity requires the existence of nonnegative $y = (y^1, y^2, \ldots, y^6)$ such that*

$$\begin{pmatrix} -1 & -1 & 1 & 0 & 1 & 0 \\ 1 & 0 & -1 & -1 & 0 & 1 \\ 0 & 1 & 0 & 1 & -1 & -1 \\ p^{1\top}(x^1 - x^2) & p^{1\top}(x^1 - x^3) & 0 & 0 & 0 & 0 \\ 0 & 0 & \cdots & \cdots & 0 & 0 \\ 0 & 0 & 0 & 0 & p^{3\top}(x^3 - x^1) & p^{3\top}(x^3 - x^1) \end{pmatrix} y > 0.$$

Step 1: Argue from here that satisfying the condition for cyclical monotonicity implies GARP.

Step 2: Extend the argument to an arbitrary dimension.

9 Constructing a Utility Function from *E*(*p*; *y*) or *R*(*p*; *x*)

Afriat's Theorem provides a method for using observed demands and price to construct a utility function consistent with the data. Direct estimation of demand systems based on a parametric specification of either an indirect utility function or an expenditure function is another approach that is frequently pursued in applied settings. This section shows that a McKenzie expenditure function or a revenue function can be used to construct their dual utility functions. We've established that either $-d\left(0,y;g\right)$ or $-t\left(0,y;g\right)$ can be taken as a utility function. Thus, there are at least two dual procedures that can be used to recapture these representations of the preference structure from their dual manifestations.[9] One can solve:

$$\begin{aligned} u\left(y;g\right) &= -d\left(0,y;g\right) \\ &= -\min_{\frac{p}{p^{\top}g}}\left\{-E\left(\frac{p}{p^{\top}g};y\right)\right\} \\ &= \max_{\frac{p}{p^{\top}g}}\left\{E\left(\frac{p}{p^{\top}g};y\right)\right\}, \end{aligned}$$

to calculate it as the maximum willingness-to-pay for y. Or one can solve

$$\begin{aligned} -t\left(0,y;g\right) &= -\max_{\frac{p}{p^{\top}g}}\left\{-R\left(\frac{p}{p^{\top}g};y\right)\right\} \\ &= \min_{\frac{p}{p^{\top}g}}\left\{R\left(\frac{p}{p^{\top}g};y\right)\right\}, \end{aligned}$$

[9] There's actually three; the final one involves $I\left(p\right)$ and $u\left(x\right)$. For any $x \in B\left(p\right)$,

$$I\left(p\right) = u\left(x^{*}\left(p\right)\right) \geq u\left(x\right),$$

from which it follows almost immediately that, subject to weak regularity conditions,

$$u\left(x\right) = \min_{p}\left\{I\left(p\right) : p^{\top}x \leq 1\right\}.$$

to calculate it as the minimum willingness-to-accept for y. Completeness (CO), therefore, ensures that there's no gap between the individual's willingness-to-pay and willingness-to-accept in normalized dollar terms for y. That is,

$$\min_{\frac{p}{p^\top g}} \left\{ R\left(\frac{p}{p^\top g}; y\right) \right\} = \max_{\frac{p}{p^\top g}} \left\{ E\left(\frac{p}{p^\top g}; y\right) \right\},$$

and that

$$0 \in \partial R\left(\frac{p}{p^\top g}; y\right) \cap \partial E\left(\frac{p}{p^\top g}; y\right).$$

Problem 47. *Solve*

$$u(x) = \min_p \{ I(p) : p^\top x \leq 1 \},$$

with $I(p)$ quasi-convex. Include a complete discussion of your results.

Remark 14. *Yet again, I have chosen to refer to things in terms of common economic concepts, willingness-to-pay and willingness-to-accept, with which I presume that you are familiar. In general, the difference between the two depends critically on how one defines the related variation. For example, if the variation involves situations A and B and one starts at A, the move from A to B is associated with the willingness-to-pay, while a move from B to A is associated with the willingness-to-accept. But if one starts at B, the roles are reversed and so is the terminology. So, while the difference is reference-dependent, understanding it in applied settings is both important and extremely crucial. A general treatment can be found in Chambers and Melkonyan (2009). Please also see Chapter 10 of this text.*

Remark 15. *I encourage you to consult other sources on resurrecting a utility function or $V(y)$ from $E(p; y)$. On the consumer side, Jehle and Reny (2011) give a nice treatment. On the producer side, you might look at Chambers (1988). Jehle and Reny (2011) follow the same basic approach as Chambers (1988) and then effectively solve for the utility function by "finding the production function" consistent with $V(y)$ when y is a scalar.*

You should look for several things. First, the basic principles are the same. Second, the mechanics involved are somewhat different. Where we rely on the conjugacy relationship, Chambers (1988) and Jehle and Reny (2011) rely on

Minkowski's Theorem to resurrect $V(y)$. *The conjugate approach is especially suited for economists who have grown up solving for profit maximization by choosing output to maximize the difference between revenue and cost. Third,* $\min\left\{R\left(\frac{p}{p^{\top}g};y\right)\right\}$ *can actually be measured, in principle. And fourth, a nonrhetorical question: why do Jehle and Reny (2011) need to solve a maximization problem to find the utility function?*

10 A Structural Restriction

We now turn to the consequences of imposing a specific structural restriction on $\succeq(y)$. Quite likely, you have already seen it in other contexts. Whether you recognize where is not important for now. What is important is that you intelligently judge it on its merits and that you understand its consequences. We continue to maintain that $\succeq(y)$ is continuous, reflexive, transitive, and strictly monotonic.

The new assumption (axiom) is that

$$x \succeq (y) \Leftrightarrow \alpha x + (1-\alpha)r \succeq (\alpha y + (1-\alpha)r) \text{ for all } \alpha \in (0,1] \text{ and all } r \in \mathbb{R}^N. \quad (5.17)$$

In words, expression (5.17) requires that if x is preferred to y, then the weighted averages of x and any other commodity bundle will be preferred to the weighted averages of y and that commodity bundle. You can visualize this in two-space as follows. Pick a point $x \in \mathbb{R}^2$ that is preferred to another point $y \in \mathbb{R}^2$. (You may wish to sketch in $\bar{V}(y)$ to assist in your visualization.) Now pick a third point, r, somewhere else in $\mathbb{R}^2$. The weighted averages of x and r are given by the points falling on the line segment connecting x and r. Ditto for y and r. The axiom requires that each point on the first line segment is preferred to the corresponding point (as determined by α) on the second line segment. Thus, preference rankings of points across these two line segments are determined by the preferences over x and y *independently* of the amount of r that is added in. For this reason, this axiom is often referred to as *the independence axiom.*

Exercise 23. *Following the discussion above, develop a pictorial representation of the independence axiom for x, y, and a particular r. Now incorporate another choice for r—call it r′—into that representation. What are the implications?*

Independence has a number of important consequences. We first show that independence implies that $\succeq(y)$ satisfies *CONA*. Take arbitrary $p, q, y \in \mathbb{R}^N$ such that $p, q \in V(y)$. Independence requires for $\alpha \in (0,1)$

$$\alpha p + (1-\alpha) r \succeq (\alpha y + (1-\alpha) r) \quad \text{for all } r \in \mathbb{R}^N$$

and

$$(1-\alpha) q + \alpha r' \succeq ((1-\alpha) y + \alpha r') \quad \text{for all } r' \in \mathbb{R}^N.$$

Taking $r = q$ gives

$$\alpha p + (1-\alpha) q \succeq (\alpha y + (1-\alpha) q),$$

while taking $r' = y$ gives

$$\alpha y + (1-\alpha) q \succeq (y).$$

By transitivity, these two expressions imply that

$$\begin{aligned} \alpha p + (1-\alpha) q &\succeq (\alpha y + (1-\alpha) q) \\ &\succeq (y), \end{aligned}$$

for $\alpha \in (0,1)$, which establishes that $\succeq(y)$ satisfies convexity from above (*CONA*).

Now it's your turn:

Problem 48. *Prove that if $\succeq(y)$ is continuous, reflexive, transitive, and satisfies (5.17), it satisfies CONB.*

Imposing the independence axiom requires that $\succeq(y)$ be "nicely behaved" from both above and below. *CONA* implies that you can visualize $V(y)$ associated with $\succeq(y)$ as an upturned bowl tilted to the northeast, and *CONB* implies $Y(y)$ as a downturned bowl tilted to the southwest in $\mathbb{R}^2$ as depicted in Figure 5.2.

More formally, we can now conclude:

Lemma 15. *If $\succeq(y)$ is continuous, reflexive, transitive, and satisfies (5.17), $\succeq(y)$ satisfies CONA and CONB.*

Lemma 15 communicates considerable information about the structure. Among other results, it ensures that $d(x, y; g)$ is concave in x and that $t(y, x; g)$ is convex in y. These properties ensure superdifferentiability and subdifferentiability of $d(x, y; g)$ and $t(y, x; g)$, respectively. Still, Lemma 15 does not exhaust the implications of independence. More can be said. Take $r = 0$ and observe that independence requires that for all $\alpha \in (0, 1]$

$$\frac{x}{\alpha} \succeq \left(\frac{y}{\alpha}\right) \Leftrightarrow x \succeq (y) \Leftrightarrow \alpha x \succeq (\alpha y),$$

which (because $a^{-1} \geq 1$) implies that

$$x \succeq (y) \Leftrightarrow \mu x \succeq (\mu y) \text{ for all } \mu > 0. \tag{5.18}$$

In words, expression (5.18) requires $\succeq (y)$ to be *invariant to radial transformations.* In familiar economic jargon, $\succeq (y)$ is *homothetic.*

Remark 16. *The terminology "homothetic" is borrowed from the mathematical concept of homothety that involves transforming affine spaces, such as $\mathbb{R}^N$, by a fixed point in the space and a dilation parameter. Take the time to look this up so that you understand it geometrically. In economics, I believe the terminology is attributable to Shephard's (1953) "little green book." He defined a function $f : \mathbb{R}^N \to \mathbb{R}$ to be homothetic if it could be written as a monotonic transformation of a homogeneous function. The homotheticity property characterized by (5.18) is a special case of the requirements for input homotheticity that will be developed in Chapter 6.*

Problem 49. *Prove that*

$$x \succeq (y) \Leftrightarrow \mu x \succeq (\mu y) \textit{ for all } \mu > 0,$$

implies

$$V(\mu y) = \mu V(y),$$

and

$$Y(\mu y) = \mu Y(y),$$

for $\mu > 0$.

Undoubtedly, you have already encountered homotheticity. It's a very convenient property regardless of the underlying nature of the squiggle ordering. In consumer theory, it implies that as you proceed outward from the origin along a ray in $\mathbb{R}_+^N$, the marginal rate of substitution between commodities remains constant. This property, in turn, implies "nice" income effects. Commodities have positive income effects and thus are normal.

In producer theory, homotheticity makes analysis of economies of size and economies of scale particularly easy. In the theory of decision making under uncertainty, homotheticity implies *constant relative uncertainty aversion.*

Because the independence axiom requires

$$x \succeq (y) \Leftrightarrow \alpha x + (1-\alpha) r \succeq (\alpha y + (1-\alpha) r)$$

for all possible $r \in \mathbb{R}^N$, one can always define $z = (1-\alpha) r$ and, thus, rewrite independence as requiring[10]

$$x \succeq (y) \Leftrightarrow \alpha x + z \succeq (\alpha y + z), \quad \alpha > 0, z \in \mathbb{R}^N. \tag{5.19}$$

Thus, independence not only requires that the preference order be homothetic, but it also must be *invariant to translation (translation invariant) in all directions* $z \in \mathbb{R}^N$. Setting $\alpha = 1$ in (5.19) and taking z first to be $-y$ and then $-x$ gives, respectively,

$$x \succeq (y) \Leftrightarrow x - y \succeq (0),$$

and

$$x \succeq (y) \Leftrightarrow 0 \succeq (y - x).$$

Together, the preceding arguments establish the following representation result:[11]

Theorem 12. *For* $\succeq (y)$ *continuous, reflexive, and transitive, (5.17) is satisfied if and only if*

$$x \succeq (y) \Leftrightarrow \mu x \succeq (\mu y) \text{ for all } \mu > 0,$$

[10] You may well wonder why I didn't simply just write it this way to start. If the consumer context were the only case in which we would encounter it, likely I would have. But in other areas, there is a long tradition of writing it in the fashion in which I originally introduced it. We shall return to such issues in our discussion of decision making under uncertainty.

[11] The arguments in the text demonstrate necessity. Sufficiency is relatively straightforward, and so it is left to the reader.

$$x \succeq (y) \Leftrightarrow x - y \succeq (0),$$

and

$$x \succeq (y) \Leftrightarrow 0 \succeq (y - x).$$

If preferences satisfy independence, all comparisons between x and y can be reduced to comparing the vector difference, $x - y$, to the zero vector. If the vector difference is preferred to the zero vector, x is preferred to y. If the zero vector is preferred to (minus) the difference, x is preferred to y. In this sense, independence is closely akin to the ordering of $\mathbb{R}^N \times \mathbb{R}^N$ associated with the usual greater than or equal to relation, $\geq$. In fact, it is easily established that $\geq$ satisfies Theorem 12 so that it represents a special case of the independence condition. That, of course, implies that independence can be interpreted as a generalization of $\geq$ that admits other than Leontief-type structures. This is, indeed, the case.

Turning to our cardinal preference representation, notice that independence requires that

$$\begin{aligned} d(x, y; g) &= \sup\{\beta : x - \beta g \in V(y)\} \\ &= \sup\{\beta : x - y - \beta g \in V(0)\} \\ &= d(x - y, 0; g) \end{aligned}$$

and for $\mu > 0$

$$\begin{aligned} d(\mu(x - y), 0; g) &= d(\mu(x - y), \mu 0; g) \\ &= \sup\{\beta : \mu(x - y) - \beta g \in V(\mu 0)\} \\ &= \mu \sup\left\{\frac{\beta}{\mu} : x - y - \frac{\beta}{\mu} g \in V(0)\right\} \\ &= \mu d(x - y, 0; g). \end{aligned}$$

Thus, $d(x - y, 0; g)$ is positively homogeneous in $(x - y)$. Superlinearity in $(x - y)$ follows immediately because *CONA* of $V(0)$ implies concavity of $d(x - y, 0; g)$ in $x - y$. Applying Lemma 4 now gives:

Corollary 5. *(Aumann 1962) For $\succeq (y)$ continuous, reflexive, transitive, and monotonic, (5.17) is satisfied if and only if*

$$x \succeq (y) \Leftrightarrow d(x - y, 0; g) \geq 0$$

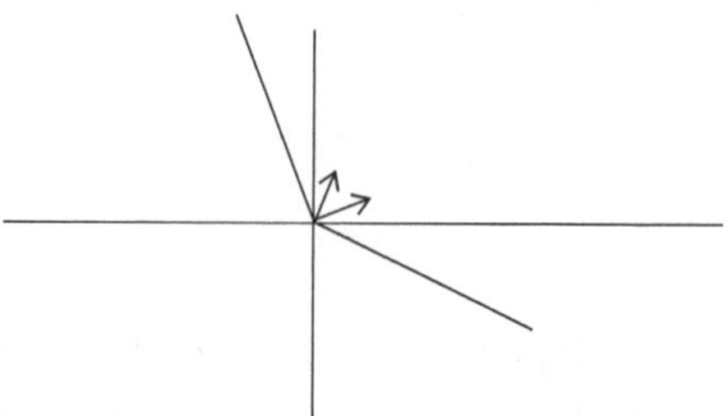

Fig. 5.4 $V(0)$ under Independence

with

$$d(x-y,0;g)=\inf_{q}\{q^{\top}(x-y) : q\in Q\}$$

where $Q\subset\mathbb{R}_{+}^{N}$ is closed and convex.

Figure 5.4 illustrates the lower boundary for $V(0)$ as the piecewise linear frontier with a kink at the origin. The arrows emanating from the origin illustrate the normals for each linear component of the frontier. Q, therefore, corresponds to the convex hull (not drawn) of these normals that can be visualized as the line segment connecting to the two arrowheads.

Problem 50. *Prove that for $\succeq(y)$ continuous, reflexive, transitive, and monotonic, (5.17) is satisfied if and only if*

$$t(y-x,0;g)=\sup\{q^{\top}(y-x) : q\in Q\}$$

where $Q\subset\mathbb{R}_{+}^{N}$ is closed and convex.

Problem 51. *Preferences are said to satisfy g-independence if for fixed $g\in\mathbb{R}_{++}^{N}$*

$$x\succeq(y)\Longleftrightarrow\alpha x+(1-\alpha)g\succeq(\alpha y+(1-\alpha)g)\ \textit{for all}\ \alpha\in(0,1]. \quad (5.20)$$

Provide an intuitive discussion of what g-independence means economically.

11 Chapter Commentary

This chapter's primary point of departure from the standard textbook treatment of consumer theoryis its use of the zero-minimum (zero-maximum) principle to characterize rational, and thus ultimately utility-maximizing, consumer behavior. That approach involves applying ideas, originally advanced by Luenberger (1992b), for characterizing general equilibria to characterizing undominated individual behavior. Luenberger's (1992b) approach shares close parallels with Fenchel's Duality Theorem and the theory of supremal and infimal convolutions (for example, Rockafellar 1970). With the exception of the *Profit Maximization and Utility Maximization* and *Revealed Preference* sections, all remaining results can be found in any sound graduate-level micro text (for example, Kreps (2013)) as augmented by Sakai (1974). The Profit and Utility Maximization discussion originally saw light as an unworked problem in an earlier version of the lecture notes used as the basis of this book. I am indebted to several cohorts of students who endured solving it. The *Revealed Preference* section was heavily influenced by Samuelson (1938) and the Chambers and Echenique (2016) monograph.

6
The (Nonstochastic) Producer Problem

A Conversation Overheard

Kid: What's an input?

Famous Production Economist: x.

Kid: What's x?

Famous Production Economist: An input.

This chapter manipulates $x's$, $y's$, $p's$, $w's$, and other real objects. As mathematical objects, they're clearly defined. But to interpret them properly, it's essential to remember what they mean. So, while you will catch me and other economists referring to inputs lackadaisically as *labor, land,* and *capital* and *apples, oranges,* and *tomatoes* as outputs, our analysis only applies to more precisely defined commodities. Each is distinguished according to time, place, quality, type, location, and all economically meaningful dimensions. The only dimension in which they can differ across observations is quantity.

Unfortunately, such precise observations on real-world quantities rarely occur. Properly controlling all potential dimensions, except quantity, in data collection remains outside our reach. Even if proper controls could be exercised, collecting data requires time, and things change as time passes. You're not the same person you were yesterday because yesterday's experiences have colored your view of the world. And neither is any other economic agent. Those changes may seem imperceptible, but over time they accrete and can affect economic choices. Thus, applied situations often require pragmatic compromises and the application of our concepts to data that differ from the setting in which the concepts were developed. Thus, gaps can be expected to appear between what our models predict and what we observe. In some sense, it's to be expected. Fortunately, such gaps often point the way for refining both our conceptual models and our empirical analysis.

The study of economic growth presents a classic example. Over six decades ago, Abramovitz (1956) observed that net national product growth in the United States between between 1870 and 1953 was primarily driven by an increase in *total factor productivity*, with the latter being defined as measured aggregate output divided by measured aggregate input. His reaction bears repeating:

Competitive Agents in Certain and Uncertain Markets. Robert G. Chambers, Oxford University Press (2021).

DOI: 10.1093/oso/9780190063016.001.0001

> This result is surprising in the lopsided importance which it appears to give to productivity increase, and it should be, in a sense, sobering, if not discouraging, to students of economic growth. Since we know little about the causes of productivity increase, the indicated importance of this element may be taken to be some sort of measure of our ignorance about the causes of economic growth in the United States and some sort of indication of where we need to concentrate our attention. (Abramovitz, 1956, p.11)

Almost exactly contemporaneously, Schultz (1956) phrased the central problem of explaining economic growth as reestablishing

> a strong and satisfactory linkage between input and output over time. In our efforts to do this, we would do well to place before us and keep in mind the characteristics of an ideal input–output formula for this purpose. It would be one where output over inputs, excluding of course, changes in their quality, stayed at or close to one. The closer we come to a one-to-one relationship in our formulation the more complete would be our (economic) explanation. (Schultz, 1956, p. 758)[1]

What clearly bothered both Abramovitz (1956) and Schultz (1956) was that the only way to reconcile observed total-factor-productivity behavior with economic theory was to attribute virtually all historic output growth to *unexplained shifts* in the aggregate production frontier. One could, of course, call this unexplained shift *technological change*. And many did, but as Jorgenson and Griliches (1967) memorably argued: "Simply relabelling these changes as Technical Progress or Advance of Knowledge leaves the problem of explaining growth in total output unsolved." Put simply, naming a phenomenon is not the same thing as explaining it. Jorgenson and Griliches (1967) were among the first to provide an answer to the apparent riddle. Its essence was that prior attempts at measuring total factor productivity had not properly utilized economic theory in translating accounting-based measures of inputs and outputs into total-factor-productivity measures. And once the resulting discrepancies were removed, input growth reemerged as the primary determinant of economic growth.[2] The theory involved was that of the profit-maximizing producer that is the core subject of much of production economics.

[1] In a footnote, Schultz (1956) attributed his phrasing to Zvi Griliches, who was his student at the time.

[2] There are exceptions, however. For example, even after the refinements made by Jorgenson and Griliches (1967) and later authors were incorporated into the analysis, aggregate input growth in U.S. agriculture since 1914 has been virtually nonexistent. But output from that industry has grown dramatically.

Production economics is perhaps the area of economics with the tightest links between theory and practice. People routinely estimate or approximate representations of technologies using observed data. Thus, reconciling theory and empirical practice is of first-order importance. That presents challenges for both data collection and for applications of theory to those data. Consequently, choosing *specific mathematical forms* for production structures is a practical problem. And in making such choices, the goal is "to allow economists to immerse themselves in their data . . . and then to choose forms which seem capable of handling this information" (William M. "Terence" Gorman as quoted by Honohan and Neary 2003). In trying to cope with the practical problem of choosing implementable structures, production economists have developed a peculiar jargon that is distinct from that, say, of consumer theorists or decision theorists.[3]

That jargon mainly extends or specializes our basic assumptions of *CA*, *CB*, *C*, *MA*, *MB*, *M*, *CONA*, *CONB*, and *CON* but with different names. The nomenclature we've been using is intended to promote a visual understanding of $\succeq(y)$ in terms of correspondences derived from it. Thus, the "above" (A) properties refer to $V(y)$ and the "below" (B) properties to $Y(x)$. This chapter reverts frequently to the production–economics jargon. That risks promoting confusion, but the intent is to make the underlying production–economics literature more accessible to you when, and if, you turn to it. But it leaves the onus on you to link the two. I will provide exercises along the way to help you, but if they're ignored much of what follows may prove relatively incomprehensible. The discussion that follows also focuses on the production–economics analogue of $Y(x)$. That is done because the consumer problem studied in Chapter 5 used $V(y)$ almost exclusively. $V(y)$, which corresponds to what production economists think of as an *input set*, is certainly essential to production economics. But I believe leaving it to you to develop the analogous properties for V and T (introduced below) using (6.1) will eventually prove more beneficial to you than if I were to recycle previously developed concepts into a producer context.

That brings us to inputs and outputs. Economists routinely distinguish between inputs and outputs. Strictly speaking, this is not formally necessary, and, worse, many times it's misleading. But it buttresses traditional intuition, which can be helpful in thinking of concrete examples. In the main, that

[3] As a production economist who often keeps company with economists from different intellectual neighborhoods, I rarely fail to be amazed when their seemingly mysterious slang (jargon) is explained to me. All too often, my response has been of the ilk "but that's what we (meaning production economists) call. . . ." Anyone who believes all economists truly speak a common language is as deluded as someone who believes Americans and Aussies share one.

distinction is maintained in this chapter. As such, this chapter follows specific notational conventions (these are the same as in Chambers [1988]): $x \in \mathbb{R}_{+}^{N}$ denotes a vector of inputs, $y \in \mathbb{R}_{+}^{M}$ denotes a vector of outputs, $w \in \mathbb{R}_{++}^{N}$ denotes a vector of input prices, and $p \in \mathbb{R}_{++}^{M}$ denotes a vector of output prices.

Remark 17. *Having decided to preserve the distinction between inputs and outputs, it's appropriate to think about why doing so may be problematic. As always, simple (albeit frequently unrealistic) examples illustrate best. Consider the generic "hog-corn" producer who grows corn that is ultimately fed to the hogs. In a similar vein, many dairy farmers traditionally grew corn, converted that corn into silage, and then fed the silage to their animals. Decide for yourself how to classify corn and silage in these examples. Are they outputs or inputs? Or do they represent something else?*

1 The Canonical Problem

The standard producer problem is to choose an input bundle, $x \in \mathbb{R}_{+}^{N}$, and an output bundle, $y \in \mathbb{R}_{+}^{M}$, to maximize the difference between revenue, $p^{\top}y$, realized from sale of the output bundle at market prices, $p \in \mathbb{R}_{++}^{M}$, and the cost of purchasing the input bundle, $w^{\top}x$, at market prices, $w \in \mathbb{R}_{++}^{N}$. Thus, the objective function is $p^{\top}y - w^{\top}x$, which in the absence of some constraint can be made arbitrarily large and positive. For the problem to be economically meaningful, something must constrain the producer's choice. That constraint is what production economists usually call the *technology*, $T \subset \mathbb{R}_{+}^{N} \times \mathbb{R}_{+}^{M}$, so that the canonical producer's problem is to find the (convex) conjugate of $-\delta(x, y \mid T)$ for $(p, -w)$. The solution to that problem requires that

$$(p, -w) \in \partial^{-}(-\delta)(x, y \mid T) \Rightarrow (x, y) \in \partial^{-}(-\delta)^{*}(p, -w \mid T)$$

with $(-\delta)^{*}(p, -w \mid T)$ a closed, sublinear function that's usually referred to as the *profit function* for T.[4] From Lemma 5, Theorem 5, and basic duality results, it follows that $(-\delta)^{*}(p, -w \mid T)$ is fully dual to the "convexified" technology associated with $(-\delta)^{**}(x, y \mid T)$ interpreted as the biconjugate of $-\delta(x, y \mid T)$ in $(p, -w)$.

[4] The notation $\partial^{-}(-\delta)(x, y \mid T)$ is certainly unsightly and perhaps confusing. It is to be read as the subdifferential operation applied to $-\delta(x, y \mid T)$. Similarly, $(-\delta)^{*}(p, -w \mid T)$ is to be read as the conjugacy operation applied to $-\delta(x, y \mid T)$. My apologies for resorting to it, but doing so allows me to operate using a common consistent definition of the indicator function.

Although it's not treated in detail here, handling a "constrained profit-maximization" problem reduces operationally to finding the intersection of T with the constraint set, call it C, and then solving for $(-\delta)^*(p,-w \mid T \cap C)$ with optimal solutions satisfying

$$(p,-w) \in \partial^-(-\delta)(x,y \mid T \cap C) \Rightarrow (x,y) \in \partial^-(-\delta)^*(p,-w \mid T \cap C).$$

So, with the essential math already developed, need we go further? Do we need to detail the properties of T and the peculiarities that separate it from $V(y)$ interpreted as an at-least-as-good set? This question is not easily answered. But it is one that can be asked about the consumer-oriented material presented in Chapter 5 and about all the chapters that follow.

For the rest of the chapter, I assume that you answered in the positive. The discussion proceeds as follows. First, I discuss what production economists mean when they talk about technologies and how they perceive them. Then I work through some restrictive versions of technologies that have received varying amounts of attention in the literature. The structural restrictions discussed often have important implications in areas beyond production economics, even though they are often called by different names. Thus, they merit independent study on their own, but for concreteness sake the conversation is cast in production-theoretic terms. The discussion then moves to an examination of the profit-maximization problem in its various guises. Each of these has been discussed in "squiggle" form in Chapter 4, so you can expect a relatively discursive treatment that highlights some of the peculiar problems production economists concentrate on. That is followed by discussion of "revealed-preference" approaches to the producer problem.

2 Defining the Technology

To initiate the discussion of the technology, I want to emphasize a fundamental perspective that most production economists take. Economists from other areas often do not adhere to this distinction in discussing production-related problems. That can result in considerable confusion when the two parties try to communicate. It's yet another instance that reminds us why the primary definition of "jargon" offered by the *Oxford English Dictionary* is "[t]he inarticulate utterance of birds or a vocal sound resembling it."

In production-theoretic terms, the "technology" consists of purely physical relationships, and it is devoid of economic content. It is a datum that producers take as given in determining their feasible reaction to market conditions, and that datum describes what can be produced at the time decisions are made. Unless we assume otherwise, the technology is known to producers and all producers have access to it. That does not mean, however, that all produce things in the same manner. For example, given the current state of knowledge, producers can choose to cut grass a variety of different ways. They can use a riding mower, a gasoline-powered push mower, a battery-powered push motor, or if they're particularly energetic, a human-powered push reel blade mower. Each procedure is possible and as such is part of the technology. The difference, of course, lies in the input combinations that are used and, perhaps, in the end product. Nevertheless, in common parlance, many would refer to each of these different methods as *different technologies*. That is not our definition. Instead, we refer to such differences as different *production processes* that are contained within the technology.

Because the technology is a datum, it is not something that producers can change. What is and what is not physically possible is determined not by producers but by the laws of Nature, so to speak. Viewed from this perspective, the technology represents the basic constraint that underlies all economic activity involving the exchange of goods and services because most goods or services can be exchanged only if they can be produced.

There are three mathematical representations of the technology, each of which is equivalent to the other two. They are the *input correspondence*, $V : \mathbb{R}^M_+ \rightrightarrows \mathbb{R}^N_+$, defined by

$$\begin{aligned} V(y) &= \{x \in \mathbb{R}^N_+ : x \text{ can produce } y \in \mathbb{R}^M_+\} \\ &= \{x \in \mathbb{R}^N_+ : x \succeq (y)\}, \end{aligned}$$

the *output correspondence*, $Y : \mathbb{R}^N_+ \rightrightarrows \mathbb{R}^M_+$, defined by

$$\begin{aligned} Y(x) &= \{y \in \mathbb{R}^M_+ : x \in \mathbb{R}^N_{++} \text{ can produce } y\} \\ &= \{y \in \mathbb{R}^M_+ : x \succeq (y)\}, \end{aligned}$$

and the *graph of the technology*, $T \subset \mathbb{R}^{M+N}_+$

$$\begin{aligned} T &= \{(x, y) : x \text{ can produce } y\} \\ &= \{(x, y) : x \succeq (y)\}. \end{aligned}$$

From these definitions, it should be apparent that $\succeq (y)$ is now a binary relation defined on $\mathbb{R}^N_+ \times \mathbb{R}^M_+$, where comparison or ordering now relate to whether x is feasible for producing y. Moreover, T corresponds to what we referred to earlier as $Gr(\succeq(y))$. For the remainder of this chapter, we'll stick with this simpler notation, hopefully with little or no confusion.

As always, these different representations of $\succeq(y)$ satisfy

$$x \in V(y) \Leftrightarrow y \in Y(x) \Leftrightarrow (x, y) \in T. \tag{6.1}$$

Pictorially, the *input set* (the image of the input correspondence) is associated with everything on or above an *isoquant*, the *output set* (the image of the output correspondence) with everything on or below a *production possibilities frontier (transformation curve)*, and the *graph of the technology* with all input–output combinations on or below the *production function.*

One way to visualize what is involved is to draw a representation of T on a piece of paper. Restricting attention to a single input and single output, many of you would likely draw something that approximates the curve emanating from the origin in Figure 1.1. $V(y)$ is then associated with fixing y, slicing T horizontally (presuming x to be on the horizontal axis), and projecting that slice onto the x axis. $Y(x)$ is associated with fixing x, slicing T vertically, and projecting that slice onto the y axis. **Please remember the projection part!** When there are two inputs, the result of this slicing procedure for $V(y)$, under appropriate regularity conditions, gives you something similar to the curved part of Figure 1.2. When there are two outputs, the slicing procedure for $Y(x)$ gives you something similar to the curved component of Figure 1.4.

2.1 Properties of Output Sets

I list these properties and then discuss their intuitive content and possible limitations. *These properties are not cast in iron.* As before, they can be interpreted as a menu of potential assumptions to be placed upon nonstochastic production technologies. Which ones are appropriate depends crucially on the applied context. In reading and thinking about them you should compare them to properties that were imposed earlier on $\succeq(y)$. In particular, you should try to identify which ones are special cases of those imposed earlier and which ones are not.

Properties of the Output Set (Y)

Y.1 $0 \in Y(x)$ for all $x \in \mathbb{R}^N_+$, $Y(0) \cap \mathbb{R}^M_{++} = \varnothing$;

Y.2 $y' \leq y \in Y(x) \Rightarrow y' \in Y(x)$ (free disposability of outputs);

Y.2.W $\lambda Y(x) \subset Y(x)$ for $0 < \lambda < 1$ (weak disposability of output);

Y.3 $x' \geq x \Rightarrow Y(x) \subset Y(x')$ (free disposability of inputs);

Y.3.W $Y(x) \subset Y(\lambda x)$ for $\lambda > 1$ (weak disposability of inputs);

Y.4 $Y(x)$ is bounded for all $x \in \mathbb{R}_+^N$ (boundedness);

Y.5. $Y(x)$ is a convex set for all $x \in \mathbb{R}_+^N$;

Y.6 $Y(x) \cap Y(x') \subset Y(\mu x + (1-\mu)x')$ for $\mu \in [0,1]$ and all $x, x' \in \mathbb{R}_+^N$ (quasi-concavity);

Y.7 $\mu Y(x) + (1-\mu)Y(x') \subset Y(\mu x + (1-\mu)x')$ for $\mu \in [0,1]$ and all $x, x' \in \mathbb{R}_+^N$ (convexity of the graph);

Y.8 $Y(x)$ is a closed correspondence, that is, if $x^k \to x^o, y^k \to y^o$ and $y^k \in Y(x^k)$ for all k, then $y^o \in Y(x^o)$.

Problem 52. *State the properties of the input set (input correspondence) and the graph of the technology (T) that are associated with Properties Y.*1 *to Y.*8.

2.1.1 No Fixed Costs and No Free Lunch (No Land of Cockaigne)

Y.1 comes in two parts. The first, $0 \in Y(x)$ for all $x \in \mathbb{R}_+^N$, says that all input bundles can produce nothing. Or put another way, output inaction is always possible. Formally, this ensures that all output sets are nonempty because each at least contains the origin. Its name, *no fixed costs*, reflects its economic consequence.

The second part of Y.1 means that failure to commit a strictly positive amount of at least one input cannot be consistent with the production of a positive amount of any output. Traditionally, the second part of Y.1 is referred to in Friedmanesque terms—there is *no free lunch*—and in more classical terms as *No Land of Cockaigne*. Either gets the basic idea across: you can't get something from nothing.

2.1.2 Disposability of Outputs

Y.2 says that a producer can choose to operate inefficiently in output space. We often refer to Y.2 as *free disposability of outputs* or output-free disposability. Output-free disposability means exactly what it says: Producers can dispose of outputs they may not desire for free. While probably a harmless assumption when outputs are "goods," that is, have a positive market value, it isn't so obviously harmless when one of the outputs is a "bad."

For example, suppose an agricultural producer wants to diminish runoff pollution without altering her overall input commitment. Then resources allocated to producing the crop presumably must be diverted to preventing the runoff. Almost inevitably, that means she will have to lower agricultural outputs. Thus, bad outputs are likely not freely disposable.

Y. 2, therefore, may be too strong. So, it's convenient to have a weaker assumption to fall back on. Y.2.W, where W stands for "weak," is one such possibility that has been widely used: we shall typically refer to it as *weak disposability of output*. Weak disposability of output implies that outputs can be costlessly disposed of along the ray on which the output bundle lies. That is, to costlessly reduce one output, the other outputs must also be reduced proportionately. The reasoning here is that if, for example, one of the outputs is an industrial good and the other is a pollutant, the resources required to abate pollution are liberated by the radial reduction in the good outputs. Hence, disposing of bad outputs like pollution no longer carries a zero opportunity cost. Instead it bears a positive opportunity cost (for a fixed-input bundle) in terms of foregone "good" outputs.

Y.2.W, however, encounters real-world problems in many settings. Both it and Y.2 may not be consistent with the requirements of *material (mass) balance*. The application of material balance in economic analysis was pioneered by the pathbreaking contribution of Ayres and Kneese (1969) and involves applying the physical principle of *conservation of mass* to production systems.

An example illustrates. Consider again the runoff–pollution problem, and in particular, nitrogen runoff from chemical fertilizer. What weak disposability literally says is that holding x constant, which in this case means holding fertilizer application constant, reducing runoff and agricultural output proportionally is possible. If true, then where does the nitrogen mass embedded in the fertilizer go? Surely, it is not embedded in the output if one can drive that to zero as one drives runoff to zero. Because that mass must be conserved, the unused nitrogen must go somewhere. Weak disposability can thus violate material balance. So, too, can Y.2.

One proposed solution to this puzzle is to relabel pollution or runoff as an input and treat it as a conventional input (that is, one that is freely disposable as described below). This is even less acceptable than weak disposability. In fact, it's silly. It supposes that relabeling something changes its essential character. Even worse, it does not get at the basic problem. Here's why. As will become clear, treating it in this fashion requires the following to be possible. Holding all outputs and all other inputs constant, increasing runoff without bound has to be technically feasible.

An example from my home state well illustrates the problem. Maryland's primary agricultural industry is *broiler* production. A broiler is a chicken grown to be broiled, although frying (especially in Maryland) and baking is also permissible. Naturally feeding chickens produces chicken meat, but much like feeding humans, it also produces a very natural by-product. That by-product when produced in massive amounts is also nasty to handle and can have negative environmental impacts on water and other natural systems. Now let's agree to rename that nasty by-product an input and treat it as though it were freely disposable. As noted, that requires it to be physically possible to hold all other inputs, including chicken feed and water and all other outputs, including the actual broilers, constant and to increase by-production of that nasty input without bound. So, where does the by-product come from if feed is held constant, as are the number of chickens? Again, material balance is obviously violated, and the proposed solution only works if one ignores physical reality.

2.1.3 Input Disposability and Input Congestion

Y.3, *free disposability of inputs* or input-free disposability, generalizes the concept of positive marginal productivities of variable inputs. Many real-world examples, however, suggest that some inputs may have negative marginal products. Typically, this happens when too much of a variable input is applied to a fixed bundle of nonvariable inputs. The additional variable input simply cannot find enough fixed inputs with which to cooperate. The fixed input becomes *congested* as increasing amounts of the variable inputs are heaped upon it.

Fertilizers provide perhaps the best-known example of input congestion. Applied at low rates, chemical fertilizer increases yield, but at excessive rates of application, the resultant chemical burning reduces yields. Another is the old saw, "too many cooks spoil the broth."

Allowing for input congestion requires a weaker version of Y.3. Y.3.W, *weak disposability of inputs*, only requires that radial expansion of an input vector capable of producing an output vector can produce that same output vector. Here the reasoning is simple. If all inputs are expanded proportionately, the crowding phenomenon that arises from increasing amounts of a variable input being applied to a fixed-input bundle will not occur. Again, chemical fertilizers are a good real-world example. If fertilizer and acreage are expanded proportionately, chemical burn is unlikely to emerge. However, as was pointed out above, problems with material balance may still intrude. The fertilizer and acreage example illustrates. In applying fertilizer to acreage results in runoff, it's highly unlikely that either Y.3 or Y.3.*W* will be consistent with material balance.

Example 10. *Lichtenberg and Zilberman (1986) argue that certain inputs, such as pesticides, do not promote output growth. Rather, they prevent output damage. The damage-control specification of an agricultural production system is the result.*

Suppose that the amount of the damage-control input applied is x_d and the nondamage-control inputs are x_p. The most common version of the damage-

control specification requires output, y_s, of crop s to be related to inputs according to

$$y_s = \left(1 - e^{-g(x_d)}\right) f\left(x_p\right),$$

where the function $g(x_d)$ is nondecreasing so that application of the damage-control input prevents damage. Here $f\left(x_p\right)$ is intuitively thought of as the maximal attainable output given use of x_p if no damage occurs. In many, if not most, instances, damage-control inputs such as pesticides will be associated with a by-product, pesticide pollution, that escapes into the environment because it does not end on the plant. Here you may want to think of spray application. Call this by-product y_p and assume it is measured in the same physical units as x_d. A more accurate representation of the damage-control model would be something like

$$y_s = \left(1 - e^{-h\left(x_d - y_p\right)}\right) f\left(x_p\right),$$

so that damage-control activity is specifically attributed to the amount of the damage-control agent that reaches the plant. Hopefully, this makes physical sense to you; if it does not, you should write out why you disagree and suggest an alternative specification.

We can now use this example to consider the plausibility of treating the by-product as a conventional input and the plausibility of weak disposability of the inputs $\left(x_p, x_d\right)$. For the first, consider what happens if y_p increases in this model, holding $\left(x_p, x_d\right)$ constant? If h is nondecreasing as we would expect, y_s should fall. The reason is simple: increasing the by-product means less of the active ingredient goes to damage control, more damage occurs, and output falls. The output falling is not what you would normally expect from increasing an input, and so treating y_p as an input in this context may be problematic. Now, it's your turn: Is the damage-control specification consistent with Y.2.W?

Remark 18. *Various attempts have been made to develop a "good model of bad outputs." Exemplars include Murty, Russell, and Levkoff (2012) and Førsund (2009), who extend ideas originally advanced by Frisch (1965) in another context. Another is Pethig (2006). Their essential idea is that practical production systems often require more detailed modeling and assumptions than are typically used in economic models of production.*

The damage-control model helps illustrate. Suppose that production of the good output obeys $y_s = \left(1 - e^{-h\left(x_d - y_p\right)}\right) f\left(x_p\right)$, where all terms are as above.

It's clear that, in this context, increases in y_p are associated with decreases in good output. That's because the by-product results from an active ingredient that is not reaching its targeted use. Thus, from the producer's perspective, it's wasted material. You can be sure that producers will take economic actions to diminish that wastage. Picture, for example, how a producer would react to a faulty sprayer that routinely wasted a measurable percentage of the active ingredient. Rationality, in the long run, would require him or her to take ameliorative action. Resources would be devoted to controlling that wastage. If producers, however, devote resources to controlling that wastage, those resources must be included in the production process. That recognition would argue for an even more detailed modeling of the production system that would properly account for those ameliorative or abating activities.

2.1.4 Bounds on Output Sets

Y.4 requires the output set to have an upper bound for any potential combination of inputs. From a practical perspective, this is a regularity condition that facilitates mathematical analysis of production systems. In a very real sense, it's also likely a "free" assumption because it's hard to imagine it being contradicted by data generated from real-world observations.

2.1.5 Curvature Properties of Output Sets

Conditions Y.5 through Y.7 each imply something about the shape of the output set. Generally, they are not equivalent. It's easy to show, however, that Y.7 implies both Y.5 and Y.6. However, neither Y.5 nor Y.6 implies Y.7, or one another. Thus, these axioms represent different curvature conditions to impose upon the output sets. But fundamentally, the rationale for each is some version of the law of diminishing returns. You should be aware by now that the concepts of diminishing returns to scale and diminishing marginal returns to an input are different. But just to be safe, perform the following exercise.

Exercise 24. *Please discuss with appropriate visual illustrations and mathematical formalisms the distinction between decreasing returns to scale, diminishing marginal productivity, diminishing marginal rate of technical substitution, and increasing marginal rate of transformation.*

Y.5 implies that output sets are convex; that is, they have production possibility frontiers that are concave to the origin and that exhibit an *increasing marginal rate of transformation between outputs*. Put another way, if inputs are held constant, successive increases in one output can only be had by increasingly large sacrifices of another output. Here you should refer to Figure 1.4 and Figure 1.6. Y.5 is equivalent to *CONB*.

Y.6 implies that $V(y)$ convex. Here you should refer to Figure 1.2 and Figure 1.6. Isoquants are shaped in their normal fashion and exhibit a *diminishing marginal rate of technical substitution between all inputs.* Or, if all outputs are held fixed, decreases in the use of one input can only be compensated by increasingly large increases in another input. Y.6 is equivalent to *CONA*.

Y.7 is referred to as *convexity of the graph,* but you should also recognize it as convexity of the order (*CON*). It implies, among other things, that both Y.5 and Y.6 are satisfied. Heuristically, it imposes the notions of diminishing marginal returns to inputs and nonincreasing returns to scale. It can be visualized using Figure 1.1 by labeling the horizontal axis x and the vertical axis y and then taking T to be everything on or below the curve emanating from the origin.

2.1.6 $Y : \mathbb{R}^N \rightrightarrows \mathbb{R}^M$ a closed correspondence

Y.8 is a continuity requirement. It's useful in establishing the existence of minima and maxima, and it's perhaps best viewed as a regularity condition. If you fix x, and consider $y^k \to y^o$ and $y^k \in Y(x^k)$, you will see it implies *CB*. It also implies *CA*. What's especially important to note is that it is impossible to contradict Y.8 based solely on the observation of any finite data set. (Put another way, for any observed body of production data, one can construct a closed output set consistent with it.) I demonstrate this claim by an important example.

Example 11. *This example has its roots in Koopmans (1951), Farrell (1957), and Afriat (1972). Let's assume that we have collected data by surveying K firms about their production practices. Denote the observations on inputs and outputs for the kth firm by*

$$(x^k, y^k) \in \mathbb{R}_+^{N+M}, \quad k = 1, ..., K.$$

Thus, you have K observations on an N-dimensional vector of inputs and an M-dimensional output vector. Now consider the following piecewise linear technology constructed from those observations:

$$T^K = \left\{(x, y) : x \geq \sum_{k=1}^{K} \lambda_k x^k, y \leq \sum_{k=1}^{K} \lambda_k y^k, \lambda_k \geq 0, k = 1, ..., K, \sum_{k=1}^{K} \lambda_k = 1\right\}.$$

This technology is often referred to as the **data envelopment analysis** *(DEA) approximation to the underlying technology induced from these observations on inputs and outputs. Because each* (x^k, y^k) *corresponds to an observed input–output combination, it must be that* $(x^k, y^k) \in T$ *for all k. The set formed as*

$$C^K = \left\{(x, y) : x = \sum_{k=1}^{K} \lambda_k x^k, y = \sum_{k=1}^{K} \lambda_k y^k, \lambda_k \geq 0, k = 1, ..., K, \sum_{k=1}^{K} \lambda_k = 1\right\},$$

is the convex hull of the observed data. As such, C^K *represents the smallest convex set in* $\mathbb{R}^{M+N}$ *containing the data.* T^K *is obtained by imposing free disposability of inputs and outputs on* C^K*.* T^K *is sometimes referred to as the* **free disposal convex hull** *(FDCH) of the observed data.*

Problem 53. *Illustrate the technology in Example 11 pictorially in the case of a single input and a single output. (Hint: Start by locating three points in input–output space. First, draw the smallest convex set containing all three points. Now impose free disposability of inputs and outputs.)*

Problem 54. *Determine which of the properties of the output sets the technology in Example 11 satisfies. Discuss all of your reasoning here.*

Problem 55. *For the case of scalar y, consider the production function derived from* T^K *as the solution to the following* **linear program***:*

$$f^K(x) = Max\{y : (x, y) \in T^K\}.$$

Show that if the output correspondence satisfies properties Y.1–Y.4, Y.6, and Y.8, f^K *is continuous, nondecreasing, and concave in x. Finally, prove that*

$$(x, y) \in T^K \Leftrightarrow y \leq f^K(x);$$

that is, the production function is a complete function representation of the technology.

3 Function Representations of the Technology

We closed the last section with an exercise demonstrating that for the scalar output case the production function for the technology in Example 11 is *a complete function representation of the technology*. The example on which that exercise is based says something deeper: namely, *for any body of observed data, one can find a technology consistent with nonincreasing returns to scale and free disposability of inputs and outputs that is consistent with it.* In other words, we can always construct from *any* observed data set on inputs and outputs a "technology" that satisfies these axioms. Moreover, in isolating this "technology," data on input and output prices are not required. So the identification strategy is not the same as that in the revealed-preference approach. One might well wonder why a similar strategy would not work in the consumer framework. The answer lies in what's observable and what's not. In the revealed-preference approach, the consumer analogue of output is utility, which is not observed. Hence, the consumer case has no observable primal measure of "input" performance. In the production case, an observable measure of "input" performance is available, and it's the observed output. That greatly simplifies matters. A large applied literature has sprouted from this observation. Much of it falls within the interstices of economics and operations research, and it often appears under the rubric of *data envelopment analysis* or *nonparametric productivity analysis.*

3.1 The directional input distance function

I used T^K to convince you that you could define and calculate a function representation of an approximation to T. Having done that, it's time to renew an old acquaintance. The *directional input distance function* is defined as

$$\begin{aligned} d(x, y; g) &= \max\{\beta \in \mathbb{R} : x - \beta g \in V(y)\}, \quad g \in \mathbb{R}_+^N \backslash \{0\} \\ &= \max\{\beta \in \mathbb{R} : y \in Y(x - \beta g)\}, \quad g \in \mathbb{R}_+^N \backslash \{0\}, \end{aligned}$$

if there is β such that $x - \beta g \in V(y)$ and $-\infty$ otherwise. It gives the largest number of units of the reference vector g that can be subtracted from the relevant input vector and keep it feasible for the relevant y. g, of course, now is interpreted as a vector of inputs, and thus g is an *input numeraire.*

You may have already guessed that if the technology satisfies free disposability of inputs, $d(x, y; g)$ is a complete function representation of the technology in the sense that

$$d(x, y; g) \geq 0 \Leftrightarrow x \in V(y).$$

Sufficiency is trivial. To see necessity, suppose that $d(x,y; g) \geq 0$; then by definition

$$x - d(x, y; g)\, g \in V(y),$$

and $x \geq x - d(x, y; g)\, g$. Now use free disposability of inputs. Given this result, it's immediate that:

Proposition 5. *The directional input distance function defined by the linear program*

$$\max \left\{ \begin{array}{c} \beta : (x - \beta g)\, x \geq \sum_{k=1}^{K} \lambda_k x^k, \\ y \leq \sum_{k=1}^{K} \lambda_k y^k, \\ \sum_{k=1}^{K} \lambda_k = 1, \\ \lambda_k \geq 0, k = 1, \ldots, K, \end{array} \right\}$$

is a complete function representation of T^K.

3.2 Properties of $d(x, y; g)$

By now, you should be able to show the following yourselves:

1. $d(x + \alpha g, y; g) = d(x, y; g) + \alpha, \alpha \in \mathbb{R}$.
2. $d(x, y; \mu g) = \mu^{-1} d(x, y; g), \quad \mu > 0$.
3. If Y.8 is satisfied, $d(x, y; g)$ is jointly continuous in inputs and outputs.
4. Free disposability of inputs implies $d(x, y; g)$ is nondecreasing in inputs.
5. Free disposability of outputs implies $d(x, y; g)$ is nonincreasing in outputs.
6. Quasi-concavity of $Y(x)$ implies $d(x, y; g)$ is concave in inputs.

Here are some easy problems or *finger exercises*. Please make sure that you do them because I use them to introduce two other directional distance functions. One you've already seen (but in a slightly different form), and the other you haven't.

Exercise 25. *Develop a graphical representation of the directional input distance function and a proof of its properties above.*

Exercise 26. *Consider the* ***radial input distance function***, $D_i(x, y)$ *defined by*

$$D_i(x, y) = \frac{1}{1 - d(x, y; x)}.$$

Exhaustively develop the properties of $D_i(x, y)$.

Exercise 27. *Consider the* ***directional output distance function***[5] *defined by*

$$\vec{D}_o(y, x; g) \equiv \max\{\theta \in \mathbb{R} : y + \theta g \in Y(x)\}, \quad g \in \mathbb{R}^M_+ \backslash \{0\}.$$

Show that under free disposability of outputs, $\vec{D}_o(y, x; g)$ is a complete function representation of the technology in the sense that

$$\vec{D}_o(y, x; g) \geq 0 \Leftrightarrow y \in Y(x).$$

Exercise 28. *Develop the properties of $\vec{D}_o(y, x; g)$ corresponding to Y.1–Y.8.*

Exercise 29. *Consider the* ***directional technology distance function*** *defined by*[6]

$$\vec{D}_T(y, x; g_y, g_x) \equiv \max\{\theta : y + \theta g_y \in Y(x - \theta g_x)\}, \quad (g_y, g_x) \in \mathbb{R}^{M+N}_+ \backslash \{0\}.$$

Show that under free disposability of inputs and outputs, $\vec{D}_T(y, x; g_y, g_x)$ is a complete function representation of the technology.

Exercise 30. *Develop the properties of $\vec{D}_T(y, x; g_y, g_x)$ corresponding to Y.1–Y.8.*

Exercise 31. *Consider the* ***radial output distance function*** *given by*

$$\vec{D}_o(y, x; y) = \frac{1 - D_o(y, x)}{D_o(y, x)}.$$

Develop its properties that derive from Y.1–Y.8.

Problem 56. *For the DEA (FDCH) technology, T^K, derive $\vec{D}_o(y, x; g)$ and exhaustively characterize its properties. Is that $\vec{D}_o(y, x; g)$ a complete function representation of T^K?*

[5] $\vec{D}_o$, while obviously related to t, is defined slightly differently. The definition of t in the current case is

$$\begin{aligned} t(y, x; g) &= \inf\{\beta : x \in V(y - \beta g)\} \\ &= \inf\{\beta : y - \beta g \in Y(x)\}. \end{aligned}$$

$\vec{D}_o$ reflects the standard definition and terminology in the current production economics literature. Unfortunately, I am in large part responsible for that situation, but *ex post* apologies don't rectify past mistakes. So, to ensure that you can translate results developed in the production-economics literature to the current context, I preserve the distinction here. However, in Chapter 9, which discusses stochastic technologies, I revert to t. And, for that, my reasoning would be that there's no sense in extending a bad precedent made in one context to another.

[6] More apologies.

4 Structure of Technology

In many instances, the restrictions on the technology that have been developed in Y.1–Y.8 suffice. For example, as we've already shown in our "Squiggly Economics" discussion, we need only a subset of those restrictions to ensure the existence of cost functions, revenue functions, and profit functions and along with them well-behaved demand and supplies. As Example 11 and the following problems and exercises clarify, a programming approximation to a convex technology for any data set is always available.

But in many instances, and particularly in econometric work, further structure is needed for empirical investigation. Econometric work typically starts with the assumption of a particular functional form. The sad fact, however, is that we do not know the true structure of economic relationships. We draw generic pictures to visualize and analyze generic functions that satisfy a set of potentially plausible criteria, such as concavity or positive homogeneity, but the theory alone does not determine specific forms for these functions. Nonetheless, for empirical work to proceed, something must be chosen to represent the "true" model. In a production setting, the form chosen necessarily imposes structure on our empirical representation of the technology, and that structure determines the types of economic parables we can tell about the underlying data. Even more importantly, those structures inform and constrain the manner in which we confront and analyze economic phenomena. Paraphrasing Gorman, the ultimate goal is to let us immerse ourselves in our data and "choose forms which seem capable of handling this information."

If we are to have any confidence in our empirical work, it's important to understand what questions that empirical work can answer. To be able to do that, you need to be able to recognize the restrictions embedded in functional structures. In applied work, it's imperative to remember that specification matters and that often specification *implies* certain results. So, if you impose a structure that implies specific results, don't be surprised to see them when they appear and don't interpret them as results. Because there are almost as many functional specifications as there are applied economists, it's impossible to survey the different possibilities in anything short of a tome. What follows represents a quick run-through of some of the most common versions intended to introduce you to the many varying possibilities.

4.1 Homotheticity

Some type of homotheticity is perhaps the most common functional restriction in economics. The Cobb–Douglas form is homothetic, and so too is the constant-elasticity-of-substitution (CES) form. In practice, one may encounter several different types of homotheticity, and, depending on the circumstances, "homotheticity" can mean different things.

Production economists, for example, worry about both outputs and inputs. Consumer-demand specialists, however, usually only worry about the consumer analogue to inputs–consumer demands. Thus, for consumer economists, "homotheticity" usually means what is referred to as input homotheticity below. Production economists, on the other hand, discriminate between input and output versions of homotheticity.

The bifurcated jargon emerges because consumer economists routinely assume that $\succeq(y)$ satisfies complete ordering (CO). That allows them to work in terms of an ordinal utility function, whose specific units are inconsequential. Consequently, their focus is mainly on the component of $\succeq(y)$ that corresponds to $V(y)$, and their jargon is developed for that case. But when CO is not satisfied, a more discriminating taxonomy is needed. If I were to be consistent with what's gone before, I might cast the following homotheticity discussion in terms of an *above* (for $V(y)$) notion and a *below* (for $Y(x)$) notion. Instead, I have followed the established tradition in production economics and used input and output notions.

Input homotheticity is the most familiar version. A technology is said to be *input-homothetic* if its input correspondence, $V : \mathbb{R}_+^M \rightrightarrows \mathbb{R}_+^N$, satisfies

$$V(y) = h(y)\, V(1)$$

where $h : \mathbb{R}_+^M \to \mathbb{R}_{++}$ and $1 \in \mathbb{R}^M$ is a *reference bundle of outputs.* Just what enters into this reference bundle will depend on the application, and so we can be a bit vague at the moment. The notation suggests that it might contain one unit of each of the outputs, and this is certainly a possibility. But that's not required. What is required is that once it is specified, it does not vary.

Exercise 32. *Show that if the technology is input-homothetic*

$$x \succeq (y) \Leftrightarrow \frac{x}{h(y)} \succeq (1).$$

Exercise 33. *Prove that* $h(1) = 1$ *and provide an economic interpretation.*

Exercise 34. *Prove that for an input-homothetic technology:*

$$d(x, y; g) = h(y)\, d\left(\frac{x}{h(y)}, 1; g\right),$$

where

$$d(x, 1; g) = \max\{\beta : x - \beta g \in V(1)\}.$$

Exercise 35. *Prove that for an input-homothetic technology*

$$\partial d(x, y; g) = \partial d\left(\frac{x}{h(y)}, 1; g\right).$$

Provide an economic interpretation of this result in terms of marginal rates of technical subsitution between inputs.

Input homotheticity implies that all input sets are either radial blow-ups or radial contractions of the reference input set $V(1)$. The degree to which the radial adjustment is made depends on the function h. As the last exercise demonstrates, superdifferentials are invariant to radial adjustments in input. Pictorially, that means marginal rates of substitution between inputs remain constant along rays from the origin. That, in turn, means that cost-minimizing expansion paths are linear. The technology is *input-homogeneous of degree* α if it is input-homothetic and

$$h(\mu y) = \mu^{\alpha} h(y), \quad \mu > 0.$$

Exercise 36. *Derive the directional output and technology distance functions for an input-homothetic technology.*

4.1.1 Output homotheticity

A technology is said to be *output homothetic* if its output correspondence, $Y : \mathbb{R}_+^N \rightrightarrows \mathbb{R}_+^M$, satisfies

$$Y(x) = y(x)\, Y(1)$$

where $y : \mathbb{R}_+^N \to \mathbb{R}_{++}$ and $1 \in \mathbb{R}^N$ is a *reference input vector*. As with input homotheticity, one natural, but not necessary, choice for this reference vector is the vector with one unit of each input in it. The output sets for an output-homothetic technology are all radial blow-ups or radial contractions of the reference output set, $Y(1)$. Output-homogeneous technologies are a special case of output homotheticity.

Exercise 37. *Show that if the technology is output homothetic*

$$x \geq (y) \Leftrightarrow 1 \geq \left(\frac{y}{y(x)}\right).$$

Exercise 38. *Derive the directional input, output, and technology distance functions for an output-homothetic technology.*

4.1.2 Quasi-input homotheticity

A technology is *quasi-input homothetic* if its input correspondence satisfies

$$V(y) = V^o + h(y)\, V^1$$

where $h : \mathbb{R}_+^M \rightarrow \mathbb{R}_{++}$, V^o, $V^1 \subset \mathbb{R}_+^N$ are reference sets, and summation is in the *Minkowski sense.* For $J, K \subset \mathbb{R}^N$, their *Minkowski sum* is the set formed by adding to each element of J all of the elements of K, or equivalently the set formed by adding to each element of K all the elements of J,

$$J + K = \{z \in \mathbb{R}^N : z = x + y, x \in J, y \in K\}.$$

Figure 6.1 illustrates the Minkowski addition of set J, drawn as a right angle oriented toward the northeast, and set K, drawn as a smooth curve connecting points a and b. Quasi-input-homothetic technologies possess input sets expressible as the Minkowski sum of two input sets. One, V^o, is independent of output. The other, $h(y)\, V^1$, is the input set for an input-homothetic technology.

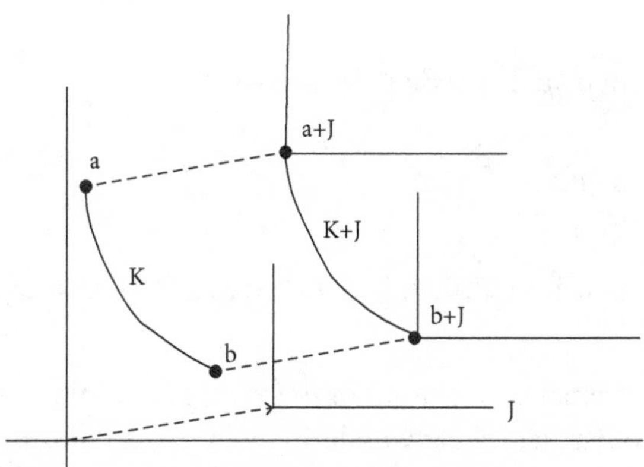

Fig. 6.1 Minkowski Addition of Two Sets

For technologies, quasi-input homotheticity results in cost-minimizing expansion paths, defined by varying output, that are straight lines which do not emanate from the origin. Consequently, they will exhibit *fixed costs,* and these will be associated with V^o. In the consumer context, the parallel property is that Engel curves are affine (not linear), and the associated fixed costs are frequently interpreted as *subsistence requirements.*

Problem 57. *Sir Richard Stone was an English economist awarded the Nobel Memorial Prize in 1984. One of his many contributions involved the popularization of the linear expenditure system (LES), which was at the forefront of attempts to model empirical demand systems consistent with consumer theory. That system was based on a utility function (the Stone–Geary function) of the form:*

$$U(y) = \prod_{n=1}^{N} (y_n - \beta_n)^{\gamma_n}$$

where β_n, γ_n for all n are parameters. The Cobb–Douglas utility function is the special case where all β_n equal to zero. Defining

$$V(u) = \{y : U(y) \geq u\},$$

prove that the Stone–Geary function satisfies quasi-input homotheticity in y. Provide an economic interpretation of all the parameters.

The directional input distance function for a quasi-input-homothetic technology is a bit complicated but ultimately familiar. Assuming free disposability of inputs

$$\begin{aligned} d(x, y; g) &= \max_{\beta} \{\beta : x - \beta g \in V^o + h(y) V^1\} \\ &= \max_{\beta^o, \beta^1, x^o, x^1} \{\beta^o + \beta^1 : x^0 - \beta^o g \in V^o, x^1 - \beta^1 g \in h(y) V^1, \\ &\qquad x^o + x^1 = x\} \\ &= \max_{x^o, x^1} \{d^o(x^o, 0; g) + d^1(x^1, y; g) : x^o + x^1 = x\}, \end{aligned}$$

which is the supremal convolution of $d^o(x^o, 0; g)$ and $d^1(x^1, y; g)$. Looking at this structure may leave you wondering why any sound-minded practical economist might be interested in quasi-input homotheticity or Stone–Geary utility structures. The answer to that question lies in the extreme tractability of its conjugate dual (2.22) representation, which corresponds to the famous Gorman polar form.

Exercise 39. *Derive the directional output and directional technology distance functions for a quasi-input-homothetic technology.*

Exercise 40. *Consider the special case of quasi-input homotheticity where*

$$V^1 = g \in \mathbb{R}_+^N.$$

This technology is ***input-translation-homothetic*** *(in the direction of g). Its input sets are parallel to V^o in the direction of g. Its directional input distance function can be written as*

$$\begin{aligned} d(x, y; g) &= \max\{\beta : x - \beta g \in V^o + h(y)\, g\} \\ &= \max\{\beta + h(y) : x - (\beta + h(y))\, g \in V^o\} - h(y) \\ &= d^o(x, 0; g^o) - h(y). \end{aligned}$$

Develop a graphical representation of this technology in terms of input sets.

Exercise 41. *Show that in the case of a scalar output, a technology is input-translation-homothetic (in the direction of g) only if its production function can be written as a monotonic transformation of a function that satisfies the Translation Property in g.*

Exercise 42. *Develop the directional output distance function for the input-translation-homothetic technology.*

Exercise 43. *Another special case of the quasi-input-homothetic technology is the* ***input affine homothetic technology*** *described by*

$$V^o = v \in \mathbb{R}_+^N.$$

This technology can be heuristically thought of as homothetic to the point $v \in \mathbb{R}_+^N$. Develop all its distance functions. Can you suggest an economic interpretation of such a technology in terms of fixed costs?

4.1.3 Quasi-output homotheticity

The technology is *quasi-output-homothetic* if its output expansion paths are affine. More formally, the technology is quasi-output-homothetic if

$$Y(x) = Y^o + y(x)\, Y^1,$$

where $y : \mathbb{R}_+^N \to \mathbb{R}_{++}$ and $Y^o, Y^1 \subset \mathbb{R}_+^M$ are reference output sets.

Problem 58. *There are obvious output analogues to input translation homotheticity and input affine homotheticity that are special cases of quasi-output homotheticity. Write these down, develop visual interpretations of each, and develop all the distance functions for the quasi-output-homothetic, output translation homothetic, and output affine homothetic technologies.*

4.2 Nonjointness

Nonjointness refers to the ability to crack the technology into separate production processes. We will study four different types of nonjointness.

4.2.1 Input nonjointness

Perhaps the most commonly recognized type of nonjointness is input nonjointness. A technology is *input-nonjoint* or *nonjoint in inputs* if

$$V(y) = \sum_{m=1}^{M} V^m(y_m),$$

with $V^m(y_m) \subset \mathbb{R}_+^N$, $m = 1, 2, ..., M$. In words, each output has its own input set. This implies

$$\begin{aligned} Y(x) &= \left\{y : x \in \sum_{m=1}^{M} V^m(y_m)\right\} \\ &= \left\{y : x^m \in V^m(y_m), m = 1, \ldots, M, \sum_{m=1}^{M} x^m = x\right\} \\ &= \left\{y : y_m \in Y^m(x^m), m = 1, \ldots, M, \sum_{m=1}^{M} x^m = x\right\} \\ &\equiv \left\{\prod_{m=1}^{M} Y^m(x^m) : \sum_{m=1}^{M} x^m = x\right\}, \end{aligned}$$

where $Y^m(x^m) \subset \mathbb{R}_+$ and $\prod_{m=1}^{M} Y^m(x^m) \equiv Y^1(x^1) \times Y^2(x^2) \times \cdots \times Y^M(x^M)$.

Figure 6.2 illustrates. For input allocation (x^1, x^2) with $x = x^1 + x^2$, $Y^1(x^1) \times Y^2(x^2)$ is the rectangle with outer vertex $(max\{Y^1(x^1)\}, max\{Y^2(x^2)\})$. The corresponding $Y(x)$ is derived by allowing (x^1, x^2) to vary across all possible allocations with the shifting outer vertex of the resulting rectangles tracing out $Y(x)'s$ outer boundary. Input nonjoint technologies played a particularly

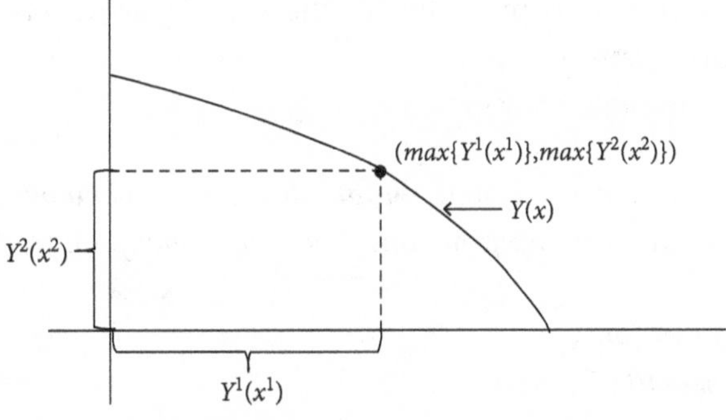

Fig. 6.2 Input-nonjoint Output Set

prominent role in the theory of international trade, where they were key to developing early versions of some of its most famous results, including the Stolper–Samuelson Theorem, the Rybczynski Theorem, and the Factor-Price Equalization Theorem.

Exercise 44. *Suppose that the technology is input-nonjoint and that each input correspondence V^m is consistent with weak diposability of output. Prove that*

$$Y(x) = \left\{ \prod_{m=1}^{M} \{y_m : y_m \le f^m(x^m)\} : \sum_{m=1}^{M} x^m = x \right\},$$

where $f^m(x^m)$ is a production function. Now discuss what this means intuitively.

The directional input distance function for an input-nonjoint technology can be derived, assuming free disposability of inputs, as (note the similarity to quasi-input homotheticity)

$$d(x, y; g) = \max\left\{\beta : \sum_{m=1}^{M} x^m - \beta g \in \sum_{m=1}^{M} V^m(y_m), \sum_{m=1}^{M} x^m = x\right\}$$

$$= \max_{\substack{\beta^1,\dots,\beta^M \\ x^1,\dots,x^M}} \left\{\sum_{m=1}^{M} \beta^m : x^m - \beta^m g \in V^m(y_m), m = 1, \dots, M, \sum_{m=1}^{M} x^m = x\right\}$$

$$= \max_{x^1,\dots,x^M} \left\{\sum_{m=1}^{M} d^m(x^m, y_m; g) : \sum_{m=1}^{M} x^m = x\right\},$$

which is the supremal convolution of the individual directional distance functions. Once again, you are encouraged to consult expression (2.22) to appreciate its economic relevance.

Exercise 45. *Derive the directional output, directional technology, radial input, and radial output distance functions for an input-nonjoint technology.*

4.2.2 Output nonjoint

A technology is *output-nonjoint* if

$$Y(x) = \sum_{n=1}^{N} Y^n(x_n),$$

with each $Y^n(x_n) \subset \mathbb{R}^M$ so that each input has its own output set. Literally, this means that inputs can be cracked into the respective outputs. I would love to give you some reasonable examples, but I've never been able to think of one that I find truly convincing. Regardless, it does have structural consequences which should be recognized.

It's easy to see (verify this on your own) that

$$V(y) = \left\{\prod_{n=1}^{N} V^n(y^n) : y = \sum_{n=1}^{N} y^n\right\},$$

where each $V^n \subset \mathbb{R}$. To visualize $V(y)$, just repeat the earlier exercise for the input-nonjoint technology replacing outputs by inputs.

Exercise 46. *Provide an economically intuitive description of the characteristics of an output-nonjoint technology.*

Exercise 47. *Derive all the distance functions for the output-nonjoint technology.*

4.2.3 Input-price-nonjoint

A technology is *input-price-nonjoint* if

$$V(y) = \prod_{n=1}^{N} V^n(y)$$

where $V^n(y) \subset \mathbb{R}_+$ is an input set for the *nth* input. The input-price-nonjoint technology is the multi-output generalization of the Leontief technology. Its input sets have L-shaped boundaries, which means that all inputs are *perfect complements.* The directional input distance function for the input-price-nonjoint technology is

$$d(x,y;g) = \sup\left\{\beta : x - \beta g \in \prod_{n=1}^{N} V^n(y)\right\}$$
$$= \sup\{\beta : x_n - \beta g_n \in V^n(y), n = 1, ..., N\}.$$

For β to be feasible, it must be true that for all $n = 1, ..., N$

$$x_n - \beta g_n \in V^n(y),$$

so that $\beta \leq d^n(x_n, y; g_n,)$ for all n where $d^n(x_n, y; g_n)$ is the distance function for V^n. Input free disposability then implies

$$d(x,y;g) = \min_{n=1,..,N}\{d^n(x_n, y; g_n,)\}.$$

Exercise 48. *Derive all the remaining distance functions associated with the input-price-nonjoint technology.*

Exercise 49. *Derive the output correspondence and the graph of the technology for input-price nonjoint technology.*

4.2.4 Output-price-nonjoint

A technology is *output-price-nonjoint* if

$$Y(x) = \prod_{m=1}^{M} Y^m(x),$$

with each $Y^m : \mathbb{R}^N \rightrightarrows \mathbb{R}$. For $M = 2$, it's written

$$Y(x) = Y^1(x) \times Y^2(x),$$

Thus, pictorially, it's represented by a rectangle with outer vertex

$$\left(\max\{Y^1(x)\}, \max\{Y^2(x)\}\right).$$

Note its similarities to and differences from the input-nonjoint technology. In higher dimensions, this rectangularity is reflected in *prism-shaped output sets.* Economically, this rectangularity implies that there is a *complete lack of substitutability between the different outputs* and that outputs are *perfect complements.* (See Chapter 10 for an applied problem using this type of technology.) One intuitive story that is told about such technologies is that they correspond to a production situation where a fixed bundle of inputs is cracked into M distinct outputs in fixed proportions. Think, for example, of an animal carcass as x; then the different outputs in this case would be the different components into which it could be rendered.

With the possible exception of the fisheries economics literature, the output-price-nonjoint technology has received relatively little attention in the nonstochastic production literature. It can be encountered but relatively rarely. On the other hand, as we shall see in Chapter 8, in the form of the *stochastic production function model,* it has proved a workhorse in the stochastic production economics literature.

We end this section with more finger exercises.

Exercise 50. *Derive the input correspondence and the graph of the technology for the output-price-nonjoint technology. Illustrate graphically.*

Exercise 51. *Derive all the distance functions associated with the output-price-nonjoint technology.*

Exercise 52. *Provide an economic interpretation of an output-price-nonjoint technology.*

5 A Closer Look at the Canonical Problem

The canonical producer problem takes $(p, w) \in \mathbb{R}^{M+N}_{++}$ as given and determines optimal supplies and derived demands as the solution to

$$\begin{aligned}\pi(p, w) &\equiv \max_{(x,y)} \{p^{\top} y - w^{\top} x : (x, y) \in T\} \\ &= (-\delta)^{*}(p, -w \mid T).\end{aligned}$$

Using (6.1) and Bellman's Principle gives

$$\begin{aligned}\pi(p, w) &= \max_{x} \left\{\max_{y} \{p^{\top} y : y \in Y(x)\} - w^{\top} x\right\} \\ &= \max_{x} \{R(p, x) - w^{\top} x\} \\ &= -R^{*}(p, w),\end{aligned}$$

where $R(p,x) = (-\delta)^*(p \mid Y(x))$ is the *revenue function*, $R^*(p,w)$ is its (concave) conjugate in w, and

$$\begin{aligned}\pi(p,w) &= \max_y \left\{p^\top y - \min_x \{w^\top x : x \in V(y)\}\right\} \\ &= \max_y \{p^\top y - c(w,y)\} \\ &= c^*(w,p),\end{aligned}$$

where $c(w,y) \equiv \delta^*(w \mid V(y))$ denotes the *cost function* for the technology and $c^*(w,p)$ is its convex conjugate in p.

The profit function for T is interpretable as a conjugate of $\delta(x,y \mid T)$, the indicator function for T, $R(p,x)$, the revenue function formed as the (upper) support function for $Y(x)$, and $c(w,y)$, the cost function interpreted as the (lower) support function for $V(y)$. As the (upper) support function for T, $(-\delta)^*(p,-w \mid T)$ is sublinear in prices, and conjugate duality ensures its dual conjugate is $(-\delta)^{**}(x,y \mid T) = -\delta(x,y \mid Co\{T\})$. In defining $\pi(p,w)$, however, the conjugacy mapping is only applied to $-\delta(x,y \mid T)$ over $(p,w) \in \mathbb{R}^{M+N}_{++}$. Hence, in reversing the argument, attention is restricted to affine half-spaces of the form

$$H(-\pi(p,w),(p,-w)) = \{(x,y) \in \mathbb{R}^N : p^\top y - w^\top x \leq \pi(p,w)\},$$

over $(p,w) \in \mathbb{R}^{M+N}_{++}$. Each such half-space is the hypograph of an affine function exhibiting free disposability of input and output. Thus, the indicator function recaptured is that associated with the *free disposal hull* of $Co\{T\}$,

$$FC_o\{T\} \equiv \{(x,y) \in \mathbb{R}^{N+M} : (x,y) \in Co\{T\} + (\mathbb{R}^N_+ \times \mathbb{R}^M_-)\},$$

and not $Co\{T\}$. But for reasons elaborated in Chapters 2 and 4, in a market setting $FC_o\{T\}$ and $Co\{T\}$ are observationally equivalent for competitive markets.

Figure 6.3 illustrates for T depicted as everything on or below the curve $0ABCD$. As drawn, T satisfies neither free disposability of inputs nor *CON*. $Co\{T\}$, which satisfies *CON*, replaces the nonconvex portions of the boundary of T along $0AB$ with the dotted line segments connecting $0A$ and AB. $FC_o\{T\}$ augments $C_o\{T\}$ by replacing CD of the boundary of T with the dotted-line segment (and its infinite extension) CE. The take-away message is that in analyzing profit-maximizing behavior, no real generality is lost by studying an $\succeq(y)$ that exhibits *CON*, free disposability of input, free disposability of output, and *C*.

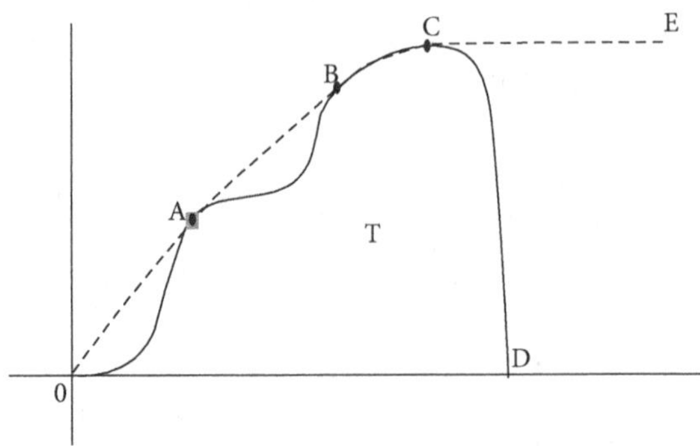

Fig. 6.3 Free Disposal Convex Hull of T

Similar arguments show that $R(p, x)$ and $c(w, y)$ are dual, respectively, to $Co\{Y(x)\}$ and to $Co\{V(y)\}$. They are also derived for positive prices. Hence, applying the conjugacy mapping to each gives, respectively, (minus) the indicator function for the free disposal hull of $Co\{Y(x)\}$ and the indicator function for the free disposal hull of $Co\{V(y)\}$. Thus, if firms maximize revenue for fixed-input prices, no true generality is lost in assuming that $\succeq(y)$ exhibits convexity of $Y(x)$, free disposability of output, and C, and if firms minimize cost nothing is lost in assuming that $\succeq(y)$ exhibits quasi-concavity of $Y(x)$, free disposability of input, and C.

Problem 59. *Show by a direct argument that* $x(w, y) \in \arg\min\{w^\top x : x \in V(y)\} \Rightarrow x(w, y) \in \partial c(w, y)$.

Problem 60. *Show by a direct argument that* $y(p, x) \in \arg\max\{p^\top y : y \in Y(x)\} \Rightarrow y(p, x) \in \partial^- R(p, x)$, *interpreted as the subdifferential of* $R(p, x)$ *in* p.

Problem 61. *For the DEA (FDCH) technology in Example 11,*

$$\pi^K(p, w) = \max\left\{p^\top y - w^\top x : x \geq \sum_{k=1}^{K} \lambda_k x^k, y \leq \sum_{k=1}^{K} \lambda_k y^k, \lambda_k \geq 0,\right.$$
$$\left. k = 1, \ldots, K, \sum_{k=1}^{K} \lambda_k = 1\right\}$$
$$= (-\delta)^*(p, -w \mid T^K).$$

This is another example of a ***linear programming problem****. It's also obviously a special case of the problems considered in detail in Chapter 2.*

Step 1: Solve this problem.
Step 2: Because T^K is a convex set and $\pi^K(p,w)$ is its (upper) support function, it follows from our basic conjugacy results that $(-\delta)^{**}(x,y \mid T^K) = -\delta(x,y \mid T^K)$. Derive $-\delta(x,y \mid T^K)$ by applying the conjugacy mapping to $(-\delta)^*(p,-w \mid T^K)$.

Problem 62. *Develop the structural consequences of input homotheticity, output homotheticity, quasi-input homotheticity, quasi-output homotheticity, input nonjointness, output nonjointness, input-price nonjointness, and output-price nonjointness for $\pi(p,w)$, $R(p,x)$, and $c(w,y)$.*

6 Comparative Statics and the LeChatelier Principle for the Canonical Problem

This discussion requires a slightly more refined notation for superdifferentials and subdifferentials than others. Therefore, let ∂_z and ∂_z^- denote, respectively, the superdifferential and the subdifferential with respect to the subscripted argument z.

Profit-maximizing supplies, denoted as $y^*(p,w) \in \mathbb{R}^M$, satisfy

$$p \in \partial_y^- c(w, y^*(p,w)) \Rightarrow y^*(p,w) \in \partial_p^- \pi(p,w)$$

and profit-maximizing derived demands for inputs, denoted as $x^*(p,w) \in \mathbb{R}^N$, satisfy

$$w \in \partial_x R(p, x^*(p,w)) \Rightarrow -x^*(p,w) \in \partial_w^- \pi(p,w).$$

As usual, the convex structure of $\pi(p,w)$ ensures that its subdifferentials exist everywhere on the relative interior of *dom* (π), and are *cyclically monotone increasing*. Thus, for all $((y^{*k}, -x^{*k}), (p^k, w^k))$,

$$[(p^1,w^1) - (p^0,w^0)]^\top (y^{*0}, -x^{*0}) + \cdots + [(p^0,w^0) - (p^K,w^K)]^\top (y^{*K}, -x^{*K}) \leq 0$$

implying, for example, that all profit-maximizing supplies are upward sloping in their own prices and that profit-maximizing demands are downward sloping in their own prices. The sublinear nature of $\pi(p,w)$ also ensures that its subdifferentials are homogeneous of degree zero in (p,w), so that purely proportional price changes have no effect on optimal choices of inputs and outputs, although they do change $\pi(p,w)$ by the same proportion. For the smoothly differentiable case, this implies that the Hessian matrix of $\pi(p,w)$

$$\begin{bmatrix} \nabla_{pp'}\pi(p,w) & \nabla_{pw'}\pi(p,w) \\ \nabla_{wp'}\pi(p,w) & \nabla_{ww'}\pi(p,w) \end{bmatrix},$$

which consists of price effects on optimal supplies and (minus) derived demands, is positive semidefinite and singular.

Recall that solutions to the cost-minimization problem, $x(w,y)$, satisfy,

$$x(w,y) \in \partial_w c(w,y),$$

while solutions to the revenue-maximization problem, denoted $y(p,x)$, satisfy

$$y(p,x) \in \partial_p^- R(p,x).$$

Hence,

Claim 4. *(Sakai 1974) Optimal solutions to the profit-maximization problem satisfy*

$$y^*(p,w) = y(p,x^*(p,w)),$$

and

$$x^*(p,w) = x(w,y^*(p,w)).$$

Problem 63. *Prove Claim 4.*

Claim 4 parallels earlier decomposition results presented for rational and Marshallian demands. Profit-maximizing supplies equal revenue-maximizing supplies evaluated at profit-maximizing demands, and profit-maximizing demands equal cost-minimizing demands evaluated at profit-maximizing supplies. This is another AS IF claim that follows from the three equivalent formulations of the profit-maximization problem and is yet another of the many consequences of Bellman's Principle.

These decompositions can be illustrated using our canonical figures in a neatly symmetric manner. The solution to the cost-minimization problem is illustrated by Figure 1.2 with the axes labeled as inputs, the curve representing an isoquant, and the illustrated tangency depicting matching the marginal rate of technical substitution to real input prices. The second-stage problem, $\max_y \{p^\top y - c(w,y)\}$, is illustrated by Figure 1.3 with the vertical axis labeled dollars, the horizontal axis labeled output, the curve representing a nicely convex (in output) cost function, and the straight line revenue from sale of output with the output price determining its slope. The solution to the second-stage problem is depicted in Figure 1.4 with the axes labeled outputs, the curve representing a level set (in y) for $c(w, y)$, and the tangency depicting equalizing the ratio of marginal costs to real output price, $p \in \partial_y^- c(w, y^*(p, w))$.

Figure 1.4 illustrates the first-stage revenue-maximization problem, with axes labeled as outputs, the curve the boundary of $Y(x)$, and the tangency depicting equating the marginal rate of transformation to real output price. The second-stage problem, $\max_x \{R(p, x) - w^\top x\}$, is illustrated in Figure 1.1, with the curve emanating from the origin representing a (concave) revenue function, the straight line input expenditure, and the distance between the two profit. The solution to the second-stage problem is then illustrated in Figure 1.2 with the axes labeled as inputs, the curve representing an *isorevenue* curve (in x), and the tangency depicting equating the ratio of marginal revenues to the real input price.

Claim 4 permits the decomposition of supply and derived-demand adjustments into two distinct components, a "substitution effect" and an "expansion effect." Here the calculus is handy, so let's assume nicely smooth supply and demand. Differentiating the equalities in Claim 4 gives for each m

$$\begin{aligned}\frac{\partial y_m^*(p, w)}{\partial p_j} &= \frac{\partial y_m(p, x^*(p, w))}{\partial p_j} + \sum_n \frac{\partial y_m(p, x^*(p, w))}{\partial x_n} \frac{\partial x_n^*(p, w)}{\partial p_j}, \\ \frac{\partial y_m^*(p, w)}{\partial w_j} &= \sum_n \frac{\partial y_m(p, x^*(p, w))}{\partial x_n} \frac{\partial x_n^*(p, w)}{\partial w_j}\end{aligned} \tag{6.2}$$

and for each n

$$\begin{aligned}\frac{\partial x_n^*(p, w)}{\partial w_j} &= \frac{\partial x_n(w, y^*(p, w))}{\partial w_j} + \sum_m \frac{\partial x_n(w, y^*(p, w))}{\partial y_m} \frac{\partial y_m^*(p, w)}{\partial w_j}, \\ \frac{\partial x_n^*(p, w)}{\partial p_j} &= \sum_m \frac{\partial x_n(w, y^*(p, w))}{\partial y_m} \frac{\partial y_m^*(p, w)}{\partial p_j}.\end{aligned} \tag{6.3}$$

Exercise 53. *Develop the discrete versions of the expressions in (6.2) and (6.3).*

In (6.2), $\frac{\partial y_m(p,x^*(p,w))}{\partial p_j}$ represents a *substitution effect* envisioned as moving along $\bar{Y}(x)$ in response to the price change. $\sum_n \frac{\partial y_m(p,x^*(p,w))}{\partial x_n} \frac{\partial x_n^*(p,w)}{\partial p_j}$ is an *expansion effect* that results from the supply adjustment driven by the price-induced change in optimal input use. Thus, $\frac{\partial y_m^*(p,w)}{\partial p_j}$ is more properly thought of as a *gross substitution effect.* Regardless of the sign or magnitude of the expansion effect, convexity of $\pi(p,w)$ ensures that $\frac{\partial y_m^*(p,w)}{\partial p_m} \geq 0$ for all m (also see below).

Similarly, $\frac{\partial x_n(w,y^*(p,w))}{\partial w_j}$ is the substitution effect envisioned as movement along $\bar{V}(y)$ in response to the price change, and $\sum_m \frac{\partial x_n(w,y^*(p,w))}{\partial y_m} \frac{\partial y_m(p,x^*(p,w))}{\partial w_j}$ is an expansion effect driven by the price-induced change in optimal supplies. Thus, $\frac{\partial x_n^*(p,w)}{\partial w_j}$ represents the gross substitution effect. The convexity of $\pi(p,w)$ ensures $\frac{\partial x_n^*(p,w)}{\partial w_n} \leq 0$. There are no Giffen input demands for profit-maximizing producers.

Exercise 54. *Discuss the decomposition in (6.3) intuitively.*

Problem 64. *The convexity of $\pi(p,w)$ implies that its Hessian matrix in prices is positive semidefinite, whence*

$$\frac{\partial^2 \pi(p,w)}{\partial p_j \partial w_k} = \frac{\partial^2 \pi(p,w)}{\partial w_k \partial p_j}.$$

Use this fact and expressions (6.2) and (6.3) to show that

$$\frac{\partial y_m^*(p,w)}{\partial w_j} = -\sum_k \frac{\partial x_j(w,y^*(p,w))}{\partial y_k} \frac{\partial y_k^*(p,w)}{\partial p_m},$$

$$\frac{\partial x_n^*(p,w)}{\partial p_j} = -\sum_k \frac{\partial y_j(p,x^*(p,w))}{\partial x_k} \frac{\partial x_k^*(p,w)}{\partial w_n}.$$

Discuss the results intuitively.

These decompositions can also be cast as reflecting the nexus between *long-run* and *short-run* supply and derived-demand response. As usual, the terms *long run* and *short run,* though evocative of temporal adjustment, refer not to adjustments made as time passes, but to responses differentiated by the presence of either fixed outputs or fixed inputs. Short-run responses are those made in the presence of either fixed inputs or output, and long-run responses are ones made when all inputs and outputs are completely variable. Because $p^\top y - c(w,y)$ necessarily maximizes profit associated with an output bundle fixed at y, it's a *short-run profit function for the fixed-output bundle y.* Similarly, $R(p,x) - w^\top x$ is the *short-run profit function for the fixed-input bundle x.* So, for example, the substitution effect, $\frac{\partial y_m(p,x^*(p,w))}{\partial p_j}$, depicts a short-run supply response, while the gross-substitution effect $\frac{\partial y_m^*(p,w)}{\partial p_j}$ is a long-run response.

An immediate consequence of our decompositions of the canonical problem is the famous *LeChatelier Principle* introduced into economics by Samuelson (1947). In the current context, it implies that the derivative of a long-run supply or derived demand in its own price is larger (in absolute value terms) than its short-run counterpart. Let's demonstrate with $\frac{\partial y_m^*(p,w)}{\partial p_j}$. From Problem 64, cross-price effects on demands and supplies are symmetric so that

$$\frac{\partial y_j^*(p,w)}{\partial w_n} = -\frac{\partial x_n^*(p,w)}{\partial p_j}.$$

Substituting this result into the right-hand side of the first expression in (6.2), we get

$$\frac{\partial y_m^*(p,w)}{\partial p_j} = \frac{\partial y_m(p,x^*(p,w))}{\partial p_j} - \sum_n \frac{\partial y_m(p,x^*(p,w))}{\partial x_n} \frac{\partial y_j^*(p,w)}{\partial w_n},$$

while using the second expression in (6.2) gives

$$\frac{\partial y_m^*(p,w)}{\partial p_j} = \frac{\partial y_m(p,x^*(p,w))}{\partial p_j} - \sum_n \sum_k \frac{\partial y_m(p,x^*(p,w))}{\partial x_n} \frac{\partial x_k^*(p,w)}{\partial w_n} \frac{\partial y_j(p,x^*(p,w))}{\partial x_k}.$$

Finally, setting $j = m$, we have

$$\frac{\partial y_m^*(p,w)}{\partial p_m} = \frac{\partial y_m(p,x^*(p,w))}{\partial p_m} - \sum_n \sum_k \frac{\partial y_m(p,x^*(p,w))}{\partial x_n} \frac{\partial x_k^*(p,w)}{\partial w_n} \frac{\partial y_m(p,x^*(p,w))}{\partial x_k}.$$

The second part of this expression, $-\sum_n \sum_k \frac{\partial y_m(p,x^*(p,w))}{\partial x_n} \frac{\partial x_k^*(p,w)}{\partial w_n} \frac{\partial y_m(p,x^*(p,w))}{\partial x_k}$, representing the expansion effect, is a quadratic form in the sub-Hessian matrix $\nabla_{ww'}\pi(p,w)$. Convexity implies that $\nabla_{ww'}\pi(p,w)$ is positive semidefinite, and the expansion effect must be positive. Hence,

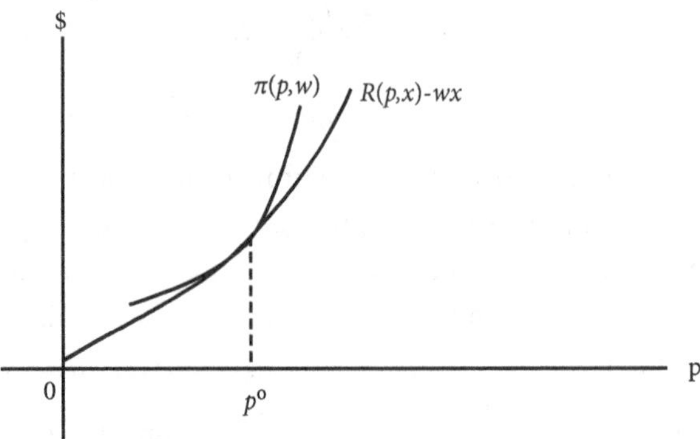

Fig. 6.4 Le Chatelier Principle

$$\frac{\partial y_m^*(p,w)}{\partial p_m} \geq \frac{\partial y_m(p,x^*(p,w))}{\partial p_m}.$$

Long-run supply response in its own price is always at least as large as the short-run supply.

The result, which is a direct consequence of $\pi(p,w)$ being the pointwise maximum of a collection of convex functions of p, is illustrated in Figure 6.4. Suppose that x has been chosen optimally for (p^o,w). Then, the short-run profit function is represented as an increasing convex function of p that coincides with $\pi(p^o,w)$ at p^o. Consider a movement to the right of p^o. The short-run supply response is captured by moving to a point on the short-run profit function with greater slope than at $R(p^o,x) - w^\top x$. This movement represents a lower bound on optimal producer response because it was achieved holding x constant. The long-run response, which allows x to vary, must satisfy $\pi(p,w) \geq R(p,x) - w^\top x$. Thus, as a function of p, $\pi(p,w)$ is "more convex" than $R(p,x) - w^\top x$, so that its slope at the higher p, the new long-run supply, must be greater than that of $R(p,x) - w^\top x$ at the higher p, the new short-run supply.

Problem 65. *Prove that*

$$\frac{\partial x_n^*(p,w)}{\partial w_n} \leq \frac{\partial x_n(w,y^*(p,w))}{\partial w_n},$$

for all n. Illustrate your answer graphically.

Problem 66. *Now consider*

$$\pi^s(p,w,x_k^o) = \max_{(x_{-k},y)} \left\{py - wx : (x_{-k},x_k^o,y) \in T\right\},$$

where the notation x_{-k} denotes the vector x with the kth element removed. Note that maximization is over (x_{-k}, y) and not (x, y), so that x_k is held fixed at x_k^o. This is a short-run profit-maximization problem, and

$$\pi(p, w) = \max_{x_k} \{\pi^s(p, w, x_k)\}.$$

Derive the LeChatelier Principle in this setting.

7 Revealed Preference and Producers

Unlike consumer theory, producer theory typically deals in observable, or potentially observable, objects. One naturally suspects that this simplifies determining "postulates" that can form the basis for a theory of producer behavior based exclusively on observables. Our basic conjugacy results clarify why this suspicion is correct.

We start by assuming that we possess K observations on the production practices of a single producer. For the sake of a compact notation, we denote the *kth* observation by $(q^k, z^k) = ((p^k, -w^k), (y^k, x^k))$ with $(p^k, w^k) \in \mathbb{R}_{++}^{M+N}$. For a data set,

$$D = \{(q^1, z^1), (q^2, z^2), ..., (q^K, z^K)\},$$

if the observations satisfy

$$q^{k\top} z^k \geq q^{k\top} z^j \text{ for all } k, j,$$

which we shall refer to as the *axiom of profit maximization (APM)*, there must exist a closed, convex $T^D \subset \mathbb{R}^{M+N}$ exhibiting free disposability of input and output such that

$$q^k \in \partial^-(-\delta)(z \mid T^D) \Leftrightarrow z^k \in \partial^-(-\delta)^*(q^k \mid T^D). \tag{6.4}$$

The argument is as follows. If APM is satisfied, then

$$\begin{aligned} z^j &\in \{z : q^k z \leq q^k z^k\} \\ &= H(-q^k z^k, q^k) \text{ for all } j \text{ and } k. \end{aligned}$$

Each $H(-q^k z^k, q^k)$ is a closed, convex subset of $\mathbb{R}^{M+N}$ that exhibits free disposability of inputs and outputs. (I leave the proof to you.) Letting

$$T^D = \cap_k H(-q^k z^k, q^k),$$

we see that T^D is also closed, convex, and exhibits free disposal of inputs and outputs. (Here you should prove that the intersection of two convex sets is itself convex.) Moreover, it follows from its definition that

$$q^k \in \partial^- (-\delta) \left(z^k \mid T^D\right) \text{ for all } k, \tag{6.5}$$

and conjugacy implies the rest.

Because observed inputs and outputs can be interpreted as images of the subdifferential correspondence, $\partial^- (-\delta)^* \left(q^k \mid T^D\right)$, observed output patterns are consistent with positively sloped supply curves and observed input patterns are consistent with negatively sloped derived demand curves. Thus, as you have likely anticipated, APM implies consistency with standard neoclassical price-taking behavior.

An immediate consequence of (6.5), Claim 4, and basic conjugacy results is that satisfaction of APM implies the existence of an $R(p, x)$ closed, concave, and nondecreasing as a function of x and the existence of a $c(w, y)$ closed, convex, and nondecreasing as a function of y interpretable, respectively, as the revenue function and the cost function for T^D that satisfy

$$w^k \in \partial_x R\left(p^k, x^k\right),$$

and

$$p^k \in \partial_y^- c\left(w^k, y^k\right).$$

$R(p, x)$ and $c(w, y)$, so derived, are naturally interpretable as the support functions for closed, convex $Y(x)$ satisfying free disposability of output and for closed, convex $V(y)$ satisfying free disposability of input. Both are naturally derived with respect to T^D.

Problem 67. *What are the implications for observed behavior if D satisfies*

$$z^{k\top} q^k \geq z^{k\top} q^j \text{ for all } k, j?$$

Given these results, it's not unnatural to think of T^D as a *data-generated technology* that envelops the observed data. In fact, that's one standard interpretation. But, as always, the economic jargon that we attach to such objects are examples of Fishburn's extramathematical interpretations of the theory. Let's recall, for example, that we've also looked at another approximation to the technology generated by the data (see Example 11), denoted T^K, that we have referred to as the DEA approximation. That representation exists regardless of whether or not *APM* is satisfied. And because it is the *smallest convex set consistent with free disposability* that encompasses the observed data, it follows immediately that if APM is satisfied, $T^K \subset T^D$ because the latter also is convex, encompasses the data, and satisfies free disposability of inputs and outputs. (For this reason, T^D is sometimes referred to as an *outer representation of the data* and T^K as an *inner representation.*) Immediate observations are that $(-\delta)^* (p, -w \mid T^K) \leq (-\delta)^* (p, -w \mid T^D)$ and $-\delta (y, x \mid T^K) = (-\delta)^{**} (y, x \mid T^K)$.

Problem 68. *Prove or disprove. For any* (p^k, w^k) *associated with D,*

$$(-\delta)^* (p^k, -w^k \mid T^K) = (-\delta)^* (p^k, -w^k \mid T^D).$$

As I have tried to emphasize repeatedly, real-world observations rarely come in the neat packages that our mathematical manipulations require. That necessarily colors how we interpret structures such as T^D. To illustrate, imagine a situation where *the only information* available on a producer is her utilization of inputs for K input price settings. Here *only* means "*only*"; nothing beyond the data are known! Lacking any further knowledge, what does satisfaction of APM allow us to say? Given only observations on inputs and their prices, *APM* requires

$$w^{k\top} x^k \leq w^{k\top} x^j \text{ for all } k, j.$$

If satisfied, exactly parallel arguments reveal that there exists a closed, convex set $V^D \subset \mathbb{R}^N$ exhibiting free disposal of inputs such that

$$w^k \in \partial\delta (x^k \mid V^D) \Leftrightarrow x^k \in \partial\delta^* (w^k \mid V^D).$$

One can now claim that observed (w^k, x^k) are consistent with minimizing the cost associated with V^D. But what is V^D? Mathematically, it's a set containing elements of $\mathbb{R}^N$, which we've been calling inputs. Thus, it seems legitimate to call it an input set. Its properties are similar to those of a $V(y)$ consistent with *CONA* and input-free disposability. Does it correspond to a $V(y)$?

Exercise 55. *Suppose that one only possesses information on output and output price for a producer over K price settings. What does satisfaction of APM in that setting imply?*

So *APM* is informative when *D* only consists of observations on inputs and input prices. But what the mathematical information conveys economically is, perhaps, unclear. In some settings, augmenting *APM* may prove informative. For example, if we normalize all observed input prices so that $w^{k\top}x^k = 1$ for all k, Theorem 11 gives

Corollary 6. *The following are equivalent:*
(a) the input data are consistent with

$$F(w) = \max\{f^{**}(x) : w^\top x = 1\}$$

for a continuous, strictly monotonic, proper concave f^{**} *;*
(b) the input data satisfy GARP; and
(c) for each (x^k, w^k) *there exist strictly positive real numbers* (λ^k, f^{**k}) *satisfying* $\lambda^k w^{k\top}(x^j - x^k) \geq f^{**j} - f^{**k}$ *for all* $j \in \{1, 2, ..., K\}$.

The consumer analogue to f^{**} was interpreted as a utility function. The knee-jerk reaction is to interpet f^{**} as a production function and $F(w)$ as its *indirect production function*. But, as usually defined, a production function is only truly meaningful in a single-output setting. As noted, single-product technologies are nice conceptually but rarely exist. That might tempt one to interpret $f^{**}(x)$ as a revenue function, $R(p, x)$, concave in x. In that case, $F(w)$ is replaced by

$$IR(p, w) = \max\{R(p, x) : w^\top x = 1\},$$

which Färe and Primont (1995) call a *cost-indirect revenue function*. I leave the interpretation of the indirect production function and the cost-indirect production function to you. The message that I am trying to redeliver is that the economic interpretation of our results reflects not only the mathematical manipulations but also their extramathematical interpretations. Different contexts may, and often do, involve identical manipulations but demand different interpretations.

Problem 69. *Suppose that D only consists of observations on outputs and output prices. Normalize all output prices so that* $p^{k\top}y^k = 1$ *for all K+1 observations. What are the economic implications of* $(y^k, -p^k)$ *satisfying GARP?*

Problem 70. *Both $F(w) - 1$ and $IR(p, w) - 1$ are examples of short-run profit functions. Explain why and then develop thoroughly their relationship to the long-run profit function.*

8 Chapter Commentary

The essential ideas established in this chapter are well and truly understood by many. If one were to replace superdifferentials and subdifferential with gradients, the substantive discussion of this chapter would not depart significantly from Samuelson's (1947) classic formulation of producer theory. Similarly, the dual approach was equally well established in Shephard (1953, 1970), McFadden (1978), and Diewert (1982). Much of that theory was summarized in Chambers (1988). If there is a difference between those developments and the ones in this chapter, it's one of form. Here, I have relied almost exclusively on the conjugate approach grounded in the use of distance functions as the cardinal representation of the underlying technology. But as Chapter 4 hopefully clarified, all of that material can be suitably recast in terms of support functions for technology sets or conjugates for indicator functions for those same technology sets.

7
Equilibrium, Efficiency, and Welfare

Economists typically focus on market "equilibrium" and "equilibrium behavior." An equilibrium occurs when a constellation of quantities and prices exists from which one does not expect economic agents to move. Our notions of equilibrium were originally borrowed from thermodynamics where an equilibrium is mathematically characterized as an extremum of a thermodynamic potential function, such as free energy or entropy. Not surprisingly, economists routinely characterize equilibria in terms of points around which no variation leads to an improvement. Optimal individual behavior, therefore, is equilibrium behavior.

For example, rational-demand behavior requires expenditure minimization. If neither prices nor income change, rational demands represent a consumer "equilibrium." And because utility maximization requires rational-demand behavior, so too does utility maximization. Similarly, producers choose input allocations to minimize cost, output allocations to maximize revenue, and both to maximize profit. Once made, these choices won't change if prices or other givens don't.

So, we already have clear notions of individual equilibria. Each is linked to optimization principles. Adam Smith famously recognized that when market participants freely interact, the resulting market "equilibrium" has desirable welfare consequences. Because market equilibria are constructed on an edifice that assumes individuals are individual optimizers, a reasonable conjecture is that variational methods may prove useful in characterizing them and that they too correspond mathematically to the solution of an appropriate optimization.

This chapter investigates interactive equilibria in the competitive (price-taking) setting that is the centerpiece of neoclassical economics. Thus, the basic ideas should be familiar to anyone with an exposure to intermediate microeconomics. The goal of the chapter is modest. It's not an attempt to provide an exhaustive presentation of modern equilibrium theory. Any number of excellent textbooks already do that. Instead, it seeks to demonstrate

Competitive Agents in Certain and Uncertain Markets. Robert G. Chambers, Oxford University Press (2021).

DOI: 10.1093/oso/9780190063016.001.0001

the linkage between our core variational arguments and the mathematical characterization of economic equilibria. Therefore, with next to no apology, this chapter treats only "nice" cases, where preferences satisfy *CONA* and *M* and technologies are convex and exhibit free disposability of output. This definitely represents a shortcut and rules out the type of problems that routinely bedevil serious students of this area. But it greatly streamlines the presentation, and as we have already argued in a number of contexts, parallel, but more notationally demanding, arguments can be developed by the by-now standard artifice of convexifying or hulling nonconvex or nonmonotonic structures. Substantive results change little. Another benefit of imposing this structure from the get-go is that it lets us sidestep the issue of equilibrium existence because it rules out all the difficulties. Again this is not done to diminish the importance of such issues but to focus attention on the problem aspects of peculiar interest to us. The take-away message from this chapter, which should be attributed to Luenberger (1994, 1995), is that characterizing equilibria recycles variational arguments made elsewhere.

1 Partial Equilibrium

We start with a simple case. We imagine K consumers, each of whom is endowed with a predetermined amount of money income that can be spent on N commodities. It's more general if we allow each consumer's income to differ, but it's much easier notationally if we don't. So assume all K have the same income and fix it at one. Each of the K consumers is rational and has preferences characterized by a transitive $\succeq^k(y)$, $k = 1, \ldots, K$, with $y \in \mathbb{R}_+^N$ that satisfies continuity from above (*CA*), monotonicity from above (*MA*), and convexity from above (*CONA*). As elsewhere, things are greatly simplified by strengthening *MA* to ensure strict monotonicity. Do so.

Attention is restricted throughout this chapter to commodity prices $p \in \mathbb{R}_+^N$ normalized so that the numeraire bundle is priced at one, that is, $p^\top g = 1$. By Corollary 3 rational demands, $x^k(p) \in \mathbb{R}_+^N$, satisfy

$$x^k(p) \in \arg\min_{x \in \mathbb{R}_+^N} \{p^\top x - d^k(x, x^k(p); g)\}, \quad k = 1, \ldots, K$$

and thus

$$x^k(p) \in \partial E^k(p; x^k(p)) \Leftrightarrow p \in \partial d^k(x^k(p), x^k(p); g) \tag{7.1}$$

Verbally, a demand is rational only if it represents the cheapest way to ensure that consumer k is at least as good as he or she would be at $x^k(p)$.[1] As we've already established, the consumer problem and its solution are illustrated by Figures 1.1 and 1.2.

Joining the K consumers in these N commodity markets are J competitive producers who take both commodity prices, p, and input prices, w, as predetermined. Their respective cost functions are denoted by $c^j(w,y)$, $j = 1, \ldots, J$. Each is strictly increasing and convex in y. The *jth* producer's optimal supplies, therefore, solve

$$y^j(p,w) \in \arg\max_{y \in \mathbb{R}^N_+} \{p^\top y - c^j(w,y)\},$$

and

$$y^j(p,w) \in \partial^- c^{*j}(w,p) \Leftrightarrow p \in \partial^- c^j(w, y^j(p,w)), \qquad (7.2)$$

where

$$c^{*j}(w,p) \equiv \max_{y \in \mathbb{R}^N_+} \{p^\top y - c^j(w,y)\}$$

as the convex conjugate of $c^j(w,y)$ (in terms of y) is the *profit function* dual to $c^j(w,y)$. The profit-maximization problem for the single-output case is illustrated by Figure 1.3, and its multi-output solution is illustrated by Figure 1.4.

A *partial equilibrium* is a configuration of profit-maximizing supplies, rational demands, and normalized commodity prices $p \in \mathbb{R}^N_+$ for which rational demands aggregated across consumers exactly balance profit-maximizing supplies *for predetermined input prices w*. The equilibrium is *partial* because it depends on predetermined input prices and the predetermined income distribution.

Notationally, partial equilibrium requires:

$$\sum_{k=1}^{K} x^k(p) - \sum_{j=1}^{J} y^j(p,w) = 0. \qquad (7.3)$$

[1] Admittedly, this sounds a bit circular. But that is mitigated by the realization that utility maximization requires that Marshallian demands satisfy

$$x^M(p) \in \partial E^H(p; u(x^M(p))),$$

which is just as circular, albeit a bit less transparently.

Thus, finding a partial equilibrium reduces to a problem of solving N equations for the N unknown real prices. If $N = 1$, a partial equilbrium p has a familiar visual interpretation. It represents the point at which the aggregate demand and the aggregate supply curves intersect. Figure 1.5 illustrates when the axes are interpreted as price and quantity, respectively.

An alternative perspective on solving (7.3) is obtained by writing it in variational form. Use expressions (7.1) and (7.2) to rewrite (7.3) as

$$0 \in \sum_{k=1}^{K} \partial E^k \left(p; x^k\left(p\right)\right) - \sum_{j=1}^{J} \partial^- c^{*j}\left(w, p\right),$$

where summation over the images of superdifferentials and subdifferentials, which are formally sets, are Minkowski sums. Under our regularity conditions, this criterion becomes

$$0 \in \partial\left(\sum_{k=1}^{K} E^k\left(p; x^k\left(p\right)\right) - \sum_{j=1}^{J} c^{*j}\left(p, w\right)\right), \tag{7.4}$$

which can be recognized as a necessary and sufficient condition for

$$p \in \max_{q}\left\{\sum_{k=1}^{K} E^k\left(q; x^k\left(p\right)\right) - \sum_{j=1}^{J} c^{*j}\left(w, q\right)\right\}. \tag{7.5}$$

For prices $q \in \mathbb{R}^N_+$, $\sum_{k=1}^{K} E^k\left(q; x^k\right)$ is the total amount that the K consumers would spend to achieve preference levels associated with $\left(x^1, \ldots, x^K\right)$. $\sum_{j=1}^{J} c^{*j}\left(w, q\right)$ is total producer profit. The difference between the two,

$$\mathcal{E}\left(q; X, w\right) \equiv \sum_{k=1}^{K} E^k\left(q; x^k\right) - \sum_{j=1}^{J} c^{*j}\left(w, q\right),$$

is the *excess expenditure for* $X = \left(x^1, \ldots, x^K\right)$ at $\left(q, w\right)$.[2] Intuitively, excess expenditure is the difference between minimal expenditure at q required to give all k individuals a level of well-being at least as good as their x^k and maximal profit at q.

[2] The trade-expenditure function expressed in terms of utility is the complete preference analogue of the excess expenditure function. Luenberger (1995) calls the complete preference analogue of $-\mathcal{E}$ the income surplus function.

Thus, a variational approach to isolating a partial equilibrium can be described as follows. First, choose a $p \in \mathbb{R}^N_+$ and find the rational demands for that p. Then for those rational demands find the $q \in \mathbb{R}^N_+$ that maximizes $\mathcal{E}(q; X(p), w)$. If that q is p, it's a potential partial equilibrium. If it's not, the process needs to be repeated until a p is found that satisfies

$$\mathcal{E}(p; X(p), w) = \max_q \{\mathcal{E}(q; X(p), w)\}.$$

Although we do not go into detail here, the essential idea behind ensuring the *existence of a partial equilibrium* is to isolate assumptions on the $E^k(\cdot)$ and the $c^{*j}(\cdot)$[3] to ensure that the correspondence (7.5), which can be rewritten as

$$p = \arg\max_q \{\mathcal{E}(q; X(p), w)\},$$

is single valued and continuous on $\{p \in \mathbb{R}^N_+ : p^\top g = 1\}$. Once that's done, an appropriate fixed-point theorem guarantees the existence of a solution. Given our applied focus, we won't go into the details behind existence.[4]

Having identified a p-variational approach to isolating a partial equilibrium, conjugate duality ensures that a matching quantity-based approach exists. Fenchel's Duality Theorem requires that

$$\max_q \{\mathcal{E}(q; X(p), w)\} =$$

$$\min_{\substack{x^1,\ldots,x^K \\ y^1,\ldots,y^J}} \left\{ \sum_j c^j(w, y^j) - \sum_k d^k(x^k, x^k(p); g) : \sum_{j=1}^J y^j = \sum_{k=1}^K x^k \right\}. \tag{7.6}$$

Thus, for p to represent an equilibrium price,

$$p \in \cap_{j=1}^J \partial_y^- c^j(w, y^j(p, w)) \cap \{\cap_{k=1}^K \partial d^k(x^k(p), x^k(p); g)\} \neq \emptyset, \tag{7.7}$$

which requires that the superdifferentials of all the consumer distance functions and the subdifferentials of all the producer cost functions must overlap. When only one good, one consumer, one producer exist, and the world is suitably smooth, Figure 1.5 with the vertical axis measuring price and the horizontal quantity illustrates the solution where the downward-sloping curve

[3] Alternatively, these assumptions can be imposed directly on the preference orderings and the cost functions. Basically, they require that demand and supply be uniquely determined and monotonic.

[4] Here you would do well to consult Aliprantis and Border (2007, Chapter 17) for more details

represents $\partial d(x(p), x(p); g)$, the consumer's price-dependent McKenzie demand, and the upward-sloping curve represents the producer's upward-sloping price-dependent supply (marginal cost) $\partial_y^- c(w, y(p, w))$. Figure 1.6, with the axes appropriately labeled, illustrates the equilibrium when there are two goods, one producer, and one consumer. All producers must share common marginal costs that are equal to common internal prices shared by all consumers. Or, in a slightly different jargon, marginal rates of substitution must be equalized across consumers and equated to a common marginal rate of transformation for commodities.

Summarizing,

Theorem 13. *If p is consistent with partial equilibrium, the following conditions are equivalent*

$$p \in \arg\max \{\mathcal{E}(q; X(p), w)\},$$

and

$$\left(x^k(p), y^j(p, w)\right)_{\substack{j=1,\dots,J \\ k=1,\dots,K}} \in \arg\min \left\{ \begin{array}{c} \sum_j c^j(w, y^j) - \sum_k d^k(x^k, x^k(p); g) : \\ \sum_j y^j = \sum_k x^k \end{array} \right\}.$$

Equating marginal rates of substitution to marginal rates of transformation, as required by (7.7), is a firmly established characteristic of *Pareto-optimal allocations* of consumption and production. Thus, a natural conjecture is that partial equilibria are Pareto optimal in some sense. To investigate the conjecture, we start with a definition:

Definition 3. *A production plan, $(y^1, \dots, y^j)$, and a consumption plan, $(x^1, \dots, x^K)$, satisfying $\sum_k x^k = \sum_j y^j$ are quasi-Pareto optimal if there exist no alternative plans $(\tilde{y}^1, \dots, \tilde{y}^j)$, $(\tilde{x}^1, \dots, \tilde{x}^K)$, $\sum_k \tilde{x}^k = \sum_j \tilde{y}^j$ such that $\tilde{x}^k \succeq (x^k)$ for all k and $c(w, \tilde{y}^j) \leq c(w, y^j)$ with at least one k or j such that $\tilde{x}^k \succ (x^k)$ or $c(w, \tilde{y}^j) < c(w, y^j)$.*

Quasi-Pareto optimality requires the absence of alternative production and consumption plans that leave all producers and consumers at least as well off as at $(x^1, \dots, x^K)$ and $(y^1, \dots, y^j)$ and that make at least one producer or consumer strictly better off. For producers, "better off" means lowering cost.

In the language of distance functions, $(x^1, \dots, x^K)$ and $(y^1, \dots, y^j)$ are quasi-Pareto optimal only if no plans exist such that $d^k(\tilde{x}^k, x^k; g) \geq d^k(x^k, x^k; g)$ for all k and $c(w, \tilde{y}^j) \leq c(w, y^j)$ for all j with at least one strong inequality and $\sum_k \tilde{x}^k = \sum_j \tilde{y}^j$. Summing over k and j, that means there cannot exist any $(\tilde{y}^1, \ldots, \tilde{y}^J)$, $(\tilde{x}^1, \ldots, \tilde{x}^K)$, $\sum_k \tilde{x}^k = \sum_j \tilde{y}^j$ such that

$$\sum_k d^k(\tilde{x}^k, x^k; g) + \sum_j c(w, y^j) > \sum_k d^k(x^k, x^k; g) + c(w, \tilde{y}^j).$$

Thus, $(y^1, \ldots, y^J)$ and $(x^1, \ldots, x^K)$ are quasi-Pareto optimal only if

$$\sum_j c(w, y^j) - \sum_k d^k(x^k, x^k; g) \leq \sum_j c(w, \tilde{y}^j) - \sum_k d^k(\tilde{x}^k, x^k; g)$$

for all $\sum_k \tilde{x}^k = \sum_j \tilde{y}^j$, or that

$$(x^k, y^j)_{\substack{j=1,\ldots,J \\ k=1,\ldots,K}} \in \arg\min \left\{ \sum_j c(w, \tilde{y}^j) - \sum_k d^k(\tilde{x}^k, x^k; g) : \sum_k \tilde{x}^k = \sum_j \tilde{y}^j \right\}. \tag{7.8}$$

Solving the right-hand side of (7.8) is, therefore, a necessary step in finding quasi-Pareto-optimal allocations.

To show that solving the right-hand side of (7.8) suffices for quasi-Pareto optimality, assume the contrary. That is, there exist allocations satisfying (7.8) that are not quasi-Pareto optimal. Allocations must then exist such that $d^k(\tilde{x}^k, x^k; g) \geq d^k(x^k, x^k; g)$ for all k, $c(w, \tilde{y}^j) \leq c(w, y^j)$ for all j, $\sum_k \tilde{x}^k = \sum_j \tilde{y}^j$, which also satisfy

$$\sum_j c(w, y^j) - \sum_k d^k(x^k, x^k; g) < \sum_j c(w, \tilde{y}^j) - \sum_k d^k(\tilde{x}^k, x^k; g)$$

which requires

$$0 < \sum_j c(w, \tilde{y}^j) - c(w, y^j) + \sum_k d^k(x^k, x^k; g) - d^k(\tilde{x}^k, x^k; g).$$

By the presumed quasi-Pareto optimality of the alternative allocations, both sums on the right must be nonpositive, and one must be strictly negative. That yields a contradiction. These arguments establish:

Theorem 14. *A production plan, $(y^1, \ldots, y^J)$, and a consumption plan, $(x^1, \ldots, x^K)$, that satisfy $\sum_k x^k = \sum_j y^j$ are quasi-Pareto optimal if and only if (7.8) is satisfied.*

Theorems 13 and 14 establish variational approaches to finding partial equilibria and to finding quasi-Pareto-optimal allocations. The approaches overlap. Thus, the existence of a partial equilibrium has welfare and efficiency consequences. If a partial equilibrium exists, the rational demands and supplies associated with it represent quasi-Pareto-optimal allocations. Conversely, the existence of a quasi Pareto optimum has partial equilibrium implications. If quasi-Pareto-optimal allocations exist, an "invisible hand" (read market price structure p) can be found that will guide rational consumers and producers to it.

2 Consumer Surplus, Producer Surplus, and Equilibrium

You probably learned in intermediate microeconomics that market equilibrium occurs at the price (quantity) that maximizes the sum of *consumer surplus* and *producer surplus*.[5] Because these surpluses are meant to measure consumer and producer well-being, this is a clear statement about the welfare consequences of market equilibrium that echoes Adam Smith's assertion that competition promotes desirable welfare outcomes. Seeing, therefore, that (partial) equilibrium occurs where excess expenditure is maximized may be puzzling. It's not, however, once consumer and producer surplus are properly recast in the current framework.

Because competitive consumers and producers react to a given price, p, their "primal" problem is usually perceived as choosing quantity, x or y, in reaction to the "dual" price. We represent those solutions functionally as $x(p)$ or $y(p, w)$. And when p and x are both scalars, mathematical convention dictates that functional relations of the form $x(p)$ are depicted visually as the ordered pair $(p, x(p))$. The independent variable, p, comes first and is measured along the horizontal axis (the ordinate), and the image of the dependent variable, $x(p)$, is measured along the vertical axis (the abcissa). The economic convention, following Marshall (1920), reverses these roles and represents the same ordered pair visually as $(x(p), p)$. Thus, price is measured along the vertical axis and quantity along the horizontal, suggesting instead that demand calls forth price. In other words, the convention in economics is to represent demand and supply in *price-dependent form*.

The traditional explanation of *consumer surplus* is cast in similar dual terms. Jules Dupuit (1844) appears to have introduced the concept, but its popularization is more properly attributed to Alfred Marshall, who defined

[5] Some writers refer to consumer surplus and producer surplus in possessive terms as consumer's surplus and producer's surplus. Unless, I am directly quoting such an author, I will use the simpler versions.

consumer surplus as "[t]he excess of the price which (the consumer) would be willing to pay rather than go without the thing, over that which (the consumer) actually does pay" (Marshall, 1920, p. 124). That "excess of the price" is generally measured as an area behind a price-dependent demand curve.

The argument that justifies its use as a welfare measure runs as follows. Compare a competitive market with a perfectly discriminating monopolist. The latter auctions off a given amount of the product, say $\hat{x}$, in finite units. The first unit sold goes for the highest price, the second unit for a slightly lower price, and so on until the last unit is purchased at the price that corresponds to $\hat{x}$ on the demand curve.

In a competitive market, all the quantity is sold at the price for $\hat{x}$ on the demand curve. Consumer surplus (which is measured in "money" terms) is thus defined as the difference between what a perfectly discriminating monopolist receives for auctioning off $\hat{x}$ and what a competitive producer receives for $\hat{x}$. The perfectly discriminating monopolist receives the area under the demand curve between 0 and $\hat{x}$. The competitive producer receives the market price (the marginal willingness-to-pay) times $\hat{x}$. Geometrically, consumer surplus is the difference between the two. Figure 7.1 illustrates demand X, price P, and demand curve ABC. The area under the demand curve between 0 and X is given by the area of the quadrilateral $0ABX$ and the market value of X by the rectangle $0PBX$, leaving consumer surplus as the area of the triangle ABP.

This auctioning process envisions price as adjusting to quantity changes instead of quantity adjusting to price change. Rather than looking at $x(p)$, one looks at its dual reflection:

$$p \in \partial d(x, x; g),$$

the associated price-dependent (inverse) demand (see Chapter 5). Consumer surplus (now measured in units of the numeraire) at $\hat{x}$ is calculated by

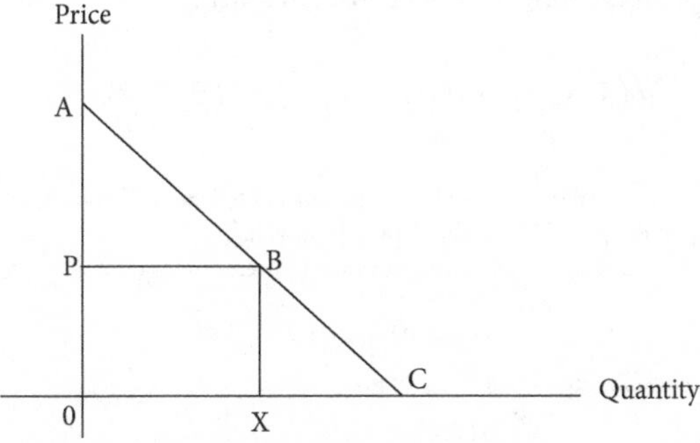

Fig. 7.1 Consumer Surplus

integrating this relationship from 0 to $\hat{x}$ and then subtracting $\partial d(\hat{x}, \hat{x}; g) \cdot \hat{x}$. That is,

$$\text{Consumer Surplus} = \int_0^{\hat{x}} \partial d(z, z; g)\, dz - \partial d(\hat{x}, \hat{x}; g) \cdot \hat{x}.$$

It's well known, however, that the presence of income effects ensures that consumer surplus is only an approximate welfare measure.[6] Basic micro theory teaches us that we can only get a true welfare measure from such an integration procedure if we use the Hicksian-compensated demand rather than Marshallian demand to ensure that "real-income" effects are washed out. The reason why consumer surplus is not an exact welfare measure is straightforward. If the consumer purchased $\hat{x}$ via the step-by-step auctioning process, he would pay more money than if he simply purchased the entire bundle at $\partial d(\hat{x}, \hat{x}; g)$. This income reduction would imply that fewer units would be purchased if the good were normal and more if it were inferior. For expenditure changes to reflect welfare changes exactly, either the marginal utility of income needs to remain constant for such moves or one needs to calibrate the auctioning process of the perfectly discriminating monopolist along the compensated (Hicksian) demand rather than the uncompensated demand curve (see Chapter 5).

Expressing demands in price-dependent terms just means that Hicksian demands are rewritten as their Antonelli (compensated demands) counterparts. Welfare calculations, therefore, should be computed using Antonelli demands rather than their rational (or Marshallian) price-dependent counterparts. Fixing original well-being at $\hat{x}$, we find that the area under the Antonelli demand between 0 and $\hat{x}$ is

$$\int_0^{\hat{x}} \partial d(z, \hat{x}; g)\, dz = d(\hat{x}, \hat{x}; g) - d(0, \hat{x}; g).$$

Thus, the appropriate consumer welfare measure is[7]

$$d(\hat{x}, \hat{x}; g) - d(0, \hat{x}; g) - \partial d(\hat{x}, \hat{x}; g) \cdot \hat{x}.$$

[6] This is one of those things that you are already presumed to know. If you are not familiar with it, you may consult, for example, Kreps (2013) and Chapter 10 of this book.

[7] Several things to note here. Given strictly monotonic preferences $d(\hat{x}, \hat{x}, g) = 0$ so that the welfare measure is

$$-d(0, \hat{x}; g) - \partial d(\hat{x}, \hat{x}, g) \cdot \hat{x}.$$

Using results developed in Chapter 5, we can reexpress this as

$$u(\hat{x}; g) - \partial d(\hat{x}, \hat{x}, g) \cdot \hat{x},$$

which is the difference between the g equivalent for $\hat{x}$ and its shadow valuation expressed in units of the numeraire.

As traditionally calculated, the sum of consumer and producer surplus is visualized in quantity-price space as the difference between the areas under the demand and supply curves. Here's why. The dual relation

$$y \in \partial^- c^* (w, p) \Leftrightarrow p \in \partial^- c(w, y)$$

shows that the price-dependent manifestation of the supply curve is the associated marginal cost. Thus, *producer surplus,* which is defined visually as the market price times the quantity less the area underneath the price-dependent supply curve is written for $\tilde{x}$ as

$$\tilde{p}\tilde{x} - \int_0^{\tilde{x}} \partial^- c(w, y)\, dy = \tilde{p}\tilde{x} - c(w, \tilde{x}),$$

which equals maximal profit at $\tilde{p}$, $c^*(w, \tilde{p})$, if $c(w, 0) = 0$ (no fixed costs). Adding consumer surplus to this expression gives for $\tilde{x}$, $\int_0^{\tilde{x}} \partial d(z, z; g)\, dz - \int_0^{\tilde{x}} \partial^- c(w, y)\, dy$, as required.

By similar reasoning, the sum of our consumer welfare measure and producer surplus at $\tilde{x}$ is[8]

$$d(\tilde{x}, \hat{x}; g) - c(w, \tilde{x}) - d(0, \hat{x}; g),$$

so that having $\hat{x}$ maximize it (for real welfare held constant at $\hat{x}$) is equivalent to having $\hat{x}$ solve

$$\min_{\tilde{x}} \{c(w, \tilde{x}) - d(\tilde{x}, \hat{x}; g)\} = \max_{p} \{E(p, \hat{x}) - c^*(w, p)\},$$

which is our excess expenditure criterion and the criterion for quasi-Pareto optimality.

Generalizing arguments shows that

$$\left\{ \sum_{k=1}^{K} d^k(\tilde{x}^k, x^k; g) - \sum_{j=1}^{J} c^k(w, y^j) : \sum_{j=1}^{J} y^j = \sum_{k=1}^{K} \tilde{x}^k \right\}$$

represents the sum of true consumer surplus and producer surplus at common total quantities. Therefore, our conjugate equilibrium calculation is also

[8] Note that the market price times the quantity sold by producers just balances the quantity purchased by consumers times the price. Thus, an alternative way of looking at the sum of consumer and producer surplus is to recognize that it equals the difference between a measure of the benefit associated with $\tilde{x}$ and the cost of producing $\tilde{x}$. Thus, one could equally think of $d(\tilde{x}, x; g) - c(w, \tilde{x})$ as a measure of *net benefits.*

interpretable as one of maximizing that measure of aggregate welfare. And, of course, we can trivially conclude that maximizing that measure of aggregate welfare results in an equilibrium allocation of demands and supplies that is quasi-Pareto optimal and supportable by a partial equilibrium.

Whether you find maximizing excess expenditure, maximizing "consumer plus producer surplus," or maximizing disposable surplus more intuitive is not particularly important. It's a matter of perspective. What is important is that you recognize the commonality of the reasoning *and* that $d(x, y; g)$ is a complete cardinal measure of $\succeq(y)$. *And if* $\succeq(y)$ *is defined by consumer preferences, that means that* $d(x, y; g)$ *is a valid cardinal welfare measure that we can identify with willingness-to-pay. Unlike consumer surplus, it needs no "real-income" correction. And unlike a utility function specified in ordinal terms, it has an interpretation in terms of concretely measurable objects.* (Chapter 10 presents a detailed treatment of how $d(x, y; g)$ can be used in applied welfare analysis.)

3 General Equilibrium and the First and Second Welfare Theorems

The goal of this section is to demonstrate how two of the fundamental results from equilibrium theory drop out as relatively straightforward manifestations of our central mathematical results. These are the First and Second Welfare Theorems. The First Welfare Theorem says that any competitive equilibrium (to be defined) is Pareto optimal (efficient). And the Second Welfare Theorem turns this statement on its head and says that any Pareto optimal (efficient) allocation and production plan can be implemented via a competitive price equilibrium.

Treating general equilibrium only requires a slight recycling of variational arguments. The essential logic remains the same, and as elswhere, Fenchel's Inequality and Fenchel's Duality Theorem drive the analysis.

There are K rational consumers with preferences that are transitive, reflexive, continuous from above, strictly monotonic from above, and convex from above. Without loss of generality, we work with prices normalized by the numeraire, $g \in \mathbb{R}^N_+ \backslash \{0\}$. Rational demands satisfy

$$E^k(q; x^k) \leq q^\top \tilde{x}^k - d^k(\tilde{x}^k, x^k; g), \quad \text{for all } (q, \tilde{x}^k) \in \mathbb{R}^{2N} \tag{7.9}$$

with $k = 1, \ldots, K$, where $q \in \mathbb{R}^N$ is a normalized price vector.

Different approaches to modeling general-equilibrium production exist. One is to introduce firms and specific assumptions concerning firm ownership. Another is to be vague about ownership structure and work instead in terms of a general *transformation set* that simply lists the consumption bundles that are "feasible" for society to consume.[9] This feasibility can arise from physical production activities, but it can also arise from other alternatives.[10] Because the latter is simpler to handle, we work with it. You can always complicate this problem later by adding more texture to it. Following Chapter 6, let's call the transformation set $T \subset \mathbb{R}^N$. For mnemonic purposes, you may wish to think of T as a technology, but as we shall note, other interpretations are definitely possible. T is nonempty, closed, bounded, and convex, and satisfies the following version of free disposability

$$y \in T \Rightarrow y' \in T \text{ for } y' \leq y$$

with $y' \in \mathbb{R}^N$.Visually, these assumptions yield a *transformation function* that is concave to the origin. See Figure 1.6.

Given the slightly different notational setup, we're (meaning you) going to develop a simple distance-based version of that transformation function, $\sigma(y)$, that we will refer to as a *shortage function*

Problem 71. *Prove that*

$$\sigma(y) \equiv \min\{\alpha \in \mathbb{R} : y - \alpha g \in T\},$$

if there exists α such that $y-\alpha g \in T$ and ∞ otherwise satisfies: nondecreasing in y; $y \in T \Leftrightarrow \sigma(y) \leq 0$ (Indication); for $\beta \in \mathbb{R}$, $\sigma(y+\beta) = \sigma(y) + \beta$ (Translation Property); σ is convex in y with $q \in \partial^{-}\sigma(y) \Rightarrow q^{\top}g = 1$.

Because T contains technically feasible y, it's linked intuitively to our discussion of $\succeq(y)$ in terms of technologies. But there are differences. For example, here there is no formal distinction between inputs and outputs. Give this some thought. Malinvaud (1972, p. 87) frames the essential issue nicely: "The classification of goods into ...categories ...complicates the exposition, but has little effect on the logical structure."

[9] Think of the production possibilities set in intermediate micro or its graphical representation as everything on or below the production possibilities frontier (transformation curve).

[10] One clear alternative that is especially important in financial economics is a competitive asset structure.

Define the convex conjugate of σ as

$$\sigma^*(p) \equiv \sup_y \{p^\top y - \sigma(y)\}, \text{ for } p \in \mathbb{R}^N.$$

By Theorem 7, the structure of T ensures that

$$\sigma(y) = \sup_p \{p^\top y - \sigma^*(p)\},$$

and

$$p \in \partial^- \sigma(y) \Leftrightarrow y \in \partial^- \sigma^*(p).$$

I am going to leave it to you as an exercise to decide precisely how you wish to think of $\sigma^*(p)$. (There's definitely more than one alternative.)

Problem 72. *Provide an economic explanation and thorough discussion of the dual relationships*

$$\sigma^*(p) = \sup_y \{p^\top y - \sigma(y)\},$$
$$\sigma(y) = \sup_p \{p^\top y - \sigma^*(p)\},$$

and

$$p \in \partial^- \sigma(y) \Leftrightarrow y \in \partial^- \sigma^*(p).$$

Problem 73. *Prove that under our assumptions*

$$y \in T \Leftrightarrow p^\top y \leq \sigma^*(p) \text{ for all } p.$$

Some necessary terminology will help us formalize our arguments.

Definition 4. *A production plan $y \in \mathbb{R}^N$ and an allocation of it to K consumers, $(x^1, \ldots, x^K)$, are feasible if $\sigma(y) \leq 0$ and $y = \sum_{k=1}^K x^k$*

Definition 5. *A feasible production plan and allocation are Pareto optimal if there is no other feasible production plan y^0 and allocation $(x^{01}, \ldots, x^{0K})$ such that $x^{0k} \succeq (x^k)$ for all k with at least one k′ such that $x^{k'} \succ (x^k)$.*

Problem 74. *Prove that a feasible production plan and allocation are Pareto optimal if there is no other feasible production plan y^0 and allocation $(x^{01}, \ldots, x^{0K})$ such that $x^{0k} \succ (x^k)$ for all k.*

The challenge now is to determine conditions characterizing Pareto-optimal production plans and allocations and to relate these conditions to a competitive equilibrium (still not defined). Previous experience suggests that this characterization involves consumer marginal rates of substitution equalized across individuals and equated to producer marginal rates of transformation and aggregate consumer demand balanced by aggregate supply. How to show this simply?

The answer, once again, lies in Fenchel's Inequality (2.16). We have

$$\sigma^*(q) \geq q^\top y - \sigma(y) \text{ for all } (q, y) \in \mathbb{R}^{2N}.$$

Adding this result to the sum of (7.9) over k gives, after slight rearrangement, that

$$\sum_k E^k(q; x^k) - \sigma^*(q) \leq \sigma(y) - \sum_{k=1}^K d^k(\tilde{x}^k, x^k; g) + q^\top\left(\sum_k \tilde{x}^k - y\right) \tag{7.10}$$

for all $(q, \tilde{x}^k, y) \in \mathbb{R}^{2N}$, $k = 1, \ldots, K$. Hence, setting $\sum_k \tilde{x}^k = y$ implies that the lower bound of the right-hand side must dominate the upper bound of the left-hand side, whence

$$\max_q \left\{\sum_k E^k(q; x^k) - \sigma^*(q)\right\} \leq \min_{(y, \tilde{x}^1, \ldots, \tilde{x}^K)} \left\{\sigma(y) - \sum_{k=1}^K d^k(\tilde{x}^k, x^k; g) : \sum_k \tilde{x}^k = y\right\}. \tag{7.11}$$

Problem 75. *Prove Theorem 15.*

Theorem 15. *A feasible production plan y and allocation $(x^1, \ldots, x^K)$ are Pareto optimal if and only if they are zero minimal for*

$$\min_{(\hat{y}, \tilde{x}^1, \ldots, \tilde{x}^K)} \left\{\sigma(\hat{y}) - \sum_{k=1}^K d^k(\tilde{x}^k, x^k; g) : \sum_k \tilde{x}^k = \hat{y}\right\}.$$

Given Theorem 15, the calculating formulas for establishing necessary and sufficient conditions for Pareto optimality reduce to a simple application of superdifferential analysis. Under our regularity conditions, $\sigma(y)$ is nondecreasing, convex in y and, each $d^k(\cdot)$ is nondecreasing, concave in $\tilde{x}^k$, so the appropriate subdifferentiability and superdifferentiability are assured. Moreover, the relevant differentials are subsets of $\mathbb{R}^N_+$. (We can easily strengthen the assumptions to ensure that they fall in $\mathbb{R}^N_{++}$). Thus, if an interior solution exists,[11] Pareto optimality requires

$$\emptyset \neq \partial^- \sigma(y) \cap \left[\cap_k \partial d^k\left(x^k, x^k; g\right)\right] \subset \mathbb{R}^N_+. \tag{7.12}$$

The intuition behind (7.12) is standard. If two consumers had different marginal rates of substitution, they can arrange a trade between them that benefits one of them while leaving the other no worse off. In fact, given continuity and strict monotonicity, they can arrange a trade that makes both of them better off. If the marginal rates of substitution differ from the marginal rate of transformation associated with $\partial^- \sigma(y)$, there's necessarily a disagreement about marginal valuation between consumers and T. That means, relative to their tastes, T is offering some commodities at terms that consumers find favorable. That will lead them to trade with T until all such differences are eliminated.

Problem 76. *Using an "Edgeworth Box" diagram, illustrate why it must be true that if an allocation leaves two consumers with differing marginal rates of substitution, at least one consumer can be made strictly better off. Now modify that diagram to include the existence of production and illustrate why all must agree on relative prices.*

What's the connection between Pareto-optimal production plans and allocations and general equilibrium? If you've guessed that the price-taking (competitive) version of the latter generates the former, you're correct. To that end, we say that $y(p)$, $x^1(p), \dots, x^K(p)$, and p represent a *competitive general (Walrasian) equilibrium* if

$$\begin{aligned} x^k(p) &\in \partial E^k\left(p; x^k(p)\right), \; k = 1, \dots, K, \\ y(p) &\in \partial^- \sigma^*(p), \end{aligned}$$

[11] Uniqueness is another matter—hence the use of the overlapping condition.

and

$$\sum_k x^k(p) = y(p).$$

But if this is true, it must also be true that general equilibrium requires

$$p \in \max_q \left\{ \sum_k E^k(q; x^k(p)) - \sigma^*(q) \right\}.$$

Using Theorem 15, expression (7.11), and recycling arguments from Section 1 (I shall leave this to you) establishes:

Theorem 16. *If p is consistent with general equilibrium, the following conditions are equivalent, p is zero maximal for*

$$\max_q \left\{ \sum_k E^k(q; x^k(p)) - \sigma^*(q) \right\},$$

and $(y(p), x^1(p), \dots, x^K(p))$ *is zero minimal for*

$$\min_{(y, \tilde{x}^1, \dots, \tilde{x}^K)} \left\{ \sigma(y) - \sum_{k=1}^K d^k(\tilde{x}^k, x^k(p); g) : \sum_k \tilde{x}^k = y \right\}.$$

Problem 77. *Prove Theorem 16 formally and then discuss it intuitively.*

Theorem 16 crystallizes the essence of the First and Second Welfare Theorems. If prices support a general equilibrium (more formally a Walrasian equilibrium), the associated production plan and distribution of that production plan across consumers is Pareto optimal. Conversely, if a production plan is Pareto optimal, there exists a general equilibrium price that supports it. The first part of Theorem 16 also establishes that general equilibrium will only occur at prices where excess expenditure is maximized at zero. Thus, consumer expenditure must be exactly balanced by the income that can be generated from T. In short, equilibrium and efficiency require that aggregate consumer expenditure respects the economy's budget constraint.

If Pareto optimality is a valid notion of efficiency, a price-taking general equilibrium ensures efficiency under some specific assumptions. But the Paretian criterion only establishes a partial ordering of welfare outcomes. In that sense, it is not unlike $\succeq(y)$ interpreted as an at-least-as-good correspondence. It can isolate production plans and allocations that are Pareto superior. But once those plans and allocations are identified, it cannot isolate a "best" plan. That is the problem of *social choice*, which is beyond the scope of our lectures.

Problem 78. *Let $K = 2$ and $N = 2$. Using a single picture, illustrate why (7.12) is necessary and sufficient.*

Problem 79. *Suppose that*

$$T = \{y \in \mathbb{R}^2_+ : y \leq \hat{y}\},$$

where $\hat{y} \in \mathbb{R}^2_{++}$ derive the necessary and sufficient conditions for Pareto optimality.

Problem 80. *Suppose that for all k,*

$$x \succeq^k (y) \Leftrightarrow x \geq y$$

with $y \in \mathbb{R}^N$ and that

$$\sigma(y) = \log\left(\sum_n b_n \exp(y_n)\right).$$

Derive $\sigma^*(p)$, conditions ensuring that $\sigma(y)$ is convex and that there are necessary and sufficient conditions for Pareto optimality.

Problem 81. *Suppose that there are J producers, each having a feasible production set $T^j \subset \mathbb{R}^N$ that is closed, convex, and nonempty, satisfies free disposability, and that*

$$T = T^1 + T^2 + \ldots + T^J.$$

Prove that

$$\sigma^*(p) = \sum_{j=1}^{J} \sigma^{*j}(p),$$

where

$$\sigma^{*j}(p) = \sup\{py - \sigma^j(y)\},$$

and

$$\sigma^j(y) \equiv \inf\{\alpha \in \mathbb{R} : y - \alpha g \in T^j\}.$$

Problem 82. *For T described in Problem 81, prove Theorem 17 and provide a thorough intuitive discussion of its economic content.*

Theorem 17. *Suppose that there are J producers, each having a feasible production set $T^j \subset \mathbb{R}^N$ so that*

$$T = T^1 + T^2 + \ldots + T^J$$

with each T^j closed, convex, nonempty, and satisfying free disposability. If p is consistent with general equilibrium, the following conditions are equivalent: p is zero maximal for

$$\max_q \left\{ \sum_k E^k(q; x^k(p)) - \sum_{j=1}^{J} \sigma^{*j}(q) \right\},$$

and $(y^1(p), \ldots, y^j(p), x^1(p), \ldots, x^K(p))$ is zero minimal for

$$\min_{(y^1\ldots,y^j,\tilde{x}^1,\ldots,\tilde{x}^K)} \left\{ \sum_{j=1}^{J} \sigma^j(y^j) - \sum_{k=1}^{K} d^k(\tilde{x}^k, x^k(p); g) : \sum_k \tilde{x}^k = \sum_{j=1}^{J} y^j \right\}.$$

4 Kinks and Equilibrium

Virtually all of our visual illustrations depict cases where consumer preferences and some version of the "technology" are nicely smooth and thus amenable to calculus manipulation and characterization. But the formal analysis admits the possibility of kinked preference maps or kinked transformation maps. Thus, at a technical level, "kinkiness" is something that we are well prepared to handle. However, one should be aware that kinks can transform an otherwise unique equilibrium.

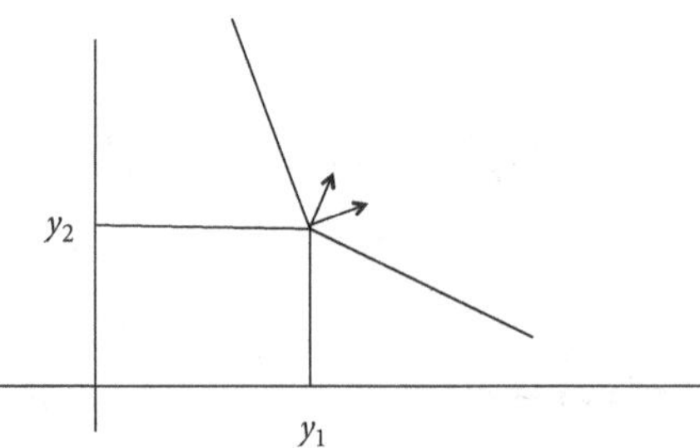

Fig. 7.2 Independent Preferences in an Endowment Economy

Figure 7.2 illustrates what is often referred to as a "pure-exchange" or endowment economy, where there is no production but consumers are "endowed" with a fixed amount of each good, and the equilibrium problem is to find a pattern of exchange where consumer demand exactly balances endowed supply. The aggregate endowment in Figure 7.2 is given by (y_1, y_2). The preferences of a "representative consumer,"[12] whose preferences are incomplete, are assumed to satisfy the independence axiom, so that her distance function satisfies (see Corollary 5)

$$d(x-y,0;g) = \inf_q \{q^\top (x-y) : q \in Q\}.$$

Equilibrium occurs where $V(y)$ for the aggregate consumer just sits on the "box" formed by (y_1, y_2) and the origin, $(0,0)$. Several things are to be noted. First, because there is no production, equilibrium price determination only involves ensuring that consumers have overlapping marginal rates of substitution. The "representative consumer" assumption slashes this Gordian Knot by assuming that all consumers have identical preferences. (Again, a willing suspension of disbelief is needed to swallow this argument.) And as long as they all operate on the same point on their respective $\bar{V}(y)$, equilibrium conditions are met. Second, the equilibrium depicted, which effectively just splits the consumption bundle among the various consumers,

[12] Representative consumers or producers are convenient analytic artifices that likely never exist. But, for us, they are immensely useful when it comes to drawing pictures of general equilibria. Moreover, they form the essential bedrock of much of modern macroeconomics that treats the economy as though it consists of such individuals.

Basically, they require that differences among consumers are so small that their differing tastes can be ignored analytically. The actual requirements for their existence, as pointed out by Gorman (1953, 1968) in different circumstances, are so extreme as to be implausible (basically everything has to be quasi-homothetic; please see Chapter 6). Thus, you would do well to treat results developed using them with extreme caution if not outright disbelief.

is supported by multiple half-spaces-each with a different price normal. The range of potential normals, Q, is illustrated by the "arrows" emanating from (y_1, y_2). Each describes a different relative price pair that will be consistent with equilibrium. As drawn, therefore, an infinity (a continuum) of such pairs exists, with each corresponding to a different arrow emanating from (y_1, y_2) whose azimuths fall between the two depicted. Finally, the "box" depicting the endowment in Figure 7.1 is isomorphic to a production economy characterized by an output-price-nonjoint technology as described in Chapter 6. Thus, conclusions drawn in studying "pure-exchange" equilibria extend directly to that setting. The reason of course is that the lack of substitutability that characterizes an output-price-nonjoint technology ensures that price signals emitted by the market have no effect on determining the equilibrium pattern of production, other than to ensure that all produced output is sold.

The equilibrium depicted in Figure 7.2 is curious but well defined. The Dubovistky–Milyutin overlapping condition for Pareto optimality

$$Q \cap \mathbb{R}^2_+ \neq \emptyset,$$

or in words that Q contain nonnegative pricing normals (this is ensured by monotonicity and is assumed in Figure 7.2). Demand equals supply, which is unique, but instead of a singleton equilibrium price vector, we find a continuum. Prices are indeterminate. Intuitively, one might think they might appear unstable in an applied setting. After all, any price normal in the range of the depicted arrows supports the same equilibrium, and so over different observations one may not be surprised to find considerable price variability even in the absence of any commodity instability. It's as though a shaky "invisible hand" is guiding the market allocation process.

Just how seriously should we take Figure 7.2 and what are the fundamental economics behind it? Perhaps the most important behavioral implication of kinks in either preference maps or production contours is that the agents associated with them will not respond smoothly to price signals. Figure 7.2 illustrates the situation where both sides of the market hesitate, so it can seem extreme, and perhaps it is. But many well-documented, real-world instances exist where either consumers or producers do not respond to price signals as smooth theory would suggest. The phenomena associated with the *home-country bias, the endowment effect, the gap between willingness-to-pay and willingess-to-accept, and the status-quo bias* provide a short list of such settings.

5 It's Obvious, Right?

The central tenet of the Arrow–Debreu–McKenzie Theorem is that if an economy consists of consumers with "nice" preferences and production characterized by "nice" technologies, it possesses a competitive equilibrium and that the competitive equilibrium is Paretian. In making the mathematical argument, we've taken the shortcut of assuming that preferences and production possibilities are "nice." And so, we've assumed that economic behavior for consumers can be modeled AS IF consumer k solves

$$\min_{\hat{x}^k} \{p^\top \hat{x}^k - d^k(\hat{x}^k, x^k; g)\}, \; k = 1, \ldots, K,$$

where $d^k(\hat{x}^k, x^k; g)$ is nicely concave. Similarly, the "representative producer" associated with T acts as if she solves

$$\max_y \{p^\top y - \sigma(y)\},$$

with $\sigma(y)$ nicely convex.

Referring back to Chapter 2's conjugate duality discussion and Lemma 8 provides some perspective. The former establishes that if "nice" dual functions, $E(\cdot)$ and $\sigma^*(\cdot)$, exist, there must exist "nice" primal functions. While there's no *a priori* guarantee that nice primal functions exist, Lemma 8 ensures that nice dual functions exist as long as individuals do indeed take prices as given and optimize. Therefore, even if the nice primal functions didn't exist in the first place, we can pretend AS IF they did if we truly believe in the existence of $E(\cdot)$ and $\sigma^*(\cdot)$.

The key assumptions required to ensure the existence of nice dual functions are monotonicity from above (MA) for consumers, economic rationality (which presumes individual's optimize), and price-taking behavior. As I've tried to emphasize elsewhere (see Chapter 2's discussion of the importance of duality), those represent abstractions about economic individuals and the decision environment they face. You can work out your own feelings about this elsewhere. What is important from an analytic perspective is that under weak regularity conditions (mainly MA) those assumptions imply that economic behavior for consumers and producers can be modeled AS IF those representations exist.

When viewed from this perspective and your accumulated knowledge of conjugate dual relations, the essential content of the Arrow–Debreu–McKenzie Theorem is in a sense an obvious consequence of Fenchel's Inequality and fixed-point theory. But in saying that, one must remember that the Arrow–Debreu–McKenzie Theorem is over 60 years old. In particular, the concept of generalized differentials as sets (correspondences) dates, independently, to Moreau (1962) and Rockafellar (1963), a decade after the Arrow–Debreu Theorem appeared. Similarly, the French version of Berge (1963), which contains the first clear statement of the Maximum Theorem, dates to 1959, half a decade after Arrow–Debreu–McKenzie. Finally, our conjugate duality relies on results developed in Rockafellar (1970). Therefore, much of our mathematical apparatus postdates the Arrow–Debreu–McKenzie contribution. It's only when things are viewed from that perspective of individuals grappling with a problem with what we would today regard as rudimentary tools can the magnitude of their intellectual achievement be fully appreciated. Perhaps nothing puts the achievement in perspective better than a quote from an interview with R. T. Rockafellar about optimization theory at the time he started his PhD work at Harvard (roughly 1958, emphasis added): "The topic was in optimization, *which as a subject was only about 8 years old at that time*."

6 Chapter Commentary

The zero-minimum (zero-maximum) approach to characterize equilibria is due to Luenberger (1992b) and has close parallels in Fenchel's Duality Theorem and the theory of supremal and infimal convolutions. As far as I am aware, the first application of the methods to characterize Pareto-optimal outcomes involving incomplete preference structures is Chambers (2014), but essentially equivalent results are available using alternative computational algorithms (see, for example, Rigotti and Shannon 2005).

8
Preferences and Production under Uncertainty

We now turn our attention to economics in an *uncertain* setting. In talking about *uncertainty*, Donald Rumsfeld famously opined (U.S. Department of Defense, 2002):

> [T]here are known knowns; there are things we know we know. We also know there are known unknowns; that is to say we know there are some things we do not know. But there are also unknown unknowns—the ones we don't know we don't know.

Uncertainty is something everyone seems to understand but that many define in subtly and not-so-subtly different ways. When pressed, however, many resort to simple games of chance as canonical illustrations of an uncertain economic setting. Figure 8.1, which represents a slightly redrawn and labeled version of Figure 1.2, illustrates one such game, the "coin-flip game" as it is typically played in the United States. It's a simple betting game that involves tossing (flipping) a coin into the air and betting on which side of the coin will face up when it settles. The two possible outcomes are a Heads, which means that the obverse side of the coin depicting the head of some historic individual (often a president, but sometimes not) will face up, and Tails, which means that the reverse side of the coin will face up. The stakes are typically all or nothing for each player. If you win, you get your opponent's *ante* and your own. If you lose, you get nothing.

In Figure 8.1, the vertical axis, labeled Heads, shows the payout that occurs when a Head occurs, and the horizontal axis the payout when a Tail occurs. There are three possibilities. One is that you refuse to play. In that case, whether a Head or a Tail occurs is irrelevant because you always keep your ante and only your ante. This outcome is illustrated by the point B with the payout $(1, 1)$ meaning that you get one dollar if a Heads comes up and one dollar if a Tails comes up. If you choose to play and have the Heads option, you will receive your ante and your opponent's ante if a Head results and nothing if a Tail comes up. This is illustrated by point A with a payout of $(0, 2)$. If

Competitive Agents in Certain and Uncertain Markets. Robert G. Chambers, Oxford University Press (2021).

DOI: 10.1093/oso/9780190063016.001.0001

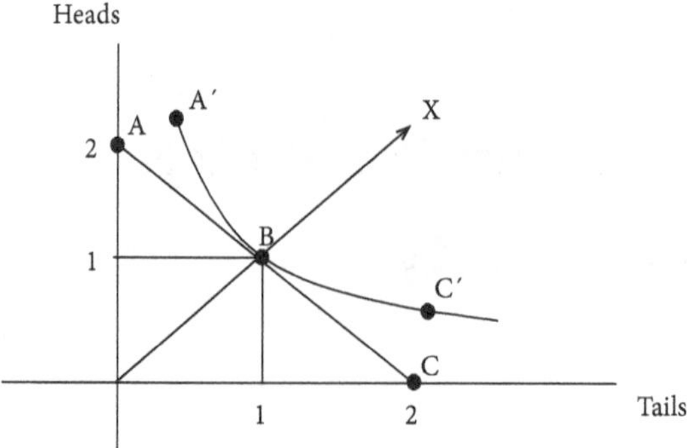

Fig. 8.1 The Coin-flip Game

you hold the Tails option, your outcome is illustrated by C with a payout of $(2,0)$. Presuming that the coin is truly *fair*, which side turns up is a matter of chance, a 50–50 proposition. If so, the expected value of A, B, and C should be the same and equal to 1. In other words, the expectation is that you simply keep your ante.

What governs choice in this setting? In particular, if there's no expected gain, why play? To study that, we need a firm grasp of the essential economic problem. If you are the caller, the choice problem is to choose between $(1,1)$, $(0,2)$, and $(2,0)$. You can say, "I don't want to play," which is represented as choosing $(1,1)$. You can say, "I want to play" and call Heads so that the choice is $(0,2)$, or Tails if you choose the reverse and pick $(2,0)$. These are *actual payments* measured as ordered pairs of real numbers (2-tuples, two-dimensional vectors), just as 1 egg and 1 orange, 0 eggs and 2 oranges, and 2 eggs and 0 oranges can be so arranged.

Viewed this way, the coin-flip game is precisely the type of choice encountered previously. What's different is not its mathematical formulation but the interpretation of that formulation. It's natural to suppose, therefore, that choice (preference) can be depicted using an order $\succeq(y)$. If we interpret the smooth curve passing through B as $\bar{V}(B)$ and everything above it as $V(B)$, it appears that the individual illustrated chooses not play.

This betting game captures the essence of many problems faced by decision makers in an uncertain setting. It contains a decision period in which you must decide whether you want to play. You must choose, Heads or Tails, without knowing which will actually occur. It also contains an outcome or settlement period, after the coin is flipped, in which real payments are made. Further, all potential outcomes of the game are known.[1]

[1] One imagines, of course, the possibility that the coin once flipped will exactly balance itself on its edge, leaving a "leansy." But having never seen that or having heard of it occurring, I rule it out without apology.

This chapter does several things. Working from the basic coin-flip game, it develops an economic framework (due to Arrow 1953, 1964, Savage 1954, and Debreu 1959) for modeling uncertain or stochastic outcomes. Once that is done, the attention turns to analyzing individual choice in that setting. A parallel production model is then developed. In reading this chapter and the one that follows, you will note that the discussion draws subject content directly from *decision theory* and the literature on producer decision making under uncertainty. However, the focus is decidedly on emphasizing the essential equivalences between our preceding discussions of consumers and producers and not on a complete exposition of either of those literatures.

Decision theory, in particular, has its own place. And while the mathematics underlying decision theory are remarkably similar to the math used here, axioms are framed and discussed from a very different perspective. Much of decision theory seeks to develop an appropriate framework for *rational choice.* As used in decision theory, the adjective "rational" typically carries a very different meaning than the one that I have used. As a result, decision theory is more focused on describing how individuals *should* behave in a particular setting than how they actually behave. Thus, while the overlap is significant, it's an area that merits its own independent study. I strongly encourage those of you who are interested to consult the ever-relevant Savage (1954), Fishburn (1972), and the remarkably accessible, but rigorous, presentation by Gilboa (2009). On the producer side of things, I suggest (immodestly) that you consult Chambers and Quiggin (2000).

Another thing that you will note is that less space is given to analyzing uncertain economic settings than has been given to nonstochastic problems. You shouldn't infer, however, that I, or anyone else, regard uncertain problems as either less important or more unrealistic than nonstochastic problems. Just the opposite is true. So why the unbalanced dichotomous treatment? My answer is that it manifests two things. First, the prior pedagogical tradition in consumer and producer economics emphasizes nonstochastic decision settings at the relative expense of uncertain (stochastic) ones. Economists have developed a relatively exhaustive knowledge of those problems—so much so that both stopped being "sexy" topics to study approximately three to four decades ago. So completeness is to be expected. The second thing, which is a primary message of this book, is that the essential tools for analyzing stochastic decision settings and the results attainable closely parallel those from nonstochastic theory. I cannot say, however, that it is either a particularly new or a particularly original message. Both Arrow (1953) and Debreu (1959) delivered the latter more than five decades ago. What I do here is to take their insights seriously and analyze them using mathematical tools largely developed in the intervening decades. Because the nonstochastic and stochastics settings do differ, changes are required. But in the main, these changes represent a subtle massaging of notation coupled with a slightly different interpretation of previous results. Most of the formal arguments have been made in earlier chapters, so there's no need for me to repeat their development. That makes for a more streamlined presentation, and, even better, encourages you to develop the needed extensions on your own.

1 The Economic Environment

To now, we have always worked in a timeless setting. Much of modern decision theory does as well. But as the coin-flip game illustrates, when we think about uncertainty, we often think in terms of things that have not yet occurred. One makes a choice before the coin settles. Farmers plant their crops without knowing what weather conditions will occur during the growing season. Investors invest in stocks, bonds, mutual funds, and exchange-traded funds (ETFs) before they know whether the market goes up or down. You place your bet before you know whether or not your opponent has filled that inside straight or not in stud poker. Because we tend to speak in such terms, there are intuitive advantages to introducing a temporal structure to choices involving uncertainty. So, in what follows, we opt for the simplest possible dynamic setting, a two-period one.

The first period, the *decision (ex ante) period,* is denoted notationally by 0 subscripts or superscripts and involves no uncertainty. Uncertainty enters in the next period, which we denote notationally by 1. The uncertainty is from the perspective of period 0 about what the economic environment will look like in period 1. For example, in the coin-flip game, will *Heads* or *Tails* be the final outcome of the coin flip? For farmers, will it rain or not? We formalize that uncertainty by saying that a set of possible states, S, exists. That set is finite and contains an exhaustive and mutually exclusive enumeration of elements. Those elements are called *states,* and each contains a complete description of the potential economic environment in period 1.

In the coin-flip game, $S = \{Heads, Tails\}$, and the states are *Heads* and *Tails.* More generally, however, there's no reason to restrict ourselves to such simple games, and we suppose instead that S is of the general form $S = \{1, 2, ..., S\}$. Hence, S does double duty notationally: It describes the set of states, and it also describes that set's cardinality. The way uncertainty about period 1 is resolved formally is to introduce a neutral player, *Nature,* which selects a single element from S *after* period 0. Once Nature makes that selection, all uncertainty about period 1 is resolved. The problem from the decision maker's perspective, of course, is that choices must be made in 0 before Nature's selection.

Note several things here. First, the concept of a state is somewhat squishy. I say squishy because the practical interpretation of a state varies over different economic problems. For example, two states suffice for the coin-flip game. But two states typically won't work for many decision situations that require a more complicated delineation of the possible ways in which the world can vary. Regarding just what information is provided by the state, Savage (1954, p. 9) writes that states leave "no relevant aspect undescribed." That leaves room for a lot to be included or a lot to be excluded, depending on the problem setting. It just depends.

Second, S is exhaustive. Thus, we're talking about uncertainty involving "known unknowns" and not "unknown unknowns," in Rumsfeld's terminology. We are specifically restricting attention to considering situations where we know what can happen, or a bit more generally, what we can imagine will happen. The things that "we don't know we don't know" are not included in the analysis. While this is not problematic in well-defined games of chance, such as the coin-flip game or poker, things change in more general economic settings where completely unanticipated outcomes are known to occur. As the ever-burgeoning literature on climate change attests, such matters are deeply relevant. Treating them, however, goes well beyond the scope of these lectures.

So what ultimately distinguishes decisions made under uncertainty is that the exact *consequences* of the decision maker's choices remain unknown until after Nature makes its selection from S. In treating *consequences*, Savage (1954) took an extremely abstract approach. He called a consequence "anything that may happen" and left it at that without specifying any further mathematical structure. We take a more concrete (and less general) approach and only treat *consequences* that fall in $\mathbb{R}^M$ for some integer M. So, consequences are anything that can happen and that can be counted in terms of real numbers. They could be apples or oranges, or they could be real-valued functions of these apples and oranges. It all depends on the setting and how you choose to interpret the mathematical arguments.[2]

The way that we relate uncertainty to these consequences is, following Savage (1954), to define an *act* as a function that maps S, the set of states, to the set of *consequences*. So, if $M = 1$ and the set of consequences is $\mathbb{R}$, then an act $f : S \to \mathbb{R}$. More generally, however, an act $f : S \to \mathbb{R}^M$. Because $S = \{1, 2, ..., S\}$, we see that in the first instance $f : S \to \mathbb{R}$ defines an S-dimensional real vector $f = (f(1), f(2), ..., f(S))^\top \in \mathbb{R}^S$ and in the second an $S \times M$ real matrix

[2] We'll return to this point when we talk about complete preference orders that satisfy the independence axiom introduced in Chapter 5.

$$f = \begin{bmatrix} f(1,1) & f(1,2) & \cdots & f(1,M) \\ f(2,1) & f(2,2) & \cdots & f(2,M) \\ \vdots & \vdots & \ddots & \vdots \\ f(S,1) & f(S,2) & \cdots & f(S,M) \end{bmatrix} \in \mathbb{R}^{S \times M}$$

The way to interpret these acts is as follows. If act f is chosen in period 0, and Nature chooses $s \in S$, then when the *consequence* space is $\mathbb{R}$, the outcome realized in period 1 is $f(s)$, and if the *consequence* space is $\mathbb{R}^M$, $(f(s,1), f(s,2), ..., f(s,M))$. Thus, $f \in \mathbb{R}^{S \times M}$ can be recognized as the objects of decision-maker choice and as a *vector-valued random variable.*[3]

2 Preferences

Our approach to modeling preferences for a two-period, stochastic setting is essentially identical to that used in the single-period, nonstochastic setting studied in Chapters 3 and 5. We must refine our notation, however, to accommodate an intertemporal and stochastic setting. What happens in period 0 needs to be distinguished from what happens in period 1. Period 0 choices for period 0 fall in $\mathbb{R}^M$ and are nonstochastic. These will be distinguished by a superscript 0, say $y^0 \in \mathbb{R}^M$. Period 0 choices for period 1 also have consequences that fall in $\mathbb{R}^M$ but are stochastic. Thus, we might naturally express $y^1 \in \mathbb{R}^{S \times M}$ visually as an $S \times M$ matrix (see above). While visually appealing, it's cumbersome notationally. So instead we express it as an $S \times M$ vector of the form

$$y^1 = \begin{pmatrix} y^1_{11} \\ \vdots \\ y^1_{1M} \\ y^1_{21} \\ \vdots \\ y^1_{2M} \\ \vdots \\ y^1_{S1} \\ \vdots \\ y^1_{SM} \end{pmatrix},$$

[3] You are probably used to seeing random variables being defined in terms of a probability distribution defined over some support. This is the statistical perspective on it, which places its focus on the probability structure. But as you will see, probabilities really have no innate place in developing a formal theory of economic decision making under uncertainty. They can serve as useful intuitive devices, to be sure, but they have little or nothing to do with formal economics. The way to translate from the probability defined over a support to the current context is to recognize that the support (the range of values the random value can take) defines our notion of an act or a random variable.

where the convention is that y^1_{sm} is the *mth* period 1 consequence that occurs if $s \in S$ is selected by Nature. Then defining

$$y = \begin{pmatrix} y^0 \\ y^1 \end{pmatrix},$$

we take $\succeq (y)$ to be a binary order, where $x \succeq (y)$ is to be read as outcome x is at least as good as outcome y.

Allowing for the domain changes, the analysis proceeds along the same lines as in Chapter 3. More formally, we assume that $\succeq (y)$ is a binary relation on $M + (S \times M) \times M + (S \times M)$ that is continuous, strictly monotonic

$$y + \delta \succ (y), \qquad \delta \in \mathbb{R}^{M+(S\times M)} \setminus \{0\},$$

reflexive, and transitive. Its cardinal representation, $d(x, y; g)$, satisfies suitably modified versions of Lemma 7 and Lemma 8. Here, as elsewhere, strict monotonicity simplifies the argument without drastically changing the economic content.

While the mathematical formalities are similar, their interpretation differs. These differences reflect the different aspects of the economic problems. Whereas before, activities were both timeless and "stateless," here activities can differ by both time and state. Such activities are potentially different economically, even if they involve identical physical entities. That ice-cream cone that seems so delicious today may be repellent tomorrow if Nature selects "cold snap" from S. Or an umbrella handy for today's rain is excess baggage for tomorrow's sunny day. Because both the state of Nature and timing matter, one needs to think in terms of substitute and complementary relationships across time and across states of Nature as well as across commodities. Very quickly, this becomes quite messy to discuss.

One way to bring some order to the resulting tangle of economic relationships is to simplify by concentrating attention on aspects of the problem that are fundamentally distinct from those that we have already studied. That means focusing on intertemporal and stochastic matters rather than on cross-commodity comparisons. This does some violence to reality, but it is sensible. So, in what follows, *the verbal discussion* focuses on $\mathbb{R}$ as the consequence space. No doubt, the substitute and complementary relationships within a given time or state are equally important. But these were the foci of the discussions in Chapters 3 and 5 and need not be repeated here. Nevertheless, the mathematical treatment in this chapter remains general, and exercises and problems are used to encourage the reader to engage more general matters.[4]

[4] In Chapter 9, we focus exclusively on an outcome space of $\mathbb{R}$.

2.1 Choosing a Numeraire

The numeraire determines the cardinal units used to frame the economic stories we tell. The essential substance of those stories does not vary with the choice of the numeraire, but the examples and intuition do. And so, in different settings, different normalizations prove both convenient and intuitive.

Recall Figure 8.1. There $M = 1$, and we referred to the resulting consequence intuitively as dollars. But the essentials of the gambling structure would not have changed if the stakes were measured in terms of a physical commodity. We would still use real numbers to measure the outcomes, and all that would be required would be relabeling the units in which the axes are enumerated. *The really fundamental aspect of Figure 1 is that the horizontal and vertical axes are denominated in the same physical units.* What differentiates the alternatives is the state of Nature in which particular consequences occur. Thus, $(2, 0)$ stands for \$2 if Tails occurs and nothing if Heads, $(0, 2)$ stands for nothing if Tails and \$2 if Heads, and $(1, 1)$ stands for \$1 regardless of Heads or Tails. Formally, the alternatives are defined as acts (*random variables*) that are subject to choice. But $(1, 1)$ is a peculiar random variable. It takes the same value regardless of which state of Nature occurs. So, it's a random variable for which uncertainty is unimportant. This leads some to refer to it as a *degenerate random variable* to distinguish it from random variables for which uncertainty matters. Economically, it's also important because it represents a choice not to expose oneself to uncertainty. That leads to $(1, 1)$ being referred to as either a *safe asset* or a *riskless* one.

In discussing uncertainty, we rely exclusively on a safe asset as our numeraire. The reason for the choice will become apparent as the argument develops. Some notation to distinguish the class of safe assets proves useful. We define

$$\mathcal{X} = \left\{x \in \mathbb{R}^{S\times M} : x_{sm} = \beta, \beta \in \mathbb{R}, s = 1, 2, ..., S, m = 1, 2, .., M\right\},$$

as the subset of $\mathbb{R}^{S\times M}$ describable as $S \times M$ vectors whose entries all equal the same real number. Without confusion, we shall write $\beta \in \mathcal{X}$ to denote the element of $\mathcal{X}$ describable as the $S \times M$ vector whose entries all equal $\beta \in \mathbb{R}$. Our choice for g is

$$\tilde{g} = \left\{ \begin{array}{c} 0 \in \mathbb{R}^M \\ 1 \in \mathcal{X} \end{array} \right\},$$

so that we do not include any period 0 consequences in the numeraire. Figure 8.1 illustrates $\mathcal{X}$ by the vector passing through the origin and B.

2.2 The Cardinal Representation

For this numeraire, $d(x, y; \tilde{g})$ represents the number of units of nonstochastic period-1 consumption that needs to be subtracted from x to leave the consumer indifferent between the result and y. Put differently, $d(x, y; \tilde{g})$ is the willingness-to-pay for moving from y to x as measured in units of the safe period 1 asset. An immediate consequence is:

Corollary 7. *Suppose that* $\succeq(y)$ *for* $y \in \mathbb{R}^{M+(S\times M)}$ *satisfies continuity, strict monotonicity, transitivity, and reflexivity; then*

$$q \in \partial d(y, y; \tilde{g}) \Leftrightarrow q^{\top}(x - y) \geq 0 \text{ for all } x \succeq (y),$$

with $q \in \mathbb{R}_{+}^{M+(S\times M)}$ *and* $q^{1\top}1 = 1$ *where* $q = (q^0, q^1)^{\top}$.

Corollary 7 recycles Lemma 8. There's merit in recycling judiciously. So, let's consider $x = (x^0, x^1)$ and $y = (x^0, y^1)$. The only difference between the two is the period 1 (the uncertain) component. Let's also suppose that $M = 1$. Then,

$$q \in \partial d(y, y; \tilde{g}) \Leftrightarrow q^{1\top}(x^1 - y^1) \geq 0 \text{ for all } (x^0, x^1) \succeq (x^0, y^1),$$

with $q \in \mathbb{R}_{+}^{1+S}$ and $q^{1\top}1 = 1$. Because each such $q^1 \in \mathbb{R}_{+}^{S}$ and $q^{1\top}1 = 1$, each can be interpreted as a *probability measure defined over* S. Thinking in these terms, we see that superdifferentiability at y requires that each $q \in \partial d(y, y; \tilde{g})$ assign a greater *expected value* to x^1 than y^1 whenever $(x^0, x^1) \succeq (x^0, y^1)$. The converse is also true.

Superdifferentiability, therefore, has probabilistic implications. But the probabilities were derived from $\succeq(y)$ *without making any assumptions about the relative frequency with which states occur*. So, what that probabilistic structure communicates about the objective likelihood of the elements of S is problematic. What is clear is that the probabilities depend on the individual's preferences and can differ across individuals. Thus, in some sense, they should reflect the individual's beliefs about the relative likelihoods of the difference states. Because individuals can disagree, those beliefs can be subjective.

It's important to emphasize, however, that this probabilistic discussion is an extramathematical interpretation of a mathematical result. In particular, you should recall that it's a different interpretation than the one I offered in a nonstochastic setting. It works well in this setting because of the convenient numeraire choice. But it would have worked, albeit with more maths, for any realistic choice. The essential point is that mathematical results originally derived in a different *intuitive* setting were recycled to make them more palatable for individuals who think in probabilistic terms. The essence has not changed; only the intuitive motivation has. Thus, the tools of economic analysis still work. There's really no need to rely on *statistics* to analyze this problem. Economics works just fine.

Problem 83. *Applying Lemma 10 establishes: Suppose that* $\succeq(y)$ *for* $y \in \mathbb{R}^{M+(S\times M)}$ *satisfies continuity, strict monotonicity, transitivity, and reflexivity, then*

$$p \in \partial^{-} t(x, x; \tilde{g}) \Leftrightarrow p^{\top}(x-y) \geq 0 \text{ for all } y \in Y(x),$$

with $p \in \mathbb{R}_{+}^{M+(S\times M)}$ *and* $p^{1\top} g = 1$*. Discuss this result intuitively.*

Problem 84. *For* $M \neq 1$,

$$q \in \partial d(y, y; \tilde{g}) \Leftrightarrow q^{1\top}(x^1 - y^1) \geq 0 \text{ for all } (x^0, x^1) \succeq (x^0, y^1),$$

with $q \in \mathbb{R}_{+}^{M+(S\times M)}$ *and* $q^{1\top}1 = 1$*. Using summation notation, we can write the main condition as*

$$q \in \partial d(y, y; \tilde{g}) \Leftrightarrow \sum_{s}\sum_{m} q_{sm}^{1}(x_{sm}^{1} - y_{sm}^{1}) \geq 0 \text{ for all } (x^0, x^1) \succeq (x^0, y^1)$$

with $q \in \mathbb{R}_{+}^{M+(S\times M)}$ *and* $\sum_s \sum_m q_{sm}^1 = 1$*. Rewrite the middle expression as*

$$\sum_{s}\left(\sum_{m'} q_{sm'}^{1}\right)\sum_{m}\frac{q_{sm}^{1}}{\sum_{m'} q_{sm'}^{1}}(x_{sm}^{1} - y_{sm}^{1}) \geq 0.$$

Develop a probabilistic interpretation of this inequality and discuss it intuitively in the general M-dimensional case. (Hint: You may wish to think intuitively in terms of conditional probability structures.)

Still holding $M = 1$, now suppose that $x^0 = y^0 + 1$ and $x^1 = y^1 - 1$ (where $1 \in \mathbb{R}$ in the first and $1 \in \mathcal{X}$ in the second). Moving from (y^0, y^1) to (x^0, x^1) involves exchanging one dollar of (riskless) period 1 consumption for a one dollar increase in period 0 consumption. If $(y^0 + 1, y^1 - 1) \succeq ((y^0, y^1))$, Corollary 7 requires that

$$q \in \partial d(y, y; \tilde{g}) \Leftrightarrow q^0 \geq 1.$$

All superdifferential shadow values for period 0 consumption, $q^0 \in \mathbb{R}$, must now exceed the shadow value of $1 \in \mathcal{X}$ (recall that $1 \in \mathcal{X}$ is the numeraire). Each such q^0 has a natural interpretation as a *marginal rate of substitution* between one unit of period 0 and one unit of (safe or riskless) period 1 consumption. And when $\partial d(y, y; \tilde{g})$ is a singleton set, q^0 is *the* marginal rate of substitution. It also measures, in terms of the numeraire, the *individual's rate of time preference* for consumption. Hence, if $q^0 \geq 1$, the individual prefers receiving one dollar today to consuming it tomorrow. Because delaying consumption is usually viewed as a sacrifice, $q^0 \geq 1$ is viewed as the normal state of affairs. It's considered so normal that

$$r^0 \equiv q^0 - 1 \tag{8.1}$$

is typically referred to as the *individual's discount rate.* The connotation is clear. Period 1 consumption enters the individual's preference structure *at a discount* relative to period 0 consumption. Because r^0 is derived from $\partial d(y, y; \tilde{g})$, it's subjective. Individuals can disagree about the rate at which period 1 consumption is discounted relative to period 0 consumption. Such differences, of course, would justify intertemporal exchanges between individuals. But because $\partial d(y, y; \tilde{g})$ is not always a singleton set, many discount rates might exist. And while $q^0 \geq 1$ is the norm, it's not implied by our assumptions. They only require that $r^0 \geq -1$.

Similar logic shows that

$$-q^1_{s'}/q^1_s \text{ for } q \in \partial d(y, y; \tilde{g}) \text{ and } s, s' \in S$$

measures the individual's marginal rate of substitution between period-1 consumption in s and s'. And $-q^1_s/q^0$ for $q \in \partial d(y, y; \tilde{g})$ measures the marginal rate of substitution between period 0 consumption and period 1 consumption in state s.

Problem 85. *As I write this chapter, the yield (interest rate) on the German government's 10-year bund (bond) is −.70. Suppose, for the sake of argument, that this yield actually reflects the average German individual's discount rate. What does it imply about her attitudes toward period 0 and period 1 consumption? What does this mean economically?*

Problem 86. *Let $M = 1$. An individual, who is initially at $y = (y^0, y^1)$, is asked to nominate a period 0 price, call it $v \in \mathbb{R}$, at which she would be willing to purchase in period 0 one unit of a stochastic asset (you might think of this as* *common stock, a government bond, or a share in the period 1 profits from a enterprise) whose uncertain period 1 payout is $b \in \mathbb{R}^S$. Show that*

$$\frac{q^{1\top} b}{q^0} \geq v,$$

for all $q \in \partial d(y, y; \tilde{g})$. Explain the result intuitively.

Remark 19. *Expressions of the generic form $\frac{q^{1\top} b}{q^0}$ are often referred to as subjective "martingale" prices—subjective because they are derived from $\succeq (y)$. In the current setting, one interpretation is that a "martingale" is an act (random variable) whose discounted expected return equals its period 0 value. Thus, denoting the expected value for b derived using q as $E_q[b]$ and using the definition of r^0, the condition becomes*

$$\frac{E_q[b]}{1 + r^0} \geq v,$$

which is the traditional present (period 0) valuation martingale formula. It follows that

$$\min \left\{ \frac{q^{1\top} b}{q^0} : q \in \partial d(y, y; \tilde{g}) \right\} \geq v,$$

so that the lower support function of $\partial d(y, y; \tilde{g})$ (in normalized terms) represents an upper bound on the willingness-to-pay.

2.3 Structural Restrictions

Returning to Figure 8.1, let's continue to interpret the smooth curve passing through B as the lower boundary of $V(B)$. As drawn, $V(B)$ satisfies *CONA*. So, convex combinations of any random variables falling in $V(B)$ are at least weakly preferred to B. Convex combinations of random variables, such as A' and B in Figure 8.1, are themselves random variables, $B + \lambda(A' - B) \in \mathbb{R}^{S \times M}$, derived as weighted averages (mixtures) of random variables with the specific weights determined by the mixing parameter $\lambda \in (0, 1)$.

To get an intuitive handle on what this means in a stochastic setting, you might want to think of mixing A' and B as *diversifying* between A' and B. Take, for example, a new homeowner who combines her home purchase with

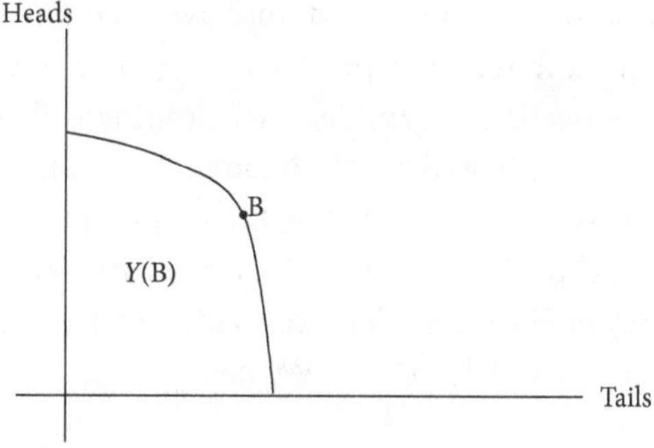

Fig. 8.2 Y(B) under CONB

a simultaneous purchase of homeowners insurance. The random variables she mixes (diversifies) are the home value or cost of home ownership and potential insurance payouts. Another example is that of an individual who allocates her financial wealth between equity (stock) investments and risk-free government bonds.[5] *CONA* requires that an individual always prefers diversifying between B and elements of $V(B)$ to holding only B. This preference for diversification is often referred to as *uncertainty aversion.*

In Figure 8.2, I have drawn a $Y(B)$ that is consistent with *CONB*. If you compare mixtures of B with points in $Y(B)$, B would dominate those mixtures. Similarly, mixtures of gambles falling in $Y(B)$ will always be dominated by B. So, instead of exhibiting a preference for diversifiying, the individual prefers to stick with B. Hence, *CONB* might be thought of as implying *mixture domination.*

Uncertainty aversion and mixture domination may appear mutually exclusive. That is, you might think an uncertainty-averse individual would only be mixture-dominating in a limiting or weak sense, and vice versa. That's certainly true if the curve passing through B in Figure 8.1 defines $\bar{V}(B)$ for an individual with complete preferences. In that case, $Y(B)$ would correspond to everything on or below the curve. It's then easy to find elements of $Y(B)$ having mixtures that dominate B, and thus violate mixture domination. But if preferences are incomplete, the lower boundary of $V(B)$ need not coincide with $\bar{Y}(B)$, the boundary of $Y(B)$. And because incompleteness permits $V(B)'s$ and $Y(B)'s$ boundaries to diverge, incomplete preference structures can exhibit both *CONA* and *CONB*. Figure 5.1, after an appropriate relabeling of the axes, illustrates.

[5] In a game-theoretic context, one interprets A' and B as pure strategies and $B + \lambda(A' - B)$ as a mixed strategy. CONA requires the mixed strategy to dominate B.

The seeming paradox of joint uncertainty aversion and mixture domination arises from the different perspectives on $\succeq(y)$ offered by $V(B)$ and $Y(B)$. $V(B)$ looks upward for gambles that dominate B, while $Y(B)$ looks for gambles that are dominated by B. Incompleteness allows individuals to make those comparisons differently. For those only familiar with complete preference structures, this can seem odd or even irrational.[6] But viewed in the light of everyday experience, it's perhaps less surprising.

Under *CO*, things are much cleaner. We have:

Theorem 18. *If $\succeq(y)$ satisfies strict monotonicity, transitivity, reflexivity, CONA, CONB, and complete ordering (CO), there exists a (unique) $q \in \mathbb{R}_+^{M+(S\times M)}$ with $q^{1\top}1 = 1$ where*

$$q^\top (x - y) \geq 0 \Leftrightarrow x \succeq (y).$$

The intuition behind Theorem 18 is illustrated using Figure 8.1. Let preferences be complete so that the curve passing through B is the indifference curve. As drawn, *CONA* applies but not *CONB*. To satisfy both and complete ordering, $V(B)$ and $Y(B)$ must share a common boundary and still be convex. That suggests a linear boundary. Theorem 18 requires precisely that. Here's a quick proof. Strict monotonicity ensures that $ri(V(y)) \cap ri(Y(y)) = \emptyset$. Because both are convex if both *CONA* and *CONB* apply, the Separating Hyperplane Theorem (Theorem 3) ensures there exists $p \in \mathbb{R}^{M+(S\times M)}$ such that

$$p^\top x \geq p^\top y \geq p^\top z$$

for all $x \in V(y)$ and $z \in Y(y)$. To show that

$$p^\top x \geq p^\top y \geq p^\top z$$

implies $x \in V(y)$ and $z \in Y(y)$, suppose to the contrary that there exists an x' such that $p^\top x' > p^\top y$ but $x' \notin V(y)$. Completeness requires that $x' \in Y(y)$, which leads to a contradiction. Establishing the signs of the elements of p and the normalization are left to you. Sufficiency is established by noting that the complete preference order defined by

$$x \succeq (y) \Leftrightarrow p^\top x \geq p^\top y$$

satisfies *CONA* and *CONB*.

[6] It's well to recall that many require rational behavior to be consistent with complete ordering. Others do not.

CONA (*CONB*) ensures that $d(x,y;\tilde{g})$ ($t(y,x;\tilde{g})$) is concave (convex) in x (y) (see, for example, Lemma 11). Lemma 2 then guarantees that $d(x,y;\tilde{g})$ ($t(y,x;\tilde{g})$) is superdifferentiable (subdifferentiable) everywhere and differentiable almost everywhere on the relative interior of its effective domain. When $M = 1$, *CONA* (*CONB*) implies the existence of probability measures, derived as superdifferentials (subdifferentials), that award higher (lower) expected values to all elements of $V(y)$ ($Y(y)$) than y.

Theorem 6 implies that a nondecreasing concave $d(x,y;\tilde{g})$ is representable in conjugate terms as

$$d(x,y;\tilde{g}) = \inf_{q\in\mathbb{R}_+^{M+(M\times S)}} \{q^\top x - d^*(q,y;\tilde{g})\}.$$

while Theorem 7 implies that an increasing convex $t(y,x;\tilde{g})$ is representable as

$$t(y,x;\tilde{g}) = \sup_{q\in\mathbb{R}_+^{M+(M\times S)}} \{q^\top y - t^*(q,x;\tilde{g})\}.$$

Cardinal representations of preferences that rely on searching over probability measures are often referred to as *multiple-prior* representations because they model the individual as "choosing" the probability measures that she uses to assess random variables with different outcomes. So, where *single-prior* models, such as the familiar expected-utility model, require the individual to use a unique prior to assess outcomes, multiple-prior models allow the individual to adjust probabilistic assessments to suit the outcome. This is not particularly hard to believe. Consider, for example, how you would judge an outcome that only involved minor monetary consequences in all states versus how you would judge an outcome that involved calamitous or life-threatening outcomes in some states.

Once again, the intuition involves extramathematical reasoning adjusted to accommodate the basic mathematical consequences of Theorems 6 and 7, which ensure that solutions to these dual problems require

$$x \in \partial d^*(q,y;\tilde{g}) \Leftrightarrow q \in \partial d(x,y;\tilde{g}),$$

and

$$y \in \partial^- t^*(q,x;\tilde{g}) \Leftrightarrow q \in \partial^- t(y,x;\tilde{g}),$$

respectively.

Problem 87. *Using the notation of Problem 84, write the conjugate dual representation $d(x, y; \tilde{g})$ as*

$$d(x, y; \tilde{g}) = \inf_{q \in \mathbb{R}_{+}^{M+(M\times S)}} \left\{ \sum_{m} q_m^0 x_m^0 + \sum_{s} \sum_{m} q_{sm}^1 x_{sm}^1 - d^*(q, y; \tilde{g}) \right\}$$

$$= \inf_{q} \left\{ \sum_{m} q_m^0 x_m^0 + \sum_{s} \left(\sum_{m'} q_{sm'}^1 \right) \sum_{m} \frac{q_{sm}^1}{\left(\sum_{m'} q_{sm'}^1\right)} x_{sm}^1 - d^*(q, y; \tilde{g}) \right\}.$$

Interpret $\sum_{m'} q_{sm'}^1$ *and* $\sum_{m} \frac{q_{sm}^1}{\left(\sum_{m'} q_{sm'}^1\right)} x_{sm}^1$ *for* $s \in S$ *when*

$$\left(q^0, q^1\right) \in \arg\inf_{q} \left\{ \sum_{m} q_m^0 x_m^0 + \sum_{s} \sum_{m} q_{sm}^1 x_{sm}^1 - d^*(q, y; \tilde{g}) \right\},$$

and illustrate your answers geometrically. Repeat the parallel exercise for $t(y, x; \tilde{g})$.

Remark 20. *Uncertainty aversion or mixture domination may ring unfamiliar. Surely, however, risk aversion doesn't. Is it the same thing as uncertainty aversion? To answer, we reach back almost a century to Frank Knight (1921) to whom we owe the economist's distinction between uncertainty and risk. Risk involves randomness "susceptible of measurement" by theoretical deduction, observed historical experience, or statistical calculation. Uncertainty is randomness not "susceptible of measurement." Knight (1921) frequently used probabilistic terms. But he was careful to discriminate between three different types of probability assessment: a priori probability assessment, statistical probability assessment, and estimates (Knight 1921, pp. 224–225).*[7] *The first two he associated with risk and the last with uncertainty. In every day terms, risk is the kind of randomness that we often associate with games of chance having clearly defined odds of good or bad outcomes. The coin-flip game is one example, as are card games, a lottery, and roulette. Risk is also associated with circumstances for which meaningful relative frequencies are calculable. Uncertainty applies for all others.*

The essential kernel of risk, therefore, is the presence of a probability measure that has an objective base. This recalls the frequentist definition of a probability as the limit toward which a relative frequency occurs in an

[7] Knight was famously suspicious of mathematics in economics. Therefore, his presentation is almost entirely verbal. For modern students of economics, that often makes for tough going. It's very unlike the approach taken here but still essential reading.

*arbitrarily large number of trials. Different criticisms have been leveled at the frequentist definition by logicians, statisticians, and mathematicians. They question, among other things, the logical possibility of performing such trials and the mathematical existence of such limits. Many reject the frequentist approach. For example, de Finetti's (1974) classic treatise, A Theory of Probability, opens by opining "**PROBABILITY DOES NOT EXIST**." And Savage's (1954) The Foundation of Statistics, on which much of our setup is based, was an attempt to provide a rigorous formulation of a theory of personal (subjective) probability.*

Putting epistemic issues asides, a probability measure is represented for a finite state space S as a mathematical object, p, satisfying

$$p \in \mathbb{R}_+^S \text{ and } p^\top 1 = 1.$$

That definition also fits our definition of a random variable when the consequence space is $\mathbb{R}$. In particular, it's a random variable that sums to one. This might seem odd. But it's yet another example of seemingly disparate conceptual objects having identical mathematical representations. We witnessed this for prices and quantities. There we referred to it in dual terms. Now we see it again for probabilities and random variables. Because probability measures belong to the dual space for $\mathbb{R}^S$, they are duals for random variables, but because random variable space $\mathbb{R}^S$ is self dual, they also can be interpreted as random variables.

Any such $p \in \mathbb{R}_+^S$ generates a family of hyperplanes, $\bar{H}(\alpha, p) \subset \mathbb{R}^S$, and associated half-spaces, $H(\alpha, p)$. Figure 8.3 illustrates. The vector labeled p depicts the probability measure defining the normal, and (α, α) equals $\bar{H}(\alpha, p) \cap \mathcal{X}$. Because all points in $\bar{H}(\alpha, p)$ satisfy $p^\top x = \alpha$, p is a probability

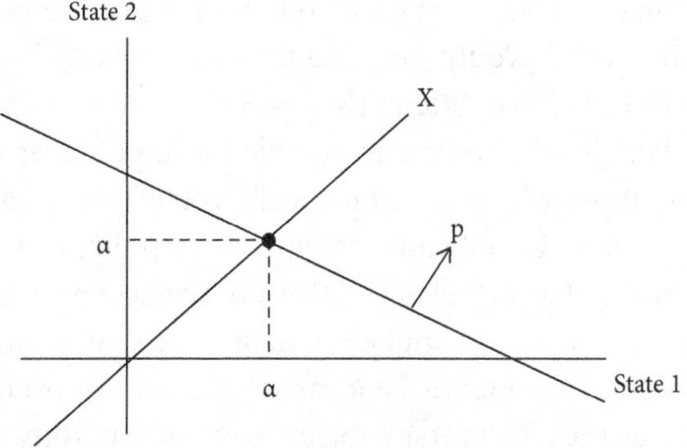

Fig. 8.3 Equal-mean Sets as a Hyperplane

measure, and (α, α) *is a degenerate random variable.* $\bar{H}(\alpha, p)$ *is the set of random variables sharing the common mean* α.

Risk aversion, according to one definition,[8] *is a preference for receiving the mean of a random variable with certainty to receiving the random variable itself. So, in these terms, risk aversion requires that* (α, α) *be at least weakly preferred to all the other elements of* $\bar{H}(\alpha, p)$. *A bounding case occurs when* (α, α) *is just weakly preferred to all elements of* $\bar{H}(\alpha, p)$. *Then the individual's* $\bar{V}(\alpha, \alpha)$ *is* $\bar{H}(\alpha, p)$. *That is often referred to as risk neutrality. A little bit of geometric experimentation will convince you that, when preferences are complete, CONA ensures risk aversion for arbitrary probability measures. Risk preference is often defined analogously as a preference for receiving a random variable to receiving the mean of the random variable with certainty. The bounding case is also risk neutrality. And some geometric experimentation will convince you that, when preferences are complete, CONB suffices to ensure risk preference for arbitrary probability measures.*

Some comments. First, discussions of risk only apply to economic problems where an objective probability measure exists. Many such situations exist, but they also form a small subset of the economic problems faced under uncertainty. Many simply do not permit a frequentist approach to be applied because they are one-off decisions made in highly specific, and likely nonreplicable, settings. Second, all risk-aversion definitions are specific to a particular objective probability measure. Yaari (1969) emphasized this reliance by showing that risk aversion is best understood relatively as being more risk averse than the linear preference structure characterized by a particular p.

CONA is frequently taken as a primitive assumption in studying uncertain decision making. This is despite the fact that we routinely observe individuals engaging in games of chance, such as the coin-flip game or lotteries, that consistency with *CONA* would not countenance. It's long been understood that people seem to behave differently when the stakes are large and when they are small. People will hesitate to gamble for large stakes when they will happily play coin flips or lotteries. Thus, while you might be mildly surprised by someone refusing to gamble on a *penny ante* coin flip, you might expect it for a *million ante* flip. Nevertheless, *CONA* doesn't accommodate both types of behavior, so that it seems unlikely that it applies globally. Our general theory works perfectly well, but be aware that many common models that use *CONA*, such as the risk-averse subjective expected utility model, do not.

[8] There are actually many, but covering them goes well beyond the scope of this book.

Remark 21. *Recall that CONA is also maintained in most discussions of consumer preference in nonstochastic settings. Consumer theory only works both ways if CONA is assumed. While price-taking suffices to generate well-behaved expenditure functions, indirect utility functions, compensated demands, and uncompensated demands, reversing the argument, requires CONA. If CONA doesn't apply, the "convexified version" of the individual's* $\succeq(y)$ *is obtained, and its usefulness is predicated upon the fact that it exhaustively characterizes the behavior of price-taking individuals. In the typical nonstochastic decision setting, price-taking behavior reflects an assumption about the market structure being studied. In many stochastic decision settings, existing market structures do not specify given probability measures at which you can reasonably make fair trades. Hence, we cannot rely on that avenue for justifying the use of CONA.*

Unlike standard consumer theory, in many instances neither *CONA* nor *CONB* suffices to predict behavior confidently. Two particularly prominent stumbling blocks inhibit analytic developments in a stochastic setting. One is the frequent lack of a linear pricing structure.[9] Another is the difficulty of predicting behavior as the individual moves across (rather than along) level sets for $\succeq(y)$. We've seen the latter before. Compensated demand curves have predictable slopes, whereas uncompensated demands do not. Income effects are always messy, and they are even messier when the underlying pricing structure is not linear.

The economist's natural reaction to unpredictability is further abstraction. Roughly put, the logic is that if we can't understand what happens in general, perhaps we can in an appropriately controlled situation. And once that is done, comparing observed behavior with controlled behavior may offer some clues about more general principles. That process of abstraction frequently uses the same strategies used to develop empirically implementable functional forms. Either place restrictive assumptions on the market setting (for example, perfect competition), individual preferences, or the prevailing technology. As a result, two particular restrictive preference classes have received special attention in the literature on stochastic decision making.

These preference classes are commonly referred to as *constant absolute risk-averse* and *constant relative risk-averse* preferences. I won't use this terminology. It leaves the impression that the concepts require a risk setting and that *CONA* is required. Neither is true. In their place, I will use *constant absolute uncertainty averse (CAUA)* and *constant relative uncertainty averse*

[9] I would note, however, that later developments will show that this concern may be overstated.

(*CRUA*), while explicitly noting that neither *CONA* nor *CONB* is required for the definitions to work.[10]

Both restrict how preference attitudes toward uncertain choices change as real-income changes. There are two standard ways to view real-income or real-wealth changes for stochastic outcomes. One is as a purely nonstochastic addition to consumption. The other is as radially changing consumption. Thus, $\succeq(y)$ exhibits *constant absolute uncertainty aversion* if

$$x \succeq (y) \Leftrightarrow x + \begin{pmatrix} 0 \\ \beta \end{pmatrix} \succeq \left(y + \begin{pmatrix} 0 \\ \beta \end{pmatrix}\right) \text{ for } \begin{pmatrix} (0,0,\ldots,0)^{\top} \\ \beta \end{pmatrix} \in \begin{pmatrix} \mathbb{R}^M \\ \mathcal{X} \end{pmatrix}$$

and *constant relative uncertainty aversion* if

$$x \succeq (y) \Leftrightarrow \begin{pmatrix} x^0 \\ \mu x^1 \end{pmatrix} \succeq \left(\begin{pmatrix} y^0 \\ \mu y^1 \end{pmatrix}\right) \text{ for } \mu > 0.$$

Preferences that exhibit *CAUA* and *CRUA* simultaneously are *constant uncertainty averse* (*CUA*).

CAUA requires that mixing x and y with degenerate random variables does not change their relative preference ranking. *CAUA* coincides with *translation homotheticity* in the direction of $\tilde{g} = \begin{pmatrix} 0 \\ 1 \end{pmatrix}$. *CRUA* requires that radially changing two period 1 gambles does not change relative preference rankings. *CRUA* is the notion of *homotheticity* of $\succeq(y)$ developed in Chapter 5. That terminology, however, reflects production and consumer economics jargon, and it is useful to say the same thing in a different way. *CAUA* requires the ranking of x and y to be independent of each being mixed with the same safe asset. So, preference rankings are *independent with respect to mixing with safe assets.* Gilboa and Schmeidler (1989) refer to this as *certainty independence. CRUA* requires that the ranking of x and y be independent of scaling either up or down by the same proportion. Rescaling x downard in this manner is equivalent to mixing x with 0, and rescaling outward is equivalent to mixing it with arbitrarily large positive multiples of itself. As a consequence, it is common to see this restriction also referred to as *radial independence* (see the discussion of the independence axiom in Chapter 5). Thus, preferences that satisfy *CUA* exhibit both certainty independence and radial independence.

[10] Presumably, therefore, I might call them something like *constant absolute uncertainty preference* and *constant relative uncertainty preference.* But doing so threatens to erase entirely the already tenuous link between my terminology and what's most common in the literature.

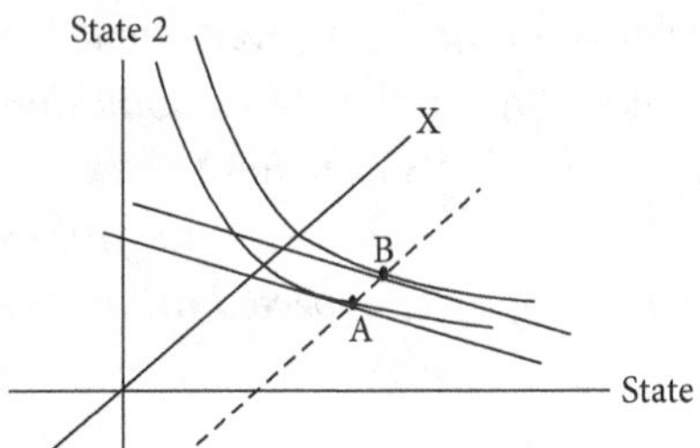

(b) Constant Relative Uncertainty Aversion

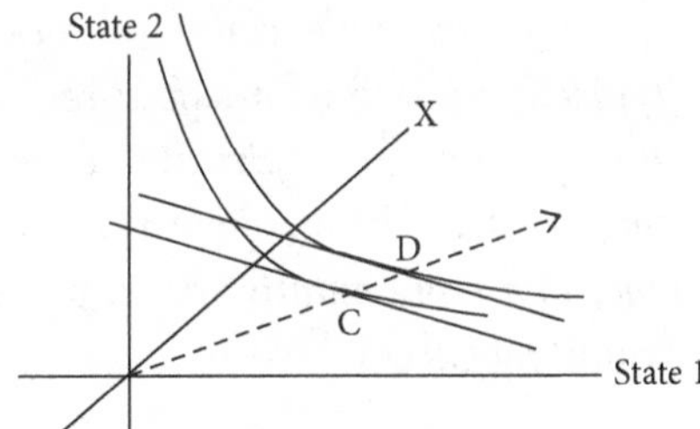

Fig. 8.4

I leave it to you to develop the structural consequences *CAUA* and *CRUA* for *d* and *t*. Visually, *CAUA* implies that as you proceed parallel to $\mathcal{X}$ from *A* to *B* in Figure 8.4a (and beyond), you encounter level sets of *d* and *t* with equal slopes. *CRUA* requires encountering points of equal slope as one proceeds along rays from the origin as illustrated in Figure 8.4b by points C and D. In Figure 8.4a *CUA* requires that as one proceeds along the ray connecting *A* and the origin, one always encounters level sets having the same slope as points *A* and *B*. Conversely, if one translates *C* in the direction of $\mathcal{X}$ in Figure 8.4b, one must always encounter level sets having the same slope as at *C* and *D*.

Problem 88. *Derive the consequences of CAUA, CRUA, and CUA for* $t(y, x; \tilde{g})$. *Explain the results intuitively.*

The various panels of Figure 8.4 should convince you that *CUA* represents an extreme abstraction. You might wonder, for example, if *CUA* would seem plausible if encountered in the context of standard consumer theory. Or even more personally, do you behave in this manner? Likely, many would say no.

Mind you, that's not necessarily a bad thing. It only means that real-life behavior may not accord with the behavior of someone with quite stylized responses to real-wealth changes. As an economist, you should be used to that, even if you're not particularly comfortable with it. Just remember that the purpose of such stylized models is not always to describe true behavior. Instead, it provides a benchmark against which real behavior can be compared.

Remark 22. *Some observations from the finance and macroeconomics literature help illustrate. At the end of the twentieth century, and even today, one of the most important empirical puzzles was the "equity-premium puzzle"* *identified by Mehra and Prescott (1985). Briefly, the puzzle is that returns on equity (for example, common stocks) relative to those on government bonds (typically viewed as a safe asset) are much higher than a combination of "theory" and our empirical knowledge of individual's aversion to risk would suggest. That "theory," however, was predicated on models assuming the existence of a representative agent possessing an objective expected utility model exhibiting CRUA.*

The stochastic world often turns out to be so difficult to analyze that much of the theoretical and empirical research undertaken on decision making under uncertainty imposes more structure than *CUA*. Specifically, much of it relies on a version of the the *independence restriction* that we introduced in Chapter 5. In the current setting, independence requires that $\succeq(y)$ satisfy

$$x \succeq (y) \Leftrightarrow \alpha x + (1-\alpha) r \succeq (\alpha y + (1-\alpha) r) \text{ for all } \alpha \in (0,1] \text{ and all } r \in \mathbb{R}^{M+(M\times S)}. \tag{8.2}$$

The structural consequences of imposing (8.2) are summarized by Lemma 15, Theorem 12, and Corollary 5. A little algebra should convince you that those results imply that these preferences exhibit *CONA*, *CONB*, and *CUA* and are invariant to translations in arbitrary directions $r \in \mathbb{R}^{M+(M\times S)}$. That's a lot to swallow. So some healthy skepticism is merited. But don't forget that for us assumption (8.2) depicts a benchmark case and should be interpreted in that light.[11]

Instead of revisiting the math that we slogged through in Chapter 5, let's take a closer look at the underlying idea. Let me present you with some hypothetical choice situations. I ask that you respond to them honestly *but without* reading ahead. The setting is $S = 2$ and $M = 1$, so there are two states of Nature and the consequence space is $\mathbb{R}$. Refer to the consequences as dollars. You are first asked to choose between A and B in the following table, where columns denote the gambles and rows the payouts for the respective states in period 1, and we assume that A and B have the same payout for period 0:

[11] Specialists from other areas may object strenuously to this interpretation. Depending on one's epistemic viewpoint, such disagreement is to be expected. For example, if one believes axioms should adhere closely to observed behavior, one might conclude that independence is irrelevant. On the other hand, if axioms are regarded as something that is required for, say, "rational behavior," independence might pass with flying colors. For example, Savage, when confronted with evidence that he had fallen prey to the Allais Paradox and thus violated independence, admitted that he had behaved irrationally but insisted that independence was an appropriate criterion for rational choice.

Choice 1	A	B
State 1	1	3 .
State 2	3	1

Now that you've made that choice, I want you to make another one that is conditional on that choice. If you chose *B*, you are asked to choose between

If B	C	D
State 1	4	6 ,
State 2	4	2

and if you chose *A* you are asked to choose between

If A	E	F
State 1	2	4 .
State 2	6	4

If you chose *A* and then *E*, or if you chose *B* and then *D*, your choices are consistent with independence. But if you chose *A* and then *C* or *B* and then *F*, they are not. Figure 8.5 illustrates why. When you depict *A*, *B*, *C*, and *D*, it's clear that *A* and *B* are simple permutations of one another. As such, they are *perfect hedges for one another* in the sense that when you add them together, you get the degenerate random variable $(4, 4) \in \mathcal{X}$. On the other hand, having two units of *B* gives a stochastic payout of $(6, 2)$. Thus, if you initially chose *B*, your actual second round choice was between

$$C = B + A \quad \text{and}$$
$$D = B + B.$$

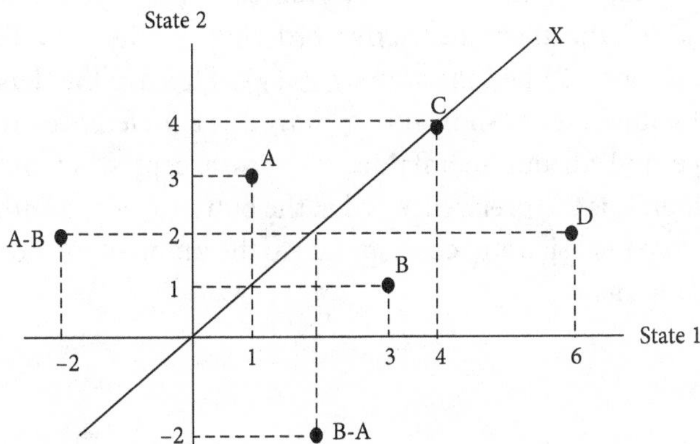

Fig. 8.5 Independence?

If independence were true and you originally chose B, you should choose $B + B$ because your choices between A and B should exactly match your choice between $B+A$ and $B+B$ and vice versa. The fly-in-the-ointment is that individuals placed in such a setting often choose B and then C. One potential reason is that A and B hedge one another.

Try thinking of it this way. When asked to choose between two stochastic choices, such as A and B, when little information is provided about the states, some individuals are observed to base their choice on relatively arbitrary grounds. Examples of such behavior abound from the well-known "flip-a-coin" choice rule to the continuing controversy as to whether *abacab* or *bacaba* is the better strategy for answering a multiple-guess exam that you have not studied for.[12] Choosing between C and D instead of A and B, however, is slightly different because it offers a choice between a degenerate, but safe, random variable, C, and a nondegenerate random variable, D. Degenerate or not, some people prefer safety to the nondegenerate but also unsafe choice.

Either direct arguments or Theorem 12 will establish that independence requires both $V(0)$ and $Y(0)$ to be closed, convex cones (recall Figure 5.2).[13] Independence also requires that $B \succeq (A)$ if and only if $B-A \succeq (0)$ and that $B-A \succeq (0)$ if and only if $0 \succeq (A-B)$. Thus, $B-A \in V(0)$ if and only if $A-B \in Y(0)$. Because this is true for arbitrary pairs, $Y(0)$ must be the mirror image of $V(0)$. Figure 8.6 illustrates. The gray-shaded "butterfly" depicts the gambles that cannot be compared to 0 because of preference incompleteness. $V(0)$ is everything lying to the northeast of the butterfly, and $Y(0)$ is everything to its southwest.

As Figure 8.6 illustrates, $\mathbb{R}_{+}^{M+(S\times M)} \subset V(0)$ and $\mathbb{R}_{-}^{M+(S\times M)} \subset Y(0)$. Because we maintain monotonicity, this is expected. But another perspective is obtained by noting that imposing monotonicity on $\succeq (y)$ requires that all choices made for the more restrictive ordering $\geq$ (the very first one we discussed in Chapter 2) be inherited by $\succeq (y)$. I'll leave the demonstration to you, but it's quite easy to show that $\geq$ judged as a preference order satisfies independence and all our maintained axioms except strict monotonicity. Moreover, when $\geq$ is the preference order, the butterfly-shaped area in Figure 8.6 attains is maximal size and corresponds to the union of the northwest and southeast quadrants.

[12] I first encountered this controversy roughly three decades ago upon overhearing a conversation between one of my sons and his friends.

[13] Also recall that a set $K \subset \mathbb{R}^N$ is a *cone* if $x \in K \Rightarrow \lambda x \in K$ for $\lambda > 0$.

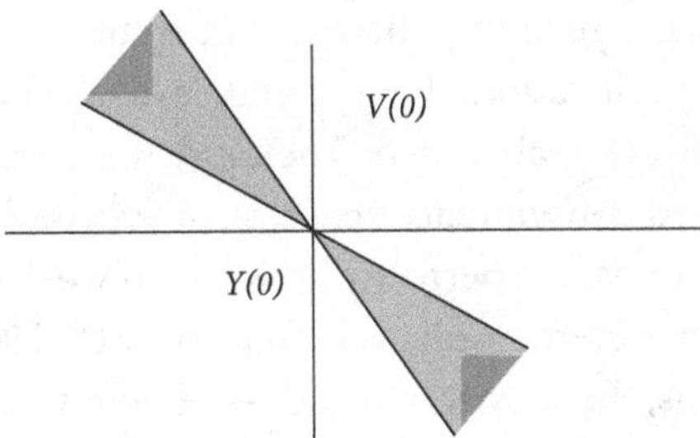

Fig. 8.6 $V(0)$ and $Y(0)$ under Independence

Intuitively, these observations suggest that $\geq$ is the order belonging to the subset of orders satisfying our basic axioms and independence that exhibits *maximal incompleteness.* Similarly, the natural conjecture is that the class of independent preference structures exhibiting *minimal incompleteness* would be those for which the wings of the butterfly narrowed to a single line so that both shaded areas disappeared. If minimal incompleteness is interpreted as requiring that $\succeq (y)$ completely order $\mathbb{R}^{M+(S\times M)}$, the conjecture follows trivially from Theorem 18.

Problem 89. *Theorem 18 was derived using Theorem 3. Other demonstrations are possible. In particular, one alternative is to use results developed in Chapter 5 for complete ordering (CO) and independence. Use Theorem 10, Corollary 5, and Problem 50 to prove Theorem 18.*

Given all the structure imposed on $\succeq (y)$ and the geometric depiction in Figure 8.6, the emergence of a linear preference structure under complete ordering should not be too surprising. Still, it might strike some as unsettling. That's because when $M = 1$, Theorem 18 implies that

$$\begin{aligned} u(y;g) &= -d(0,y;\tilde{g}) = \min\{\gamma \in \mathbb{R} : \gamma\tilde{g} \in V(y)\} \\ &= q^{\top}y \\ &= q^0y^0 + q^{1\top}y^1, \end{aligned}$$

which is an affine transformation of a *(Subjective) Expected Value (SEV)* function and not a *(Subjective) Expected Utility (SEU)* function, which many economists treat as their go-to model for analyzing uncertain decisions. For those schooled in the SEU paradigm, an SEV function reflects what is commonly viewed as *risk-neutral behavior for the subjectively derived probability measure,* q^1. But standard *SEU,* which relies on a form of independence, does not require risk neutrality. Is there a contradiction?

The answer is no. The seeming difference in results emerges from a divergence between our specification of $\succeq(y)$ and Savage's (1954). Recall that our consequences are always real-valued. Therefore, acts were defined as maps from S to a real-valued consequence space, $\mathbb{R}$ or $\mathbb{R}^M$. Savage (1954) didn't do that. His consequence space is perfectly arbitrary. If we denote it by $\mathfrak{C}$, his acts map $S \to \mathfrak{C}$, and his preference order is defined over $\mathfrak{C}^S$. He then demonstrates that, under his axioms, there exists a $u : \mathfrak{C} \to \mathbb{R}$, and then he derives an SEU representation in terms of that u. So our approach, as I pointed out earlier, represents a short cut to Savage's (1954) "constructing the numbers with his bare hands" (Gilboa, 2009, p. 95).

I don't want to apologize for taking that shortcut for several reasons. First, things are complicated enough without it. Second, even decision theorists routinely resort to similar shortcuts in their analysis. For example, the deservedly famous Anscombe–Aumann (1963) "simplified" derivation of the SEU model uses a similar shortcut. Where we work with $\mathbb{R}^M$ as the consequence space, they work with an arbitrary mixture space that defines lotteries over outcomes.[14] The similarity between the Anscombe–Aumann (1963) structure is further clarified by using the notation defined in Problem 84 to write the M-dimensional analogue of $u(y;\tilde{g})$ as

$$
\begin{aligned}
u(y;\tilde{g}) &= \sum_m q_m^0 y_m^0 + \sum_s \left(\sum_{m'} q_{sm'}^1\right) \sum_m \frac{q_{sm}^1}{\left(\sum_{m'} q_{sm'}^1\right)} y_{sm}^1 \\
&= u_0\left(y^0\right) + \sum_s \pi_s u_s\left(y_{s\cdot}\right),
\end{aligned}
$$

where $\pi_s = \left(\sum_{m'} q_{sm'}^1\right) \in \mathbb{R}_+$, $u_0\left(y^0\right) = \sum_m q_m^0 y_m^0$, $u_s\left(y_{s\cdot}\right) = \sum_m \frac{q_{sm}^1}{\left(\sum_{m'} q_{sm'}^1\right)} y_{sm}^1$, and $\sum_s \pi_s = 1$. Third, in any case, all that's been claimed is that the outcomes are counted in real units. As an example, in many applied settings using the expected utility framework, it's common to specify an *ex post* utility function that maps income (measured in real units) into utility or utils (also measured in real units). Doing that in our setting is equivalent mathematically to making change of variables from y to u as follows,

$$
u = u(y)
$$

with $u : \mathbb{R} \to \mathbb{R}$ to obtain the *SEU* model.

[14] An arbitrary space K is a mixture space if it has a convex structure. $\mathbb{R}$ and $\mathbb{R}^N$ for arbitrary N are special cases of mixture spaces.

Savage's (1954) derivation of the *SEU* model represents an important landmark in our understanding of uncertain decision making whose importance cannot be overemphasized. Nevertheless, it's not needed to develop the most basic results for producer or consumer decision making under uncertainty—this despite its importance in developing a rational model for choice and in providing a basis for a probabilistic approach that does not depend on the often-criticized frequentist notion.

Exercise 56. *Consider the coin-flip game with $M = 1$ and $S = \{Heads, Tails\}$. Suppose that in period 0 you decide to devote 1 of period 0 consumption to earning money for period 1. Also suppose that your preferences satisfy Theorem 18 with $q_H^1 = \frac{3}{4}$. What would be your choice? Illustrate your answer geometrically, and explain it intuitively.*

3 Production

Interpreting $\succeq (y)$ as a stochastic production technology requires some notational changes. We continue to work in a two-period setting with 0 not subject to uncertainty and 1 uncertain. The technology, as described by the binary relation $x \succeq (y)$, works as follows. In period 0, the producer chooses input bundle $x \in \mathbb{R}^N$ and stochastic output bundle $y \in \mathbb{R}^{S\times M}$. *After* the producer makes this choice, Nature makes her choice from S, and that choice resolves all the uncertainty about period 1. If the producer chooses $(x, y) \in \mathbb{R}^N \times \mathbb{R}^{S\times M}$ in period 0 and Nature chooses $s \in S$, the realized period-1 output vector is $y_{s\cdot} = (y_{s1}, y_{s2}, ..., y_{sM})^{\top}$.

Apart from the time dimension and uncertainty, this version of $\succeq (y)$ as a technology operates similarly to its nonstochastic analogue. (In fact, the nonstochastic analogue studied in Chapter 6 is the special case where $S = \{1\}$, so that Nature faces a degenerate choice.) It is a datum that defines what is technically possible, that producers know but cannot affect, and for which all possible outcomes are known. Again we are talking known unknowns and not unknown unknowns. For intuitive purposes, we maintain a split between inputs and outputs. The former are nonstochastic and chosen in period 0, and the latter are stochastic and while chosen in 0 are only realized in period 1. This is easily extended to more general cases. So, for example, by altering notation and monotonicity (disposability) assumptions, the same framework can accommodate nonstochastic outputs chosen and realized in period 0, stochastic inputs chosen in period 0 but realized in period 1, and netputs of either variety.

We maintain the same notation as in Chapter 6 while changing its domain to accommodate y's stochastic nature. Thus, the *input correspondence* $V : \mathbb{R}^{S\times M} \rightrightarrows \mathbb{R}^{N}$ is defined by

$$\begin{aligned} V(y) &= \{x \in \mathbb{R}^N : x \geq (y)\} \\ &= \{x \in \mathbb{R}^N : x \text{ can produce } y \in \mathbb{R}^{S\times M}\}, \end{aligned}$$

the *(stochastic) output correspondence*, $Y : \mathbb{R}^N \rightrightarrows \mathbb{R}^{S\times M}$, is defined by

$$\begin{aligned} Y(x) &= \{y \in \mathbb{R}^{S\times M} : x \geq (y)\} \\ &= \{y \in \mathbb{R}^{S\times M} : x \in \mathbb{R}^N \text{ can produce } y\}, \end{aligned}$$

and the *graph of the technology*, $T \subset \mathbb{R}^{N+(S\times M)}$, is

$$\begin{aligned} T &= \{(x, y) : x \geq (y)\} \\ &= \{(x, y) : x \text{ can produce } y\}. \end{aligned}$$

The true difference between the stochastic and nonstochastic production models lies not in their mathematical formalisms but in their interpretations. For the most part, those differences revolve around $Y(x)$ and not $V(y)$. In fact, with few exceptions, everything said in Chapter 6 about $V(y)$ and $c(w, y)$ applies to the current case with little or no change.[15] Any recycling of that discussion that is necessary is left to the interested reader.

Figure 8.7 depicts $Y(x)$ when $M = 1$. The horizontal and vertical axes measure the same output but in different states of Nature. $Y(x)$, which corresponds to everything on or below the curve, is drawn to satisfy monotonicity from below (*MB*), or in the jargon of production economics, free disposability of output. Notice that $Y(x)$ has a nonempty intersection with $\mathcal{X}$. Thus, for this $x \in \mathbb{R}^N$, choosing to produce nonstochastically is feasible. Exposing oneself to production uncertainty is a choice and not a necessity. This may or may not be realistic. Much depends on the actual production process. Realistic or not, it is a consequence of imposing *MB* because that requires for any $0 \leq y \in Y(x)$ that $\mathcal{X} \ni 0 \in Y(x)$. So *MB* may be problematic in modeling stochastic technologies. But don't forget that Proposition 4 shows that *MB* is

[15] It was not always realized that this was true. In particular, until the mid-1990s, certain areas of applied economics maintained that standard production analysis had little to no applicability under uncertainty. Agricultural economics was a particular hotbed, and it made for some pretty silly claims. But reason eventually prevailed, and the insights of Arrow and Debreu were recognized to apply there as well.

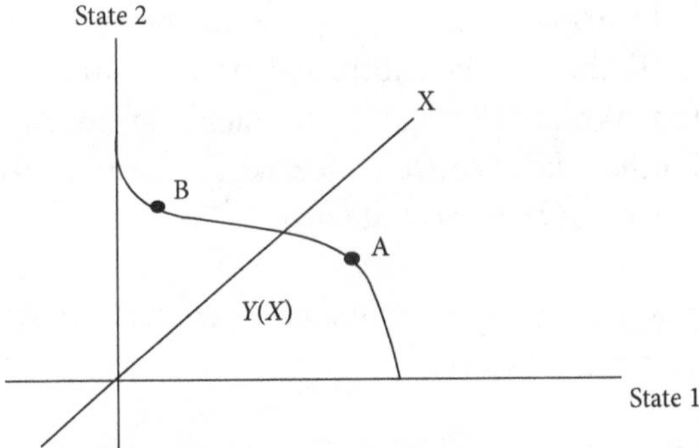

Fig. 8.7 A Stochastic Output Set

what's required for $c(w, y)$ to exhibit positive marginal costs, which is clearly both desirable and intuitive. Thus, an analytic tension exists. At the margin, having $c(w, y)$ exhibit positive marginal cost seems plausible, if not probable. But placing sufficient global structure on $Y(x)$ to ensure that outcome holds globally also ensures that foregoing uncertain production is possible.

Figure 8.7 also depicts a situation where neither 1 nor 2 is necessarily the "good" state. If one chooses to produce above $\mathcal{X}$ in $Y(x)$, state 2 is the one with the largest output and state 1 the one with the smallest. The reverse happens if one chooses to produce below $\mathcal{X}$ in $Y(x)$. Depending on the technology, this may or may not be plausible. But it illustrates that what distinguishes between good and bad economically often depends on how one prepares. Suppose, for example, that a farmer lives next to a waterway from which she can draw irrigation water. Also suppose that she devotes all available labor at planting time to maintaining irrigation ditches but none to maintaining flood-control levees. If excessive rain occurs, flooding can destroy the crop. In hindsight, maintaining the irrigation ditches wasted labor. But if flooding doesn't occur, all is well. Now reverse the effort allocation decision. That also reverses the good and bad states. Unless there's flooding, the effort was wasted. So, it depends.

3.1 The Cardinal Measure

Our cardinal representation of $\succeq(y)$, interpreted as a stochastic technology, is

$$t(y, x; 1) = \min\{\beta \in \mathbb{R} : y - \beta \in Y(x), \beta \in \mathcal{X}\},$$

where $1 \in \mathcal{X}$.[16] In words, $t(y, x; 1)$ represents the smallest amount of the safe output, $1 \in \mathcal{X}$, that can be subtracted from y while leaving $y - \beta$ still producible using x. While *MB* might be problematic globally for the reasons just alluded to, for the sake of convenience, we choose to maintain it. We then recycle Lemma 10 to the current context as

Corollary 8. *Suppose that $\succeq(y)$ (as a binary order on $\mathbb{R}^N \times \mathbb{R}^{S\times M}$) satisfies CB and MB, then for $y \in \bar{Y}(x)$*

$$p \in \partial^- t(y, x; g) \Leftrightarrow p^\top (y - \hat{y}) \geq 0 \text{ for all } \hat{y} \in Y(x),$$

with $p \in \mathbb{R}_+^{S\times M}$ and $p^\top 1 = 1$.

Figure 8.7 illustrates Corollary 8. There the curve through A and B represents $\bar{Y}(x)$ ($\{y : t(y, x; 1) = 0\}$). It's smooth everywhere on $\mathbb{R}_{++}^{S\times M}$ signaling that $t(y, x; 1)$ is differentiable at all points in $\bar{Y}(x)$. However, $t(y, x; 1)$ is subdifferentiable at A but not at B, because $Y(x)$ is supported (from above) by a half-space at A but not at B. Different metaphors can be used to explain the normal to the supporting halfspace at A. It represents shadow prices for period 1 stochastic production that would make y the revenue maximizer for $Y(x)$. These shadow prices, when expressed in real terms by dividing one element of p by another, also define marginal rates of stochastic transformation that measure the rate at which one stochastic output can be transferred into another. Or, finally, when $M = 1$ so that $\mathcal{X} \subset \mathbb{R}^S$, p has the same characteristics as a *probability measure that ensures y has the highest expected value among all the elements of $Y(x)$*.

Let's pursue the latter. Because any such p is derived from $\succeq(y)$, which we now view as a stochastic technology reflecting the laws of Nature, it has *objective content.* That objective content, however, may not provide information about the relative likelihood of different states occurring. In this, p is not inherently different from the subjective probability measures derived from $d(x, y; \tilde{g})$ for the preference structure. But where the latter measures provide information about the rate at which individuals would exchange consumption across states of Nature, those from $t(y, x; 1)$ convey information about the physical possibilities of transforming income in one state of Nature into another. This can be visualized using Figure 8.7. As drawn, $\bar{Y}(x)$ contains a continuum of points where it is subdifferentiable. Each has its own unique p

[16] As I said, the focus is on $Y(x)$, and for that reason I will only discuss $t(y, x; 1)$. However, $d(x, y; g)$ works equally well. But I will leave it to the interested to work through those derivations, which simply repeat with minor variations those derived earlier.

associated with it. Once a point in that continuum is chosen, there are only two possible production outcomes. We could count the relative frequencies of those two outcomes to get a frequentist probability. But that relative frequency doesn't reflect the normal to the supporting half space at A. Instead, the normal reflects the physical process of transferring income or output across states of Nature. The relative frequency, on the other hand, reflects Nature's choices, which being drawn for a neutral player cannot depend on the point chosen. There's no apparent reason that they should coincide. So, while the subdifferentials generated by $t(y, x; 1)$ look like probabilities and act like probabilities, after a fashion, they do not have a frequentist interpretation.

3.2 Structure

What was said about the structure of nonstochastic technologies applies with equal force to stochastic technologies. Obtaining results will often depend critically on imposing structure. Practical data limitations ensure that this becomes particularly important in applied analyses. So much so that the default representation of a stochastic technology in both the empirical and theoretical literatures traditionally imposed a structure that in any other economic context would have been recognized as extreme. That structure, usually identified with a *stochastic production function,* is a special case of the *output-price nonjoint (OPNJ) technology* identified in Chapter 6. In the current context, it is written as

$$Y(x) = \prod_{s} Y^s(x),$$

with each $Y^s : \mathbb{R}^N \rightrightarrows \mathbb{R}^M$, $s \in S$. For $M = 1$, under *MB*

$$Y^s(x) = \{y_s \in \mathbb{R} : y_s \leq f_s(x)\},$$

where each $f_s : \mathbb{R}^N \to \mathbb{R}$ has the natural interpretation of a production function specific to state s (*state-contingent production function*). Because Nature's choice of s is not known when x is chosen, maximal potential output for each state is the random variable $(f_1(x), \ldots, f_S(x))^{\top} \in \mathbb{R}^S$. Hence,

$$\begin{aligned} t(y, x; 1) &= \min\{\beta : y_s - \beta \leq f_s(x) \text{ for all } s \in S\} \\ &= \max_{s \in S}\{y_s - f_s(x)\}. \end{aligned}$$

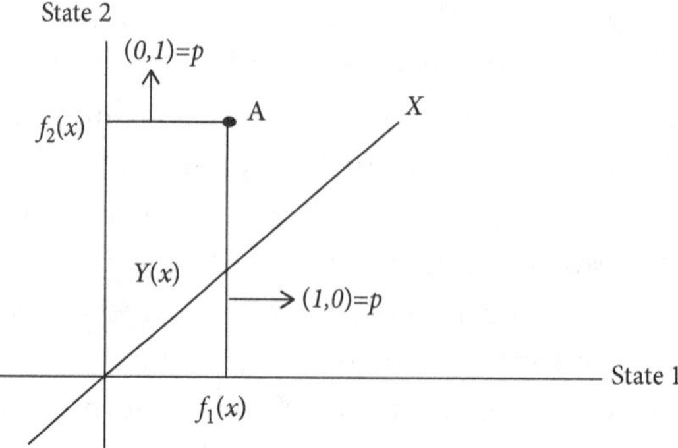

Fig. 8.8 Stochastic Production Function

Figure 8.8 illustrates $Y(x)$ for the OPNJ technology. Outputs in different states are perfect complements for one another. Consequently, this representation of $Y(x)$ rules out the possibility of redirecting fixed-input allocations to different tasks that would permit efficient transformation of output across different states of Nature. The only way to change the mix of outputs realized across different states of Nature is to choose a different input bundle. At points such as A, $\partial^{-}t\left(y, x; 1\right) = \Delta$, the S-dimensional probability simplex, and elsewhere $\partial^{-}t\left(y, x; 1\right)$ is the $s_{\max}$-element of the usual orthonormal basis where

$$s_{\max} = \arg\max_{s \in S} \{y_s - f_s(x)\},$$

which, of course, manifests the kink occurring at A. In the nonstochastic case, OPNJ approximates a technology in which the fixed-input bundle is cracked in fixed components into distinct components. That metaphor in a stochastic setting would require that you get varying portions of the fixed bundle in each of the different states. One way to visualize this simply would be to think of the fixed-input bundle as a pie that has been cut into different-sized slices, with each slice corresponding to a state. Nature then chooses which slice you receive.

Despite its odd structure, this technology represents a default specification for stochastic technologies. One important reason stems from the fact that observed economic data do not represent random variables. Instead, they represent observations on *realized* values of random variables. Notationally, $y \in \mathbb{R}^S$ represents a random variable, and y_s represents the realization if Nature picks $s \in S$. Data on random variables correspond to the latter and not the former. Associating y_s with the y from which it is drawn is a *classical statistical identification problem.*[17]

Viewed from that perspective, the OPNJ framework is a natural consequence of two distinct analytic traditions. The first is the single-product production function familiar from intermediate micro theory. The second is Haavelmo's (1943) classic identification of the "econometric error" with the equation as a whole and not any single variable in the set of dependent and independent variables. The most common version of the OPNJ model melds these ideas into the generic form

$$y_s = f_s(x) \equiv g(x, \varepsilon_s), \qquad s \in S$$

where $\varepsilon \equiv (\varepsilon_1, \varepsilon_2, ..., \varepsilon_s)^{\mathsf{T}} \in \mathbb{R}^S$ is an exogenously determined random variable and $g : \mathbb{R}^{N+1} \to \mathbb{R}$. The assumption is that, prior to choosing x, the producer knows g and ε but not its specific realization. Hence, choosing x immediately results in the unique choice of rational y as $\left(g(x, \varepsilon_1), ..., g(x, \varepsilon_S)\right)^{\mathsf{T}}$. How ε is determined is rarely broached and even less rarely explained. Typically, ε is chosen to satisfy analytically convenient *statistical properties* rather than with regard to the actual decision setting. In econometric terms, ε provides the "sample space" for the stochastic factors affecting production.[18]

The cost of econometric tractability, however, may be economic plausibility. Chambers and Quiggin (2000) provide a detailed critique of the economic implications of the stochastic production function model, which they refer to as *output-cubical,* and an axiomatic derivation of it in a decision-theoretic setting. Not the least of their critiques is the lack of analytic tractability that the "kinky" nature of this specification imposes on function representations such as $t\left(y, x; 1\right)$.

But there are also other conceptual problems. To give a flavor of some of these, yet another agricultural example is useful. Let y correspond to a stochastic crop output, x to the vector of inputs controlled by the producer, and ε to a composite of inputs beyond the producer's control such as natural moisture (m), radiation (r), and pest infestation (b) that may take S distinct realizations. More formally, set

$$\varepsilon_s = \varphi(m_s, r_s, b_s), \quad s \in S$$

[17] Italics are used here to discriminate this notion from the more specialized identification notions commonly used in econometric discussions.

[18] Most applications treat the case where S is infinite dimensional and thus take ε to be an interval of the real line. In this setting, the corresponding random variable y will also be an interval of the real line over which the probability distribution function is defined.

so that

$$y_s = g(x, \varphi(m_s, r_s, b_s)), \qquad s \in S.$$

This specification requires the state-specific inputs, (m_s, r_s, b_s), to be weakly separable from x. So, for example, if x contains pesticides, the marginal rate of substitution between pest infestation and moisture must be independent of the amount of pesticides applied. Similarly, if x contains chemical fertilizer, the marginal rate of substitution between natural moisture and radiation must be independent of fertilizer. Both are restrictive, if not implausible. But as we've seen before, incorporating observed data into our models makes for some nasty choices, and compromises are to be expected. One important reason that the OPNJ has proven so popular is that it works in applied circumstances. Its analytic advantages, however, are far less apparent.

4 Chapter Commentary

This chapter recycles concepts from decision theory and producer theory into our mathematical framework. The contributions of Arrow (1953), Savage (1954), Debreu (1959), and Shephard (1970) provide the intellectual foundation on which the edifice is built, whereas the contributions of Blackorby and Donaldson (1980) and Luenberger (1992, 1995), when coupled with conjugacy theory, provide the analytic apparatus. It's dangerous to parse the relative contributions of one's predecessors, and so I won't try. But the take-away message is that analyzing uncertain decisions involves virtually identical principles as analyzing certain decisions. This is clearly stated in both Arrow (1953) and Debreu (1959), and it is routinely reiterated in advanced microeconomics texts (see, for example, Jehle and Reny 2011). Still, I have learned and borrowed much from Fishburn (1972), Kreps (1990), and Gilboa (2009) on preferences. And I owe much of my production material to my joint work with John Quiggin (for example, Chambers and Quiggin, 2000) over the last several decades.

9
Decision Making and Equilibrium under Uncertainty

This chapter analyzes decision making under uncertainty using the preference and production models developed in Chapter 8. I maintain the same basic assumptions as in Chapter 8: strict monotonicity, continuity, and transitivity of preferences and MB (free disposability of output (FDO)) for the technology. As elsewhere, sharp assumptions promote a cleaner analysis, and the interested reader is urged to extend the analysis to a weaker suite of assumptions as a means of flexing one's analytic muscles.

The analytic techniques mirror those discussed in Chapters 4–7. Tools developed there are repurposed to characterize rational uncertain decision making. I intentionally try to minimize the differences between the certainty and uncertainty cases. After all, the former is just a special case of the latter. Granted, it's simpler and thus easier to analyze. But both share the same basic challenges. Individuals need to decide, and those decisions are guided by their preferences and the constraints they face. In both cases, the constraints determine how resources can be marshaled to satisfy those preferences. The nonlinear structures that can arise from the uncertain constraints can raise some difficulties, but these are relatively minor. In the end, the economics of uncertainty is just economics.

Rational behavior is analyzed in a variety of settings. To focus on aspects of the problem peculiar to the uncertain setting, the consequence space in all cases is $\mathbb{R}$. Thus, the preference order is defined over $\mathbb{R}^{1+S} \times \mathbb{R}^{1+S}$, and the technology order is defined over $\mathbb{R}^{N} \times \mathbb{R}^{S}$. To distinguish between consumption and production activities, we use $c = \left(c^0, c^1\right)^{\top} \in \mathbb{R}^{1+S}$ to denote period 0 and period 1 consumption, $x \in \mathbb{R}^N$ to denote period 0 inputs, and $y \in \mathbb{R}^S$ to denote the period 1 stochastic output.

Three decision settings are examined. The first, often cast as the *standard portfolio problem*, parallels Chapter 5's analysis of the consumer problem. But instead of allocating income over commodities, the decision maker now allocates period 0 income over current period consumption and different means of financing period 1 consumption using financial markets.

Competitive Agents in Certain and Uncertain Markets. Robert G. Chambers, Oxford University Press (2021).

DOI: 10.1093/oso/9780190063016.001.0001

The second setting treats an individual generating period 1 consumables via a stochastic technology. This extends Chapter 6's treatment to cover the stochastic case. This analysis transforms the standard consumer and standard portfolio problems posed in terms of linear budget sets into one with nonlinear budget sets. All else essentially remains the same.

The final setting is for an individual having access to both financial markets and a physical, but stochastic, production technology.[1] It makes the rather obvious point that financial markets and stochastic physical technologies are both special cases of a more general "technology," not unlike the T treated in Chapter 7, that transforms period 0 resources into different means of generating period 1 consumables. And, just as obviously, rationality requires eliminating any potential arbitrages between the two.

A very brief discussion of the decision maker's problem in the presence of complete ordering (CO) is then followed by a characterization of Pareto optimal equilibria in a stochastic setting. As Debreu (1959) showed long ago, transiting from the nonstochastic to the stochastic equilibrium setting is simply a matter of reinterpreting variables and notation. So, the discussion is relatively terse, and its primary focus is on the ability of financial markets to support Pareto optimal outcomes.

1 The Portfolio Problem

The standard formulation of the *portfolio problem* examines how individuals allocate their period 0 wealth to satisfy their wants and needs in periods 0 and 1. Wealth is predetermined and is denoted by $m \in \mathbb{R}_+$. Individuals allocate that wealth between period 0 consumption and period 0 investment in assets that generate stochastic period 1 payouts. There are J such assets. Each can be purchased in period 0 at a cost of one dollar and carries a period 1 stochastic return of $A_j \in \mathbb{R}^S, j = 1, 2, \dots, J$. You can think of these assets as including bonds, equities, futures contracts for commodities, insurance instruments, ETFs, and options contracts. The assumption that their period 0 price and their period 1 returns are fixed means that individuals react to them in a competitive or price-taking manner.

Denote by $A \in \mathbb{R}^{S \times J}$ the matrix formed as $[A_1, A_2, \dots, A_J]$ and by A_{sj} the payout in state $s \in S$ on the *jth* asset. A is assumed to be of full column rank. The amount of the *jth* asset purchased in period 0 is denoted by $h_j \in \mathbb{R}$. Total

[1] Magill and Quinzii (1996) refer to this as the sole-proprietor model.

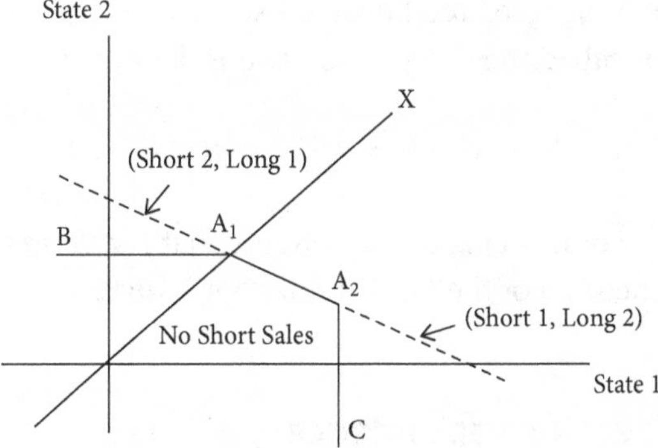

Fig. 9.1 Asset Market

period 0 expenditures on the individual's asset portfolio are thus $1_J^{\top} h$ where 1_J is the J-dimensional vector with $1 \in \mathbb{R}$ in each entry and $h = (h_1, \ldots, h_J)^{\top}$ is the vector of period 0 asset purchases (*the portfolio*). Stochastic period 1 return for those portfolio purchases is $Ah \in \mathbb{R}^S$. Figure 9.1 illustrates the case where there are two assets: $A_1 \in \mathcal{X}$ representing a *safe asset* and A_2 representing an *uncertain asset.*

The notational decision to set the period 0 price of each asset to one dollar implies that each A_j is interpreted in "returns form." It involves no-loss of generality. Suppose that, instead, asset prices were given by $v \in \mathbb{R}^J$ and payouts by $A_j^*, j = 1, \ldots, J$. Then period 0 expenditure on portfolio $h^* \in \mathbb{R}^J$ is

$$\sum_j v_j h_j^*$$

and period 1 payouts are $A^* h^*$. Setting $h_j = v_j h_j^*$ and letting $A_j = A_j^* / v_j$ denote return per dollar invested gives

$$\sum_j v_j h_j^* = \sum_j h_j,$$

and $Ah = A^* h^*$.

Assuming that A has full column rank also involves no loss of generality. If its rank were less than J, some of the columns of A could be expressed as linear combinations of the remaining columns. These collinear columns carry no information that is not embedded in the remaining columns. Deleting them while working with the remaining columns gives identical results to working with all J columns. Thus, assuming that A is full column rank is equivalent to eliminating the redundant assets and only working with the ones (*the basis assets*) that form a basis for the linear subspace of $\mathbb{R}^S$ generated by A. That linear subspace is called the *market span* and is denoted by

$$\mathcal{M} = \{y : y = Ah, \qquad h \in \mathbb{R}^J\}.$$

For the remainder of this chapter, we assume that $J < S$, so that markets are *incomplete* and the span of the market does not *span* $\mathbb{R}^S$.

1.1 The Budget Correspondence

The individual faces budget constraints in both periods. In period 0, consumption and expenditures on assets cannot exceed wealth, and in period 1, consumption in each state $s \in S$ must be covered by asset income for that state. Thus,

$$\begin{aligned} 1_J^\top h + c^0 &\leq m, \\ c^1 &\leq Ah. \end{aligned}$$

Two alternative representations are commonly considered. Rather than viewing them as realistic alternatives, they are better seen as polar cases describing different assumptions about market access. In the *frictionless* case, each h_j can be either positive or negative. The *no-short-sales* case allows the individual to purchase assets but not to sell them so that all h_j are nonnegative. The no-short-sales language is borrowed from the finance literature where an individual who purchases an asset is said to go *long* while a seller is said to go *short.* When short-selling restrictions exist, $\frac{h_j}{m-c^0}$ represents the percentage of $m - c^0 > 0$ spent on the jth asset. Thus, $\frac{h}{m-c^0} \in \mathbb{R}^J$ is the vector containing the percentages of available wealth devoted to each of the J assets. These percentages are positive and sum to one so that $A\frac{h}{m-c^0}$ represents a convex combination of $A_1, ..., A_J$, and $\left\{A\frac{h}{m-c^0} : 1_J^\top \frac{h}{m-c^0} = 1\right\}$ is their convex hull, $Co\{A_1, ..., A_J\}$. In Figure 9.1, the line segment connecting A_1 and A_2 represents $Co\{A_1, A_2\}$. Assuming for simplicity that $c^0 = 0$, the budget feasible c^1 falls in the region lying to the southwest of the frontier described by BA_1A_2C. The corresponding frontier in the frictionless case is the hyperplane passing through A_1 and A_2, and the feasible set is the half-space falling to its southwest.

The budget correspondence, $\mathcal{B} : \mathbb{R}^{S\times J} \times \mathbb{R}_+ \rightrightarrows \mathbb{R}^{1+S}$, is defined in the frictionless case by

$$\mathcal{B}(A, m) = \left\{c : 1_J^\top h + c^0 \leq m, c^1 \leq Ah, h \in \mathbb{R}^J\right\},$$

and in the no-short-sales case by

$$\mathcal{B}^+(A, m) = \left\{c : 1_J^\top h + c^0 \leq m, c^1 \leq Ah, h \in \mathbb{R}_+^J\right\}.$$

The associated budget-shortage functions are, respectively,

$$\mathfrak{b}(c; A, m) \equiv \inf\{\beta \in \mathbb{R} : (c^0, c^1 - \beta) \in \mathcal{B}(A, m), \beta \in \mathcal{X}\},$$

and

$$\mathfrak{b}^+(c; A, m) \equiv \inf\{\beta \in \mathbb{R} : (c^0, c^1 - \beta) \in \mathcal{B}^+(A, m), \beta \in \mathcal{X}\}.$$

These budget-shortage functions are the natural analogues of Chapter 5's budget-shortage function, $b(x, p; g)$. They offer function representations of the budget correspondences for the portfolio problem.

Exercise 57. *Show that* $c \in \mathcal{B}(A, m) \Leftrightarrow \mathfrak{b}(c; A, m) \leq 0$ *and that* $\mathfrak{b}(c; A, m)$ *is convex in* c.

Exercise 58. *Show that*

$$\mathfrak{b}(c; A, m) = \inf_{h \in \mathbb{R}^J}\left\{\max_s\{c_s^1 - A_{s\cdot}h\} : 1_J^\top h + c^0 \leq m\right\},$$

where $A_{s\cdot}$ *denotes the sth row of* A.

Exercise 59. *Show that* $c \in \mathcal{B}^+(A, m) \Leftrightarrow \mathfrak{b}^+(c; A, m) \leq 0$ *and that* $\mathfrak{b}^+(c; A, m)$ *is convex in* c.

Exercise 60. *Show that*

$$\mathfrak{b}^+(c; A, m) = \inf_{h \in \mathbb{R}_+^J}\left\{\max_{s \in S}\{c_s^1 - A_{s\cdot}h\} : 1_J^\top h + c^0 \leq m\right\}.$$

Remark 23. *Neither the frictionless nor the no-short-sales market structures are completely realistic. Everyday experience teaches us that few, if any, individuals can assume unboundedly large short positions in period 0 for period 1 assets as required by the frictionless case. On the other hand, many individuals in developed and undeveloped markets routinely borrow* *money in period 0 while promising to repay it plus interest at a later date. Borrowing and promising to repay a fixed interest is equivalent to shorting a safe asset. Moreover, many individuals count among their period 0 wealth some financial assets that can be liquidated in that period to finance period 1 consumption. Here you may wish to think of an individual rejiggling his or her stock portfolio to take advantage of changing market developments.*

Remark 24. *Example 11 in Chapter 6 describes a convex technology that can be derived from K observations on inputs and outputs* (x^k, y^k), $k = 1, 2, \dots, K$. *Take* $K = 2$, *let* $x^1 = x^2 = x$, *and* $y^1, y^2 \in \mathbb{R}^N$. *Then using the representation in Example 11 gives*

$$Y(x) = \{y : y \leq y^1 + \lambda(y^2 - y^1), \lambda \in [0, 1]\},$$

as the set of vectors dominated by the convex hull of y^1, y^2. *Sketching this* $Y(x)$ *in* $\mathbb{R}^2$ *gives a representation similar to that presented in Figure 9.1 for the no-short-sales case.*

1.2 Arbitrages and the Land of Cockaigne

Cockaigne (spellings vary) was a mythical land where you could get something for nothing. When financial economists talk about arbitrages or money pumps, that's what they mean. Getting something for nothing. More formally, they would say that an *arbitrage* exists if there is an h such that $1_J^\top h = 0$ with $Ah \in \mathbb{R}^S_+ \backslash \{0\}$, or an h exists such that $1_J^\top h < 0$ with $Ah = 0$. In the first instance, zero expenditure in period 0 earns a strictly positive return in some period 1 state. And in the second, you can arrange your portfolio transactions to make a strict profit in period 0 without affecting period 1 returns.

The presence of an arbitrage, depending on your perspective, has pleasant, if unbelievable, implications. For example, suppose that one of the first form exists. Then for zero current period cost you can generate positive income in at least one state of Nature. But that also means that you can repeatedly replicate that transaction an arbitrarily large number of times, generating the same positive returns. This is the classic definition of *money pump*, where arbitrarily large returns are available for free. It presents a nice, but implausible, world because it simultaneously implies that whoever is taking the opposite side of your transaction is making arbitrarily large negative losses.

And so, in what follows, we always assume that the financial markets permit no arbitrages (don't fall in the Land of Cockaigne). There are several different, but ultimately equivalent, ways of determining the consequences of this assumption. One is to recognize that if no arbitrages exist then

$$\begin{pmatrix} y^0 \\ y^1 \end{pmatrix} = \begin{bmatrix} -1_J^\top \\ A \end{bmatrix} h.$$

cannot fall in $\mathbb{R}^{1+S}_{++}$. Thus, by the Theorem of the Alternative (Theorem 4) the absence of an arbitrage implies the existence of $[v, p^\top] \in \mathbb{R}^{1+S}_{++}$, with $v + \sum_s p_s = 1$ such that

$$[v, p^\top] \begin{bmatrix} -1_J^\top \\ A \end{bmatrix} = 0,$$

whence $\left(\frac{p}{v}\right)^\top A = 1_J^\top$. Here, $\frac{p}{v}$ as an element of the dual space for $\mathbb{R}^S_+$ is intuitively interpretable as a *linear pricing functional* for A that ensures each asset in A is valued at its period 0 acquistion cost.

Alternatively, multiplying $\frac{p}{v}$ by one in the form $\frac{1^\top p}{1^\top p}$ with $1 \in \mathcal{X}$ gives

$$\frac{p}{v} = \delta\pi$$

with $\pi = \frac{p}{1^\top p} \in \Delta$ and $\delta = \frac{1^\top p}{v}$. Because v is a price that the no-arbitrage condition ensures exists for period 0 income and p is an analogous stochastic price for period 1 income, δ is the ratio of the no-arbitrage valuation of period 1 safe income relative to its valuation of period 0 income. So, just as $\frac{1}{1+r^0}$ is the individual's subjectively discounted price (discounted value) of $1 \in \mathcal{X}$ received in period 1 in period 0 units, δ is a discounted value of $1 \in \mathcal{X}$ implied by the absence of an arbitrage. Put simply, the absence of an arbitrage implies the existence of a (strictly positive) martingale pricing functional of the type discussed in Remark 19 for period 1 assets.

Another technical perspective on the consequences of the no-arbitrage assumption, which I leave to the reader, is offered by using conjugacy theory and the properties of $\mathfrak{b}$:

Problem 90. *In the frictionless case, the absence of an arbitrage requires that* $\mathfrak{b}((m, c^1); A, m) > 0$ *for all* $c^1 \in \mathbb{R}^S_+ \setminus \{0\}$ *and* $\mathfrak{b}((c^0, 0); A, m) > 0$ *for* $c^0 > m$. *(Prove this.) For* $(q^0, q^1) \in \mathbb{R}^{1+S}_+$ *and* $q^1 \in \Delta$, *the convex conjugate of* $\mathfrak{b}(c; A, m)$ *is defined*

$$\mathfrak{b}^*(q; A, m) = \sup_c \{q^\top c - \mathfrak{b}(c; A, m)\}.$$

Characterize the solution to this problem. Then characterize directly the solutions to

$$\mathfrak{b}^{**}(c; A, m) = \sup_q \{q^\top c - \mathfrak{b}^*(q; A, m)\},$$

for (m, c^1) *with* $c^1 \in \mathbb{R}^S_+ \backslash \{0\}$ *and* $(c^0, 0)$ *with* $c^0 > m$. *Discuss the results intuitively and compare them with those obtained by applying the Theorem of the Alternative.*

Regardless of the way you look at it technically, assuming the absence of an arbitrage effectively requires the financial market as represented by A to be in a zero-profit "equilibrium." I use scare quotes on equilibrium because our specification of the financial market details no equilibrating mechanism. Moreover, I won't discuss an equilibrating mechanism for the financial market. In what follows, I simply take it as given. So, calling it an equilibrium is technically misleading but hopefully suggestive intuitively. In essence, the assumption is the true equilibrating mechanism.

1.3 Rational Behavior

The analytic differences between the frictionless and the no-short-sales versions of the budget correspondence are encapsulated in $\mathfrak{b}(c; A, m)$ and $\mathfrak{b}^+(c; A, m)$. They differ, and generally $\mathfrak{b}(c; A, m) \leq \mathfrak{b}^+(c; A, m)$ because $\mathcal{B}^+(A, m) \subset \mathcal{B}(A, m)$. But the approach to identifying rational behavior in both instances is essentially identical. Therefore, attention is focused on $\mathcal{B}(A, m)$, and it is left to the reader to tweak the analysis to cover $\mathcal{B}^+(A, m)$.

Rational Portfolio Behavior A feasible consumption vector $c \in \mathcal{B}(A, m)$ is *rational* for the frictionless portfolio problem only if there exists no $\hat{c} \in \mathcal{B}(A, m)$ such that

$$\hat{c} \succ (c).$$

Using a proof strategy analogous to that for Theorem 9, you can establish:[2]

[2] Note that the rationality criterion, after a suitable adjustment, is presented here as one of zero maximality rather than zero minimality. Don't let this confuse you, or if it does, hopefully your confusion won't persist. It facilitates the analytic approach that I pursue here and later in this chapter.

Theorem 19. *c is rational for the frictionless portfolio problem if and only if it is zero maximal for*

$$\max_{\hat{c}} \left\{ d\left(\hat{c}, c; \tilde{g}\right) - \mathfrak{b}\left(\hat{c}; A, m\right) \right\}.$$

Describing rational behavior recycles arguments made in Chapters 5 and 7. So, let's do it quickly. Rational c in the frictionless problem is characterized differentially by

$$\partial d\left(c, c; \tilde{g}\right) \cap \partial^{-} \mathfrak{b}\left(c; A, m\right) \neq \emptyset.$$

The decision maker's shadow prices, as a consumer, overlap with the shadow prices generated by the budget correspondence. When $d\left(\hat{c}, c; \tilde{g}\right)$ is concave in $\hat{c}$, Fenchel's Duality Theorem (expression (2.24)) also requires that

$$\max_{\hat{c}} \left\{ d\left(\hat{c}, c; \tilde{g}\right) - \mathfrak{b}\left(\hat{c}; A, m\right) \right\} = \min_{q} \left\{ \mathfrak{b}^{*}\left(q; A, m\right) - d^{*}\left(q, c; \tilde{g}\right) \right\},$$

which gives the parallel overlapping condition for rationality

$$\partial^{-} \mathfrak{b}^{*}\left(q; A, m\right) \cap \partial d^{*}\left(q, c; \tilde{g}\right) \neq \emptyset.$$

As elsewhere, $d^{*}\left(q, c; \tilde{g}\right)$ is interpretable as a McKenzie expenditure function, and its superdifferential as the associated demands (for c^{0}, c^{1}). Interpreting $\mathfrak{b}\left(c; A, m\right)$ as a "transformation function" for incomes in period 0 and period 1 implies that $\mathfrak{b}^{*}\left(q; A, m\right)$ can be interpreted as the associated "revenue function" whose subdifferential yields consumable income in periods 0 and 1. Visually, one depicts the rational choice as the level set for $d\left(c, c; \tilde{g}\right)$ forming a tangency with the boundary of the budget correspondence depicted in Figure 9.1. Alternatively, it looks like Figure 1.2 with the axes relabeled.

Your solution to Problem 90 should show that

$$\mathfrak{b}^{*}\left(q; A, m\right) = \sup_{h} \left\{ q^{0} c^{0} + q^{1\top} c^{1} \, : \, c^{0} = \left(m - 1_{J}^{\top} h\right), c^{1} = A h \right\},$$

and

$$\left(c^{0}, c^{1}\right) \in \partial^{-} \mathfrak{b}^{*}\left(q; A, m\right) \Leftrightarrow q \in \partial^{-} \mathfrak{b}\left(c; A, m\right) \Leftrightarrow \frac{q^{1\top}}{q^{0}} A = 1_{J}^{\top}.$$

Putting arguments together gives

$$q \in \partial d\left(c, c; \tilde{g}\right) \Leftrightarrow \frac{q^{1\top}}{q^0} A = 1_J^\top,$$

as the differential requirement for rationality. You will note that this is the subjective martingale pricing rule to which you were introduced in Remark 19. In words, it requires that elements of the superdifferential of d evaluated at rational $\left(c^0, c^1\right)$ define stochastic discount factors for period 1 incomes which ensure that discounted values of the income streams from each of the financial assets exactly equal its period 0 price of one.

Remark 25. *The subjective martingale pricing rule required for rationality and the requirement for the absence of arbitrage are markedly similar. Recall that if no arbitrages are present, there must exist $p/v \in \mathbb{R}_{++}^S$ such that*

$$\frac{p^\top}{v} A = 1_J^\top.$$

This is not a coincidence. Give it some thought. You might start by asking yourself how a rational individual would respond to an arbitrage if one existed.

We could stop here. But the assumption that preferences are *strictly monotonic* lets us develop the argument from a slightly different perspective that enchances the connection with arguments made in earlier chapters.[3] Strict monotonicity ensures that rational choices for $\left(c^0, c^1\right)$ satisfy

$$c^1 = Ah,$$
$$1_J^\top h + c^0 = m.$$

In both instances, if the equality is replaced with $>$, c is not feasible. And if the equality were replaced by $<$, strict monotonicity of $\succeq(y)$ ensures that there exist larger values of $\left(c^0, c^1\right)$ dominating c, thus contradicting presumed rationality. The first S equalities require that rational c^1 fall in $\mathcal{M}$. The *Orthogonal Projection Theorem* yields the unique solution for the associated portfolio as

[3] If $\succeq(y)$ interpreted as a preference order is not strictly monotonic, c^1 need not lie in $\mathcal{M}$. Arguments made prior to this point continue to apply, but the following arguments need not. In a related context, see Problem 98 below.

$$h = \left(A^{\top}A\right)^{-1} A^{\top}c^{1},$$

where $\left(A^{\top}A\right)^{-1} A^{\top}$ is the familiar OLS matrix that projects $\mathbb{R}^S$ onto $\mathcal{M}$.[4] Substituting this result into the period 0 budget constraint gives

$$\begin{aligned} c^0 &= m - 1_J^{\top}\left(A^{\top}A\right)^{-1} A^{\top}c^1 \\ &\equiv m - Pc^1 \end{aligned}$$

with $P \equiv 1_J^{\top}\left(A^{\top}A\right)^{-1} A^{\top}$ and $\mathfrak{b}(c; A, m) = 0$. The zero maximality problem thus reduces to demonstrating c's zero maximality for

$$\max_{\hat{c}}\left\{d\left(m - P\hat{c}^1, \hat{c}^1, c; \tilde{g}\right)\right\}.$$

The associated differential requirement for an interior solution is

$$0 \in \partial_1 d\left(c, c; \tilde{g}\right) - \partial_0 d\left(c, c; \tilde{g}\right) P^{\top}, \tag{9.1}$$

where $\partial_1 d$ denotes the superdifferential of d with respect to c^1 and $\partial_0 d$ the superdifferential with respect to c^0.

The random variable $P \in \mathbb{R}^S$ is known variously as the *pricing kernel* or *ideal stochastic discount factor.* It converts consumption or income streams falling in $\mathcal{M}$ into period 0 units. It does this by taking a random variable falling in the span of the market, using the projection matrix $\left(A^{\top}A\right)^{-1} A^{\top}$ to construct the unique asset portfolio that exactly replicates it,[5] and then valuing that portfolio using period 0 acquisition prices of A, $1_J^{\top}$. By construction, therefore, Pc^1 gives the period 0 cost of constructing a portfolio that exactly covers $c^1 \in \mathcal{M}$. The elements of P, which we shall denote $P(s)$ for $s \in S$, establish period 0 prices, derived from A, for income in each of the S states of Nature in period 1. The common name for a period 0 price for period 1 income in state $s \in S$ is an *sth state-claim price.* These particular state-claim prices are determined via the financial market and reflect the *marginal costs* at which A transforms income in one state of Nature into

[4] By standard vector-space results, for a linear subspace $\mathcal{M} \subset \mathbb{R}^S$, $\mathbb{R}^S$ can be "split" into $\mathcal{M}$ and into the subspace of vectors in $\mathbb{R}^S$ orthogonal to $\mathcal{M}$. The latter subspace is called $\mathcal{M}'$*s orthogonal complement* and is denoted $\mathcal{M}^{\perp}$. Thus, $\mathbb{R}^S = \mathcal{M} + \mathcal{M}^{\perp}$, where addition is now in the Minkowski sense. The *orthogonal projection of* $x \in \mathbb{R}^S$ onto $\mathcal{M}$ is the point in $\mathcal{M}$ lying closest (in a least-squares sense) to x and equals the part of x that falls in $\mathcal{M}$. It equals $\left(A^{\top}A\right)^{-1} A^{\top}x \in \mathcal{M}$, and the component falling in $\mathcal{M}^{\perp}$ is $\left(I - \left(A^{\top}A\right)^{-1} A^{\top}\right)x$. (For more on orthogonal complements and orthogonal projections see Luenberger 1969, pp. 52–65.)

[5] Uniqueness is guaranteed by the Orthogonal Projection Theorem.

another. Accordingly, when considered in relative terms, $\frac{P(s)}{P(s')}$, they measure *marginal rates of transformation.*

The pricing kernel, however, only accurately prices random variables falling in $\mathcal{M}$ because those are the ones it can exactly price. For $y \notin \mathcal{M}$, the financial market can be used to construct a portfolio that dominates y, that is, $Ah \geq y$, but that does not "replicate" it. Consequently, the financial market can be used to create "bounds" within which period 0 prices for assets falling outside $\mathcal{M}$ must fall, but not exact prices.[6]

Rewriting expression (9.1) gives the following requirement for rational behavior

$$\frac{q^{1\top}}{q^0} = \frac{q^{1\top}}{1 + r^0} = P \text{ for some } q \in \partial d\left(c, c; \tilde{g}\right) \tag{9.2}$$

where the subjective discount rate, r^0, is defined as in (8.1). In Chapter 8's language, rationality requires that at least one of the individual's *subjectively discounted subjective probability measures* agrees with the market-determined state-claim prices, P.

Figure 1.2 illustrates expression (9.2) if one takes the axes to depict income (consumption) in states 1 and 2, the straight line to depict the budget hyperplane with normal P, and the curve representing a level set of $d\left(c, c; \tilde{g}\right)$. In brief, expression (9.2) and Corollary 3 are exact analogues. Where Corollary 3 requires equating marginal rates of substitution for nonstochastic commodities to market prices, expression (9.2) requires marginal rates of substitution for stochastic consumption to be equated to P. The inescapable conclusion is that rational c for the Portfolio Problem are interpretable as McKenzie demands for $\succeq(y)$ interpreted as a binary ordering of stochastic consumption alternatives. Taking $E\left(q^0, q^1, c\right)$ to be the associated McKenzie expenditure function that is positively homogeneous in $\left(q^1, q^0\right)$ gives

[6] More generally, take an arbitrary random variable y and decompose it into two parts

$$y = y^{\mathcal{M}} + y^{\perp}.$$

Because $y^{\perp}$ is constructed to be orthogonal to A, $Py^{\perp} = 0$, so that $Py = Py^{\mathcal{M}}$, leaving part of the random variable unpriced. A primary concern of financial economics is the accurate pricing in period 0 units of period 1 financial assets both inside and outside of $\mathcal{M}$. LeRoy and Werner (2001) is an excellent introduction, and successively more advanced treatments are Cochrane (2001) and Duffie (2001). The standard bounds for assets outside of the span are given by the support functions

$$\min\left\{1_J^{\top} h : Ah \geq y\right\}$$

and

$$\max\left\{1_J^{\top} h : y \geq Ah\right\}.$$

$$(1, P) \in \partial d(c, c; \tilde{g}) \Leftrightarrow c \in \partial E(1, P, c),$$

where we use the fact that expenditure-minimizing demands are homogeneous of degree zero in prices. These rational demands satisfy the same properties in $(1, P)$, as do Chapter 5's consumer demands in market prices, p. We won't reiterate these properties, but you can extend arguments developed in Chapter 5 to this case.

Problem 91. *Suppose that* $\succeq(y)$ *interpreted as the preference order satisfies the independence restriction (8.2) so that*

$$d(\hat{c}, c; \tilde{g}) = \inf_q \{q^\top (\hat{c} - c) : q \in Q\}$$

where $Q = \partial d(0, 0; \tilde{g})$ *is closed convex. What is required for c to be rational for the portfolio problem? Is it possible that the set of rational demands can be empty? If so, why?*

Problem 92. *Suppose that*

$$d(\hat{c}, c; \tilde{g}) = \inf_q \{q^\top (\hat{c} - c) : q \in Q\}$$

and that the preference order satisfies complete ordering (CO). Describe optimal behavior and contrast it with the solution to Problem 91.

2 The Producer Problem

This section studies a decision maker whose only alternative for covering stochastic consumption in period 1 is a stochastic production technology. If it helps intuitively, you might want to think of a farmer facing an uncertain Mother Nature. The preference structure is the same as in the Portfolio Problem, and available wealth is still $m \in \mathbb{R}_+$. The stochastic technology, as represented by $t(y, x; 1)$, satisfies *MB* (free disposability of stochastic output), where $y \in \mathbb{R}^S$ denotes stochastic period 1 production and $x \in \mathbb{R}^N$ inputs committed in period 0 to production. A competitive period 0 market exists for inputs, and they are priced at $w \in \mathbb{R}^N_{++}$.

Remark 26. *Although the portfolio problem was cast in the form of an investor engaging a financial market, it is equivalent mathematically to a producer* *who faces a linear, but stochastic, production technology that converts the period* 0 *commodity into stochastic period* 1 *output. In that setting, the inputs are the period* 0 *asset purchases, and the asset-specific payouts are* $h_j A_j \in \mathbb{R}^S$. *This parallels Koopmans's (1951) activity-analysis model where each* A_j *would represent a stochastic activity, and* h *the levels at which the* J *activities operate.*

In Koopmans's (1951) framework, $h \in \mathbb{R}^J_+$. *Under that interpretation, the analogue to the producer cost function,* $c(w, y)$ *is*

$$\mathfrak{v}(y) \equiv \min\left\{1_J^\top h : Ah \geq y\right\}.$$

$\mathfrak{v}(y)$ *is the support function for the closed convex set,* $\{h : Ah \geq y\}$, *formed as the intersection of J half-spaces. Thus, it possesses the essential properties of a cost function, and the technology's linear nature ensures that* $\mathfrak{v}(\lambda y) = \lambda \mathfrak{v}(y)$ *for* $\lambda > 0$ *(see, for example, LeRoy and Werner 2001).*

Remark 27. *The current problem has been posed as one of an individual using a stochastic technology to cover period* 1 *consumption. With virtually no change in the mathematics, the same setup can be reinterpreted as an individual facing a nonlinear pricing mechanism for covering period* 1 *consumption claims. Moreover, harking back to Chapter 5, one also finds that a closely parallel model handles the consumption decision problems for an individual facing a nonlinear budget constraint. I will not discuss either in detail, but it follows immediately that Figures 1.5 and 1.6 depict those problems as well and that the differential representation of equilibria for those settings mirrors those developed below.*

The budget constraints are now

$$c^0 + w^\top x \leq m,$$
$$c^1 \leq y,$$

and $w^\top x$ replaces $1^\top h$ from the portfolio problem in the budget constraint. The definition of rationality that accommodates the changed problem structure is:

Rational Producer Behavior (c^0, c^1, x, y) satisfying $t(y, x; 1) \leq 0$ and the budget constraints is rational for the producer problem if there exists no $(\hat{c}^0, \hat{c}^1, \hat{x}, \hat{y})$ such that the budget constraints are met, $t(\hat{y}, \hat{x}; 1) \leq 0$, and $(\hat{c}^0, \hat{c}^1) \succ ((c^0, c^1))$.

For a strictly monotonic preference order, an equivalent definition is to say that (c^0, c^1, y) satisfying

$$\begin{aligned} c^0 + \gamma(w, y) &\leq m, \\ c^1 &\leq y, \end{aligned} \tag{9.3}$$

is rational for the producer problem if no $(\hat{c}^0, \hat{c}^1, \hat{y})$ satisfying (9.3) exists with $(\hat{c}^0, \hat{c}^1) \succ ((c^0, c^1))$, where

$$\gamma(w, y) = \min\{w^\top x : t(y, x; 1) \leq 0\}$$

represents the minimal cost of producing stochastic y (see also Chapter 6, where the same concept is denoted $c(w, y)$).[7]

To prove the equivalence, note that any (x, y, c) meeting the constraints with x not cost minimizing for y leaves $w^\top x - \gamma(w, y)$ available for consumption in period 0 without affecting feasibility. Hence, it cannot be rational.

I leave the formulation of the budget correspondence in functional terms and the characterization of rational (c^0, c^1, y) in terms of an extremum problem to you.

Problem 93. *The budget correspondence now becomes*

$$\mathcal{B}^T(w, m) \equiv \{c \in \mathbb{R}^{1+S} : c^0 + \gamma(w, y) \leq m, c^1 \leq y, y \in \mathbb{R}^S\}$$

and gives all $c \in \mathbb{R}^{1+S}$ that can be financed out of wealth m with prevailing input prices $w \in \mathbb{R}^N$. Define

$$\mathfrak{b}^T(c, w, m) = \inf\{\beta \in \mathbb{R} : (c^0, c^1 - \beta) \in \mathcal{B}^T(w, m), \beta \in \mathcal{X}\}.$$

Prove that if $\gamma(w, y)$ is quasi-convex in y that $\mathfrak{b}^T(c, w, m)$ is convex in c^{1}. Compare $\mathfrak{b}^T(c, w, m)$ with

$$\inf\{\beta : \gamma(w, c^1 - \beta) \leq m - c^0\}.$$

Problem 94. *Show that (c^0, c^1, y) is rational for the producer problem if and only if $c = (c^0, c^1)$ is zero maximal for*

$$\max_{\hat{c}}\{d(\hat{c}, c; \tilde{g}) - \mathfrak{b}^T(\hat{c}, w, m)\}.$$

[7] My apologies for the midstream change in notation. It was necessitated by the need to discriminate between c used to denote consumption in this chapter and c to denote cost.

Characterize the solution differentially and develop an alternative representation for the case where CONA applies for preferences and $\gamma(w, y)$ is quasi-convex in y. (Hint: Fenchel's Duality Theorem)

Strict monotonicity of the preference order ensures that attention can be restricted to (c, y) satisfying

$$c^0 + \gamma(w, y) = m,$$
$$c^1 = y$$

whence

$$c^0 + \gamma(w, c^1) = m.$$

Applying the Indication Property of $d(\hat{c}, c; \tilde{g})$ establishes:

Theorem 20. (c^0, c^1, y) *is rational for the producer problem if and only if* $c^1 = y$, $c^0 = m - \gamma(w, y)$, *and* c^1 *is zero maximal for*

$$\max_{\hat{c}^1} \{d(m - \gamma(w, \hat{c}^1), \hat{c}^1, c; \tilde{g})\}$$

From Theorem 20, rational behavior requires that there exist some $q \in \partial d(c, c; \tilde{g})$ for which

$$\frac{q^1}{q^0} \in \partial_y^- \gamma(w, y), \tag{9.4}$$

where $\partial_y^- \gamma(w, y) \subset \mathbb{R}^S$ denotes γ's subdifferential in y. That subdifferential has a natural intepretation in terms of period 0 marginal cost of raising income in each of the respective states of nature. So, not surprisingly, rational producer behavior requires matching marginal rates of substitution between period 0 consumption and period 1 consumption (the individual's internal prices of period 1 consumption in period 0 units) with the technology's marginal costs. Figure 1.6 depicts the smooth version of the solution as the standard "kissing" tangency with the axes now interpreted as measuring $c_1(y_1)$ and $c_2(y_2)$, the convex to the origin curve as representing the level set for $d(c, c; \tilde{g})$, and the concave to the origin curve as representing the isocost curve (level set) for $\gamma(w, c^1)$.

Theorem 20, expression (9.4), and standard conjugate duality results imply that stochastic production, y, consistent with rational behavior must satisfy

$$y \in \partial_q^- \gamma^*\left(w, \frac{q^1}{q^0}\right),$$

for $q \in \partial d(c, c; \tilde{g})$ where $\gamma^*(w, q^1)$ is the convex conjugate of $\gamma(w, y)$. Thus, rational supply, y, must be consistent with supply chosen to maximize $\frac{q^{1\top}}{q^0}y - \gamma(w, y)$, and rational (c^0, c^1) must be McKenzie demands for q. From Chapter 8, one interpretation of $\frac{q^{1\top}}{q^0}y$ is as subjectively discounted subjective expected output. Thus, rational y has a natural interpretation as maximizing *subjectively discounted expected profit* from production for $\frac{q^{1\top}}{q^0}$, while (c^0, c^1) is expenditure minimizing for q.

This observation is a manifestation of the *Fisher Separation Theorem*. It implies that *once* $\frac{q^1}{q^0}$ *is determined*, the individual's actions as a producer can be *separated* from his actions as a consumer. Similarly, *once* $\frac{q^1}{q^0}$ *is determined*, the individual's actions as a consumer can be *separated* from his actions as a producer. It's yet another AS IF result. It's not that decision maker necessarily makes decisions in this fashion. What it means is that rational agents always act as if on the production side they maximize their *subjective value* of profits from production and on the consumption side they act to minimize their *subjective value* of expenditure required to cover their desired consumption bundle. That *subjective value*, however, is personal and ensures that marginal attitudes toward uncertainty are matched with marginal costs of creating state-contingent income.

A natural consequence is that comparative-static analyses derived for profit maximizers apply here. Thus, rational stochastic supply is nondecreasing in $\frac{q^1}{q^0}$, and the associated cost-minimizing demands are nonincreasing in w. It's equally true that comparative-static analyses for expenditure minimizers also apply. The important *caveat*, however, is that c, y, and $\frac{q^1}{q^0}$ are jointly dependent, so that $\frac{q^1}{q^0}$ cannot be viewed as "given" to the producer. Therefore, while these comparative-static properties are of analytic interest, they contain little essential economic content.

Remark 28. *This approach to the producer problem differs substantially from Sandmo (1971) and a number of subsequent writers. That tradition works in a single period (timeless) setting and treats the producer as a "firm" pursuing maximal benefit (expected utility) from stochastic profit. In our notation, treating output to be the numeraire commodity, stochastic profit* *is* $y - \gamma(w,y) \in \mathbb{R}^S$ *(with* $\gamma(w,y) \in \mathcal{X}$*). For a treatment in terms of general monotonic (but complete) preferences, you can consult Chambers and Quiggin (2000).*

How does one reconcile the Sandmo (1971) model with ours? The essential difference is that we treat $\gamma(w,y)$ *as being incurred in period 0, while Sandmo (1971) counts it in the same period 1 units as* y*. For the two to be equivalent, there must exist a safe way of transferring costs incurred in period 0 into period 1 income terms, so that*

$$c^0 \leq m + \gamma(w,y)$$
$$c^1 \leq y - \gamma(w,y).$$

Formally, this is equivalent to postulating the existence of a safe asset $1 \in \mathcal{X}$ *priced at 1 in period 0 which the producer sells* $\gamma(w,y)$ *units of in period 0 (perhaps to himself or herself) and pays back* $\gamma(w,y)$ *in period 1 with certainty.*

Problem 95. *Suppose that*

$$d(\hat{c}, c; \tilde{g}) = \inf_q \{q^\top (\hat{c} - c) : q \in Q\}$$

where $Q = \partial d(0,0;\tilde{g})$ *is closed convex. What characterizes rational producer behavior? Suppose that the same preference order also satisfies complete ordering (CO). What then characterizes rational behavior? Compare that behavior with what emerges when CO is not imposed.*

Problem 96. *Suppose that* $\succeq(y)$ *is interpreted as the preference order that satisfies*

$$\hat{c} \succeq (c) \Leftrightarrow \hat{c} \geq c.$$

Describe the conditions required for (c, y) *to be rational for the producer problem.*

3 Production and Portfolio Decisions

This section melds the producer problem and the portfolio problem into a single problem. We now let individuals have at least three different ways in period 0 to cover stochastic consumption in period 1. They include relying solely on financial markets, relying solely on $t(y, x; 1)$, or relying on both.

Before moving to the manipulation, I want to note that all three versions of these problems can be reformulated in perfectly general terms using something like $t(y, x; 1)$. So, in a sense, the principles of what follows have already been covered.

As I've described it, $t(y, x; 1)$ is derived from a subset of $\mathbb{R}^N \times \mathbb{R}^S$, which I've called the technology set. Virtually all of the intuitive discussion of it (apart from Chapter 7) has been in terms of physical technologies of the type economists usually treat with production functions. That's all perfectly legitimate extramathematical reasoning, but the mathematical representation also covers much more general objects.

As a simple example, consider an individual with a full-time job paid at the going wage rate who also runs a small side business selling objects that he or she produces. One way to set this situation up analytically would be to specify a production function for the side business and parallel to it a wage mechanism for hired workers.

This adds economic "texture" that complicates the problem. But it also captures an economic effect that might be otherwise ignored, the labor-leisure trade-off. Still, in the end, to paraphrase Malinvaud (1972, p. 87), adding this texture "has little effect on the logical structure." It's easy to see, for example, that by suitably massaging T to permit hiring out your own labor, we can account for such effects under the general rubric of $t(y, x; 1)$, just as Remark 26 shows that the financial asset allocation problem can be recast in production-theoretic terms. When all is said and done, the economic song remains the same. Equate marginal benefit to marginal costs.

So, why bother? My best answer is: *furphy*[8] *removal.* It so happens that furphies abound in many areas of applied economics. And perhaps no area demonstrates this better than much of the applied analysis on producer decision making under uncertainty, where many appear convinced, traditional economic analysis doesn't apply. This extra texture is being added to ensure that you don't fall for these furphies, if and when you encounter them. Simple economics gets the job done even in an uncertain decision setting.

[8] According to Wikipedia: "A furphy is Australian slang for an erroneous or improbable story that is claimed to be factual. Furphies are supposedly 'heard' from reputable sources, sometimes secondhand or thirdhand, and widely believed until discounted." I have many things to thank John Quiggin for, not the least of which is the introduction to some wonderful Aussie slang, including this particular one.

3.1 The Budget Constraints and Arbitrage

The budget constraints are now expressed as

$$w^{\top}x + 1_J^{\top}h + c^0 \leq m,$$
$$c^1 \leq Ah + y. \tag{9.5}$$

Decision opportunities are broadened in multiple directions. For example, financial markets can be used to *finance* production opportunities that might have otherwise gone unexploited if all production costs were solely financed from m. Period 0 borrowing for production loans is modeled as selling (shorting) a safe asset with a period 1 payout of $1 + r$ in return for a period 0 sale price of one dollar. The money borrowed relaxes the period 0 budget constraint while tightening the period 1 constraint.

It's also apparent that devoting resources in period 0 to production "creates" a period 1 asset y that will be priced nonlinearly at cost of $\gamma(w, y)$. That created asset may or may not fall in $\mathcal{M}$. To the extent that those production opportunities do not fall in the market span, they effectively extend the span of the financial market beyond the bounds defined by A. Thus, the simultaneous existence of investment and production alternatives allows the individual to expand "investment" horizons beyond $\mathcal{M}$ while also permitting the financing of larger than otherwise available production opportunities.

Yet another is that the decision maker can use financial and production markets to create self-insurance opportunities. Common examples are futures contracts that give the purchaser the ownership to the returns generated from a given amount (contract amount) of a specific commodity in period 1. If the commodity is the same as the numeraire for y, that futures contract can be used to hedge production directly. If it's for another commodity, it can still hedge other sources of income. Commodity options and stock options function similarly.

In treating the portfolio problem, we assumed away arbitrages. That was natural. In fact, absence of an arbitrage is sometimes referred to as the *Iron Law of Financial Economics*. That's because if arbitrages exist, the linear nature of $\mathcal{M}$ ensures that the individual's choices are effectively unconstrained. This remains true in the current setting. And so we continue to maintain the assumption that no arbitrages exist for A.

Eliminating the potential for arbitrages in A doesn't mean that potential arbitrages cannot exist between investment opportunities and physical production opportunities. In fact, what follows basically presumes the existence of some such opportunities, and a focus of our interest is how a rational individual seeks to exploit them. We say that (x, y, h) with $t(y, x; 1) \leq 0$ *admits an arbitrage* if there exists an (x^o, y^o, h^o) with $t(y^o, x^o; 1) \leq 0$ such that $Ah + y \leq Ah^o + y^o$ and $1_J^\top h + w^\top x \geq 1_J^\top h^o + w^\top x^o$ with at least one strict inequality.

3.2 Rational Production Decisions

Rational production and portfolio decisions satisfy:

Rational Production and Portfolio Behavior (x, y, h, c) satisfying $t(y, x; 1) \leq 0$ and (9.5) are *rational for the production and portfolio problem* only if there exists no $(\hat{x}, \hat{y}, \hat{h}, \hat{c})$ satisfying $t(\hat{y}, \hat{x}; 1) \leq 0$ and (9.5) with

$$\hat{c} \succ (c).$$

Strict monotonicity of $\succeq (y)$ interpreted as a preference order again suffices to ensure that any rational choice must exhaust both budget constraints

$$w^\top x + 1_J^\top h + c^0 = m,$$
$$c^1 = Ah + y,$$

and, moreover, that

$$w^\top x + 1_J^\top h = \min_{(x,h,y)} \left\{ w^\top x + 1_J^\top h : Ah + y = c^1, t(y, x; 1) \leq 0 \right\}.$$

The first two equalities follow as before. If they held as inequalities, without changing (x, y, h) a $\hat{c} \succ (c)$ is available. The third equality follows similarly. If it were not true, then holding c^1 constant, an $(\hat{x}, \hat{y}, \hat{h})$ can be found that is technically feasible, satisfies $A\hat{h}+\hat{y} = c^1$ and for which $w^\top \hat{x}+1_J^\top \hat{h} < w^\top x+1_J^\top h$ implying that $\hat{c}^0 > c^0$ exists, which is budget feasible.

This argument also establishes that rational (x, y, h, c) cannot admit an arbitrage for (x, y, h) precisely because an arbitrage implies unexploited opportunities to raise c. A rational individual always acts to exploit any such opportunities available, and that exploitation eliminates them. If it does not, that signals that the rational producer's problem is unbounded and thus poorly defined mathematically. We cheerfully assume those away. Eliminating arbitrages ensures that cost-minimizing principles apply.

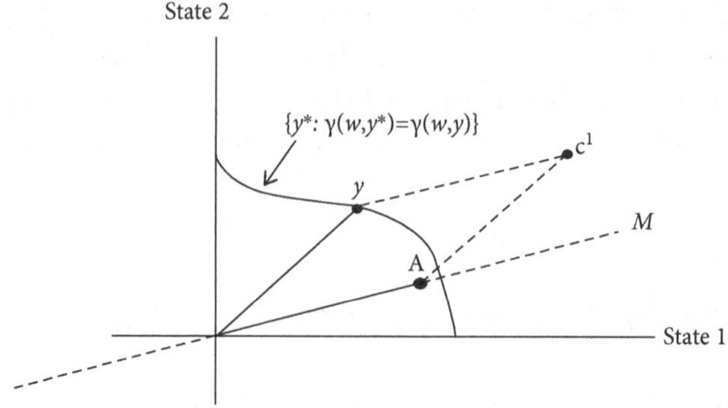

Fig. 9.2 Production and Portfolio Problem

Figure 9.2 illustrates the cost-minimizing choice (arbitrage-elimination) problem. The incomplete asset market is represented by a single asset labeled A. $\mathcal{M}$ is represented by the graph of the linear function defined by either radially expanding or radially shrinking A (toward $-\infty^S$). Short sales fall in $\mathbb{R}^2_-$ and longs in $\mathbb{R}^2_+$. P (not drawn) is represented as the vector orthogonal to A. Let the desired period 1 consumption bundle be represented by c^1. If a single unit of A were purchased, $c^1 - A \in \mathbb{R}^S$ must be covered by stochastic production. That involves incurring a cost of $\gamma(w, y)$ as illustrated by the isocost curve passing through point y. Generally speaking, purchasing a single unit of A isn't a rational investment choice, so further adjustment from y and A is required.

Define the *arbitrage cost function* as the period 0 minimal cost of assembling a production-investment portfolio that *exactly* covers period 1 consumption of c^1.[9]

$$C\left(w, P, c^1\right) \equiv \min_{(x,h,y)} \left\{w^\top x + 1_J^\top h : Ah + y = c^1, t\left(y, x; 1\right) \leq 0\right\}.$$

Successively applying Bellman's Principle using Remark 26 reveals that

$$\begin{aligned} C\left(w, P, c^1\right) &= \min_{(x,h,y)} \left\{w^\top x + 1_J^\top h : Ah + y = c^1, t\left(y, x; 1\right) \leq 0\right\} \\ &= \min_{(x,y)} \left\{w^\top x + \min_h \left\{1_J^\top h : Ah + y = c^1\right\}, t\left(y, x; 1\right) \leq 0\right\} \end{aligned}$$

[9] Chambers and Quiggin (2008, 2009) define a version of the arbitrage cost function that only requires the portfolio cover c^1. That version always provides a lower bound to the one defined here and is applicable when preferences are not strictly monotonic. It has similar generic properties, but it cannot be as completely decomposed as the one developed here. You're asked to analyze it more fully in Problem 98 below.

$$= \min_{(x,y)} \left\{ w^\top x + \mathfrak{v}\left(c^1 - y\right) : t\left(y, x; 1\right) \leq 0, c^1 - y \in \mathcal{M} \right\}$$

$$= \min_{y} \left\{ \min_{x} \left\{ w^\top x : t\left(y, x; 1\right) \leq 0 \right\} + \mathfrak{v}\left(c^1 - y\right) : c^1 - y \in \mathcal{M} \right\}$$

$$= \min_{y} \left\{ \gamma\left(w, y\right) + \mathfrak{v}\left(c^1 - y\right) : c^1 - y \in \mathcal{M} \right\}.$$

The individual's production–investment decision reduces to choosing an asset portfolio, h, to cover $c^1 - y \in \mathcal{M}$ exactly and stochastic output y to maximize discounted profit (discounting done using P).

Rational production choices are governed by $t\left(y, x; 1\right)$, w, and P. This may strike some as perplexing because a common perception is that uncertainty attitudes govern stochastic production choices. To counter that intuition, note that individual preferences are defined over c and not $\left(x, y\right)$. Producers, of course, care about $\left(x, y\right)$ but only because they affect the ability to cover c. Thus, producer preferences over $\left(x, y\right)$ as well as h are indirect. If the decision maker must rely exclusively on the stochastic technology to cover c^1, $c^1 = y$, and uncertainty attitudes are reflected in production choices. But when financial markets can also be used to cover c^1, the producer needs to choose rationally between covering c^1 via production or via the financial market. That means eliminating arbitrages between the two, and that ensures matching marginal opportunities between the two.

The result manifests a basic insight that I trace to Holbrook Working (1953). In studying commodity futures markets, he observed that hedging behavior was "not properly comparable with insurance. It is a sort of arbitrage." So rather than being driven by risk concerns, hedgers strive to exploit opportunities for increasing sure profit. Rational decision makers behave similarly, and this is precisely what it means to eliminate or exploit an arbitrage.

Marginal arguments help illustrate. Suppose that the decision maker considers selling in period 0 one unit of A_j in the financial market, while using the stochastic technology *to offset exactly* the potential change in consumption. The sale realizes one dollar. Assuming for simplicity that $\gamma\left(w, y\right)$ is convex in y, the marginal cost of producing one unit of A_j, via Lemma 2, is

$$\lim_{\lambda \downarrow 0} \frac{\gamma\left(w, y + \lambda A_j\right) - \gamma\left(w, y\right)}{\lambda} = \sup\left\{ q^\top A_j : q \in \partial^- \gamma\left(w, y\right) \right\}.$$

Because these changes offset, c^1 remains unchanged. Thus, uncertainty attitudes are not involved in making this decision, and what drives it are attitudes toward c^0. The individual, naturally, wants to make this as big as possible. If marginal cost exceeds $1 = PA_j$, the proposed move is a bad deal, while if the reverse is true, it's a good one. Rational behavior ensures that such jockeying to exploit potential arbitrages eliminates disagreements between P and $\partial^- \gamma(w, y)$.

Theorem 21. *(x, h, c, y) is rational for the producer problem if c^1 is zero maximal for*

$$\max_{\hat{c}^1} \left\{ d\left(m + c^* (w, P) - P\hat{c}^1, \hat{c}^1, c; \tilde{g}\right) \right\},$$

with

$$\begin{aligned} x &\in -\partial_w \gamma^* (w, P), \\ y &\in \partial_{\bar{P}} \gamma^* (w, P), \\ h &= \left(A^\top A\right)^{-1} A^\top \left(c^1 - y\right), \text{ and} \\ c^0 &= m + \gamma^* (w, P) - Pc^1. \end{aligned}$$

Rational period 1 consumption, therefore, can satisfy the same differential condition as in the Portfolio Problem,

$$\partial_1 d\left(c, c; \tilde{g}\right) \cap \partial_0 d\left(c, c; \tilde{g}\right) P \neq \varnothing.$$

At least one of the individual's subjective stochastic discount factors as determined by $\frac{q^{1\top}}{q^0}$ for $q \in \partial d\left(c, c; \tilde{g}\right)$ can agree with the market-determined stochastic discount factor, P. It follows immediately that rational c^1 can satisfy

$$c^1 \in \partial_P d^* \left(1, P, c; \tilde{g}\right) = \partial_P E\left(1, P, c\right),$$

just as rational y can satisfy

$$y \in \partial_{\bar{P}} \gamma^* (w, P).$$

Rational individuals with strictly monotonic preferences facing an active financial market then separate their production decisions from their consumption decisions. Stochastic production decisions are made AS IF to maximize discounted expected profit using the market-determined stochastic discount factor P. Consumption decisions are made AS IF to minimize discounted expected expenditure (as defined via P) required to dominate c.

A take-away message is that the decision criteria of individuals in uncertain settings manifest virtually identical principles to those used in nonstochastic settings. Basic principles apply, and equating marginal rates of substitution to marginal rates of transformation still holds sway. When preferences are strictly monotonic and active financial markets are available, those decision criteria mimic the behavior of competitive consumers and producers facing nonstochastic markets and nonstochastic price structures. The primary difference is that consumer and producer prices are not those that clear period 1 markets. Instead, the relevant "output prices" are the state-claim prices, P, that are derived from the financial market's implicit valuation of incomes that fall within $\mathcal{M}$.

Problem 97. *State conditions sufficient to ensure that the rational choice involves the producer not using the stochastic technology to cover period 1 consumption. State conditions sufficient to ensure that the producer only uses the stochastic technology and not financial markets to cover period 1 consumption.*

Problem 98. *Suppose that* $\succeq(y)$ *is monotonic but not strictly monotonic. Show that any rational choice must involve*

$$w^{\top}x + 1_J^{\top}h = \min_{(x,h,y)} \left\{ w^{\top}x + 1_J^{\top}h \,:\, Ah + y \geq c^1, t(y, x; 1) \leq 0 \right\},$$

and that, in this instance,

$$C\left(w, P, c^1\right) = \min_{y,r} \left\{ \gamma\left(w, y\right) + \mathfrak{v}\left(r\right) \,:\, r + y \geq c^1 \right\}.$$

Characterize the optimal solution to this problem and illustrate your solution visually. Prove that if $c^1 \in \mathcal{M} + \partial\gamma^*\left(w, P\right)$, *Theorem 21 applies.*

So far, we have viewed the process as one of market-determined P driving the determination of c^1 and y. But as with all our equilibrium results, alternative interpretations are possible. Notice that both $\partial d\left(c, c; \tilde{g}\right)$ and $\partial^{-}\gamma\left(w, y\right)$ represent "internal price" structures. The first arises from the decision maker's preference structure, and the latter from the available technology. In rational equilibrium, they must overlap or, put another way, agree in at least one element. Thus, both offer natural mechanisms for creating internal prices for period 1 assets as either preference or producer-driven opportunity costs to the decision maker. This is the fundamental observation lying behind the "consumption-based" and "production-based" approaches to empirical asset pricing (see, for example, Cochrane 2001). To illustrate, notice that $P \in \partial^{-}\gamma(w,y) \cap \partial_1 d(c,c;\tilde{g})$ ensures that there exists a common random variable, interpretable as a stochastic discount factor, for which

$$PA_j = 1,$$

can be interpreted as requiring either that the period 0 marginal cost of replicating A_j or that the subjectively discounted subjective expected value of A_j equal one.

4 Complete Ordering and Production–Portfolio Decisions

The assumptions on $\succeq(y)$ interpreted as a preference order when augmented by complete ordering (CO) ensure that the decision maker possesses a continuous and strictly monotonic utility function representable by (see Chapter 5)

$$u(c;\tilde{g}) = -d(0,c;\tilde{g}).$$

Because $u(c;\tilde{g})$ represents the number of units of the safe asset $1 \in \mathcal{X}$ required to ensure that $(0,u(c;\tilde{g})) \succeq (c^0,c^1)$, it's often referred to as a *certainty equivalent.* Define

$$E^H(q^0,q^1,u) \equiv \inf_{\hat{c}^0,\hat{c}^1}\{q^0\hat{c}^0 + q^{1\top}\hat{c}^1 : u(\hat{c};\tilde{g}) \geq u\}$$

as the Hicksian expenditure function associated with $u(\hat{c};\tilde{g})$, when period 0 prices of (c^0,c^1) are (q^0,q^1). Any (Hicksian) demand vector, c, that solves this problem when $u = u(c;\tilde{g})$ must be rational so that $E^H(q^0,q^1,u(c;\tilde{g})) = E(q^0,q^1,c)$. The *investment–expenditure function,*

$$IE(w,q^0,q^1,u) \equiv E^H(q^0,q^1,u) - \gamma^*(w,q^1),$$

is the difference between Hicksian expenditure required to yield u and the profit function dual to $\gamma(w,y)$ evaluated at q^1.[10] $IE(w,q^0,q^1,u)$ is superlinear in (w,q^0,q^1), so that applying Lemma 4 gives:

[10] The parallel concept in the international trade literature, on which the definition of the *IE* is based, is *the trade expenditure function* (see, for example, Neary and Schweinberger 1996).

Proposition 6. *$IE(w,q^0,q^1,u)$ is the (lower) support function for the closed, convex set*

$$\mathcal{A}(u) \equiv \{(x,z^0,z^1) \in \mathbb{R}^{N+1+S} : w^\top x + q^\top z \geq IE(w,q^0,q^1,u) \text{ for all } (w,q^0,q^1)\}.$$

$\mathcal{A}(u)$ is similar to the at-least-as-good sets generated by an ordinal utility function, with two specific differences. First, $\mathcal{A}(u)$ contains inputs and outputs, and second, it reflects both preferences and the technology. The z^0 elements of $\mathcal{A}(u)$ represent period 0 consumption, but the z^1 elements represent stochastic "excess demands," $c^1 - y \in \mathbb{R}^S$.

Problem 99. *As a support function for $\mathcal{A}(u)$, $IE(w,q^0,q^1,u)$ is the (concave) conjugate of $\delta(x,z^0,z^1 \mid \mathcal{A}(u))$. Use the conjugacy relationship to develop an expression for $\delta(x,z^0,z^1 \mid \mathcal{A}(u))$.*

By Theorem 6,

$$w \in \partial_x \delta(x,z^0,z^1 \mid \mathcal{A}(u)) \Leftrightarrow x \in \partial_w IE(w,q^0,q^1,u),$$
$$q^0 \in \partial_{z^0} \delta(x,z^0,z^1 \mid \mathcal{A}(u)) \Leftrightarrow z^0 \in \partial_{q^0} IE(w,q^0,q^1,u), \text{ and}$$
$$q^1 \in \partial_{z^1} \delta(x,z^0,z^1 \mid \mathcal{A}(u)) \Leftrightarrow z^1 \in \partial_{q^1} IE(w,q^0,q^1,u).$$

As noted, z^0 is interpretable as rational period 0 consumption and z^1 as the difference between optimal period 1 consumption, c^1 and production y. We won't pursue it, but these demands and "excess demands" are cyclically monotone in (w,q^0,q^1).

When coupled with the budget constraint, IE induces an indirect utility structure that gives the utility attainable by efficiently combining financial markets operations and the stochastic production technology. The *indirect investment utility function,* which abusing notation we denote by $I(w,q^0,q^1,m)$, is the implicit solution to

$$IE(w,q^0,q^1,I(w,q^0,q^1,m)) = m.$$

$I(w,q^0,q^1,m)$ is analogous to the indirect utility function, $I\left(\frac{p*}{m}\right)$, derived in Chapter 5. By the superlinearity of IE

$$IE\left(\frac{w}{m},\frac{q^0}{m},\frac{q^1}{m},I(w,q^0,q^1,m)\right) = 1,$$

thus ensuring I is homogeneous of degree zero in (w,q^0,q^1,m). A slight modification of the argument used in Chapter 5, left to you as an exercise, shows that $I(w,q^0,q^1,m)$ is quasi-convex in (w,q^0,q^1).

Exercise 61. *Prove that* $I(w, q^0, q^1, m)$ *is quasi-convex in* (w, q^0, q^1).

Just as $I\left(\frac{p^*}{m}\right)$ characterizes optimal consumer behavior for the standard consumer problem, $I(w, q^0, q^1, m)$ characterizes the individual's optimal behavior as a consumer, investor, and producer in the production–portfolio model. That means that the comparative-static results developed in Chapter 5 for $\frac{p^*}{m}$ and those in Chapter 6 for w all have direct analogues in the production–portfolio problem. Again, I leave it to you to develop these on your own.

5 Equilibrium

In the equilibrium analysis, I treat the input vector, x, as a scalar that is counted in units of the period 0 commodity. That means the period 0 commodity is treated as if it were suitable for both personal consumption and production purposes. It's a notational shortcut that lets me avoid specifying N separate markets for the inputs in the equilibrium setup. As elsewhere, you are free to make the necessary extensions. Notation will change; the substance does not.

As in Chapter 7, there are K agents, each with a strictly monotonic and continuous preference order $\succeq^k (y)$. Each agent's ability to convert the period 0 commodity into a stochastic period 1 income stream is characterized by a period 0 cost function, $\gamma^k(1, y)$. The "1" notation is to remind you that x is a singleton whose period 0 price is 1 (the period 0 commodity is the numeraire). Each individual is endowed with a fixed period 0 income, m^{k0}, and a claim on period 1 consumption $m^{k1} \in \mathbb{R}^S$. This represents a slight change from the portfolio and production–portfolio problems where no m^{k1} exists. Again it's not a substantive change, but it's used here to accommodate an equilibrium specification that works equally well in an endowment economy (pure exchange) framework and a production–exchange framework.

The exchange setting is characterized by the K individuals agreeing in period 0 to make trades involving the period 0 commodity *and* claims for period 1 consumption. The trades in the period 1 claims are thus properly viewed as *contingent trades.* That is, if an individual purchases c^1 and $s \in S$ is Nature's selection, she will receive c_s^1 from her trading partner. Once the contingent trades are agreed upon in period 0, they are assumed to be enforceable in period 1. Moreover, to avoid complications arising from hidden action and hidden information, information is assumed perfect and shared by all. In particular, *ex post*, all know Nature's choice from S.

Following Chapter 7, define:

Definition 6. *A production plan* $(y^1 \ldots, y^K)$ *and an allocation plan* $((\hat{c}^{10}, \hat{c}^{11}), \ldots, (\hat{c}^{K0}, \hat{c}^{K1}))$ *are feasible if*

$$\sum_k m^{k0} = \sum_k \gamma^k (1, y^k) + \sum_k \hat{c}^{k0},$$
$$\sum_k m^{k1} + \sum_k y^k = \sum_k \hat{c}^{k1}.$$

Definition 7. *A feasible production plan and allocation plan are Pareto optimal if there are no other feasible plans* $((\tilde{c}^{10}, \tilde{c}^{11}), \ldots, (\tilde{c}^{K0}, \tilde{c}^{K1}))$ *such that* $(\tilde{c}^{k0}, \tilde{c}^{k1}) \succeq ((\hat{c}^{k0}, \hat{c}^{k1}))$ *for all k with at least one k′ satisfying* $(\tilde{c}^{k0}, \tilde{c}^{k1}) \succ ((\hat{c}^{k0}, \hat{c}^{k1}))$.

Slightly modifying the proof of Theorem 15 establishes:

Theorem 22. *A feasible production plan* $(y^1 \ldots, y^K)$ *and an allocation plan* $((\hat{c}^{10}, \hat{c}^{11}), \ldots, (\hat{c}^{K0}, \hat{c}^{K1}))$ *are Pareto optimal if and only if they are zero maximal for*

$$\max_{\tilde{c},y} \left\{ \begin{array}{c} \sum_{k=1}^{K} d^k \left((\tilde{c}^{k0}, \tilde{c}^{k1}), (\hat{c}^{k0}, \hat{c}^{k1}); \tilde{g} \right) : \\ \sum_k m^{k0} = \sum_k \gamma^k (1, y) + \sum_k \tilde{c}^{k0} \\ \sum_k m^{k1} = \sum_k \tilde{c}^{k1} - \sum_k y^k \end{array} \right\}.$$

The familiar differential characterization of an interior optima involves overlapping superdifferentials and subdifferentials:

$$\begin{aligned} \partial_0 d^1 (\hat{c}^1, \hat{c}^1; \tilde{g}) \cap \partial_0 d^k (\hat{c}^k, \hat{c}^k; \tilde{g}) &\neq \emptyset \quad \text{for all } k \neq 1, \\ \partial_0 d^1 (\hat{c}^1, \hat{c}^1; \tilde{g}) \cap \partial_0 d^k (\hat{c}^k, \hat{c}^k; \tilde{g}) &\neq \emptyset \quad \text{for all } k \neq 1, \text{ and} \\ \partial_0 d^1 (\hat{c}^1, \hat{c}^1; \tilde{g})\, \partial^- \gamma^k (1, y^k) \cap \partial_1 d^1 (\hat{c}^1, \hat{c}^1; \tilde{g}) &\neq \emptyset \quad \text{for all } k. \end{aligned}$$

The first $K - 1$ conditions require that all K individuals share a common subjective valuation for period 0 consumption. The second $K - 1$ conditions require that they share common subjective valuations for consumption in all S states. The last K conditions require that all K marginal costs for the S states satisfy

$$\frac{q^1}{q^0} \in \partial^- \gamma^k \left(1, y^k\right) \quad \text{for all } k$$

with $\left(q^0, q^1\right) \in \cap_k \partial d^k \left(\hat{c}^k, \hat{c}^k; \tilde{g}\right)$.

Allowing for the change in the notation, these are the same as in Chapter 7. You can think of them as saying that all K individuals must agree on common period 0 prices (state-claim prices) for period 1 contingent trades for the outcome to be Pareto optimal. Or, equivalently, you can think of them as saying that Pareto optimality requires that all individuals share the same subjective stochastic discount factor for period 1. The Second Welfare Theorem and Theorem 16 imply the converse result. If a $p \in \mathbb{R}^S_{++}$ exists such that

$$\sum_k m^{k1} = \sum_k \partial_p E^k \left(1, p, c\right) - \partial_p^- \gamma^{*k} \left(1, p\right),$$
$$\sum_k m^{k0} = \sum_k \partial E^k \left(1, p, c\right) - \partial^- \gamma^{*k} \left(1, p\right)$$

the resulting exchange equilibrium is Pareto optimal.

The ultimate sticking point, however, is that this exchange setting demands that contingent trades can be agreed upon and, more importantly, enforced. The enforcement part is particularly tricky because trades that seem mutually advantageous before Nature makes her choice may become unattractive once the choice is made. Yet for the results to hold, the trades still need to go through. One can imagine legal settings in which this occurs, but the practical difficulties should not be minimized.

Agreeing upon enforceable contingent exchanges may also prove problematic. Our fundamental model of competitive markets in a nonstochastic setting is heavily colored by our observation of everyday markets for the exchange of physical commodities. We see buyers and sellers interact by agreeing or not agreeing to sell at mutually acceptable prices. You go into a store, and you come out with a bag of apples without any drama. We model such competitive arms-length interactions mathematically as buyers and suppliers reacting to a common $p \in \mathbb{R}^N$. That p is treated as given to all competitive agents, and so any commodity bundle in $\mathbb{R}^N$ is priced uniquely by it. All economically relevant information is embedded in the pricing mechanism.

For markets involving both the passage of time and uncertainty, things don't always operate in the same way. The passage of time, in and of itself, is not particularly problematic, but the existence of uncertainty is. So, while you can go into a bank and take out a loan to be repaid a year from now, there's typically some drama involved. The action is still arm's length, but the transaction will now not be anonymous. You will have to provide information on yourself, your potential earnings, and your liabilities *if* you're to qualify for the loan.

When ultimate outcomes are uncertain, individuals will feel confident only about a limited range of individual transactions. As a consequence, we observe many situations where one can make an immediate transaction but cannot arrange a transaction *contingent* upon some future state occuring. Our financial market setup recognizes this difficulty mathematically by having $\mathcal{M} \subset \mathbb{R}^S$ with $\mathcal{M}^{\perp} \neq \emptyset$. In short, period 1 outcomes exist which cannot be subjected to price discipline via period 0 transactions in A. You can interpret the nonemptiness of $\mathcal{M}^{\perp}$ as a mathematical manifestation of the difficulties involved in agreeing to and enforcing contingent exchanges. Nonempty $\mathcal{M}^{\perp}$ captures the everyday notions of *background or nondiversifiable risk.*[11]

We've seen, however, that even if $\mathcal{M}^{\perp}$ is nonempty, rational individuals with strictly monotonic preferences and access to A can choose their consumption and production choices to satisfy

$$P \in \partial^{-}\gamma^{k}\left(1, y^{k}\right), \text{ and}$$
$$0 \in \partial_{1} d^{k}\left(c^{k}, c^{k}; \tilde{g}\right) - \partial_{0} d\left(c^{k}, c^{k}; \tilde{g}\right) P^{\top} \text{ for all } k,$$

which ensures a Pareto-optimal outcome. Hence, reacting to P *can* lead to Pareto-optimal outcomes.

Don't be too hasty, however, to conclude that Pareto optimality *is to be expected* under uncertainty if financial markets exist. *Caveats* are in order. I have assumed that $\succeq(y)$ is strictly monotonic. Whereas in other settings, it's mainly an assumption that streamlines analysis, here it has substantive bite. Strict monotonicity implies that all individual budget constraints are met with equality. Normally, that simply means nothing goes to waste. But here, it carries the behavioral implication that individuals who don't produce always consume in $\mathcal{M}$ and that individuals who do produce locate their excess demands in $\mathcal{M}$. That implies that marginal production and consumption decisions are governed by P.

If the period 1 budget constraint doesn't hold as an equality, you can't conclude that individuals use financial markets to exactly cover excess demand. The existence of a financial market will guarantee Pareto-optimal outcomes

[11] Given the Knightian distinction between risk and uncertainty, it's perhaps better to think of this economically as *background or nondiversifiable uncertainty.* Regardless of semantics, it reflects the range of outcomes that cannot be covered exactly via A.

in such instances if $\mathcal{M} = \mathbb{R}^S$ (or $\mathbb{R}^{S\times M}$ when the consequence space is $\mathbb{R}^M$). In the S-dimensional case that we're treating, that requires A to have rank S, which in turn requires that contingent markets do exist for each and every state of Nature. In other words, complete contingent markets exist.

Looking at things in this manner helps explain why economists perceive individuals popularly viewed as gamblers or speculators as providing a fundamental economic service. Individuals who write the contracts associated with financial markets facilitate contingent trades that might otherwise not occur. Because of the complexity of the world, those markets may not be able to cover all outcomes, but they can cover some.

So, for example, where the person-in-the-street perceives an individual who buys a commodity futures contract (goes long) as a speculator gambling on a price rise, an economist sees someone who has made a loan to the contract seller in return for an uncertain return. That's a fundamental economic function, and it provides value to the loan recipients. Similarly, the seller of the contract provides commodity storage for the buyer, who in the absence of the contract would have to carry the physical commodity forward. Both sides to the trade can be viewed as speculative, but both produce economic value.

Popular views of such contingent contracts are frequently colored by the prism through which one views uncertainty. The reality is that all insurance activities can be viewed as gambles, and all gambles as insurance activities. They are the obverse and reverse side of the same coin. Think of it this way. If you buy trip insurance for your next vacation, you're actually gambling that something bad will happen on your trip. You only win the gamble if an insurably bad event does occur. And the insurance company instead of providing you insurance is actually gambling that nothing bad will happen to you. They lose the gamble if it does.

We close this section by noting the connection between these equilibrium results and Knight's (1921) argument that uncertainty (stochastic outcomes to which an objective probability cannot be attached) and not risk (outcomes to which an objective probability can be attached) is the source of economic profit. The fact that the pricing kernel, P, can be interpreted as a stochastic discount factor ensures that it has a probabilistic interpretation as the assessment that financial market participants agree upon for outcomes in $\mathcal{M}$. One way to interpret Knight's (1921) intuitive arguments is that as long as individuals can agree on some price structure for uncertain assets, albeit incomplete, operations within that structure should obey the normal laws of competition as we understand them.

Having said that, however, I reiterate that I haven't made any attempt to explain how A arises. Its existence was not explained but was taken for granted. Sorting through the details of what drives such markets to emerge deserves nothing less than a detailed treatise. Magill and Quinzii (1996) is a great place to start.

6 A Closing Word on Uncertainty in Economics

So, decision making under uncertainty closely parallels decision making under certainty, with the added difficulty of nonlinear budget sets. But a dash of strong monotonicity and the plausible existence of financial markets suffice to make the differences vanishingly small. Why, therefore, is there often so much more drama associated with analyzing uncertain markets rather than certain markets?

In my mind, the essential difference is observability. If you were to ask small children what an apple or an orange is, you could be reasonably certain to obtain reasonably coherent and accurate answers. On the other hand, if you were silly enough to ask them to describe a random variable, you'd deserve the gobblydegook you got back. The underlying reason is that apples or oranges are things that we observe, while random variables reflect our conceptualizations of things perceived as being beyond our control. Even if I gussied up the audience and asked a group of undergraduate micro students to perform the same tasks, I'd wager dollars to donuts that I would not get answers along the lines that we've developed.[12]

The gap between what we observe and what we conceptualize is an important roadblock to applying our AS IF treatment of decision making under uncertainty. At least in principle, the same gap doesn't exist in a nonstochastic world. For example, it's easy enough to convince even deeply unsophisticated thinkers that "peanut butter isn't really peanut butter" by asking them to compare the smooth and crunchy varieties. With enough care and patience, one could presumably design data collection practices that clearly discriminate between all different varieties.

Nature's intervention changes things. We conceptualize individuals as choosing, for example, $y \in \mathbb{R}^S$, but absent tightly controlled experiments, we can only observe $y_s \in \mathbb{R}$ that convolutes Nature's choice with the individuals. For example, you might conclude from this chapter that the

[12] But then again, I could be wrong. I never fail to be amazed at the answers that my undergraduates come up with.

Revealed-Preference Theory discussed in Chapter 5 might be applied by simply replacing market prices there with P, as defined here. That is true, but the conclusion is empirically empty. In any realistic setting, there will never be observations for the random demand that belongs to $\mathbb{R}^S$.[13]

As in the case of stochastic technologies, one can add more structure to *identify* the precise mathematical relationship between *ex ante* and *ex post* variables. This makes the problem more tractable. But it also makes any potential answer you might get more unrealistic because it adds yet another AS IF layer to our existing structure of assumptions.

Thus, even though the nonstochastic and stochastic problems can be treated using virtually identical conceptualizations, they are not both equally tractable empirically, at least as far as I know. What I have learned, however, is that failing to exploit that equivalence is the intellectual equivalent of failing to exploit an arbitrage. As much of the applied literature on production decisions under uncertainty demonstrates, the result is a farrago of models that promotes confusion, blind alleys, and dead ends.

7 Chapter Commentary

Much of the analysis in this chapter has appeared in somewhat different form in Chambers and Quiggin (2000, 2008, 2009). What differentiates the present discussion from those earlier contributions are the reliance on conjugacy-based arguments and the relaxation of complete ordering to admit incomplete preference structures. The latter was facilitated by applying the ideas of Luenberger (1992b) to characterize rational behavior, and thus mirrors arguments made in Chapter 4 and elsewhere throughout the book. Although the style of argument is different, much of what is presented here was influenced by Magill and Quinzii (1996), Cochrane (2001), Duffie (2001), and LeRoy and Werner (2001).

[13] As a practical matter, you can't even expect to have observations on P.

10
Quality, Valuation, and Welfare

The origins of this chapter lie in the "applied detours" that the course on which this book is based took over the years. Those detours typically arose from the need to introduce our first-year students to applied areas that were of special interest in our program. Over the years, the subject matter varied as the fashionable areas of microeconomics changed. To a large extent, the topics were those of central interest in agricultural economics, resource economics, or environmental economics. Sometimes those interests overlapped, sometimes they did not. What didn't change, however, was that each topic reflected a reworking of basic microeconomic principles into a more specialized context that reflected practical problems. Those practical problems often carried with them significant texture that's not present in more abstract models based on stylized notions of firms, consumers, or both. That texture frequently cut two ways. In one direction, it enriched our understanding of poorly understood areas or neglected areas of microeconomics. In the other, textural differences were often mistaken for substantive differences that rendered microeconomic theorizing meaningless. I always viewed my job as an instructor as one of striking a balance between these competing forces by clarifying when a changing texture reflected a need to rework the extramathematical reasoning that we attach to our basic models and when it called for completely new analysis. Surprisingly often, just as we've seen with decision making and equilibrium analysis under uncertainty, existing models worked just fine once they were appropriately repurposed and relabeled to fit the changing texture.

Over time, two themes proved consistently important to our students: the economics of quality and consumer-based welfare or valuation analysis. I should say from the start that neither of these is an area in which I focused my research. Therefore, what follows is best viewed as an attempt to recast important aspects of those literatures into the integrated perspective laid out in this book. I make no attempt to be encyclopedic. Each problem area involves some twists and turns of either the standard consumer problem or the standard producer problem. Usually, with the benefit of hindsight, those twists and turns can be handled using the same mathematical structure of the

Competitive Agents in Certain and Uncertain Markets. Robert G. Chambers, Oxford University Press (2021).

DOI: 10.1093/oso/9780190063016.001.0001

basic producer and consumer models developed in previous chapters, just viewed a bit differently. Basic lessons learned in one context frequently can be applied in others, even though they seemingly differ.

I first take up the economics of quality. This chapter looks at it from two perspectives: (1) the producer side and the simple economics of quality-differentiated production, with emphasis on "the simple"; and (2) the consumer side and the famous household production model that treats pricing items or characteristics that may not be marketed directly. That model, which derives basically from Gorman (1956, 1980) and Lancaster (1966), is the basis for a remarkable variety of hedonic analyses throughout applied economics. Following that discussion, I turn to welfare and valuation in both nonstochastic and stochastic settings.

1 Quality-Differentiated Production

Any of you who have visited a grocery store likely know that hamburger meat is priced and sold according to its leanness, that milk is priced and sold according to its milk-fat content, and that numerous other generically similar grocery products are differentiated by price according to either quality or perceived quality.

The same is true about products before they reach the store. Many fruits, for example, are sorted on the basis of their outward appearance into fruit suitable for sale after further processing (for example, orange juice) and fruits suitable for immediate consumption (for example, oranges). Typically, the fruit intended for immediate sale fetches a higher price than the fruit intended for processing—this despite the fact that in many instances the *mesocarp*[1] of a fruit intended for immediate consumption and that for processing may be indistinguishable. What matters is the appearance of the *epicarp*.[2] Sometimes, the epicarp is commonly consumed (for examples, grapes and apples); other times, it's not (for example, bananas).

Producers, of course, are aware of this, and in many instances, they can take actions that affect the mix of quality produced. So, let's set ourselves a *simple* problem: determine how a rational producer chooses the appropriate quality mix. We look at the problem in two settings: one in which prices are assigned according to quality differences, and one in which producer revenue is determined as the result of a sampling process.

[1] The tasty inside part.
[2] The outside layer or the skin.

This problem definitely involves production, and so deciding on a reasonable representation of the technology seems like a good initial step. From the producer's perspective, different qualities of the same generic product are different products and should be treated as such. So while skim milk and whole milk are both milk, they are not the same, and they are priced differently. Hence, a multiple-output technology is appropriate.

To be concrete while keeping it simple, let's think in terms of a fruit producer producing for two markets: fruit for immediate consumption (y_c) and fruit for processing (y_p). The producer's problem is to choose what mix of (y_c, y_p) to produce and what mix of inputs ($x \in \mathbb{R}^N_+$) to use. Byproducts are a clear possibility here, but for the moment, let's ignore them to keep the analysis as narrowly focused as possible.

We thus write

$$Y(x) = \{(y_c, y_p) : x \in \mathbb{R}^N \text{can produce } (y_c, y_p)\}.$$

My personal next step would be to draw $Y(x)$ and its lower inverse, $V(y)$. Personally, I would draw the former as everything below a "production possibilities frontier,"[3] so that it would be akin to the lower curve in Figure 1.6 (the one concave to the origin), and I would label the axes as y_p and y_c. Do you agree or disagree? If you disagree, draw what you think is a better representation. Once you've done that, also draw its lower inverse, $V(y)$.

At the moment, there is no right or wrong. We don't know enough about the technology to depict it visually. We're trying to build a simple model, so it shouldn't surprise you that there may be departures from reality. But what we're hoping for is something both reasonable and intuitive. I find the picture in Figure 1.6 intuitive, even though I know the true frontier may involve kinks or nonconvex portions, I am happy enough for the moment to skip over them.

Let's first consider the case where the two products can be sorted and, therefore, priced according to their quality. One way to formulate the producer's problem is to solve for a fixed x the revenue-maximization problem

$$R(p_c, p_p, x) = \max_{(y_c, y_p)} \{p_c y_c + p_p y_p : (y_c, y_p) \in Y(x)\}.$$

This is the first stage of the profit-maximization problem. Its solution ensures that the producer gets the maximal revenue from a given x. Visually, one

[3] AKA, transformation function, transformation frontier, transformation curve, production possibilities set, among others.

expects a price line, whose slope is determined by the relative values of $\left(p_c, p_p\right)$ to be tangent to the transformation curve.

Almost inevitably, some computation will be involved in characterizing the optimal solution here. A function representation of $Y(x)$ would prove convenient. The one that I would suggest is $t\left(y_c, y_p, x; g\right)$. If you prefer another, feel free to use it. Regardless, you will need some disposability properties (monotonicity from below in this case), but feel free to use them. With this in hand, you likely would represent the first-order conditions for the revenue-maximization problem as something like:

$$\frac{p_c}{p^{\top}g} \leq \frac{\partial t\left(y_c, y_p, x; g\right)}{\partial y_c}; y_c \geq 0,$$
$$\frac{p_p}{p^{\top}g} \leq \frac{\partial t\left(y_c, y_p, x; g\right)}{\partial y_p}; y_p \geq 0.$$

Subdifferentials or superdifferentials are, of course, more general, but this is my guess as to what you might do. Regardless, the economic intuition is standard. Optimal behavior requires the producer to equate the marginal rate of transformation to the price ratio. And we know immediately from our visual representation that if p_c rises, we expect the producer to produce more of y_c and less of y_p from a fixed bundle of inputs. That's because the point of tangency changes as the slope of the price line changes. The economic intuition is that resources that were formerly devoted to producing y_p now receive a lower return than resources that are devoted to producing y_c. Hence, resources will be diverted to y_c.

Once we've derived $R\left(p_c, p_p, x\right)$, the next step is to choose inputs to solve the profit-maximization problem

$$\pi\left(p_c, p_p, w\right) = \max_x \left\{R\left(p_c, p_p, x\right) - w^{\top}x\right\}.$$

Again, the conditions for an optimum are standard: make sure marginal revenues from varying inputs agree with their factor prices. Moreover, in the smooth case, we know from Chapter 6 that profit-maximizing supplies are given by

$$y_c\left(p_c, p_p, w\right) = \frac{\partial \pi\left(p_c, p_p, w\right)}{\partial p_c} = \frac{\partial R\left(p_c, p_p, x\left(p, w\right)\right)}{\partial p_c}, \text{ and}$$
$$y_p\left(p_c, p_p, w\right) = \frac{\partial \pi\left(p_c, p_p, w\right)}{\partial p_p} = \frac{\partial R\left(p_c, p_p, x\left(p, w\right)\right)}{\partial p_p},$$

respectively, where $x(p, w)$ denotes the profit-maximizing vector of derived demands. These, in turn, can be subjected to the same comparative-static analyses developed in Chapter 6.

When different qualities are priced differently, the analysis is pretty standard once you make the obvious connection with the multiple-output case. All of this is easily extended to an arbitrary number of different qualities of an arbitrary number of different generic products without introducing any fundamentally new concepts. You can also add differing degrees of economic texture to the model to accommodate any specific information about the applied setting that promises to be relevant. I will leave it to you to make the necessary extensions.

In some settings, it's reasonable to assume that similar generic products are sorted and priced according to quality differences. In others, it's not. A pricing process that I witnessed illustrates. The "generic" commodity was a specific type of wine grape produced in a specific region of Italy. The quality dimensions included sugar content (degrees brix) and appearance. The buyer was a wine cooperative.[4]

The process began with the farmer delivering the grapes to the cooperative in a trailer-cart. The trailer-cart was first moved to a scale where it was weighed, and the load was probed in different locations by a device that measured its degrees brix (its sugar content). The load was visually inspected by an individual, and a score was assigned. The producer's payment was based on the load's weight, brix score, and subjective evaluation. No attempt was made to sort the load into quality lots to be priced separately.

Clearly, sorting grapes, either by bunches or by single pieces of fruit, is costly. As a result, the cooperative has evolved a mechanism other than single-fruit pricing to accommodate quality differentials. What I observed involved weighing, sampling, and judgment. My admittedly uninformed guess would be that two different loads of the same quality could receive different valuations if they were packed differently or delivered on different trailer-carts. In fact, I would be hard pressed to believe otherwise. Thus, my inclination is to view the valuation process as stochastic.

Analyzing producer behavior for a stochastic reward scheme requires altering the model. To keep things simple, I stick with the two-quality setting and ignore production uncertainty. The latter is unrealistic in an agricultural setting, but it works as a first cut and lets us focus on the valuation process. As always, you can complicate this at your leisure. I don't know enough to write down an exact model of the valuation process. Nevertheless, it's reasonable

[4] I won't name the cooperative, but I've been assured that its pricing practice is not unique.

to believe the amount of both qualities delivered affect the ultimate payment, if for no other reason than total weight matters. Given my ignorance, I don't want to go too far beyond that. So, as a first cut, I will adapt the stochastic production function (OPNJ) technology discussed in Chapter 8 and model the producer's stochastic revenue, $r \in \mathbb{R}^S$, as a function of the two outputs and a random variable $\varepsilon \in \mathbb{R}^S$, $r\left(y_c, y_p, \varepsilon(s)\right)$, where $\varepsilon(s) \in \mathbb{R}$ is the *sth* realization of ε.

To accommodate the stochastic setting, we use the same decision setting as described in Chapters 8 and 9. There are two periods and S states in period 1. Just as in Chapter 8, the producer's period 0 problem is to allocate a fixed amount of wealth, m, to current period consumption, c^0, and period 1 consumption, $c^1 \in \mathbb{R}^S$. Preferences over $\left(c^0, c^1\right)$ are again represented by $d\left(\hat{c}, c; g\right)$ developed in Chapter 8. For simplicity, assume that the only source of period 1 income is production of y_c and y_p. The budget constraints are

$$
\begin{aligned}
c^0 &= m - w^\top x \\
c_s^1 &= r\left(y_c, y_p, \varepsilon(s)\right) \text{ for all } s \in S,
\end{aligned}
$$

and the technology constraint continues to be characterized by $t\left(y_c, y_p, x; g\right) \leq 0$.

Rational producers act as cost minimizers and thus solve (see Chapter 8 for the formal argument)

$$
\hat{C}(w, r) = \min_{x,y} \left\{ w^\top x : t\left(y_c, y_p, x; g\right) \leq 0, r\left(y_c, y_p, \varepsilon(s)\right) \geq r(s) \text{ for all } s \in S \right\}.
$$

By Bellman's Principle:

$$
\begin{aligned}
\hat{C}(w, r) &= \min_{(y_c, y_p)} \left\{ \min_x \left\{ w^\top x : t\left(y_c, y_p, x; g\right) \leq 0 \right\} : r\left(y_c, y_p, \varepsilon(s)\right) \right. \\
&\qquad \left. \geq r(s) \text{ for all } s \in S \right\} \\
&= \min_{(y_c, y_p)} \left\{ c\left(w, y_c, y_p\right) : r\left(y_c, y_p, \varepsilon(s)\right) \geq r(s) \text{ for all } s \in S \right\},
\end{aligned}
$$

where $r = (r(1), \ldots, r(S))^\top$. $\hat{C}(w, r)$ is the minimal cost of generating the period 1 stochastic revenue $r \in \mathbb{R}^S$, given the technology described by t and the stochastic revenue function, $r\left(y_c, y_p, \varepsilon(s)\right)$. $\hat{C}(w, r)$ is analogous to $C\left(w, P, c^1\right)$. Its properties in w are standard, superlinearity, and Shephard's Lemma.

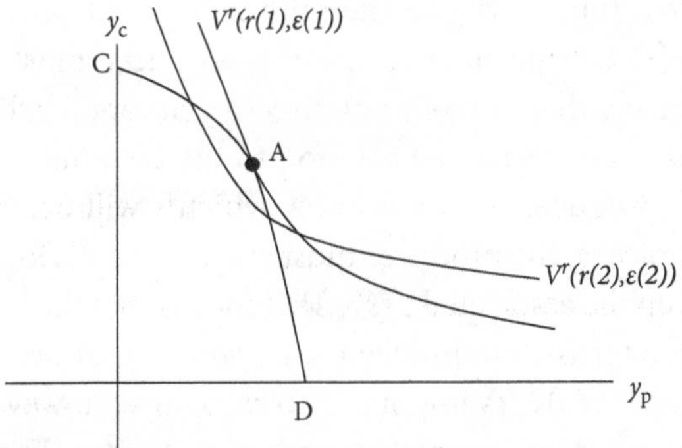

Fig. 10.1 Cost Minimization of Stochastic Return

Figure 10.1 illustrates the derivation of $\hat{C}(w,r)$ for $S = 2$. The curve labeled CD is a level set (isocost curve) for $c\left(w, y_c, y_p\right)$, and the other curves represent the lower boundaries of

$$V^r\left(r(s), \varepsilon(s)\right) = \left\{\left(y_c, y_p\right) : r\left(y_c, y_p, \varepsilon(s)\right) \geq r(s)\right\}$$

for $s = 1, 2$. For visual clarity and familiarity, I have drawn each V^r boundary to mimic traditional isoquants. That structure is not required. The revenue-feasible $\left(y_c, y_p\right)$ combinations are those falling above *both* of these boundaries and are given by

$$V^r\left(r(1), \varepsilon(1)\right) \cap V^r\left(r(2), \varepsilon(2)\right).$$

Therefore, the cost-minimizing solution occurs at A, where CD is tangent to the boundary of the revenue-feasible $\left(y_c, y_p\right)$ set.

I drew Figure 10.1 so that A lies inside $V^r\left(r(2), \varepsilon(2)\right)$ but on the boundary of $V^r\left(r(1), \varepsilon(1)\right)$. Thus, in this instance, $\hat{C}(w,r)$ corresponds to the cheapest way possible of producing $r(1)$ given $\varepsilon(1)$. Because $V^r\left(r(2), \varepsilon(2)\right)$ doesn't present a binding constraint at the optimal solution, arbitrarily small changes in $r(2)$, which leave $V^r\left(r(1), \varepsilon(1)\right)$ unchanged, have no effect on the optimal solution. But arbitrarily small changes in $r(1)$ do. One can, of course, redraw these boundaries so that just the opposite is true.

To get an analytic handle on what's going on, let's define the *ex post* cost functions for each specific state of Nature as

$$\hat{C}^s\left(w, r(s)\right) = \min_{\left(y_c, y_p\right)} \left\{c\left(w, y_c, y_p\right) : r\left(y_c, y_p, \varepsilon(s)\right) \geq r(s)\right\}, \; s = 1, 2, \ldots, S.$$

These *ex post* cost functions give the minimal cost of producing, say, $r(s)$ knowing that $\varepsilon(s)$ will occur. Because the producer must choose (y_c, y_p) before $\varepsilon(s)$ is known, they're likely not directly relevant for the producer. But they can help us characterize the solution to the cost-minimizing problem. In period 0, the producer does not know which s will occur. Regardless of what Nature's choice is, the producer must ensure that period 0 expenditures *cover all* $r(s)$ given the associated $\varepsilon(s)$. That means that the best the producer can possibly hope for is to minimize the *ex post* cost of producing the *most expensive* $r(s)$ *given* $\varepsilon(s)$. It's important to recognize, however, that $r(s)$ *can be be more expensive than, say,* $r(s')$ even if $r(s') > r(s)$. That's because cost minimization is always conditional on $\varepsilon(s)$. Thus, even if $r(s') > r(s)$, if $\varepsilon(s)$ is bad enough it can cause $\hat{C}^s(w, r(s)) > \hat{C}^{s'}(w, r(s'))$.

Figure 10.1 is drawn to illustrate the case where covering the maximal *ex post* cost of producing the most expensive revenue is the best strategy. More generally, however, it's easy to envision cases where that strategy only provides a lower bound so that in general

$$\hat{C}(w, r) \geq \max\{\hat{C}^s(w, r(s)) : s = 1, \ldots, S\}.$$

The inequality is strict if for the most expensive $r(s)$ given $\varepsilon(s)$

$$[\cap_{s \in S} V^r(r(s), \varepsilon(s))] \cap \arg\min\{c(w, y_c, y_p) : r(y_c, y_p, \varepsilon(s)) \geq r(s)\} = \emptyset.$$

Regardless of whether or not the minmax inequality is strict, it's generally the case that arbitrarily small changes in the less expensive $r(s)$ realizations will have no effect on $\hat{C}(w, r)$ so that the typical isoscost curve for this stochastic revenue scheme can be illustrated as in Figure 10.2.

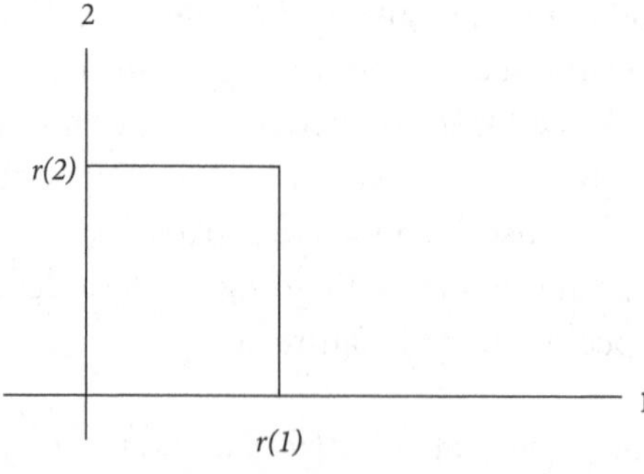

Fig. 10.2 Isocost Stochastic Revenue

Exercise 62. *Redraw Figure 10.1 to illustrate a case where* $\hat{C}(w,r) > \max\{\hat{C}^1(w,r(1)), \hat{C}(w,r)\}$.

Following the discussion and results from Chapter 8, it should be easy for you to show that, given this setup, a rational producer chooses r to ensure that it is zero maximal for

$$\max_{\hat{r}}\{d((m-\hat{C}(w,\hat{r}),\hat{r}),(m-\hat{C}(w,r),r);\tilde{g})\}.$$

And as usual, the associated differential condition for rationality requires that marginal rates of substitution between consumption agree with properly discounted marginal costs, so that

$$\frac{q^1}{q^0} \in \partial_r^- \hat{C}(w,r)$$

for some $q \in \partial d(c,c;\tilde{g})$ characterizes the interior solution. The solution is illustrated visually as a tangency between the level set for $d(c,c;\tilde{g})$ and the rectangular isocost structure in Figure 10.2. If preferences are strictly monotone, the tangency occurs at the kink point, where $\hat{C}^1(w,r(1)) = \hat{C}^2(w,r(2))$ and where the cost structure is *not smoothly* differentiable. The kinked isocost curve is a direct consequence of using a stochastic revenue function to model the producer's reward scheme. You can dispense with it by making different assumptions to remove the kink. If that's done, the same basic result holds, and the kissing tangency in Figure 1.6 illustrates.

Regardless of how you choose to specify $\hat{C}(w,r)$, our developments show that the producer's quality-choice problem, when quality is exactly priced and when it is stochastically priced, mimics our standard setup. There are notational differences, but these are not substantive. In short, the production economics of quality choice is standard production economics. And the economic song remains the same: Equate marginal benefits to marginal costs.

Remark 29. *While the structure that we've used doesn't strike me as particularly problematic, another specification has received some traction in the applied economics literature. That specification requires that the output set, which I now denote as* $Y^{TTQM}(x)$, *satsify*

$$Y^{TTQM}(x) = Y^c(x) \times Y^p(x)$$

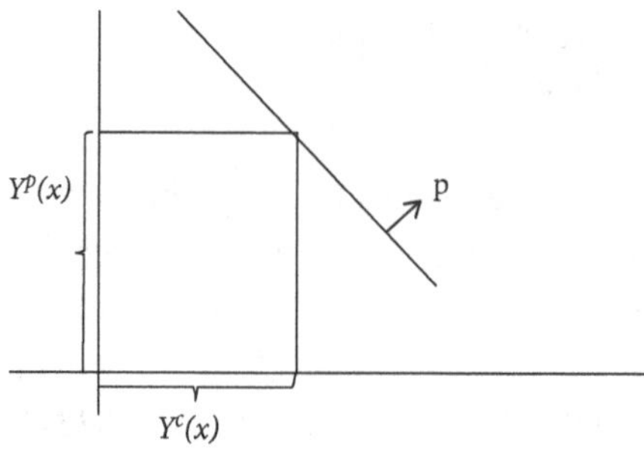

Fig. 10.3 Teeter-Totter $Y(x)$

where $Y^c : \mathbb{R}^N \rightrightarrows \mathbb{R}$ *and* $Y^p : \mathbb{R}^N \rightrightarrows \mathbb{R}$. *This is an output–price nonjoint set (OPNJ; see Chapter 6). Instead of a nice smooth curve as in Figure 1.6, the output set is rectangular with a kink at* $(\max\{Y^c(x)\}, \max\{Y^p(x)\})$, *as in Figure 10.3.*

This restriction on the technology implies at least three things. First, the revenue-maximization problem is more complicated to solve formally. Subdifferential analysis is now required. Fortunately, you are well prepared. Second, the intuitive solution remains the same and is easily visualized. Locate where the price line is just tangent to the output set. Third, y_c *and* y_p *are pure complements.*

Equating the marginal rate of transformation to the price ratio, however, no longer works as a decision rule because the former is no longer well defined. The line segment illustrating the price ratio will just touch the outer frontier of $Y(x)$ *at the kink point. If you change the price ratio, the slope of the line segment changes, but the tangency does not (unless of course you make one price zero while holding the other positive). Changing prices evinces no change in the quantity supplied. Instead, the price line just teeters up or down a bit. For that reason, I always think of this as the Teeter-Totter Quality Model (TTQM).*

Most economists feel uncomfortable with a model that forces price effects to zero—understandably so. If price effects don't matter, economists are not needed to predict and measure them. A basic message of economics is that if you change economic incentives, individuals will respond. This model rules that out.

Problem 100. *Prove that the revenue function for the TTQM assumes the form*

$$R^{TTQM}\left(p_c, p_p, x\right) = p_c \max\{Y^c(x)\} + p_p\{Y^p(x)\}.$$

Exercise 63. *Suppose that*

$$Y(x) = \left\{\left(y_c, y_p\right) : y_c \leq c(x)f(x) \text{ and } y_p \leq g(x)f(x)\right\}.$$

Prove that $Y(x)$ is a special case of the TTQM.

Problem 101. *Provide strong intuitive reasons why revenue-maximizing supply choice should (or should not) be independent of output prices. Whichever position you take, please provide something approaching real-world examples to buttress that position.*

Problem 102. *One might hope that things get simpler if you pursue the cost-function approach to modeling profit maximization. Let's see how that works. The cost function associated with the TTQM is defined by*

$$c^{TTQM}\left(w, y_c, y_p\right) = \min\left\{w^{\top}x : \left(y_c, y_p\right) \in Y^c(x) \times Y^p(x)\right\}.$$

You are to:
(a) Prove that

$$\begin{aligned} c^{TTQM}\left(w, y_c, y_p\right) &= \min\left\{w^{\top}x : x \in V^c\left(y_c\right) \cap V^p\left(y_p\right)\right\} \\ &\geq \max\left\{c^c\left(w, y_c\right), c^p\left(w, y_p\right)\right\}, \end{aligned}$$

where, for example,

$$c^c\left(w, y_c\right) = \min\left\{w^{\top}x : x \in V^c\left(y_c\right)\right\}.$$

(b) Solve

$$\max_{\left(y_c, y_p\right)} \left\{p_c y_c + p_p y_p - c^{TTQM}\left(w, y_c, y_p\right)\right\}$$

using superdifferential methods and characterize formally the conditions required for an interior solution.

Problem 103. *Suppose that the TTQM model applies and that the producer's revenue is stochastic and obeys the $r\left(y_c, y_p, \varepsilon(s)\right)$ setup. Develop a complete model of rational producer behavior in this setting.*

2 Household Production

The previous section looked at the quality problem from the producer's perspective. This section turns things around and looks at them from the consumer's perspective. Specifically, it constructs an economic model of how consumers value different aspects of quality. This section using our setup, introduces you to the "basics" of an especially important valuation model. The basic idea, which traces back at least to Waugh (1928), is simple. Consumers value different characteristics of commodities. For example, fruits or vegetables are typically examined prior to purchase for their color, consistency, and overall appearance. Because consumers value those characteristics, the prices they will pay for a piece of fruit or a vegetable should reflect that valuation. Thus, if characteristics are denoted by c and the price of the vegetable p, it seems plausible that

$$p = f(c).$$

While sound, this reasoning is not very scientific. All that it really says is that some relationship should exist between p and c. Therefore, even though we might cast it in "regression" form, it is not a "causal" relationship. Instead, it is one of association and can't pretend to explain prices. What's needed is an economic model that rationalizes the specification.

The "household production" model is perhaps the most important of these rationalizations. Its essence "marries" producer and consumer theory in a single decision framework. Thus, the formalisms of the household production model parallel those developed in Chapter 8 for an uncertain decision setting. Interpretations and notation differ, but the basic economics are the same. Its variants and extensions are legion. The basic ideas have formed an important component of the applied economist's toolbox for attacking problems as diverse as the valuation of nonpriced environmental amenities, the pricing of real estate, the construction of human-capital indices, as well as the incorporation of new products into existing consumer and producer price and quantity indices. Rather than try to provide a backdrop to all these areas, in the following I present a streamlined version that assumes all commodities are priced according to their characteristics. At the expense of a more detailed notation and more complicated expressions, this simple model is easily generalized to a more general setting. Once again, I'll leave that to your future endeavor, while urging you to consult the ingenious papers of Gorman (1956, 1980) and Lancaster (1966) for more details. Deaton and Muellbauer (1980, Chapter 10) provides a textbook treatment.

As you read the development, it's well to remember that we're again talking in AS IF terms. It's really not necessary that you believe that individuals actually behave in the manner described. Instead, the goal is to develop an analytic perspective that allows economists to gain some insight into how consumers value quality. To proceed, we need two different orders. I present these in terms of two correspondences. The first gives the at-least-as-good set for a set of characteristics, $c \in \mathbb{R}_+^N$, $V : \mathbb{R}_+^N \rightrightarrows \mathbb{R}_+^N$,

$$V(c) = \{c' : c' \text{ is at least as good as } c\}.$$

Feel free to impose as much structure on this as you like. To make our way, minimal assumptions are needed. Visually, however, you probably should keep in mind the upturned bowls in Figure 1.2 and Figure 1.6. The characteristics, c, are to be interpreted in a general sense. For example, the pleasure derived from a candy bar comes from its ingredients and the way in which the ingredients are combined. The ingredients satisfy different sensations: taste, feel,[5] smell, hunger, and so on. So, viewed this way, the candy bar is actually a delivery mechanism for taste, feel, smell, and hunger alleviation. Those sensations can be associated with the $c's$. Similarly, a cup of coffee can be viewed as delivering stimulation and other characteristics. The ultimate idea is that personal valuation is based on the characteristics and not the products.

The next step is to relate these characteristics to marketed goods, which we denote by $y \in \mathbb{R}_+^M$. There is a very small market for "taste of chocolate," but there is a large market for chocolate. The device that the "household production" model uses to connect the marketed goods and the characteristics is a "household technology." We represent that technology by a producible output correspondence, $P : \mathbb{R}_+^M \rightrightarrows \mathbb{R}_+^N$,

$$P(y) = \{c : y \text{ can "produce" } c\},$$

which, of course, has associated with it an input correspondence described by $P's$ lower inverse as

$$P^-(c) = \{y : c \in P(y)\}.$$

The intuitive idea is that marketed products, y, produce a range of different characteristics, c. Again, minimal properties are required to make this work,

[5] If you don't believe "feel" is an important characteristic for a candy bar, consider that M&Ms© were traditionally advertised as the milk chocolate that "melts in your mouth and not in your hand."

continuity from below and monotonicity from below. But the basic idea is captured visually by the downturned bowls facing the origin in Figures 1.4 and 1.6.

It's now clear that Figure 1.6 will be important in representing the equilibrium for the model. To get there, we need to link market activities with the preferences and the technology. To that end, assume that the commodities y are for sale in a competive market at prices p and that the typical consumer has money income that we set to 1. Thus, the decision maker's problem is to allocate money income at market prices p to the purchase of commodities y that deliver characteristics c to the consumer.

In this setting, a rational decision maker will never choose a y and a c for which there exist a y' and a c' such that

$$\begin{aligned} p^{\top}y = p^{\top}y' &= 1, \\ c \in P(y), c' &\in P(y'), \text{ but} \\ c' &> c. \end{aligned} \tag{10.1}$$

(Explain why.) Similarly, rationality ensures that the decision maker never chooses y and c for which there exists a y' and c' such that

$$\begin{aligned} c' &\geq c, \\ c \in P(y), c' &\in P(y'), \text{ but} \\ p^{\top}y' &< p^{\top}y. \end{aligned} \tag{10.2}$$

(Explain why.) I focus attention on (10.2) and leave developing a discussion of (10.1) to you.

Problem 104. *Solve the problem posed in (10.1).*

Decision makers behaving in accordance with (10.2) necessarily solve

$$m(p,c) \equiv \min\{p^{\top}y : c \in P(y)\} = \min\{p^{\top}y : y \in P^{-}(c)\}. \tag{10.3}$$

The *portfolio* of market goods is chosen to minimize the cost of c that will be "produced" via the household technology. If the decision makers acted differently, then under mild monotonicity restrictions upon $V(c)$, they could be made better off by rearranging their market choices, thus violating rationality.

You should recognize several points. First, after suitable choice of a numeraire bundle of market goods and an appropriate renormalization of market prices with respect to that numeraire (to conserve notation, set $p^{\top}g = 1$), Problem (10.3) can be recast as

$$m(p, c) = \min_{y} \{p^{\top}y - d^{P^{-}}(y, c; g)\},$$

where $d^{P^{-}}$ is the distance function derived from P^{-}. The necessary and sufficient condition for an interior solution is the familiar Dubovitsky–Milyutin overlapping condition

$$p \in \partial_y d^{P^{-}}(y, c; g), \tag{10.4}$$

and under appropriate regularity conditions its dual reflection is

$$y \in \partial_p m(p, c). \tag{10.5}$$

In words, expression (10.4), which is a version of Wold's Identity, tells us that market-price ratios are equated to marginal rates of technical substitution for y, and expression (10.5) is a version of Shephard's Lemma.

Second, the set of c that can be "manufactured" via purchases of y in the market, given a budget of 1, is given by the budget correspondence

$$B^{P^{-}}(p) = \{c : m(p, c) \leq 1\}.$$

Unlike $B(p)$ developed in Chapter 5, $B^{P^{-}}(p)$ is not a closed half-space. But it should not involve too much drama to convince you that if $P(y)$ is a convex set, $B^{P^{-}}(p)$ is a convex set that satisfies *MB*. Imposing those properties brings us to a $B^{P^{-}}(p)$ that can be illustrated by the downturned (concave to the origin) bowl in Figure 1.6, after properly labeling the axes. Thus, instead of operating in the world of linear budget constraints illustrated by Figure 1.2, we now operate with a nonlinear budget constraint.

Associated with $B^{P^{-}}(p)$ is a generalization of the *budget-shortage functions* developed in Chapters 5 and 9 (see, in particular, Problem 93):

$$b^{P^{-}}(c, p; g) = \min\{\beta : m(p, c - \beta g) \leq 1\}$$

Having assembled all the tools, we can state:

Proposition 7. *$c \in B^{P^-}(p)$ is rational if and only if it is zero minimal for*

$$\min_{\hat{c}} \left\{ b^{P^-}(\hat{c}, p; g) - d^V(\hat{c}, c; g) \right\},$$

where $d^V(\hat{c}, c; g) \equiv \max\{\beta : \hat{c} - \beta g \in V(c)\}$.

Problem 105. *Develop the properties of $d^V(\hat{c}, c; g)$ and prove Proposition 7.*

Happy marriages of preferences and the technology occur where a $V(c)$ just "kisses" $B^{P^-}(p)$. Figure 1.6 illustrates. In differential terms we have the standard overlapping equilibrium condition for an interior solution

$$\partial^- b^{P^-}(c, p; g) \cap \partial d^V(c, c; g) \neq \emptyset. \tag{10.6}$$

When b^{P-} and d^V are suitably smooth, these equilibrium conditions can be solved to obtain a system of reduced-form behavioral relations of the generic form

$$c = F(p),$$

or

$$p = f(c),$$

where f is the inverse mapping of F. Either way, prices paid for marketed goods, p, are related to the vectors of characteristics, c, so we've achieved our goal of developing a behavioral model relating p and c. Because market prices for the commodities, p, are the primitives (givens) in this problem and c the choice variables, the quantity-dependent form is the more traditional form. But the hedonic literature more typically uses the price-dependent form.

How one interprets these expressions is subtle and a matter of perspective. Because they were derived from V and P^-, they manifest characteristics of both the preference correspondence, $V(c)$, and the "technology," $P^-(c)$, that converts marketed goods into those characteristics. Thinking in terms of the former, one is tempted to think of $f(c)$ as manifesting the individual's *willingness-to-pay* for the characteristics. Thinking in terms of the latter, a more appropriate interpretation, perhaps, is in terms of the individual's *marginal cost* of creating the characteristic via the "technology." The ultimate solution necessarily convolutes the two.

To illustrate one way to rationalize an interpretation of these relations, assume that

$$d^{V}(c', c; g) = q^{\top}(c' - c),$$

for fixed $q \in \mathbb{R}^{N}_{++}$. (Use this form to induce the corresponding $V(c)$ on your own.) Using (10.6), we find that smooth equilibrium now requires

$$q = \nabla_{c} b^{P-}(c, p; g).$$

I'll leave econometric issues of how you might go about estimating such an expression to you. But if you can estimate this expression for a suitable parametrization of $b^{P-}(c, p; g)$, the resulting estimates can be used to make inferences about

$$\nabla_{cp} b^{P-}(c, p; g)\, \nabla p = -\nabla_{cc} b^{P-}(c, p; g)\, \nabla c,$$

which characterizes how equilibrium p responds to changes in c (assuming that the implicit function theorem is satisfied). Because q is determined parametrically in this instance, the information gleaned from those marginal price changes reflects the b^{P-}, which is derived from the technology, and not d^{V}. It's important to emphasize, however, that this b^{P-} is not typically associated with a physical technology. Rather, it's a conceptualization of part of the consumer's subjective valuation process in terms intuitively familiar to economists. So while we use the term "technology," we mean a component of the individual's preference structure.[6]

I developed this rationalization by making a reductionist assumption on $V(c)$ to which many practitioners would object. More traditional thinking takes the opposite view. It accomplishes a parallel version of identification via a reductionist assumption (identification by assumption) on $P(y)$. Working through the following problem will introduce you to the basics.

Problem 106. *It takes some effort to set this problem up. So please read through it carefully before you start. The actual question is only posed at the very end.*

Gorman (1980) and Lancaster (1966) both treated an activity-analysis formulation of the household that is commonly referred to as the linear in

[6] I have had it argued to me that $P(y)$ is physically meaningful and thus a true technology. So you're reading my opinion here, but as you may guess, I've not found those arguments very convincing except in the most stylized instances.

characteristics model (LCM). (Note its formal similarity to our financial market model in the portfolio problem.) The basic idea is that one unit of every market good has embedded in it a fixed amount of each characteristic. For the mth market item, we will call the amount of the kth characteristic embedded in it $a_{km} \geq 0$. Thus, if an individual purchases y_1 units of good 1 and y_2 units of good 2, his or her "production" of the kth characteristic would be $y_1 a_{k1} + y_2 a_{k2}$, the amount embedded in both. More generally, the relationship between purchased goods and characteristics is written

$$Ay \geq c,$$

where A is a $K \times M$ whose typical element is a_{km}.

The minimal cost of assembling a portfolio of characteristics c is thus given by the linear program

$$m(p, c) = \min_y \{p^\top y : Ay \geq c\}.$$

Clearly, $m(p, c)$ is a support function for

$$\{y : Ay \geq c\}$$

that describes the portfolios of the marketed goods that will yield the vector of characteristics, c. Because this set is formed as the intersection of closed half-spaces, it's convex.

When $K = M$ and A is of full rank, the solution to the minimization problem is

$$m(p, c) = p^\top A^{-1} c.$$

We can then interpret

$$B^{p^\top}(p, M) = \{c : p^\top A^{-1} c \leq 1\}$$

as a budget correspondence for the "prices" $p^\top A^{-1}$ of the characteristics. These "prices" are parametric to the problem and correspond to the marginal costs of the characteristics. In this version of the LCM, there is an exact correspondence between the theory of consumer demand developed in Chapter 2, where commodity prices are now replaced by the vector of characteristic price $p^\top A^{-1}$.

Now for the actual problem. For the case, $K \neq M$, develop a complete theory of the determination of optimal c for the LCM. (Hint: Recall our discussion of the portfolio problem in Chapter 8.)

Exercise 64. *For the case where $K = M$ with A full rank, develop the consequences of Afriat's Theorem for the LCM model.*

3 Welfare, Real Benefits, and Valuation

The notion of constructing an internally consistent social-welfare function was long ago deflated by Arrow's famous *Impossibility Theorem.* We won't pause to discuss that result here, but needless to say it forced many to realize that social decision making is, at best, an arbitrary, flawed, and imprecise process. Still, social decisions need to be based on some criteria. One practical concept that economists have frequently relied on is the *Kaldor Compensation Principle* (Kaldor 1939). Roughly put, it requires adoption of a project or a social change if the gainers from the change can *potentially* compensate the losers from the change.

There are catches. First is the potential part. That means that compensation does not have to be paid, only that it *could be* paid. The Kaldor Principle also counts individuals equally regardless of their place in society. So, if a proposed tax change disproportionately benefits the richest in society, the Kaldor Principle would suggest adoption if their gains allowed them to cover everyone else's losses. My current job isn't to argue either in favor or against such a weighting scheme; that's best left to social-choice theorists. But it's essential to keep such matters in mind when assessing welfare evaluations grounded in a comparison of *total benefits* to *total costs (benefit-cost or cost-benefit analysis).*

Another catch, which is the subject matter of what follows, is that the Kaldor Principle presumes gains and losses can be meaningfully measured and compared. Because even economists who believe in complete preference structures do not believe in interpersonal comparisons of utility, this is problematic for consumers because comparing gains and losses requires agreement on a common cardinal yardstick. The knee-jerk reaction of economists was to use money income as that yardstick, and that led directly to calculating consumer and producer surplus. But, as we saw in Chapter 7, it's well known that consumer surplus is a problematic welfare measure. Hicks (1946, p. 38), for example, opined: "The doctrine of Consumer's Surplus has caused more trouble and controversy than anything else in book iii of Marshall's *Principles*."

Samuelson (1947, p. 197) was outright dismissive: "My ideal *Principles* would not include consumer's surplus...except possibly in a footnote." Such criticisms led economists to replace consumer surplus with the Hicksian notions of *compensating variation* (*CV*) and *equivalent variation* (*EV*) in applied welfare analyses.

In the following, I introduce, in sketch form, the basic principles of CV/EV analysis. The various intricacies of the CV/EV approach to welfare analysis are readily available in text form (see, for example, Deaton and Muellbauer 1980; Kreps 2013; Freeman, Herriges, and Kling 2014; Phaneuf and Requate 2017) to which I feel confident in referring interested readers. So after that introductory sketch, attention focuses on an alternate approach, which I attribute to Allais (1943, 1989) and Luenberger (1996), that performs welfare computations in real and not money-income terms.

Before starting the discussion, I offer a caution. Applied welfare analysis is particularly calculus-ridden, almost obsessively so. Besides limiting its generality, that makes it difficult for the uninitiated to penetrate the analysis, all the more so because the jargon is frequently cast in differential terms. It's easy to get lost among the myriad ratios of elasticities and partial derivatives. It's even easier to lose sight of the underlying economics. With the exception of a quick discussion on the welfare implications of integrating under an Antonelli price-dependent demand, I follow a different approach that relies stylistically on the index-number literature. Hopefully, the argument, which is more general, is also revealing.

3.0.1 Real Benefit Measures

CV and EV are both dollar-denominated measures. Surprisingly, therefore, welfare measurement is done in *nominal* and not *real* terms. The fundamental idea is to calculate an individual's indirect utility function and then use it to determine income adjustments required to leave the individual indifferent between the situations being compared. The most basic treatment is dedicated to developing a money measure of welfare change caused by price changes, and so we start there. The Hicksian *compensating variation* for moving from prices and income (p^0, m^0), framed as the *status quo,* to prices and income (p^1, m^0), framed as the *alternative,* is

$$I(p^0, m^0) = I(p^1, m^0 - CV),$$

while the *equivalent variation* is

$$I(p^0, m^0 + EV) = I(p^1, m^0),$$

where $I(p,m)$, with an abuse of notation, denotes the indirect utility function for (p,m).

The difference between CV and EV lies in where the income adjustment is calculated. The compensating variation calculates it as the dollar amount required to bring the individual's welfare at prices p^1 to the welfare obtained at p^0. The equivalent variation calculates it the other way around as the money income needed to bring the individual facing p^0 to the welfare level for p^1. Thus, both CV and EV are distance functions associated with $I(p,m)$ whose common numeraire is m. By the way, the distinction drawn here between the *status quo* and the *alternative* reflects extramathematical reasoning attached to the mathematical manipulations. Nothing of substance changes by switching the roles of (p^0, m^0) and (p^1, m^0), which of course switches the definitions.

Using (5.3), as expressed in nominal prices and income, reveals the equivalent definitions of CV and EV as

$$CV = E^H(p^1, u^0) - E^H(p^0, u^0),$$

and

$$EV = E^H(p^1, u^1) - E^H(p^0, u^1),$$

where $u^0 = I(p^0, m^0)$ and $u^1 = I(p^1, m^0)$. The positive homogeneity of $E^H(p,u)$ in p ensures that both CV and EV are also positively homogeneous in p, reflecting their nominal nature. For differentially small price changes, the concavity of $E^H(p,u)$ ensures that CV and EV are representable as directional derivatives

$$\begin{aligned} CV &= E^{H\prime}(p^0, u^0; p^1 - p^0) \\ &= \inf\left\{(p^1 - p^0)^\top x : x \in \partial E^H(p^0, u^0)\right\}, \end{aligned}$$

and

$$\begin{aligned} EV &= -E^{H\prime}(p^1, u^1; p^0 - p^1) \\ &= -\inf\left\{(p^0 - p^1)^\top x : x \in \partial E^H(p^1, u^1)\right\}, \end{aligned}$$

so that differential welfare effects are captured by Hicksian compensated demands evaluated at either (p^0, u^0) or (p^1, u^1).

Instead of relying on nominal welfare measures, Allais (1989) pursues welfare measurement in terms of the *disposable surplus* (*surplus distribuable)* of a numeraire commodity, defined as the change in the quantity of the numeraire required to leave utility unchanged after a change occurs.[7] Luenberger (1996) extended Allais's analysis by permitting welfare measurement in terms of a numeraire bundle of commodities (our $g \in \mathbb{R}^N$) and defining real analogues to the nominal CV and EV.

Luenberger's (1996) analysis centers on the special case of $d(x, y; g)$ derived under CO. Define the *benefit function* by

$$B(x, u) \equiv \sup\{\beta : u(x - \beta g; g) \geq u\},$$

where following the notation developed in Chapter 5, $u(x; g) \equiv -t(0, x; g)$. It is obvious, for example, that $d(x, y; g) = B(x, u(y; g))$. An immediate consequence of this identity is that $B(x, u)$ inherits the properties of $d(x, y; g)$ in x. Thus, it satisfies the Translation Property, Indication, and is concave in x when $\succeq(y)$ satisfies $CONA$. Under monotonicity of $\succeq(y)$, it's also nonincreasing in u, a fact that I leave to you to demonstrate.

Taking y as the *status quo* and x as the *alternative*, Luenberger (1996) defines the *compensating benefit* (CB) associated with x and y as the number of units of a numeraire bundle of quantities, g, required to make x indifferent to $u(y; g)$

$$x - CBg \sim (y).$$

The *equivalent benefit* (EB) is defined as the number of units of the numeraire bundle required to bring an individual at the *status quo* to $u(x; g)$:

$$x \sim (y + EBg).$$

Thus,

$$CB(x, y; g) = B(x, u(y; g)),$$

and

$$EB(x, y; g) = -B(y, u(x; g)).$$

[7] *Le surplus distribuable relatif à un bien (U) et à une modification réalisable de l'économie laissant tous les indices de préférences inchangés est défini comme la quantité de ce bien qui peut être libérée à partir de cette transformation* (Allais 1989).

A trivial consequence of preceding developments is that $x \succeq (y)$ if and only if $CB(x, y; g)$ and $EB(x, y; g)$ are both positive. Moreover, because $B(z, u(z, g)) = 0$, for $z \in \mathbb{R}^N$, we can define both in forms analogous to CV and EV.

$$CB(x, y; g) = B(x, u(y; g)) - B(y, u(y; g)),$$

and

$$EB(x, y; g) = B(x, u(x; g)) - B(y, u(x; g)).$$

For differentially small quantity changes, taking $B(x, u)$ to be concave ensures that

$$\begin{aligned} CB &= B'(y, u(y; g); x - y) \\ &= \inf\{p^\top (x - y) : p \in \partial B(y, u(y; g))\}, \end{aligned}$$

and

$$\begin{aligned} EB &= -B'(x, u(x; g); y - x) \\ &= -\inf\{p^\top (y - x) : p \in \partial B(x, u(x; g))\}, \end{aligned}$$

so that differential welfare effects are captured by Antonelli price-dependent demands. (Throughout this discussion, I normalize units so that $p^\top g = 1$ to avoid the necessity of writing all price-dependent demands as $\frac{p}{p^\top g}$.) Thus, where the CV/EV approach measures welfare differentially in terms of $\partial E^H(p, u)$, the CB/EB approach evaluates welfare differentially in terms of $\partial B(x, u)$. Simply put, the essential economic behavior analyzed is the same; all that differs is whether welfare differences are measured along the price (money) axis or the quantity axis for a standard demand curve.

As Figure 10.4 illustrates, when $x \neq y + \alpha g$ for some $\alpha \in \mathbb{R}$, CB and EB generally differ. The same is true for the CV and EV measures. In fact, evidence from studies on stated preferences and behavioral experiments suggest that differences between CV and EV are to be expected and can be quite large. (We return to this issue below.) Figure 10.4 clarifies what's required for CB and EB to coincide. The distance between $\bar{V}(y)$ and x and the distance between $\bar{V}(x)$ and y need to be the same. This observation immediately leads us to claim (the proof is left to you):

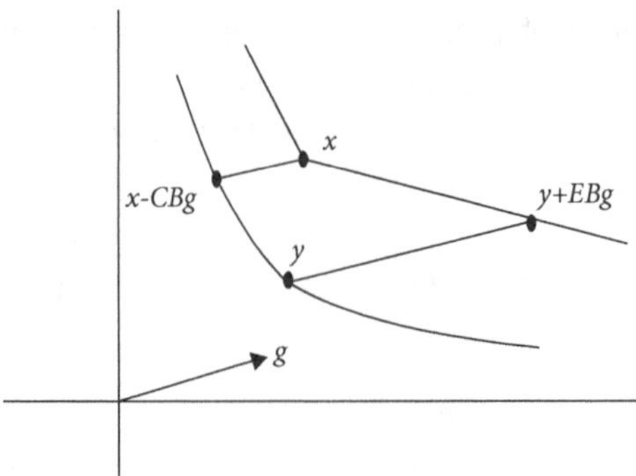

Fig. 10.4 Compensating and Equivalent Benefits

Proposition 8. *Assume $\succeq(y)$ satisfies M and C, then (a) and (b) are equivalent:*
(a) For all (x, y), $x \succeq (y) \Leftrightarrow x + \alpha g \succeq (y + \alpha g)$, $\alpha \in \mathbb{R}$.
(b)

$$CB(x, y; g) = EB(x, y; g)$$

for all $x, y \in \mathbb{R}^N$.

The structural restriction in Proposition 8 requires that the preference ordering between x and y be independent of translations of both in the direction of g. It weakens the independence axiom from Chapter 5 in two ways. The new axiom does not require the preference ordering of x and y to be independent of radial contractions or expansions of x and y, and where the independence axiom requires invariance to translations in all directions, it only requires invariance to translation of the numeraire. Adapting the terminology of Gilboa and Schmeidler (1989), we refer to it as *g-independence* (*GI*). Chambers and Färe (1998) and Chambers (2002) refer to *GI* as translation homotheticity in the direction of g. See also Chapter 6's discussion of translation homotheticity (especially Exercise 40) and Chapter 8's discussion of constant absolute uncertainty aversion for parallel concepts.

Setting $\alpha = -1$ in the definition of *GI* gives

$$x \succeq (y) \Leftrightarrow x - g \succeq (y - g).$$

Under *GI*, preference judgments made at (x, y) (relative to the traditional origin of 0) are identical to preference judgments made with respect to a new origin of g, $(x - g, y - g)$. The potential choices for g are myriad, literally infinite. That implies great flexibility in deploying *GI* in applied settings. In particular, because *g* only needs to contain one nonzero element, *GI* may only require independence to a relatively slight renormalization of the commodity space.

Geometrically, *GI* requires that all rays parallel to the numeraire, *g*, cut indifference curves at points of equal slope, leaving marginal rates of substitution between goods invariant to translations in the direction of *g* (again see Chapter 6). That, in turn, has the behavioral implication that income expansion paths are affine in the direction of *g*. As with the Gorman polar form, to which it is related, income effects are "nice."

3.1 From Observed Behavior to Practical Measures

CB and *EB* can be elicited experimentally or by asking individuals to make direct comparisons between alternatives (stated preference studies). Frequently, however, welfare judgments must rely on "observed" behavior.[8] When that information comes in the form of "observed" market demand and prices, the practical problem is to relate those "observed" phenomena to our definitions that are cast in terms of $B(x, u)$, which we emphasize depends on u that is not "observed." Analogous problems confront *CV* and *EV* analysis. This is natural. As our duality results show, in a competitive setting and under appropriate regularity conditions, nothing of substance changes by working in primal rather than dual space. The only difference is one of perspective. The hope is that, just as dual methods have enlightened traditional analysis rooted in primal terms, analyzing welfare in real (primal) terms may bring insights overlooked in nominal (dual) terms.

Before proceeding, let me explain why I used quotes on "observed." Normally, data are available for prices, quantities, and expenditure. But one does not "observe" quantity-dependent or price-dependent demand functions. Typically, statistical analysis is needed to obtain approximations to these functions. This isn't always easy and usually is far from exact. I am putting those problems to the side in what follows and assuming that "observed" means that one has obtained appropriate representations of the underlying demand functions. This lets us focus on the underlying analytic issues without getting bogged down on fundamentally statistical issues.

[8] In the welfare literature, this is often referred to as a *revealed-preference* approach. While related intuitively, this is a slightly different definition of revealed preference than the one used in Chapter 5. To avoid conflating the two, I use the "observed" terminology in the following.

As I said, applied welfare analysis typically relies heavily on calculus arguments. Let me first illustrate why this makes sense in the smooth case. The *CB* criterion judges marginal welfare effects via $\partial B(x, u(y; g))$, while the *EB* criterion uses $\partial B(y, u(x; g))$. By Wold's Identity (5.1), these superdifferentials represent utility-compensated (Antonelli) price-dependent demand correspondences (after normalizing so that $p^{\top} g = 1$). For small changes in y, these welfare effects are captured by the uncompensated price-dependent demands[9] because rational y satisfies

$$\begin{aligned} p^*(y) &= p(y, y) \\ &= \partial B(y, u(y; g)) \\ &= \nabla_x B(y, u(y; g)) \end{aligned}$$

for B smooth. But in most practical cases, the problem is not to measure marginal changes but discrete changes. That requires integrating the marginal changes holding u at $u(y; g)$, whence

$$\begin{aligned} \int_y^x p(v, y)\, dv &= \int_y^x \nabla_x B(v, u(y; g))\, dv \\ &= B(x, u(y; g)) - B(y, u(y; g)) \\ &= CB. \end{aligned}$$

Because the integrand, $\nabla_x B(v, u(y; g))$, is a gradient function in v, the value of the integral is independent of the path of integration between y and x. The *CB*, thus, corresponds to the area under the Antonelli demand curve between x and y. (The analogous *CV* measure is obtained by integrating the Hicksian demands between the corresponding prices.)

The practical problem is that we observe the uncompensated price-dependent demand, $p^*(v)$, and not $p(v, y)$. Integrating $p^*(v)$ over the same interval gives:

$$\begin{aligned} \int_y^x p^*(v)\, dv &= \int_y^x p(v, v)\, dv \\ &= \int_y^x \nabla_x B(v, u(v; g))\, dv \\ &\neq B(x, u(y; g)) - B(y, u(y; g)). \end{aligned}$$

[9] Luenberger (1996) refers to the analogue of $p(x, y)$ as an adjusted price-dependent demand.

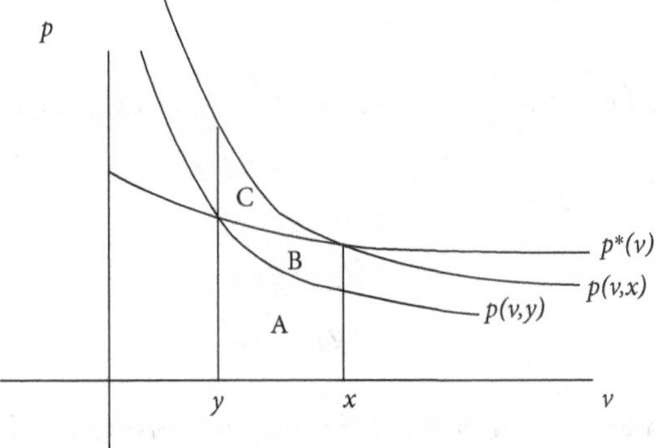

Fig. 10.5 Compensating and Equivalent Benefit

Figure 10.5 illustrates. The area A measures CB, the area $A + B$ measures $\int_y^x p^*(v)\,dv$, and the area $A + B + C$ measures EB. (Although the expressions and areas considered differ, the essential problem here is identical to that encountered in CV or EV analysis.) The area under an observed price-dependent demand curve does not correspond to either of our purported benefit measures. There are two technical problems. One involves the real-income effect incorporated in p^*. The second is that, because $p^*(v)$ is not a gradient in the variable of integration, the path of integration between y and x matters.

A large literature treats "how bad" an approximation consumer surplus is to CV or EV. Different devices have been developed for either directly measuring or approximating CV or EV using consumer surplus. Key references are Willig (1976), Hausman (1981), Randall and Stoll (1980), and Vartia (1983). Similar methods are available for approximating CB and EB using observed price-dependent demands (Randall and Stoll 1980).[10] Rather than pursue such matters, I want to focus on other lessons to be learned from viewing welfare measurement in real rather than nominal terms.

Figure 10.5 suggests that as EB approaches CB, the difference between CB and the area under $p^*(v)$ disappears. It's a good guess, therefore, that when EB and CB always correspond, the difference between CB and the area under $p^*(v)$ will also disappear. We now show that this is true.

[10] Randall and Stoll (1980) conduct quantity-based welfare measurement by substituting price-dependent demands for p in $I(p, m)$. Under regularity conditions that ensure that both $B(x, u)$ and $E^H(p, u)$ are arbitrarily smooth, their approach yields results parallel to ours. These regularity conditions, however, are quite restrictive and rule out (among others) either perfect complements or perfect substitutes.

Under *GI*,

$$\begin{aligned} u(x+\alpha g; g) &= -\sup\{\beta : -\beta g \geq (x+\alpha g)\} \\ &= -\sup\{\beta : -\alpha g - \beta g \geq (x)\} \\ &= -d(-\alpha g, x; g) \\ &= -d(0, x; g) + \alpha \\ &= u(x; g) + \alpha, \end{aligned}$$

where the fourth equality follows by Translation Property. Hence,

$$\begin{aligned} B(x,u) &= \sup\{\beta : u(x-\beta g; g) \geq u\} \\ &= \sup\{\beta : u(x-(\beta+u)g; g) \geq 0\} \\ &= \sup\{\beta + u : u(x-(\beta+u)g; g) \geq 0\} - u \\ &= B(x,0) - u \end{aligned}$$

(compare with Exercise 40 in Chapter 6). Thus, under *GI*

$$B(x, u(y; g)) = B(x, 0) - u(y; g)$$

so that

$$p^*(y) = \nabla_x B(y, u(y; g)) = \nabla_x B(y, 0),$$

whence

$$\begin{aligned} \int_y^x p^*(v)\, dv &= \int_y^x \nabla_x B(x, 0)\, dv \\ &= B(x,0) - B(y,0) \\ &= B(x, u(y,g); g) - B(y, u(y,g); g). \end{aligned}$$

The final equality establishes that the area underneath the uncompensated price-dependent demand, which is observable, equals the area underneath the Antonelli demand. Thus, *GI* ensures that *CB* (and *EB* by a symmetric argument) can be obtained by integrating $p^*(v)$. The economic reason that *GI* resolves the issues associated with $p^*(v)$ is that it ensures that real-income effects, when measured in units of an appropriately chosen numeraire, always equal one.[11]

[11] Note that this is also true in the quantity-dependent structure, so that *GI* preferences generate uncompensated demands that can be integrated to obtain valid welfare measures (Samuelson 1947). Also see Problem 107 that follows.

Let's look at this from another perspective. The practical problem is that welfare measures are defined in terms of $B(x, u)$, which is not observable because u is not observable. In other words, to do the calculations, you need to know $u(y, g)$. But if you do know $u(y; g)$, there's no need to use observed demands to assess welfare effects. The trick is to measure welfare effects while observing $p^*(v)$ but not u.

An obvious place to look, therefore, is for instances where

$$B(x, u(y, g)) - B(y, u(y, g))$$

is independent of $u(y; g)$. Setting $u(y; g) = u$ that requires the compensating benefit to be independent of u, whence

$$B(x, u) - B(y, u) = \varphi(x, y) \tag{10.7}$$

where the Translation Property of B requires that $\varphi(x + \alpha g, y + \alpha g) = 0$. Expression (10.7) is a *functional equation. Functional equations* are equations in which some of the unknowns are equations. So, instead of using them to solve for variables, they're *used to solve for equations.* Perhaps the most famous examples are the three *Cauchy equations* that characterize linear, exponential, and logarithmic functions.[12] Here, the equation we wish to solve for is $B(z, u)$. Setting $y = 0$ establishes that

$$B(x, u) = \varphi(x, 0) + B(0, u).$$

We already know, however, that in our numeraire $B(0, u) = -u$. Finally, setting $u = 0$ gives

$$B(x, 0) = \varphi(x, 0),$$

[12] Other special cases of functional equations with which you should now be familiar include the conjugate function

$$f^*(q) = \inf\{q^\top x - f(x)\},$$

where the unknown is f^*, and its inverse

$$f(x) = \inf\{q^\top x - f^*(q)\},$$

where the unknown is f. Bellman's Principle is yet another instance.

These basic techniques provide the fundamental mathematics used in the study of functional structure, including separability analysis, basic duality theory, and aggregation analysis. Each of these topics is central to applied welfare analysis. The ultimate go-to source on functional equations is Aczél (1966), which details the history of this field of mathematics and an encyclopedic coverage of the basic results.

so that the functional equation is satisfied only if

$$B(x,u) = B(x,0) - u.$$

Sufficiency follows trivially.

We conclude, therefore, that a real-based approach to compensatory or equivalent payments closely parallels *CV* and *EV* analysis. This is not surprising. We've simply recycled Theorem 6, assuming that $B(x, u(y;g)) = d(x,y;g)$ is concave in x so that *CONA* applies.[13] We have also identified a class of preferences, *GI*, for which the real welfare measures can be obtained, without error, from uncompensated price-dependent demand structures. It won't be explored here, but Chambers (2001) has shown that *GI* also ensures that Bennet (1920) cost-of-living indexes computed using appropriately normalized prices provide exact and superlative measures of $CB(x,y;g)$. Parallel results apply for *EB*. Real welfare evaluation is not only possible, but easy, given *GI*.

That said, catches exist. For *GI* to be useful, you need to know the g for which it applies, and that same g must be used to construct B. Moreover, *a priori,* I can think of no reason why preferences should satisfy *GI*. Having said that, however, I can think of no reason that general preferences should satisfy any particular functional restriction. But existing empirical practice requires specific functional forms, and they involve restrictions that, albeit familiar, aren't particularly believable. The same is often true conceptually. (If you don't believe me, don't resort to a Cobb–Douglas example the next time you work out an unfamiliar problem.) *GI* carries the advantage that it is clearly articulated, conceptually meaningful, and empirically testable.

Problem 107. *Under GI*

$$\begin{aligned} E^H(p,u) &= \min_x \{p^\top x : B(x,0) \geq u\} \\ &= \min_x \{p^\top x : B(x - ug, 0) \geq 0\} \\ &= E^H(p,0) - up^\top g, \end{aligned}$$

You are to:

(a) Develop the indirect utility function associated with the GI preference structure.

[13] Again, with no true loss of generality, because if the E^H required to compute *CV* and *EV* exists, a concave d conjugate to it must also exist.

(b) Derive explicit forms for both CV and EV in this setting.
(c) Convert both CV and EV from nominal to real terms by taking $p^{\top}g = 1$ and compare the results.

Remark 30. *A natural conjecture is that if CV and EV were always identical, one could infer welfare measures from consumer surplus in a similar manner. Unfortunately, this is not possible. (Here I would suggest that you revisit your answer to Problem 43 in Chapter 5.) The problem lies in the numeraire. Another simple functional equation argument reveals why. For CV and EV to always coincide*

$$E^H(p^1,u^0) - E^H(p^0,u^0) = E^H(p^1,u^1) - E^H(p^0,u^1),$$

for all (p^1,p^0,u^1,u^0). But this requires

$$E^H(p^1,u^0) - E^H(p^1,u^1) = E^H(p^0,u^0) - E^H(p^0,u^1)$$

Define $m(u^1,u^0,p) \equiv E^H(p,u^1) - E^H(p,u^0)$, and note that it is positively homogeneous in p. Thus, we need

$$m(u^1,u^0,p^1) = m(u^1,u^0,p^0),$$

for all (p^1,p^0,u^1,u^0). Suppose that this held for one such combination, (p^1,p^0). Then it would also have to hold for all $(p^1,\mu p^0)$ with $\mu > 0$, whence

$$\begin{aligned} m(u^1,u^0,p^1) &= m(u^1,u^0,\mu p^0) \\ &= \mu m(u^1,u^0,p^0) \quad \mu > 0. \end{aligned}$$

where the second equality follows by the positive homogeneity of m. This can only happen if $m(u^1,u^0,p^0) = 0$ or ∞. As is apparent, using a nominal numeraire handicaps rather than promotes an empirical resolution. Willig's (1976) approach to bounding the "error" associated with using consumer surplus exploits the necessary discrepancy between CV and EV to develop the resulting bounds.

Here a distinction drawn in the "index number" and the "indicator" literatures helps clarify matters. When working with scalars, the ratio, $\frac{p^1}{p^0}$, and the difference, $p^1 - p^0$, convey the same information because $\geq$ satisfies complete ordering (CO) for $\mathbb{R}_+$. That's not true for $\mathbb{R}^N_+$. Two distinct approaches have evolved to making comparisons over changes not well-ordered by $\geq$. Perhaps the most familiar is the index-number approach which relies on *ratios of real valued functions of* p^1 *divided by real-valued functions of* p^0. *The Laspeyres true cost of living index, defined as* $E^H(p^1, u^o)/E^H(p^o, u^o)$, *and the Paasche true cost of living index,* $E^H(p^1, u^1)/E^H(p^o, u^1)$, *illustrate. Popularly interpreted as price indexes, being ratio versions of the CV and EV, they are also welfare indexes. The indicator literature addresses the same problem by relying on differences between a real-valued function of* p^1 *and a real-valued function of* p^0. *So CV and the EV, being difference based, are welfare indicators, as are CB and EB. You will notice, however, that where the true cost of living indexes are invariant to rescaling of prices (as a result of the homogeneity properties of* E^H*), CV and EV are not. That, of course, reflects the nominal nature of CV and EV, while the raison d'être of price indexes is to convert nominal price changes to real terms.*

CB and EB, by the Translation Property, are invariant to translations of x and y in the direction of the numeraire. We derived GI by requiring CB = EB everywhere and saw that it offers a nicely tractable framework for applied welfare calculations. What happens if we try a similar trick for the Paasche and Laspeyres welfare indexes? (You should be able to convince yourself that this is not the same as requiring CV − EV = 0). The answer is that it's well known that the Paasche and Laspeyres will coincide for all (p^1, p^0, u^1, u^0) *if and only if* $\succeq(y)$ *is homothetic. A simple functional equation argument demonstrates. For them to always agree,*

$$\frac{E^H(p^1, u^o)}{E^H(p^o, u^o)} = \frac{E^H(p^1, u^1)}{E^H(p^o, u^1)},$$

must hold for all (p^1, p^0, u^1, u^0). *The right-hand side is zero homogeneous in* (p^1, p^0), *as is the left-hand side. The right-hand side, however, depends on* u^0 *and the left on* u^1. *Thus, the equality will always hold only if both ratios equal a common zero homogeneous function* $m(p^1, p^0)$. *Hence,*

$$E^H(p^1, u^1) = m(p^1, p^0)\, E^H(p^0, u^1).$$

Now the left-hand side only depends on p^1 *and* u^1, *so setting* $p^0 = 0$ *gives*

$$E^H(p^1, u^1) = m(p^1, 0)\, E^H(0, u^1),$$

which is the homothetic form. The reverse, which is easy, is left to you.

Problem 108. *As long as expenditures are positive, it's immediate that* $CV \geq 0 \Leftrightarrow \ln E^H(p^1, u^0) - \ln E^H(p^0, u^0) \geq 0$. *Using Shephard's Lemma, we have that*

$$s(p,u) = \nabla_{\ln p} \ln E^H(p,u)$$

with typical element, $\frac{\partial \ln E(p,u)}{\partial \ln p_k}$, *representing the vector of expenditure shares allocated to the kth commodity. Letting* $s^*(p,m) \equiv s(p, V(p,m))$, *prove that if* $\succeq (y)$ *is homothetic,* $CV \geq 0 \Leftrightarrow \int_{\ln p^0}^{\ln p^1} s^*(v,m)\,dv \geq 0$.

3.2 Benefits and the Kaldor Compensation Criterion

Now that we have individual welfare measures, it's time to see whether they can be used to determine if a proposed change satisfies the Kaldor criterion. Let there be K consumers, whose original positions are given by $(y^1, y^2, \ldots, y^K)$ with $y \equiv \sum_k y^k$. We want to determine, for example, whether a move to $(x^1, x^2, \ldots, x^K)$ with $x \equiv \sum_k x^k$ satisfies the Kaldor compensation criterion. That raises the question of how compensation, if needed, is to be paid. In CV or EV analysis, compensation is in nominal units (money income). The Allais–Luenberger approach, however, works in real and not nominal terms, so that any needed compensation associated with it should be paid in real terms. We, therefore, consider compensation in the form of redistributing $(x^1, x^2, \ldots, x^K)$ across the K consumers. We say that: *The allocation* $(x^1, x^2, \ldots, x^K)$ *satisfies the Kaldor criterion for compensation relative to* $(y^1, y^2, \ldots, y^K)$ *if there exists a reallocation of* $(x^1, x^2, \ldots, x^K)$ *across these K consumers,* $(\tilde{x}^1, \tilde{x}^2, \ldots, \tilde{x}^K)$ *with* $x = \sum_k \tilde{x}^k$, *such that* $u^k(\tilde{x}^k; g) \geq u^k(y^k; g)$ *for all k with at least one inequality holding strictly.*[14]

For $(x^1, x^2, \ldots, x^K)$ and $(u^1(y^1;g), u^2(y^2;g), \ldots, u^K(y^K;g))$, define the *aggregate benefit by*

$$AB = \sum_k B^k(x^k, u^k(y^k;g)) = \sum_k d^k(x^k, y^k; g).$$

The key result is:

Theorem 23. $(x^1, x^2, \ldots, x^K)$ *satisfies the Kaldor criterion relative to* $(y^1, y^2, \ldots, y^K)$ *if and only if there exists a reallocation of it,* $(\tilde{x}^1, \tilde{x}^2, \ldots, \tilde{x}^K)$, *such that*

$$AB = \sum_k B^k(\tilde{x}^k, u^k(y^k;g)) > 0.$$

[14] This is a strong version of the Kaldor criterion because it requires that a reallocation of x exists that Pareto dominates y. A weaker version would only require that an allocation of x exists that is not Pareto dominated by y. You can work that out on your own.

To demonstrate, assume first that $(x^1, x^2, \ldots, x^K)$ satisfies the Kaldor criterion relative to $(y^1, y^2, \ldots, y^K)$. By Indication, a reallocation must exist such that $B^k(\tilde{x}^k, u^k(y^k; g)) \geq 0$ for all k with at least one $B^j(\tilde{x}^j, u(y^j; g)) > 0$. Summing establishes necessity. To show sufficiency, now assume that a reallocation, $(\tilde{x}^1, \tilde{x}^2, \ldots, \tilde{x}^K)$, exists with $AB > 0$. From that reallocation define the further reallocation $(\hat{x}^1, \hat{x}^2, \ldots, \hat{x}^K)$:

$$\begin{aligned}\hat{x}^1 &= \tilde{x}^1 + \left(AB - B^1\left(\tilde{x}^1, u^1\left(y^1; g\right)\right)\right)g\\ \hat{x}^2 &= \tilde{x}^2 - B^j\left(\tilde{x}^2, u^2\left(y^2; g\right)\right)g\\ &\vdots\\ \hat{x}^K &= \tilde{x}^K - B^j\left(\tilde{x}^K, u^K\left(y^K; g\right)\right)g.\end{aligned}$$

Clearly, $\sum_k \hat{x}^k = \sum_k \tilde{x}^k = x$ so that $(\hat{x}^1, \hat{x}^2, \ldots, \hat{x}^K)$ is also a reallocation of $(x^1, x^2, \ldots, x^K)$. Because $AB > 0$, $\hat{x}^1 \geq \tilde{x}^1 - B^1(\tilde{x}^1, u^1(y^1; g))g$ and $\hat{x}^1 \neq \tilde{x}^1 - B^1(\tilde{x}^1, u^1(y^1; g))g$, and strict monotonicity implies $\hat{x}^1 \succ^1 (\tilde{x}^1 - B^1(\tilde{x}^1, u^1(y^1; g))g) \succeq^1 (y^1)$, given transitivity. Individual 1 is strictly better off under $\hat{x}^1$ than y^1. And for $k \neq 1$, the definition of B^k requires $\hat{x}^k \succeq^k (y^k)$. The Kaldor criterion is met.

In practice, Theorem 23 is not particularly convenient. To use it, we need to search over the potential reallocations of $(x^1, x^2, \ldots, x^K)$ to determine if we can find one for which $AB > 0$. Luenberger's (1996) ingenious solution is to recognize that, under mild restrictions, Theorem 23 is satisfied if and only if the supremal convolution associated with AB

$$\diamond B(x) = \max\left\{\sum_k B^k\left(\tilde{x}^k, u^k\left(y^k; g\right)\right) : \sum \tilde{x}^k = x\right\},$$

is positive. This yields a tractable computational algorithm for determining whether $(x^1, x^2, \ldots, x^K)$ satisfies the Kaldor criterion.

That algorithm requires isolating a $p \in \mathbb{R}^N_+$ and $(\tilde{x}^1, \tilde{x}^2, \ldots, \tilde{x}^K)$ with $\sum \tilde{x}^k = x$ such that

$$p \in \cap_{k=1,2,\ldots,K} \partial B^k\left(\tilde{x}^k, u^k\left(y^k; g\right)\right)$$

and $\sum_k B^k(\tilde{x}^k, u^k(y^k; g)) > 0$. Intuitively, this requires finding a price vector that supports all K individual indifference curves for their original endowment, y^k. Applying (2.23), the dual version of this result requires that p and x satisfy

$$x = \sum_{k=1,2,\dots,K} \partial B^{*k}\left(p, u^k\left(y^k; g\right)\right)$$
$$= \sum_{k=1,2,\dots,K} \partial E^{Hk}\left(p, u^k\left(y^k; g\right)\right),$$

with $\sum_k B^k\left(\tilde{x}^k, u^k\left(y^k; g\right)\right) = p^\top \sum_{k=1}^{K} \tilde{x}^k - \sum_{k=1,2,\dots,K} B^{*k}\left(p, u^k\left(y^k; g\right)\right) > 0$. The Kaldor criterion is met if and only if a price vector exists that ensures x equals the sum of the Hicksian-compensated demands (for the $u^k\left(y^k; g\right)$) and for which the market value of x is strictly greater than the sum of the Hicksian expenditures (for the $u^k\left(y^k; g\right)$). When each $B^k\left(\tilde{x}^k, u^k\left(y^k; g\right)\right)$ is concave in $\tilde{x}^k$, expression (2.22) and Theorem 6 let us rewrite the criterion in precisely those terms because $\Diamond B(x)$ is then its own biconjugate, whence,

$$\Diamond B(x) = \min_{\frac{p}{p^\top g}} \left\{\frac{p^\top x}{p^\top g} - \sum_{k=1}^{K} B^{k*}\left(\frac{p}{p^\top g}, u^k\left(y^k; g\right)\right)\right\}$$
$$= \min_{\frac{p}{p^\top g}} \left\{\frac{p^\top x}{p^\top g} - \sum_{k=1}^{K} E^{Hk}\left(\frac{p}{p^\top g}, u^k\left(y^k; g\right)\right)\right\}.$$

The connection with Theorem 15 is immediate. If x is replaced with y in the definition of $\Diamond B(x)$ to obtain $\Diamond B(y)$, an equivalent way of expressing Theorem 15 in the endowment economy setting (no production, pure exchange) is to require y to be zero-minimal for $\Diamond B(y)$.

It's worth emphasizing that it is not required that $\sum_k B^k\left(x^k, u^k\left(y^k; g\right)\right)$, aggregate benefit evaluated at $\left(x^1, x^2, \dots, x^K\right)$, be positive for the Kaldor criterion to be satisfied. Theorem 23 shows that this suffices, but it's not necessary. Instead, all that's required is x can be redistributed to ensure a Pareto superior outcome to y.

Remark 31. *Among the many sources of criticism of CV or EV for welfare evaluative purposes is the Boadway Paradox (Boadway 1974). I won't consider it in detail,*[15] *but its essence is that movement from one Pareto-optimal allocation of the same aggregate endowment to another Pareto-optimal allocation can result in a positive sum of CVs across individuals. Blackorby and Donaldson (1990) demonstrate that, apart from exceptional circumstances,*

[15] Blackorby and Donaldson (1990) contains a thorough treatment as well as a number of generalizations.

this is generally true. That means that summing CVs or EVs cannot yield an appropriate criterion for determining whether the Kaldor Compensation Criterion is met. If it is used as the criterion, then situations can arise where it requires moving from one Pareto-optimal allocation of the same endowment to another Pareto-optimal allocation of it. But that's nonsense because the defining characteristic of a Pareto optimum is the absence of an efficiency loss.

The AB criterion does not suffer a similar shortcoming. Consider any two Pareto-optimal distributions of the same aggregate amount y, $(\tilde{y}^1, \tilde{y}^2, \ldots, \tilde{y}^K)$ *and* $(\hat{y}^1, \ldots, \hat{y}^K)$. *By Theorem 15,*

$$
\begin{aligned}
0 &= \sum_k B^k\left(\tilde{y}^k, u^k\left(\tilde{y}^k; g\right)\right) \\
&\geq \max\left\{\sum_k B^k\left(y^k, u^k\left(\tilde{y}^k; g\right)\right) : \sum y^k = y\right\} \\
&\geq \sum_k B^k\left(\hat{y}^k, u^k\left(\tilde{y}^k; g\right)\right),
\end{aligned}
$$

for any redistribution $(\hat{y}^1, \ldots, \hat{y}^K)$.

3.3 Nontraded Goods and Services

Many of the most important applications of welfare analysis involve not price changes but changes in public goods or public projects. For example, what's the value to consumers of a clean living environment or an extensive system of national parks? Neither is actively traded in markets. Nevertheless, both have value.

Valuing such nontraded goods has proven particularly challenging. The problem is that welfare analysis works by linking welfare concepts to observed behavior. But when some commodities are not traded, the linkage for those commodities is indirect. Observed demand behavior, of course, is conditional on the nontraded commodities, but unraveling its welfare linkages has proven tricky.

That trickiness has contributed to a stunning proliferation of special-purpose models (see, for example, Freeman, Herriges, and Kling 2014). Each provides different insights into how different types of nontraded goods affect consumer behavior, and how these differences can be used to make inferences about the value of nontraded goods. Rather than attempting to shed light on the myriad nooks and crannies of these models, I will focus on the key issues for real, rather than nominal, measurement.[16] I first treat the case where it's reasonable to assume that marketed-goods purchased, x, do not respond to changing the nontraded good. Then I move on to the case where they do.

3.3.1 Marketed Goods Fixed

Let $x \in \mathbb{R}^{N_x}$ denote the observed demand for the marketed goods and $q \in \mathbb{R}^{N_q}$ the nontraded goods. Both are treated as vector variables and not as scalars. The practical problem is to infer from observed behavior of market demand $x^*(p, q)$ and its price-dependent counterparts $p^*(x, q)$ welfare effects associated with q^0 and q^1. (Here it is understood that p refers to market prices for x normalized so that $p^\top g = 1$.) The problem is to determine whether or not

$$\begin{pmatrix} x \\ q^1 \end{pmatrix} \succeq \left(\begin{pmatrix} x \\ q^0 \end{pmatrix} \right).$$

In utility terms, that translates into whether or not $u^1 = u(x, q^1; g) \geq u(x, q^0; g) = u^0$. Abusing notation slightly, define

$$B(x, q, u) \equiv \sup\{\beta : u(x - \beta g, q) \geq u\},$$

for $g \in \mathbb{R}_+^{N_x} \backslash \{0\}$ as a benefit function that uses only marketed goods in its numeraire. Using $B(x, q, u)$ gives several equivalent ways of checking whether $u^1 \geq u^0$. For example, if $u^1 \geq u^0$, the monotonicity properties of B in u require that

$$B(x, q^1, u^1) - B(x, q^1, u^0) \leq 0, \tag{10.8}$$

and

$$B(x, q^0, u^1) - B(x, q^0, u^0) \leq 0.$$

Alternatively, if $u^1 \geq u^0$, it must be true that

$$B(x, q^1, u^0) - B(x, q^0, u^0) \geq 0, \tag{10.9}$$

[16] Interested readers should consult more authoritative sources for peculiar details on the different models (Freeman, Herriges, and Kling 2014; Phaneuf and Requate 2017).

and

$$B\left(x,q^{1},u^{1}\right)-B\left(x,q^{0},u^{1}\right)\geq 0.$$

To streamline the presentation, I focus on (10.8) and (10.9) and leave extensions to you. Expression (10.8) poses the problem as determining directly whether u^1 is larger than u^0. Expression (10.9) instead uses the compensating benefit for (x,q^1) relative to (x,q^0). Because $B(x,q^0,u^0)=0$, satisfaction of (10.9) requires that $B(x,q^1,u^0)\geq 0$. The tests are equivalent, but each offers a different perspective on the empirical problem and how to tackle it.

Because the traditional focus is on compensation terms, I treat (10.9) first. Let 0 denote a reference value for x (for the moment you can think of it as zero, but more generally it's just some fixed value of the marketed goods subvector). Using this notational device, we can rewrite expression (10.9) as requiring that

$$B\left(x,q^{1},u^{0}\right)-B\left(0,q^{1},u^{0}\right)-\left[B\left(x,q^{0},u^{0}\right)-B\left(0,q^{0},u^{0}\right)\right]$$

be positive *provided that*

$$B\left(0,q^{1},u^{0}\right)=B\left(0,q^{0},u^{0}\right),$$

so that at the reference value (10.9) holds as an equality.

We rewrite the problem this way because it lets us view $B(x,q^1,u^0)-B(x,q^0,u^0)$ as the difference between two compensating benefits for marketed commodities. One is the compensating benefit for moving from $(0,q^1,u^0)$ to (x,q^1,u^0), the other is for moving from $(0,q^0,u^0)$ to (x,q^0,u^0). Measuring compensation for marketed commodities is a problem we've already solved. Thus, this decomposition permits us to use those techniques to value the changes in q.

Nice, neat, and simple: The catch, of course, is that it only works if $B(0,q^1,u^0)=B(0,q^0,u^0)$. In what follows, we refer to this as the *q-restriction*. It requires the ability to identify a reference-marketed good bundle, 0, such that $(0,q^1)$ and $(0,q^0)$ must be translated by exactly the same amount (in the direction of g) to fall in $\bar{V}(u^0)$. Thus, if x is held fixed at its translated level, the u^0-marketed-commodity indifference curve conditioned by q^0 and that conditioned by q^1 must share a common point. Figure 10.6a illustrates by having the curves intersect. Once that's done, we simply compute the respective compensating benefits relative to 0 and take the difference.

Turning to (10.8), setting x to the reference level 0 allows the criterion to be rewritten as determining whether

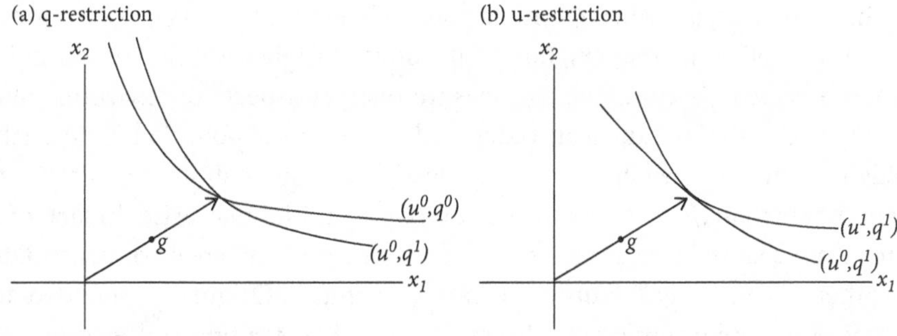

Fig. 10.6

$$B\left(x, q^1, u^1\right) - B\left(0, q^1, u^1\right) - \left[B\left(x, q^1, u^0\right) - B\left(0, q^1, u^0\right)\right] \leq 0,$$

provided that $B\left(0, q^1, u^1\right) = B\left(0, q^1, u^0\right)$, which we call the *u-restriction.* Once again, the welfare criterion is expressible as the difference between two compensating benefit measures. The restriction, however, is slightly different. Now we need to be able to identify a reference marketed-good bundle, 0 (not necessarily the same one as with the q-restriction), such that translated $\left(0, q^1\right)$ must lie on both $\bar{V}\left(u^0\right)$ and $\bar{V}\left(u^1\right)$. That means that the marketed-commodity indifference curves conditioned by q^1 for u^0 and u^1 must share a common point.

Although related, the criteria are different. The *q-restriction* requires that translated $\left(0, q^0 + \delta\right)$ fall on the same indifference curve as translated $\left(0, q^0\right)$, where $\delta = \left(q^1 - q^0\right)$. Relative to $\left(0, q^0\right)$, the variation δ carries no welfare benefit. Hence, the compensating benefits are computed relative to a reference bundle for which the δ variation has no welfare effect. The u-restriction says that translated $\left(0, q^1\right)$ falls on the indifference curve for both u^1 and u^0. All that says is that translations of $\left(0, q^1\right)$ are not required to move between u^1 and u^0. Which indifference curve translated $\left(0, q^1 - \delta\right)$ falls on remains unclear.

When q is a scalar and $\succeq (y)$ is monotonic in q, $\left(u^1 - u^0\right)\left(q^1 - q^0\right) \geq 0$. Both the u- and the q-restriction then require tangency of the marketed-goods indifference curve at the translation of 0. Figure 10.6b illustrates for the u-restriction case.

More generally, nontrivial intersections are permitted. At least two cases spring to mind. One is where q remains a scalar, but it is not assumed that $\succeq (y)$ is strictly monotone in q. Consider how a person whose economic circumstances do not permit air travel would value locating an airport in her village. Since the person is unable to afford air travel, the nuisance value likely outweighs benefit. On the other hand, if he or she could afford air travel, having an airport close by might prove beneficial.

The second occurs when q is not a scalar. Generally, treating q as a vector is seen as complicating matters, but it can convey insights as well. For example, suppose vector $q's$ components measure distinct aspects of environmental quality such as clean air, clean water, and lack of noise pollution. One easily imagines situations where q^1 is more desirable in some dimensions but less so in others than q^0, so that substitution opportunities may arise. In fact, one often finds that policies designed to address one problem create or contribute to others. *No-till agriculture* is a handy example. Originally intended to promote the environmentally desirable goal of preventing soil erosion, its implementation often contributed to increased pollution of groundwater sources. Only rarely are environmental policies, or any policies for that matter, uniformly beneficial. In such cases, crossing marketed-goods indifference curves conditioned by different $q's$ is not particularly exceptional. If there are trade-offs between the nontraded goods, it can happen.

I won't argue that either the q-restriction or u-restriction is more compelling or that either is particularly plausible. That's going to depend on the setting. But they do represent ways to immerse ourselves in messy data and design tractable solutions. No doubt alternatives are available, and I encourage you to explore them.

In doing so, keep several points in mind. I used 0 as the reference level to avoid introducing more notation. There's no need that it be the origin. The restrictions I described do not require that the origin be so translatable, only that some x can. Recall too that g is only defined in empirically vague terms as a numeraire bundle. You have an infinity of choices from which to choose. Flexibility abounds to accommodate different practical circumstances. Ultimately, therefore, the issue is whether properly defined indifference curves can share a common point. At least locally, that's not too difficult to believe. Finally, for any restrictions found, they don't need to hold exactly, but they shouldn't do "too much" damage to reality. The real battle is deciding what constitutes "too much."

Problem 109. *Suppose that* $\succeq(y)$ *obeys GI with*

$$B(x,q,u) = B(x,q,0) - u,$$

and

$$B(x,q,0) = b(x) + \sum_k \sum_n \alpha_{kn} q_k (x_n - \bar{x}_n)$$

with $b(x)$ translatable in the direction g and $\sum_n \alpha_{kn} g_n = 1$ for all k. Use the q-restriction to derive an exact measure of $B(x, q^1, u^0) - B(x, q^0, u^0)$ that can be derived from observed data.

Remark 32. *The notion of "weak complementarity" (Mäler 1974) provides the conceptual backdrop for both the q-restriction and the u-restriction. Weak complementarity requires two things: the existence of a "choke price" for a marketed demand at which none of that commodity is purchased; and the marginal utility of q to be zero when the marketed demand is zero. Partitioning x as $x = (x^a, x^b)$, the choke price condition requires that there exist $\hat{p}$ and $\hat{x}^b$ such that*

$$\begin{aligned} \hat{p} &= p(0, \hat{x}^b, q, u) \\ &= \nabla_x B(0, \hat{x}^b, q, u), \end{aligned}$$

where 0 now stands for zero, while the marginal utility condition requires

$$B_q(0, \hat{x}^b, q, u) = 0,$$

or in our discrete setup the special case of the q-restriction

$$B(0, \hat{x}^b, q^1, u^0) - B(0, \hat{x}^b, q^0, u^0) = 0.$$

The intuitive idea is that q only has value when it's consumed in conjunction with positive amounts of x^a (typically treated as a scalar). Detailed discussions of the merits of weak complementarity are available in textbook form (for example, Freeman, Herriges, and Kling 2014; Phaneuf and Requate 2017).

3.3.2 Marketed Goods Variable

In most practical situations, individuals respond to changing q by varying their consumption of x, the marketed goods. Let x^k $(k = 0, 1)$ denote consumption of the marketed goods when the nontraded goods are q^k and $u^k = u(x^k, q^k; g)$. The practical problem is to infer from observed behavior of x^0 and x^1 welfare effects associated with q^0 and q^1. At least two comparisons seem of immediate interest. Whether

$$\begin{pmatrix} x^0 \\ q^1 \end{pmatrix} \succeq \left(\begin{pmatrix} x^0 \\ q^0 \end{pmatrix} \right),$$

or whether

$$\begin{pmatrix} x^1 \\ q^0 \end{pmatrix} \succeq \begin{pmatrix} x^1 \\ q^1 \end{pmatrix}?$$

$B(x^0, q^1, u^0) - B(x^0, q^0, u^0)$ makes the former comparison and $B(x^1, q^1, u^1)$ $-B(x^1, q^0, u^1)$ the latter. We refer to them, respectively, as the *CB* and *EB* for the remainder of this section. If either $q^1 \geq q^0$ or $q^0 \geq q^1$, both give the same qualitative answer *provided that* $\succeq (y)$ *is monotonic in* q. For example, given monotonicity, $q^1 \geq q^0$ requires both to be positive. But if q^1 and q^0 are not ordered using $\geq$, the qualitative answers can differ.

Will realistic situations arise where q^0 and q^1 *are not* ordered using $\geq$? Quite often, I would think. For example, in environmental applications, the different elements of q might measure distinct aspects of environmental quality such as clean air, clean water, and lack of noise pollution. Therefore, it's easy to imagine situations where a particular mix of q^1 is more desirable than q^0 given x^0, but the reverse is true for x^1. As a result, the existence of nonscalar q introduces a potentially important analytic wrinkle to the evaluative problem. For while *CO* ensures that either

$$\begin{pmatrix} x^1 \\ q^1 \end{pmatrix} \succeq \left(\begin{pmatrix} x^0 \\ q^0 \end{pmatrix}\right),$$

or

$$\begin{pmatrix} x^0 \\ q^0 \end{pmatrix} \succeq \left(\begin{pmatrix} x^1 \\ q^1 \end{pmatrix}\right),$$

is true, it does not ensure that both the *CB* and *EB* agree with the ranking given by u^1 and u^0.

The fact that these benefit measures can yield different answers is a reality that needs to be accommodated in many applied welfare analyses. The ultimate problem is that how one values things depends on one's perspective. We've all dealt with situations requiring a change that we were initially hesitant to make but would never dream of reversing. Imagine, for example, a new q that involves introducing a new road system near where you live. Before its introduction, you might oppose it because of the inevitable increase in congestion and noise. But after it's been introduced and you've adapted your x purchases to its presence, you may be opposed to reversing things because that would mean increased commuting time and less convenient shopping. Nostalgia for the "old days" is something we all experience, but many don't allow it to dictate current choices. Some may, but others may not. There's nothing contradictory or irrational about this.

Not surprisingly, issues such as these have led some to debate whether the CV (CB) or EV (EB) (benefit) is "more appropriate" as *a welfare measure.* Frequently, the argument involves extramathematical reasoning that rarely lends itself clear resolution. For example, some have argued that relying on the CV (CB) measure gives undue weight to the *status quo* (the starting point). As such, using it may cause a failure to adopt policies that may ultimately prove beneficial. Others argue the converse. I leave it to you to decide whom to believe.

The current problem we're tackling is how to use knowledge of (x^0, x^1, q^0, q^1) to make inferences about the welfare implications of changing q. We know from having actually observed (x^0, x^1, q^0, q^1) and our definition of B that $B(x^1, q^1, u^1)$ and $B(x^0, q^0, u^0)$ both equal zero. In other words, our data start on one indifference curve and end on another. Hence, $B(x^1, q^1, u^1) - B(x^0, q^0, u^0) = 0$. While obvious, it defines a route for determining what welfare implications information on $B(x^1, q^1, u^1) - B(x^1, q^0, u^1)$ and $B(x^0, q^1, u^0) - B(x^0, q^0, u^0)$ possesses. Here I focus on $B(x^1, q^1, u^1) - B(x^1, q^0, u^1)$ and the EB, and (once again) leave the related manipulations for $B(x^0, q^1, u^0) - B(x^0, q^0, u^0)$ to you.

The $B(x^1, q^1, u^1) - B(x^0, q^0, u^0)$ difference decomposes as

$$\begin{aligned} B(x^1, q^1, u^1) - B(x^0, q^0, u^0) &= B(x^1, q^1, u^1) - B(x^1, q^0, u^1) \\ &\quad + B(x^1, q^0, u^1) - B(x^0, q^0, u^1) \\ &\quad + B(x^0, q^0, u^1) - B(x^0, q^0, u^0). \end{aligned}$$

There are three distinct components. (1) $B(x^1, q^1, u^1) - B(x^1, q^0, u^1)$ is the EB for (q^1, q^0). (2) $B(x^1, q^0, u^1) - B(x^0, q^0, u^1)$ is a compensated price-dependent demand adjustment evaluated at (q^0, u^1) that represents a marketed-good substitution effect induced by the change in q. It can be recognized as the compensating benefit for moving from (x^0, q^0, u^1) to (x^1, q^0, u^1). And (3) $B(x^0, q^0, u^1) - B(x^0, q^0, u^0)$ is a cardinalization of the real-wealth adjustment (u^1, u^0) induced by the change in q. Let's call them, respectively, EB, X^1, and U^1. (The reason for the superscripts will soon become apparent.)

Because $B(x^1, q^1, u^1) = B(x^0, q^0, u^0)$,

$$-U^1 = EB + X^1,$$

so that the real-wealth effect is the sum of our valuation measure *and* the induced substitution effect. In and of itself, *EB* does not determine whether $u^1 > u^0$ or vice versa. To know that, one must also know X. Thus, *EB* is perhaps best viewed as a *partial welfare indicator* that determines whether q^0 when combined with x^1 can guarantee a level of well-being at least as large as u^1. It makes no judgment about whether (x^1, q^0) or (x^1, q^1) can guarantee u^0. To reach a conclusion about U^1, we also need to know X^1.

Having discovered that $B(x^1, q^1, u^1) - B(x^1, q^0, u^1)$ and $B(x^0, q^1, u^0) - B(x^0, q^0, u^0)$ are more properly viewed as possibly disagreeing partial welfare indicators, it's important to realize that U^1 does not uniquely measure the u change. We can also decompose the $B(x^1, q^1, u^1) - B(x^0, q^0, u^0)$ difference as follows:

$$\begin{aligned} B(x^1, q^1, u^1) - B(x^0, q^0, u^0) = {} & B(x^1, q^1, u^1) - B(x^1, q^0, u^1) \\ & + B(x^1, q^0, u^1) - B(x^1, q^0, u^0) \\ & + B(x^1, q^0, u^0) - B(x^0, q^0, u^0). \end{aligned}$$

Viewed this way, slightly different substitution and real-wealth effects are matched with *EB*. The substitution effect is now, $X^0 = B(x^1, q^0, u^0) - B(x^0, q^0, u^0)$ and the real-wealth effect is $U^0 = B(x^1, q^0, u^1) - B(x^1, q^0, u^0)$. As before, *EB* remains a partial welfare indicator.

Both U^1 and U^0 are conceptually sound welfare measures that give the same qualitative answer. But because they are computed relative to different bases, they can differ numerically. This is an unavoidable complication involved in welfare accounting based on observed changes in (x^1, x^0) and (q^1, q^0).[17] The base matters.

Undoubtedly, this nonuniqueness will make many uncomfortable because it implies a degree of arbitrariness in welfare evaluation. It certainly doesn't lend itself to a black-box approach that can be applied regardless of the setting. But that arbitrariness also carries advantages because choosing between U^1 or U^0 requires evaluating different strategies for making welfare calculations.

Problem 110. *Choose either U^1 or U^0. Develop your restriction that allows your choice to be computed. Derive the associated measures and discuss relevant problems you would expect to face empirically..*

[17] Making B smooth doesn't make the problem disappear. Instead it reappears but couched in terms of integrals.

Another pragmatic alternative for dealing with the seemingly arbitrary nature of U^0 and U^1 is to borrow an idea from the index number literature. As discussed in Remark 30, the Laspeyres and Paasche true cost of living indexes generally give different results. Fisher's (1922) reasoned compromise to the dilemma was to create the *ideal index* as a geometric average of the Paasche and the Laspeyres,

$$\left(\frac{E^H(p^1,u^0)}{E^H(p^0,u^0)}\cdot\frac{E^H(p^1,u^1)}{E^H(p^0,u^1)}\right)^{\frac{1}{2}}.$$

The averaging tradition established by Fisher (1922) has been widely followed in both the index number and indicator number literatures, where geometric averages are used to accommodate indexes defined for different bases and simple averages for difference-based indicators (see, for example, Diewert 1976; Caves, Christensen, and Diewert 1982; Diewert 1992; and Chambers 2002). Because we are now talking indicators, the parallel solution would be to rely on $\frac{U^0+U^1}{2}$.

3.4 Willingness-to-Pay and Willingness-to-Accept Discrepancies: Anomaly or Artifact?

Many studies have uncovered evidence that individuals commonly demand much higher selling prices for goods than they are willing to pay to acquire them. The evidence comes from different settings, including stated-preference studies, laboratory experiments, field experiments, and observed trading behavior of individuals.

The average person-in-the-street probably wouldn't be too surprised to learn about such behavior. After all, "buy low and sell high" is so famous a *dictum* for business success that many of us almost view it as innate. Economists, however, reacted with a mixture of surprise and skepticism. Framing matters formally explains why.

Let me start by clarifying a semantic issue. Elsewhere, I've frequently spoken of distance functions as measuring a willingness-to-pay. The motivating idea is that they are a cardinal measure (in units of the numeraire) of what's required to achieve some objective. Identical terminology is used elsewhere (particularly in experimental and environmental economics) for a related, but slightly different, concept. There as with the general literature on welfare measurement, the numeraire is money.

The nontraded-goods problem provides an ideal metaphor for discussing this notion of willingness-to-accept (WTA) and willingness-to-pay (WTP).[18] As usually cast, the *willingness-to-pay* for moving from q^0 to q^1 is defined as

$$WTP \equiv E^H\left(p, q^1, u^0\right) - E^H\left(p, q^0, u^0\right),$$

and the *willingness to accept* as

$$WTA \equiv E^H\left(p, q^1, u^1\right) - E^H\left(p, q^0, u^1\right),$$

where u^0 represents utility achieved when q^0 is available and u^1 when q^1 is available. You will note, of course, that WTA is closely related to the CV measure and WTP to the EV.

At a quick glance, the only seeming difference between WTP and WTA is that WTP is evaluated at u^0 and WTA at u^1. So if $u^1 - u^0 \approx 0$, one naturally expects $WTA \approx WTP$. On the other hand, if $u^1 - u^0$ is large, bigger differences might be easily countenanced.

The empirical evidence didn't agree. Instead, large relative differences between WTA and WTP were observed for items as small as candy bars, coffee cups, pens, and pencils—hence, the apparent paradox. Either the experimental subjects[19] associated apparently freakishly large income effects for everyday items, or our theories were problematic.

Slightly rewriting WTA as

$$WTA = -\left[E^H\left(p, q^0, u^1\right) - E^H\left(p, q^1, u^1\right)\right]$$

helps identify another explanation. The formulation above, albeit implicitly, casts WTA as a movement from $\left(p, q^0, u^1\right)$ to $\left(p, q^1, u^1\right)$. This way casts it as a movement from $\left(p, q^1, u^1\right)$ to $\left(p, q^0, u^1\right)$. That might seem unimportant, but choosing different starting points can lead to different results in evaluating functional differences.[20]

[18] Here again, the ordering of the original and new commodity bundle lies outside of the mathematical model. Changing the commodity ordering doesn't change any of the mathematical formalities, but it does change how effects are labeled. Don't let it confuse you, or better yet, when it does, remember that it's a matter of semantics.

[19] Often, university students tested in a laboratory setting.

[20] It's well beyond the scope of this section to go into such matters in detail, but the whole idea behind what is often called *the endowment effect* or the *status-quo bias* is precisely this. They have often been cast as "new models" of consumer behavior, but as the math shows, they are special cases of our general setup. So, too, with the idea of *loss aversion*, which posits that individuals respond asymmetrically to losing and gaining. Put in terms of Chapter 2, that simply means $f'(x; v)$ and $-f'(x; -v)$ need not agree. As we've seen elsewhere, "new" theories were thought to be needed to accommodate the common practice of conflating differentiability with rationality. Once that's done, anything that departs from smoothness is easily mistaken for irrationality.

To see why, let's evaluate both *WTA* and *WTP* at a common u (to approximate zero real-income differences) for $v = q^1 - q^0$ in differential terms. That gives the local versions as

$$\begin{aligned} WTP &= \lim_{\lambda \downarrow 0} \frac{E^H(p, q^0 + \lambda v, u) - E^H(p, q^0, u)}{\lambda} \\ &\equiv E^{H\prime}(p, q, u; v) \end{aligned}$$

and using the second formulation

$$\begin{aligned} WTA &= -\lim_{\lambda \uparrow 0} \frac{E^H(p, q^0 + \lambda v, u) - E^H(p, q^0, u)}{\lambda} \\ &\equiv -\left[E^{H\prime}(p, q, u; -v)\right]. \end{aligned}$$

So, now we're talking differences between (essentially) right-hand and left-hand derivatives.[21] We know from Chapter 2 that the two are not always equal. Differences can emerge even for v small.

Differences are one thing; large relative differences are another. One naturally wonders, therefore, how large the differences can be between these two *differential measures*. The next problem walks you through a simple example for a very familiar preference model that shows that the ratio between the two can be arbitrarily large (that is, only exist in a limiting sense at ∞).

Problem 111. *Let x and q be scalars and*

$$-t(0, x, q; g) = \min\left\{\frac{x}{g_x}, \frac{q}{g_q}\right\}$$

with $g_x, g_q > 0$. Set $q^0 = g_q u$. a) Derive $E^H(p, q^0, u)$. b) For $q^1 - q^0$ positive, but very small, calculate both WTP and WTA.

The preferences in Problem 111 exhibit perfect complementarity. Is the natural inference that the empirical evidence is explained by a lack of substitutability? That appears to be the position many take. But as you may have already guessed, once you free yourself from the intellectual straitjacket that the calculus imposes on economic reasoning, other opportunities present themselves. What's really required is not a lack of substitutability, but a

[21] Our treatment of course applies to the case where q is multidimensional, and they're really one-sided directional derivatives. The standard treatment of this problem reduces q to a scalar and $v = 1$.

discontinuous change in substitutability. Another worked example should help illustrate.

Problem 112. *Suppose that*

$$(x,q) \succeq ((x^0,q^0)) \Leftrightarrow \min_{\alpha\in\left[\frac{1}{4},\frac{3}{4}\right]}\{q+\alpha(x-q)\} \geq \min_{\alpha\in\left[\frac{1}{4},\frac{3}{4}\right]}\{q^0+\alpha(x^0-q^0)\}.$$

Calculate WTP and WTA for a small change in q at $(x,q)=(1,1)$.

4 Valuation under Uncertainty

Many, if not most, public policy problems involve uncertainy. For example, as I write, what to do about climate change is the subject of intense public debate. One side argues that climate change is the most important social and economic issue that our planet faces. The other side is often actively dismissive and has even labeled climate change a hoax. An important contributing factor to the acrimony is that many of the potential changes stretch beyond human experience. Consequently, uncertainty pervades every aspect of the debate. A short list of the things that we are uncertain about includes the possible consequences of climate, the underlying physical processes, the appropriate way to model the physical processes, and how to discount far-distant consumption and income flows.[22]

This section introduces you to the basics of cost-benefit and valuation analysis in an uncertain setting. Originally, I intended to use climate change to illustrate the intuitive argument. But didactics is better served by starting with a simpler problem. Once grasped, extensions can be attempted at your leisure. And so, the problem we treat is evaluating the benefit derived from public expenditure on a *public good* that conveys stochastic period 1 benefits.

Our definition of a public good is one that is not traded and that is *nonexcludable*. Nonexcludable means that all members of society have equal access to it and that one agent's consumption of it does not impinge upon another's. Mathematically, we interpret the latter to mean that the same level of the public good enters all individual preference orderings. In practice, nonexcludability limits the range of applications. For example, you might

[22] A good place for economists to start looking at such issues is the *Stern Review* (Stern 2007). Its analysis and conclusions have been heavily criticized, but it's also very user friendly. Those wishing more scientific background would do well to consult the doorstop resource Intergovernmental Panel on Climate Change (2014).

think of public museums or public zoos as being public goods. But visiting either or both on a crowded day and noncrowded day will likely change your mind. Standard examples of public goods usually include lighthouses, national defense, clean air, and a clean environment. One can quibble with these examples, but hopefully you get the general idea.

Other than the public good, the basic setup is the same as Chapter 9's equilibrium analysis. There are two commodities. One is a commodity (the numeraire) that all individuals consume privately. Period 0 consumption of the commodity is denoted by scalar c^0 and period 1 stochastic consumption $c^1 \in \mathbb{R}^S$ with $c = (c^0, c^1) \in \mathbb{R}^{1+S}$. The other is a public good, consumed by all, denoted by $q \in \mathbb{R}^S$ whose stochastic outcome is realized in period 1. There are K individuals. Preferences for agent k are represented by a strictly monotonic and continuous binary ordering defined over $(c^{k0}, c^{k1}, q) \in \mathbb{R}^{1+2S}$ for $k = 1, 2, \ldots, K$. I want to emphasize that what follows does not require *CO* and works whether preferences are complete or incomplete.[23] Each individual is endowed with $m^k = (m^{k0}, m^{k1}) \in \mathbb{R}^{1+S}$ as in Chapter 9. For simplicity, assume that no way exists to transfer income between the two periods or to write period 0 contracts contingent upon, for example, state $s \in S$ being chosen by Nature. Thus, given strict monotonicity, individual k's consumption bundle is $(m^{k0}, m^{k1}, 0)$ in the absence of a public good.

The stochastic production process for the public good is governed by the input correspondence, $X^q : \mathbb{R}^S \to \mathbb{R}$,

$$X^q(q) = \{x \in \mathbb{R} : x \geq \hat{x}(q)\},$$

where $\hat{x}(q)$ is interpretable either as a period 0 *input-requirement* function or cost function for producing q. It's assumed strictly increasing and smooth in q. This process operates under the same basic principles as our canonical stochastic production model. In period 0, $x \in \mathbb{R}$ and $q \in \mathbb{R}^S$ are chosen, but only $q(s) \in \mathbb{R}$ is realized in period 1 after Nature makes its draw.

Formally, we ask whether a *public investment plan*, $(x^1, \ldots, x^K)$, and a *consumption plan* (c^{k0}, c^{k1}, q), $k = k = 1, 2, \ldots, K$ with $\sum_k x^k \in X^q(q)$ exist that satisfy the Kaldor criterion relative to the no-public-good case. Such plans are *feasible* if $c^{k0} = m^{k0} - x^k$ and $c^{k1} = m^{k1}$ for all k. The basic idea is that feasible public investment and consumption plans involve individuals

[23] For example, Chambers and Melkonyan (2017) contains an explicit welfare analysis for an incomplete preference structure that satisfies the independence axiom.

sacrificing period 0 consumption of the numeraire to finance production of the public good.[24]

Relative to $(m^{k0}, m^{k1}, 0)$, the *kth* agent's *CB* for (c^{k0}, c^{k1}, q) is, following the notation developed in Chapters 8 and 9,

$$d^k\left(\left(c^{k0}, c^{k1}, q\right), \left(m^{k0}, m^{k1}, 0\right); \tilde{g}\right)$$

Define the aggregate benefit for (c^{k0}, c^{k1}, q) relative to $(m^{k0}, m^{k1}, 0)$, $k = 1, 2, \dots, K$ as

$$AB = \sum_{k=1}^{K} d^k\left(\left(c^{k0}, c^{k1}, q\right), \left(m^{k0}, m^{k1}, 0\right); \tilde{g}\right).$$

Using essentially the same arguments used for Theorem 23, we obtain

Corollary 9. *If there exists a feasible public investment and consumption plan satisfying $AB > 0$, it satisfies the Kaldor criterion relative to the public investment plan $(0, 0, \dots, 0)$ and consumption plan $(m^{k0}, m^{k1}, 0)$, $k = 1, 2, \dots, K$.*

The proof is left to you. As in the nonstochastic case, an easy way to determine if the Kaldor criterion is met is to solve

$$\max_{x^1, \dots, x^K, q} \left\{\sum_{k=1}^{K} d^k\left(\left(m^{k0} - x^k, m^{k1}, q\right), \left(m^{k0}, m^{k1}, 0\right); \tilde{g}\right) : \sum_{k=1} x^k = \hat{x}(q)\right\}, \tag{10.10}$$

and then check whether $\sum_k d^k\left(\left(m^{k0} - x^k, m^{k1}, q\right), \left(m^{k0}, m^{k1}, 0\right); \tilde{g}\right) > 0$. If it is, then any public investment $(\tilde{x}^1, \dots, \tilde{x}^K)$ and consumption plan $(m^{10} - \tilde{x}^1, \dots, m^{K0} - \tilde{x}^K)$, which is a reallocation of the solution will also satisfy the Kaldor criterion.

You are invited to complicate this problem by providing more economic texture. For example, an obvious extension is to assume that an active financial market exists in which individuals are allowed to exchange period 0 claims on period 0 consumption in return for payouts in the form $A \in \mathbb{R}^{S \times M}$ as in Chapter 9. While that complicates things a bit and brings different issues to the fore,[25] the principles of how to evaluate the Kaldor criterion remain

[24] Here we intentionally abstract from problems associated with executing the implicit levy on agents. Issues of deadweight loss surely affect the potential range of outcomes, but they do not affect the basic strategy for analyzing the problem. Thus, we ignore them to keep the analytics as simple as possible.

[25] For example, how should the public good be financed. Should it be financed via a public investment scheme or via the market itself?

unchanged. Extending welfare arguments made in a nonstochastic setting to a stochastic one involves simply relabeling and reinterpreting the basic model used to develop *CB* and *EB* techniques.

The same cannot be said for *CV* and *EV* methods. Standard practice is to treat valuation and welfare matters differently in applied stochastic settings than they are treated in nonstochastic settings. The problem in translating nonstochastic welfare analysis to the stochastic case is frequently the former's reliance on nominal measures. *CV* and *EV* measures are developed and refined in a *dual setting* (price and income terms). To calculate them, information is needed on prices, in particular state-claim prices, that may not exist in the absence of complete markets. The applied cost-benefit and welfare literatures responded to this challenge by evolving a largely distinct set of tools to use in stochastic settings. Much of that literature, which is formulated in expected-utility terms, requires both *CO* and the independence axiom and is crucially dependent on that superstructure. As a consequence, some of its key concepts (for example, "risk prevention" and the "value of a statistical life") are only directly relevant for risky situations and expected-utility preferences.[26]

5 Chapter Commentary

This chapter recycled tools developed through the first nine chapters to examine the production and pricing of quality and several challenges encountered in applied welfare analysis. The presentation of the household production model draws on Gorman (1956, 1980), Lancaster (1966), Deaton and Muellbauer (1980), and Freeman, Herriges, and Kling (2014). The welfare analysis draws most directly from Hicks (1946), Samuelson (1947), Allais (1989), Luenberger (1996), Chambers (2001, 2002), Deaton and Muellbauer (1980), Graham (1981, 1992), Kreps (2013), Freeman, Herriges, and Kling (2014), and Phaneuf and Requate (2017).

[26] Important exceptions are the pathbreaking treatments of Graham (1981 and 1992), from which all can benefit by reading. Note, however, that his terminology departs from ours. In particular, his benefit function and ours are distinct concepts. If you're interested in other alternatives used in applied settings, nice introductory treatments are offered in Freeman, Herriges, and Kling (2014) or Phaneuf and Requate (2017), both of which provide ample references to more basic treatments.

Bibliography

[1] *Oxford English Dictionary*, 2d ed. 1989. Oxford: Oxford University Press.

[2] Abramovitz, M. 1956. Resource and Output Trends in the United States since 1870. *American Economic Review* 46: 5–23.

[3] Aczél, J. 1966. *Lectures on Functional Equations and Their Applications.* New York: Academic Press.

[4] Afriat, S. 1967. The Construction of Utility Functions from Expenditure Data. *International Economic Review* 8: 67–77.

[5] ——. 1972. Efficiency Estimation of Production Functions. *International Economic Review* 13: 568–598.

[6] Aliprantis, C. D., and K. C. Border. 2007. *Infinite Dimensional Analysis: A Hitchhiker's Guide*, 3d ed.. Berlin: Springer-Verlag.

[7] Allais, M. 1989. *La théorie générale des surplus.* Grenoble: Presses de l'Universitaire de Grenoble.

[8] Allais, M. 1943. *Traité d'Économie Pure*, Vol. 3. Paris: Imprimerie Nationale.

[9] Anscombe, F. J., and R. J. Aumann. 1963. A Definition of Subjective Probability. *Annals of Mathematics and Statistics* 34: 199–205.

[10] Antonelli, G. B. 1886. *Sulla Teoria Matematica della Economia Politica.* Pisa: Nella Tipognafia del Folchetto.

[11] Arrow, K. J. 1964. The Role of Securities in the Optimal Allocation of Risk Bearing. *Review of Economic Studies* 31: 91–96.

[12] Arrow, Kenneth. 1953. *Le Role des Valeurs Boursiers pour la Repartition la Meilleur des Risques.* Cahiers du Seminair d'Economie. Paris: CNRS.

[13] Aubin, J.-P. 2007. *Mathematical Methods of Game and Economic Theory: Revised Edition.* New York: Dover.

[14] Aumann, R. J. 1962. Utility Theory without the Completeness Axiom. *Econometrica* 30: 445–62.

[15] Ayres, R. U., and A. W. Kneese. 1969. Production, Consumption, and Externalities. *American Economic Review* 59: 282–97.

[16] Baumol, W. J. 1961. *Economic Theory and Operations Analysis.* Englewood Cliffs: Prentice-Hall.

[17] Bellman, R. 1957. *Dynamic Programming.* Princeton, NJ: Princeton University Press.

[18] Bennet, T. L. 1920. The Theory of Measurement of Changes in Cost of Living. *Journal of the Royal Statistical Society* 83: 445–62.

[19] Berge, C. 1963. *Topological Spaces.* New York: Macmillan.

[20] Blackorby, C., and D. Donaldson. 1980. A Theoretical Treatment of Indices of Absolute Inequality. *International Economic Review* 21, no. 1: 107–36.

[21] Blackorby, C., and D. Donaldson. 1990. The Case Against the Use of the Sum of Compensating Variations in Cost-Benefit Analysis. *Canadian Journal of Economics* 23: 471–94.

[22] Boadway, R. 1974. The Welfare Foundations of Cost Benefit Analysis. *Economic Journal* 84: 926–39.

[23] Caves, D. W., L. R. Christensen, and W. E. Diewert. 1982. The Economic Theory of Index Numbers and the Measurement of Input, Output, and Productivity. *Econometrica* 50: 1393–414.

[24] Chambers. C. P., and F. Echenique. 2016. *Revealed Preference Theory*. Cambridge: Cambridge University Press.

[25] Chambers, R. G. 1988. *Applied Production Analysis: A Dual Approach*. Cambridge: Cambridge University Press.

[26] ——. 2001. Consumers' Surplus as an Exact and Superlative Cardinal Welfare Measure. *International Economic Review* 42: 105–20.

[27] ——. 2002. Exact Nonradial Input, Output, and Productivity Measurrement. *Economic Theory* 20: 751–67.

[28] ——. 2014. Uncertain Equilibria and Incomplete Preferences. *Journal of Mathematical Economics* 55: 48–54.

[29] Chambers, R. G., Y. Chung, and R. Färe. 1996. Benefit and Distance Functions. *Journal of Economic Theory* 70: 407–19.

[30] Chambers, R. G., and R. Färe. 1998. Translation Homotheticity. *Economic Theory* 11: 629–41.

[31] Chambers, R. G., and T. A. Melkonyan. 2017. Ambiguity, reasoned determination, and climate-change policy. *Journal of Environmental Economics and Management* 81: 74–92.

[32] ——. 2009. Buy Low, Sell High: Price Gaps and Neoclassical Theory. *Journal of Mathematical Economics* 45: 720–29.

[33] Chambers, R. G., and J. Quiggin. 2007. Dual Approaches to the Analysis of Risk Aversion. *Economica* 74: 189–213.

[34] ——. 2000. *Uncertainty, Production, Choice, and Agency: The State-Contingent Approach*. New York: Cambridge University Press.

[35] ——. 2008. Narrowing the No-Arbitrage Bounds. *Journal of Mathematical Economics* 44, no. 1: 1–14.

[36] ——. 2009. Separability of Stochastic Production Decisions from Producer Risk Preferences in the Presence of Financial Markets. *Journal of Mathematical Economics* 45: 730–737.

[37] Clarke, F. H. 1983. *Optimization and Nonsmooth Analysis*. New York: Wiley.

[38] Cochrane, J. H. 2001. *Asset Pricing*. Princeton: Princeton University Press.

[39] Coursey, D., J. Hovis, and W. Schulze. 1987. The Disparity between Willingness to Accept and Willingness to Pay Measures of Value. *Quarterly Journal of Economics* 102: 679–90.

[40] de Finetti, B. 1974. *Theory of Probability*. New York: Wiley.

[41] Deaton, Angus, and John Muellbauer. 1980. *Economics and Consumer Behavior*. Cambridge: Cambridge University Press.

[42] Debreu, G. 1951. The Coefficient of Resource Utilization. *Econometrica* 19, no. 3: 273–92.

[43] ——. 1959. *The Theory of Value*. New Haven, CT: Yale University Press.

[44] Diewert, W. E. 1982. Duality Approaches to Microeconomic Theory. *Handbook of Mathematical Economics*. eds. K. Arrow, and M. Intriligator, 535–600. Vol. II. New York: North-Holland.

[45] ——. 1976. Exact and Superlative Index Numbers. *Journal of Econometrics* 4: 115–45.

[46] ——. 1992. Exact and Superlative Welfare Indicators. *Economic Inquiry* 30: 565–82.

[47] Duffie, D. 2001. *Dynamic Asset Pricing Theory*, 3d ed. Princeton, NJ: Princeton University Press.

[48] Dupuit, A. J. E. J. 1844. De la measure de l'utilité des travaux publics. *Annales Des Pont Et Chaussées* 8.

[49] Edgeworth, F. Y. 1881. *Mathematical Psychics: An Essay on the Application of Mathematics to the Moral Sciences*. London: G. Kegan Paul.

[50] Färe, R., and D. Primont. 1995. *Multi-Output Production and Duality: Theory and Applications*. Boston: Kluwer.

[51] Farrell, M. J. 1957. The Measurement of Productive Efficiency. *Journal of the Royal Statistical Society* 129A: 253–81.

[52] Fishburn, P. C. 1972. *Mathematics of Decision Theory*. The Hague: Mouton.

[53] Fisher, I. 1922. *The Making of Index Numbers: A Study of Their Varieties, Tests, and Reliability*. Boston: Houghton Mifflin.

[54] Førsund, F. 2009. Good Modeling of Bad Outputs; Pollution and Multi-output Production. *International Review of Environmental and Resource Economics* 3: 1–38.

[55] Freeman, A. M., J. Herriges, and C. Kling. 2014. *The Measurement of Environmental and Resource Values*. Abingdon: RFF Press.

[56] Frisch, R. 1965. *Theory of Production*. Dordrecht: D. Reidel.

[57] Gale, D. 1960. *The Theory of Linear Economic Models*. Chicago: University of Chicago Press.

[58] Gilboa, I. 2009. *Theory of Decision under Uncertainty*. Cambridge: Cambridge University Press.

[59] Gilboa, I., and D. Schmeidler. 1989. Maxmin Expected Utility with Non-unique Prior. *Journal of Mathematical Economics* 18: 141–53.

[60] Gorman, W. M. 1953. Community Preference Fields. *Econometrica* 21: 63–80.

[61] ——. 1968. *Measuring the Quantities of Fixed Factors: Value, Capital and Growth*. ed. J. N. Wolfe Edinburgh: Edinburgh University Press.

[62] ——. 1980. A Possible Procedure for Evaluating Quality Differentials in the Egg Market. *Review of Economic Studies* 47: 843–56.

[63] ——. 1956. A Possible Procedure for Examining Quality Differentials in the Egg Market. Working Paper, Iowa Agricultural Experiment Station.

[64] Graham, D. A. 1981. Cost-Benefit Analysis under Uncertainty. *American Economic Review* 71: 715–25.

[65] ——. 1992. Public Expenditure under Uncertainty: The Net Benefit Criteria. *American Economic Review* 82: 822–46.

[66] Haavelmo, T. 1943. The Statistical Implications of a System of Simultaneous Equations. *Econometrica* 11: 1–12.

[67] Hausman, J. 1981. Consumer's Surplus and Deadweight Loss. *American Economic Review* 71, no. 662–76.

[68] Hicks, J. R. 1946. The Generalized Theory of Consumers' Surplus. *Review of Economic Studies* 13: 68–74.

[69] Hicks, J. R., and R. G. D. Allen. 1934. A Reconsideration of the Theory of Value: Part I and Part II. *Economica* 1: 52–76 and 196–219.

[70] Hiriart-Urruty, J.-B., and C. LeMaréchal. 2001. *Fundamentals of Convex Analysis*. Heidelberg: Springer Verlag.

[71] Honohan, P., and J. P. Neary. 2003. W. M. Gorman (1983–2003). University College Dublin.

[72] Intergovernmental Panel on Climate Change. 2014. *Climate Change 2013: The Physical Science Basis*. Contribution of Working Group I to the Fifth Assessment Report of the Intergovernmental Panel on Climate Change. New York: Cambridge University Press.

[73] Jehle, G. A., and P. Reny. 2011. *Advanced Microeconomic Analysis*, Third Edition. Chicago: Addison-Wesley.

[74] Jorgenson, D. W., and Z. Griliches. 1967. The Explanation of Productivity Change. *Review of Economic Studies* 34, no. 99: 249–83.

[75] Kaldor, N. 1939. Welfare Propositions and Interpersonal Comparisons of Utility. *Economic Journal* 49: 549–52.

[76] Knight, F. H. 1921. *Risk, Uncertainty, and Profit*. New York: Augustus M. Kelley.

[77] Konüs, A. A. 1939. The Problem of the True Index of the Cost of Living. *Econometrica* 7: 10–29.
[78] Koopmans, T. C. 1951. *Activity Analysis of Production and Allocation*. New York: Wiley.
[79] Kreps, D. 1990. *A Course in Microeconomic Theory*. Princeton, NJ: Princeton University Press.
[80] ——. 2013. *Microeconomic Foundations I: Choice and Competitive Markets*. Princeton, NJ: Princeton University Press.
[81] Lancaster, K. 1966. A New Approach to Consumer Theory. *Journal of Political Economy* 74: 132–57.
[82] LeRoy, S. F., and J. Werner. 2001. *Principles of Financial Economics*. Cambridge: Cambridge University Press.
[83] Lichtenberg, E., and D. Zilberman. 1986. The Econometrics of Damage Control: Why Specification Matters. *American Journal of Agricultural Economics* 68: 261–73.
[84] Luenberger, D. 1969. *Optimization by Vector-Space Methods*. New York: Wiley.
[85] ——. 1992a. Benefit Functions and Duality. *Journal of Mathematical Economics* 21: 461–81.
[86] ——. 1994. Dual Pareto Efficiency. *Journal of Economic Theory* 62: 70–84.
[87] ——. 1995. *Microeconomic Theory*. New York: McGraw-Hill.
[88] ——. 1992b. New Optimality Principles for Economic Efficiency and Equilibrium. *Journal of Optimization Theory and Applications* 75, no. 2: 221–64.
[89] ——. 1996. Welfare from a benefit viewpoint. *Economic Theory* 7: 445–62.
[90] Magill, M., and M. Quinzii. 1996. *Theory of Incomplete Markets*. Cambridge: MIT Press.
[91] Malinvaud, E. 1972. *Lectures on Microeconomic Theory*. North Holland: Amsterdam.
[92] Malmquist, S. 1953. Index Numbers and Indifference Surfaces. *Trabajos De Estatistica* 4: 209–42.
[93] Marshall, A. 1920. *Principles of Economics*, 8th ed. London: Macmillan.
[94] McFadden, D. 1978. *Cost, Revenue, and Profit Functions. Production Economics: A Dual Approach* to Theory and Applications. Eds. M. Fuss, and D. McFaddenAmsterdam: North-Holland.
[95] ——. 1963. Further Results on C.E.S. Production Functions. *Review of Economic Studies* 30: 73–83.
[96] McKenzie, L. W. 1957. Demand Theory without a Utility Index. *Review of Economic Studies* 24: 185–89.
[97] Mehra, R., and E. Prescott. 1985. The Equity-Premium Puzzle. *Journal of Monetary Economics* 15: 145–61.
[98] Moreau, J. 1962. Fonctions duales convexes et points proximaux dans un espace hilbertien. *Comptes Rendus De L'Académie Des Sciences De Paris* A255: 2897–99.
[99] Murty, S., R. R. Russell, and S. Levkoff. 2012. On Modeling Pollution-Generating Technologies. *Journal of Environmental Economics and Management* 64: 117–35.
[100] Mäler, K.-G. 1974. *Environmental Economics: A Theoretical Inquiry*. Baltimore: Johns Hopkins Press.
[101] Neary, J., and A. G. Schweinberger. 1986. Factor-Content Functions and the Theory of International Trade. *Review of Economic Studies* 53: 421–32.
[102] Nerlove, M. L. 1963. Returns to Scale in Electricity Supply. *Measurement in Economics: Studies in Mathematical Economics and Econometrics in Memory Yehuda Grunfeld*. C. L. Christ et al. Stanford, CA: Stanford University Press.
[103] Nikaido, H. 1968. *Convex Structures and Economic Theory*. New York: Academic Press.
[104] Ok, Efe. A. 2007. *Real Analysis with Economic Applications*. Princeton, NJ: Princeton University Press.

[105] Pethig, R. 2006. Nonlinear production, pollution, abatement and materials-balance reconsidered. *Journal of Environmental Economics and Management* 51: 185–204.

[106] Phaneuf, D., and T. Requate. 2017. *A Course in Environmental Economics*. Cambridge: Cambridge University Press.

[107] Pólya, G. 1945. *How to Solve It: A New Aspect of Mathematical Method*. Princeton, NJ: Princeton University Press.

[108] Randall, A., and J. Stoll. 1980. Consumer's Surplus in Commodity Space. *American Economic Review* 70: 449–55.

[109] Rigotti, L., and C. Shannon. 2005. Uncertainty and Risk in Financial Markets. *Econometrica* 73: 203–43.

[110] Rockafellar, R. T. 1970. *Convex Analysis*. Princeton, NJ: Princeton University Press.

[111] ——. 1963. *Convex Functions and Dual Extremum Problems*. Cambridge: PhD Thesis, Harvard University.

[112] ——. 2011. *Convexity, Optimization, Risk*. Singapore: NUS.

[113] Rockafellar, R. T., and R. J. B. Wets. 1998. *Variational Analysis*. Heidelberg: Springer.

[114] Sakai, Y. 1974. Substitution and Expansion Effects in Production Economics: The Case of Joint Products. *Journal of Economic Theory* 9: 255–74.

[115] Samuelson, P. 1938. A Note on the Pure Theory of Consumer Behavior. *Economica* 5: 61–71.

[116] ——. 1947. *Foundations of Economic Analysis*. Cambridge, MA: Harvard University Press.

[117] ——. 1972. The Consumer Does Benefit from Feasible Price Stability. *Quarterly Journal of Economics* 86: 476–93.

[118] Sandmo, A. 1971. On the Theory of the Competitive Firm under Price Uncertainty. *American Economic Review* 61: 65–73.

[119] Savage, L. J. 1954. *The Foundations of Statistics*. New York: Wiley.

[120] Schultz, T. W. 1956. Reflections on Agricultural Production, Output, and Supply. *Journal of Farm Economics* 48: 748–62.

[121] Shephard, R. W. 1953. *Cost and Production Functions*. Princeton, NJ: Princeton University Press.

[122] ——. 1970. *Theory of Cost and Production Functions*. Princeton, NJ: Princeton University Press.

[123] Slutsky, E. 1915. Sulla teoria del bilancio del consummatore. *Giornale degli Economisti* 51: 1–26.

[124] Stern, R. 2007. *The Economics of Climate Change: The Stern Review*. Cambridge: Cambridge University Press.

[125] U.S. Department of Defense. 2002, February 12. DoD News Briefing: Secretary Rumsfeld and Gen. Myers.

[126] Vartia, Y. 1983. Efficient Methods of Measuring Welfare Change and Compensated Income in Terms of Ordinary Demand Functions. *Econometrica* 51: 79–88.

[127] Waugh, F. V. 1928. Quality Factors Influencing Vegetable Prices. *Journal of Farm Economics* 10: 185–96.

[128] ——. 1944. Does the Consumer Benefit from Price Stability? *Quarterly Journal of Economics* 58: 602–14.

[129] Willig, R. D. 1976. Consumer's Surplus without Apology. *American Economic Review* 66: 589–97.

[130] Yaari, M. 1969. Some Remarks on Measures of Risk Aversion and on their Uses. *Journal of Economic Theory* 1: 315–29.

Notation

$\mathbb{R} = (-\infty, +\infty)$ the real numbers

$\bar{\mathbb{R}} = [-\infty, +\infty]$ the extended real numbers

$\mathbb{R}^N$ N-dimensional real space

$\varnothing$ empty set

$\Gamma : \mathbb{R}^M \rightrightarrows \mathbb{R}^N$ correspondence

$f : \mathbb{R}^N \to \mathbb{R}$ function

Γ^+ upper inverse of Γ

Γ^- lower inverse of Γ

f^{-1} inverse mapping of f

Gr graph

∂f superdifferential correspondence

$\partial^- f$ subdifferential correspondence

∇f gradient

$x^\top y$ inner product of $x \in \mathbb{R}^N, y \in \mathbb{R}^N$

hyp hypograph

epi epigraph

$\mathit{eff}(\partial f) = \{x \in \mathbb{R}^N : \partial f(x) \neq \varnothing\}$

δ indicator function

Co convex hull

$\bar{H}(\alpha, p)$ affine hyperplane

$H(\alpha, p)$ half space defined by $\bar{H}(\alpha, p)$

dom effective domain

ri relative interior

$f'(x; v)$ directional derivative of f in direction v

lim limit

inf infimum

sup supremum

f^* conjugate (concave or convex) of f

f^{**} biconjugate (concave or convex) of f

arg inf argument infimum

arg min argument minimum

sup inf argument supremum

arg max argument maximum

u_C upper bound function for C

$\Diamond f$ supremal convolution

$\bigvee f$ infimal convolution

$x \succeq (y)$ binary relation (order) defined on $\mathbb{R}^N \times \mathbb{R}^M$

$V(y) = \{x \in \mathbb{R}^N : x \succeq (y)\}$

$\bar{V}(y)$ boundary of $V(y)$

$Y(x) = \{y \in \mathbb{R}^M : x \succeq (y)\}$

$\bar{Y}(x)$ boundary of $Y(x)$

$d(x, y; g)$ distance function for $V(y)$

$t(y, x; g)$ distance function for $Y(x)$

$E(q; y)$ McKenzie expenditure function

$R(p, x)$ revenue function

$\pi(p, q)$ profit function

$E^H(q, u)$ Hicksian expenditure function

$I(p)$ indirect utility function

$c(w, y)$ cost function

$x(q; y)$ McKenzie demand

$p(x; y)$ Antonelli demand

$B^*(p^*, m)$ budget correspondence nominal prices and income

$B(p)$ budget correspondence normalized prices

$b(x, p; g)$ budget shortage function

$\bar{B}(p)$ boundary of $B(p)$

$x(p)$ rational demand

$p(x)$ rational price dependent demand

$u(y; g)$ g equivalent utility function

$U(y)$ ordinal utility function

$x(p; u)$ Hicksian compensated demand

$x^*(p)$ Marshallian (Walrasian) demand

$p^*(x)$ Marshallian (Walrasian) price-dependent demand

$\preceq$ revealed-preference binary relation

T graph of technology (technology set)

T^K DEA approximation to T

$\vec{D}_o(y, x; g)$ directional output distance function

$J + K$ Minkowski sum *for* $J, K \subset \mathbb{R}^N$

$\mathcal{E}$ excess expenditure function

$\sigma(y)$ shortage function

$\mathcal{X}$ set of constant acts (degenerate random variables)

$\tilde{g} = \begin{Bmatrix} 0 \in \mathbb{R}^M \\ 1 \in \mathcal{X} \end{Bmatrix}$

$A = [A_1, A_2, \ldots, A_J] \in \mathbb{R}^{S \times J}$ asset matrix

$\mathcal{M}$ market span

$\mathcal{B}(A, m)$ frictionless portfolio budget correspondence

$\mathcal{B}^+(A, m)$ no-short-sales portfolio budget correspondence

$\mathfrak{b}$ shortage function for $\mathcal{B}$

$\mathfrak{b}^+$ shortage function for $\mathcal{B}^+$

$P \equiv 1_J^\top (A^\top A)^{-1} A^\top$ ideal stochastic discount factor

$\mathcal{B}^T(w, m)$ budget correspondence stochastic production

$\mathfrak{b}^T$ shortage function for $\mathcal{B}^T$

$C\left(w, P, c^1\right)$ arbitrage cost function

$B(x, u)$ benefit function

AB aggregate benefit

Index